# ANTIGONE'S GHOSTS

# ANTIGONE'S GHOSTS

*The Long Legacy of War and Genocide in Five Countries*

MARK A. WOLFGRAM

BUCKNELL UNIVERSITY PRESS

*Lewisburg, Pennsylvania*

Library of Congress Cataloging-in-Publication Control Number: 2018026287

A British Cataloging-in-Publication record for this book is available from the British Library.



∞ The paper used in this publication meets the requirements of the American National Standard for Information Sciences—Permanence of Paper for Printed Library Materials, ANSI Z39.48-1992.

www.bucknell.edu/UniversityPress

Manufactured in the United States of America

*For Vesna*

*The other states are all convulsed with hate.*
*Their mangled sons receive their final rites*
*from dogs and beasts, or else some wingéd bird*
*defiles the city's hearth with putrid flesh.*
—Tiresias to Creon, *Antigone* (1080–1084)*

* Sophocles, *Antigone*, trans. David Mulroy (Madison: University of Wisconsin Press, 2013), 55, lines 1080–83.

# Contents

# Note on Translations

All translations in this book are the author's, unless otherwise noted.

# ANTIGONE'S GHOSTS

# *Introduction*

*In contrast to revenge, which is a natural, automatic reaction to transgression and which because of the irreversibility of the action process can be expected and even calculated, the act of forgiving can never be predicted.*

—Hannah Arendt, *The Human Condition*[1]

*The gods may judge my sentence good, and I*
*will learn by suffering how I've sinned; but if*
*these men are wrong, I wish them nothing worse*
*than what they most unjustly do to me.*

—Antigone in *Antigone*[2]

*They were sisters,*
*born from the same race; one dwelt in Greece,*
*her home by lot; the other, non-Greek land.*

—Atossa in *Persians*[3]

Something spectacular happened in human history in 472 BCE. The Athenians produced Aeschylus's new play *Persians* at the Great Dionysia as part of their annual theater festival. The play is about the battle of Salamis and its aftermath, where the vastly larger forces of Xerxes and the Persians were crushed by the Athenian navy. Aeschylus was a veteran of the war, and he knew what battle looked like, how it sounded, how it felt afterward. Instead of their entire civilization having been destroyed, the Athenians had survived. That such a military triumph should have been the subject of a dramatic theater play should not strike us as surprising until we realize that Aeschylus wrote the play from the perspective of the defeated Persians. Indeed, when Phrynichus had produced his trilogy four years earlier about the same victory, it had been from the Athenian perspective, but the play had failed miserably and the playwright was fined for having traumatized the audience.[4] What led the ancient Greeks to embrace a dramatic presentation of their military victory from the perspective of those whom they had defeated?

Karen Armstrong has helped to popularize the research of Karl Jaspers, the German philosopher and scholar of religions, who wrote about the Axial Age, a period from about 800 to 200 BCE, during which there was a fundamental transformation in human consciousness through the development of religious and philosophical thought. There are two key aspects of this transformation that have a direct bearing on the present study. First, the Axial Age philosophers and religious scholars sought to confront the increasing violence in their society by opening up the possibility of empathizing with the other side and transcending one's own ego. Second, these thinkers created the possibility of questioning the givenness of one's society. At roughly the same time, these independent developments can be found within the teachings of Confucius in China, the Buddha in India, the Hebrew prophets of ancient Israel, and the Greek philosophers. The reasons for this breakthrough in human consciousness have been the result of much scholarly inquiry, but two components appear essential. First, the increasing wealth of human civilizations at the time allowed for a certain class of people to dedicate themselves to thought and reflection rather than mere daily survival. Second, the Iron Age had unleashed new scales of violence that humanity had not experienced before. The thinkers of the Axial Age began to reflect on the nature of human existence and to question the givenness of their societies. As Jaspers put it, the Axial breakthrough was the new human capacity for "questioning all human activity and conferring upon it a new meaning."[5]

*Antigone*, written by Sophocles just three decades after *Persians* in 441 BCE, is another play from the Axial Age that has a direct bearing on the problems discussed in this book. Sophocles's play is probably one of the most discussed in the Western world, with its themes of war, death, divided loyalty to the state and family, and the lead character's disobedience of state authority. In parallels that are remarkably striking and insightful for our present concerns, King Creon, uncle to Antigone, Ismene, Eteocles, and Polyneices, orders, after a civil war, that those who fought for the city should receive a proper burial, but those who fought against the city should be left to rot in the sun and have their bodies eaten by the dogs and vultures. Antigone's two brothers have fought on opposite sides in the war, and they have killed each other, but Eteocles is to receive an honorable burial, while Polyneices is to be dishonored for having fought against the city. Indeed, all those who fought with Polyneices are to be left unburied.

Antigone knowingly disobeys Creon's order, and when she is captured and challenged by Creon, she says, "It wasn't Zeus who issued that decree. The justice that resides with gods below has never sanctioned practices like yours. I didn't think a mortal man's decrees possessed sufficient strength to nullify the deities' secure, unwritten laws."[6] Creon feels compelled to enforce his law, least his authority be questioned and the fragile stability of the city, already riven by civil war, be further endangered. And in the tragic turn of the play, Antigone forces his hand by humiliating Creon in public. Both characters remain overcommitted to their original positions, unwilling to recognize any justice or reason in the actions of the other. They fail the test of the Axial Age: empathetic and compassionate identification with the other person and their situation.

Creon orders that Antigone be entombed alive in a cave. He makes his fateful and tragic decision, even though he is warned by the chorus and his son, Haemon, not to do so. Haemon recognizes Creon's vengeful and humiliated state of mind and counsels, "Step back from anger. Let your feelings change."[7] Haemon and Antigone are to be married and thus symbolize the hope and the promise of the future. But Creon pushes forward and buries that future in the cave. Three suicides are the result. Antigone hangs herself before she can be rescued, once Creon changes his mind; Haemon tries to stab Creon and then kills himself when he discovers Antigone's suicide; and Eurydice, Creon's wife, kills herself upon learning of Haemon's death. Creon has his kingdom, for the time being, and the political power, but his decisions have destroyed his family and thrown the future of his city into doubt.

While the play ends with Creon's grief-stricken words, Tiresias has issued a warning earlier that even worse may yet follow: "The other states are all convulsed with hate."[8] Not only has Creon denied a proper burial for Polyneices but also for all those who fought with him. The desire for revenge and the Furies are still loose in the world as the play closes. Too many remain unburied, unmourned.

Just as Haemon cautions Creon, "Step back from anger. Let your feelings change," Ismene becomes frightened in the face of Antigone's wild and irrational passion to bury Polyneices at the very opening of the play; Ismene tries unsuccessfully to calm Antigone's passions. Indeed, Antigone speculates about her own "madness." Aeschylus pushed his Athenian audience to move past this vengeful state in *Persians*, and Sophocles's tragic play unfolds in large part because Antigone and Creon both remain overcommitted to their positions. It is Haemon and Ismene who plead for a return to balance, for a compassionate identification with the other, for *both* Antigone and Creon to back away from their maximalist positions. The way out of the tragedy, however difficult and improbable, exists in the voices of Haemon and Ismene.

The many ghosts of *Antigone* continue to haunt the world of the play and our present reality as well. By denying an honorable burial for all those who have fought in the civil war, Creon sets in motion part of the tragedy of the play. But Antigone also plays her role in the tragedy by making it nearly impossible for Creon to back down and reverse his judgment by humiliating him in front of others, even when doubt begins to enter his mind. The moderating voices of Haemon and Ismene are swept aside in the violent storm.

To put Creon's decision into the language of the present study, which I develop in this introductory chapter, he represents the overwhelming prevalence of the *ethnocentrism of death*, which remains a key barrier to dealing with the legacy of violence today. All human societies focus on their own suffering and loss, often to such an extent that they fail to realize or deny the harm that they have caused others or the suffering that others have experienced. The intense sense of rage and grief unleashed by mourning a loved one's death, especially violent death at the hands of other humans, has the potential to blind us. When we deny one side in a conflict the right to bury their dead honorably, to mourn their losses openly, and to grieve, we set up exactly one side of the tragedy that Sophocles is warning us about in *Antigone*. But Sophocles is also warning us against the passionate overcommitment of Antigone as well. In mourning and burying our own dead, as Antigone does, which is legitimate and necessary, we need to be careful not to humiliate the other side in the process. Both sides have to grope their way forward toward what the future might look like. As will become clear throughout this book, the ethnocentrism of death is a very powerful and destructive force, one of which the ancient Greeks were well aware and associated with the Furies, the spirit of revenge. It is a spirit that destroys the possibility of the future and buries it in the cave.

The hope of this book is that by studying five cases of states and societies that have engaged their difficult histories in a self-critical manner, we can begin to explore some of the social mechanisms that are at work, and to understand the process of collective memory formation, which gives us a shared sense of the past. I chose the cases so as to provide some variation along three key dimensions on which I will elaborate in this introduction: the type of conflict within which the mass violence occurred (external imperialism or civil war), the political regime that governed the period after the conflict (democratic, transitional, authoritarian), and the general cultural tradition within which to situate the case (Western or non-Western). The cases of postwar East and West Germany, Japan, Spain, Yugoslavia, and Turkey provide variation across these three different dimensions.

The contemporary relevance of this research is not limited to the cases studied here, each of which remains, to varying degrees, unsettled. The world is filled with examples of strained international relations and lingering internal divisions. The case selection provided here offers an opportunity to take an extended view of how these societies have dealt with the long legacy of war and genocide. This provides us with some insight into what we can expect to deal with once the fighting has ended in Syria, which will eventually happen. The cases of Spain and Yugoslavia can provide important lessons especially for Syria. Turkey remains the most troubled of the five cases, and its continued democratization is currently in serious doubt. Japan continues to experience strained relations with South Korea and China in a region of the world where antagonism regarding the past remains far less settled than on the European continent.

As much as these problems remain contemporary, they are also eternal to the human condition. *Persians* and *Antigone* were not the only spectacular cultural events of those years; they are also two examples that are directly related to the concerns of this book and our own modern age. Indeed, the current relevance of these two plays from ancient Greece for the modern context should remind us that there is less that separates us from the ancients than we might sometimes assume. The anthropologist Mary Douglas once lamented the artificial division between the ancient world and the modern, writing, "So little has been done to extend the analysis across modern and primitive cultures that there is still no common vocabulary. Sacraments are one thing, magic another; taboos one thing, sin another. The first thing is to break through the spiky verbal hedges that arbitrarily insulate one set of human experiences (ours) from another set (theirs)."[9] In *Persians*, the Athenian playwright asks his fellow citizens to seek a compassionate perspective on the recent defensive war they have successfully fought against the vastly larger invading forces from Persia. In this manner, Persia fought an outward-directed, expansionist war similar to that which Germany and Japan fought during World War II. For the modern reader to gauge the massive emotional task that Aeschylus set for his audience, look for a modern-day film about World War II in which the audience is offered a chance to identify with the suffering of the Germans or Japanese. While such perspectives dominate in domestic German and Japanese cinema, reflecting the ethnocentrism of death, it is very rare to find such perspectives from those who suffered at their hands. In *Antigone*, the audience is asked to wrestle with the consequences of a civil war, where brother has slain brother, not unlike the wars that Spain, Yugoslavia, and Turkey have experienced in the twentieth century or the current situation in Syria. The concerns of the ancient Greeks are not so unlike our own. How are we to deal with the legacy of violent conflict and the potential that the Furies will remain loose in the world?

Since the end of World War II, and especially in the Western world, there has been an increasing trend toward societies engaging and debating their difficult histories and reflecting, in a self-critical manner, on the harm that they have caused others, even while perhaps fighting wars that appeared as necessary as the Athenian defense of their civilization against the Persians. This sort of self-critical reflection is very much an Axial Age exercise in empathy and a renewed concern about placing constraints on our capacity to commit horrible acts of violence against each other, even if those acts are deemed as a necessary part of warfare.

While there is some evidence of this process unfolding in each of the cases, they vary a great deal with regard as to how each society has dealt with its difficult history, from a near full acknowledgment of the crimes of National Socialism by the German state and broader society, to the long-term denial of the Armenian genocide by the Turkish state, although, as we will see, more segments of Turkish civil society today are prepared to recognize the genocide as part of Turkish history. As Armstrong has observed, the ancient Greeks understood that they needed to take responsibility for the legacy of violence in their society: "In their long-term effects, the dark deeds of the past live on in the polis, so Athenians must acknowledge them and make place for them in their minds and hearts; they can then transform these primitive passions into a force for compassion."[10] A failure to do so would leave the spirit of revenge, represented by the Furies, loose in the society and remain a threat for any future peace.

In the rest of this introduction, I develop a basic model for collective memory formation to help create a clear sense of the different processes and forces that are at work as a society deals with its legacy of mass violence. We can then use this basic model and set of concepts to help us see the similarities and differences that exist in the five cases that form the core of this book. By studying these five cases in depth and setting them into comparison with each other, we can gain some insight into what we can expect to happen in Syria or other similar cases in the coming years. We can also come to better appreciate the challenges that exist in helping societies to deal with their violent pasts, as this becomes more of the policy-making agenda in the coming years.

## A Basic Model for Collective Memory Formation

Let's begin our discussion with Figure 1, which offers a visual overview of how collective memory formation takes place and the different forces at work. We will start with a highly abstract model and then begin adding different layers of specification. One point that we will want to return to again and again is an understanding of how these different factors either tend to open up discussion about the past or shut down and subvert discussion about the past.

We begin with the individual and their encounter with some cultural expression, which is a representation of the past. This cultural expression can take many different forms. It could be a physical object, such as a film, book, or painting, or it could be a social practice, such as a dance, theater performance, or listening to someone tell a story. The individual may come to some new understanding of their relationship toward their personal past or that of their community, or to have an old understanding reconfirmed. This encounter with a representation of the past will either reconfirm an existing way of understanding the past, or it will change and transform it in some manner. This can remain an internal and personal dialogue, or it can be shared with others. If the individual choses to share their understanding with others, this has the potential to set further cultural change in motion as well.

Throughout this book, it is essential that the reader keep this dynamic understanding of culture in mind. This is certainly the intention of the author. We should avoid conceptualizing "a culture" as a bounded, homogeneous, coherent, and stable whole, which determines the behavior of individuals. Rather, individuals either reconfirm or transform their culture on a daily basis through their choices and practices. But they do so within an already-existing cultural context. By thinking about this cultural matrix within which individuals make their choices, we can work to avoid essentialist understandings of unchanging notions of "the Japanese" or "the Germans." At the same time, one must deal with the existing cultural matrix within which individuals are making these choices, and these contexts differ from one society to the next. The cultural matrix within which a Japanese individual makes daily decisions is different from the one in which a German makes their daily choices.

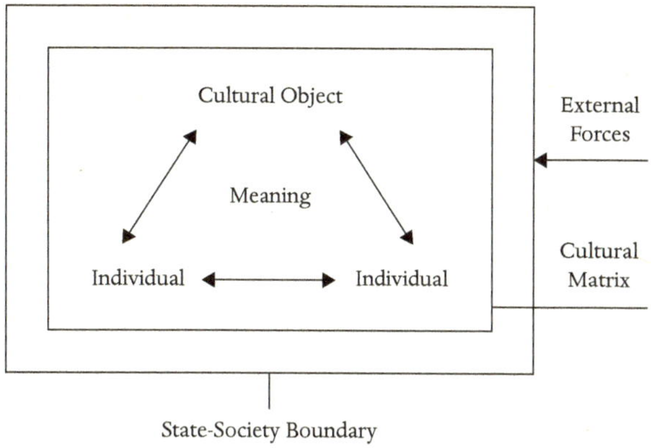


Figure 1 A basic model for collective memory formation.
*Source*: Reprinted with permission, Mark A. Wolfgram, "A Model for Comparative Collective Memory Studies: Regime Types, Cultural Traditions, and Difficult Histories," *Politička Misao* [*Croatian Political Science Review*] 51, no. 5 (2014): 13–35.

A core part of this book's argument is that the existing literature on collective memory formation largely fails to deal with cultural differences in a systematic manner.[11] A more balanced discussion of politics and culture is important for the development of this field of research. When deciding how and if one is going to engage with the nation's difficult past, people will make decisions shaped by both political and cultural power, the threat of both institutionalized violence and social sanction. The fact that most of the literature in this field is written by and for scholars located in Western countries about Western countries has led to certain blind spots regarding the role of culture in the process of confronting a difficult history. We will return to this topic in far greater detail later in this chapter.

What is of greatest interest for us is the social process that occurs when the individual engages with others and enters into a dialogue, asking the question of the other, "What do you think about that?" What then follows is an exchange of ideas about the meaning of the cultural expression. This may lead to a new, shared understanding of each individual's relationship with the past, but it could also lead to further disagreement. What matters is that the two individuals have engaged some representation of the past and entered into a discussion with each other, and as a result, old cultural understandings have either been reconfirmed or altered in some way, thus creating a new understanding.

## Psychological and Social-Psychological Processes

There are some psychological and social-psychological processes that are probably universal to the human experience, although their exact functioning and intensity may differ from case to case. The *externalization of blame* and the *ethnocentrism of death* are common to all five cases and involve, respectively, exculpating responsibility and self-focused grieving. The other three factors, *social contagion*, *reinforcement*, and *socially shared retrieval-induced forgetting* (SS-RIF) shape the manner in which narratives about the past circulate in a society and become more prevalent and salient, or fade into the background and are forgotten.

Two widely observed and interrelated phenomena are the externalization of blame for whatever has gone wrong in the past and the ethnocentrism of death in which individuals and groups focus primarily on their own victimhood and thus tend to block out the suffering they may have caused others. First, the externalization of blame appears to be a very widespread, if not perhaps a universal, phenomenon. Writing about the legacy of French colonialism in Madagascar, Jennifer Cole notes, "Like the trope of internal goodness despite violence, the externalization of blame allowed people to ignore the violence they had done to each other, to act as if it were entirely the fault of external forces."[12] We will see evidence of the externalization of blame in each of the cases in the present study. External political forces (human agency) and fate (some nonhuman force) are often used to reduce a sense of agency and responsibility for the violence that one's own group has perpetrated.

The social psychologists Bertjan Doosje and Nyla Branscombe have found that the externalization of blame intensified the more that group members strongly identified with the in-group. "We found that the more people identified with their national group, the more likely they were to explain their group's negative historical treatment of another group in terms of situational factors, and the more likely they were to point to internal or dispositional factors when they explain similar negative behavior on the part of an outgroup."[13] Although the externalization of blame can be found in all the cases studied here, it takes different forms and varies in its intensity with the passage of time. Societies that are more collectivist than individualist in nature are more likely to externalize blame.

As to the tendency to focus on one's own suffering and to have this act as a block on the recognition of the suffering that one's group may have caused others, this is again a universal phenomenon. The ethnocentrism of death means that the human need and capacity for grieving will lead first and foremost to a focus on one's own traumatic losses.[14] This is simply part of the human condition and not one that can be wished away; indeed, it may be unethical to place such a demand on anyone. Human grieving in the face of death is necessary.

In each of these cases, we can see evidence that the ethnocentrism of death weakens over time, especially as the society moves from one generation to the next. For those who directly experienced the terror of war, genocide, and mass suffering, this remains a lifelong struggle and is not easily achieved. It may become somewhat easier for the following generations to heed Haemon's warning to Creon, and Ismene's cautioning of Antigone, to step back from passionate overcommitment and to open oneself up to the possibility of a *Persian*-styled narrative. But it is far from a given that the succeeding generations will abandon the position of their forbearers. Emotional obligations to one's parents and grandparents can remain quite intense, especially when issues of family and national honor are at stake. As we will see in the following chapters, some cultures maintain a stronger bond between the living and the dead, making it more difficult to move past the ethnocentrism of death even with the passage of time.

Three additional social-psychological factors help us to appreciate how narratives about the past circulate in a society and either maintain their salience or fade into the realm of the forgotten. First, social contagion plays an important role in bringing forward difficult discussions about a country's national history. Social contagion is the spread of ideas and understandings from one person to the next. The social contagion effect does not work particularly in favor or against the engagement with a difficult history. It simply reminds us of the social aspect of the process of collective memory formation. The reinforcement effect is critical because human cognition is constantly allowing pieces of information to drift into the realm of the forgotten; our memory capacity is similar to a leaky bucket, constantly needing the inflow of new information.[15] When a topic or idea is consistently reinforced through social contagion, it becomes something that one is more likely to discuss with others.

There are elements of the process of collective memory formation that move slowly and without any clear, widespread disturbance in the society but can then in a short time burst into the national discussion. As with an earthquake, avalanche, or forest fire, there can be a largely unobserved buildup of tension, energy, or fuel that can then lead to a period of rapid and transformative change. A good example of this is the dramatic shift that occurred in West Germany in the 1980s in terms of dramatic increase in the discussion of the Holocaust and the crimes of the Nazi regime when compared to the earlier decades.[16] While by no means absent in the earlier postwar decades, the social contagion and reinforcement effects were far weaker compared to the 1980s. Each of the cases in the present study demonstrates periods of long apparent stasis or glacial movement toward confronting a violent history, followed by a period of intense activity and engagement with the same. With the aid of the *memory-market dictum*, which I discuss below, I suggest where we might best look in a society so as to appreciate where the accumulation of volatile memories might be occurring.

The final social-psychological process for us to keep in mind is SS-RIF.[17] Research on SS-RIF shows that while we are reinforcing and increasing the salience of certain understandings about the past, others are being pushed more into the realm of the forgotten. William Hirst and Gerald Echterhoff write of SS-RIF, "When people selectively remember in conversation, they are not only reinforcing existing memories, but, by not mentioning other memories, they are setting up conditions conducive for forgetting."[18] One of the most powerful effects of this process is that while it may be the case that past crimes become more widely discussed in the broader society, the identity of the perpetrators may remain very vague and unclear or carefully circumscribed by the abstraction of "the Nazis" in Germany, "the militarists" in Japan, "the Reds" in Spain, or "the fascists" in Yugoslavia. Even in a society such as Germany, where past crimes have been widely discussed for several decades, the SS-RIF effect has left the identity of the perpetrators unclear, especially within families.

All of these different effects combine to create what Marc Howard Ross has termed *psychocultural narratives* about the group's origins, fears, and history of engagement with other groups. These narratives may often strike outsiders as irrational and simply something to be dismissed, a barrier to progress on the "real" issues at stake. This is a serious mistake. As Ross notes, "While it is often easy to dismiss in-group accounts as incorrect or irrational and therefore irrelevant 'just-so' stories, to do so would be as foolish as it is for a psychoanalyst to tell a patient he or she had just recounted a stupid dream."[19] It is essential that we heed Ross's warning as we look at the different narratives that people tell about themselves and their view of their own history. This does not mean that we adopt a position of relativism but rather that we must maintain a compassionate regard for other people's fears and emotions while trying to understand how they engage or fail to engage the legacy of violence in their own society.

## Politics and Culture

Let's now begin to add in layers of specification and see how different political and cultural settings have a profound effect on our abstract model of collective memory formation. The reasons for the variations between the cases run along three different vectors: the type of conflict experienced, the political regime type, and the broad cultural tradition. This leads to two further general observations for our analysis. First, democratic political regimes with vibrant civil societies offer greater openness for discussing difficult national histories than do authoritarian political regimes. Second, Western or more individualistic societies are more likely to engage in wide-ranging, conflictual, and contentious debates about the past. For example, Japan combines the promise of openness offered by democratic institutions with a cultural tradition that seeks to minimize open, public confrontations by instead promoting harmonious relations as a social ideal. As we will see in the individual case studies, each country offers a combination of political and cultural factors that either help to enable a confrontation with a difficult history or seek to undermine and repress the same. Politics and culture are not static, but cultural norms tend to change far more slowly than formal political institutions.

### *Types of Conflicts—Internal and External*

One key comparative aspect that this research has revealed is that the type of difficult history that a society is processing matters a great deal. In terms of victims and perpetrators, are the victims of the group's violence members of their own society, or do they primarily reside in other countries? If the victims are primarily outside the state and society, then it means that the struggle to bring these past issues

Table 1 Types of Conflicts, Political Regimes, and Cultural Traditions

| *Country* | *Type of Conflict* | *Political Regime* | *Cultural Tradition* |
|---|---|---|---|
| East Germany | External Imperialism *Persians* | Authoritarian | Western |
| West Germany | External Imperialism *Persians* | Democratic | Western |
| Japan | External Imperialism *Persians* | Democratic | Non-Western |
| Spain | Civil War *Antigone* | Authoritarian / Transitional / Democratic | Western |
| Yugoslavia 1945–1992 | Civil War *Antigone* | Authoritarian / Transitional | Western |
| Turkey | Civil War *Antigone* | Authoritarian / Transitional | Non-Western |

to light in the present have to be raised more within the realm of international relations. This is primarily the case for Germany and Japan in which the victims and survivors of their wars and genocidal campaigns resided primarily outside the source country at the end of the war. This means that it is far easier for the domestic population, after the war, to focus on their own victimhood and suffering, reinforcing the ethnocentrism of death. One's own victimhood and hardship in the war or on the home front is much more immediate than any acts of perpetratorhood that occurred far from home. For the vast majority of the population, the suffering that their group caused to others is not immediately available to them in terms of face-to-face interaction. A local sense of the war's history will encourage a dissociation from narratives and stories of perpetratorhood far from home. Their encounter with the victims of their own group's violence will only develop over a longer time and often at a distance. It will be mediated through newspaper reports, war crime trials, radio reports, television programs, and films. But domestic victims can also be influential. West Germany's very small remaining Jewish community, largely concentrated in Berlin, played a critical role in prodding the German conscious about what had happened during the war from within the society. In contrast, the domestic Korean and Chinese communities in Japan remained far more marginalized and unable to organize or to express themselves.

If, on the other hand, the conflict and violence was primarily internal to the same state and society, as in a civil war, the dynamics become radically different. Local memories will be far more volatile, explosive, and divided, as victims and perpetrators will continue to live in close proximity to each other and may have to encounter each other on a daily basis. Fear and the potential for renewed violence will be far greater. Depending on how mixed the communities are, this daily face-to-face interaction may be frequent or infrequent. For example, in Spain, the violence of Spaniard against Spaniard penetrated to the village level, so that the victim and perpetrator groups found themselves in daily contact with each other for decades after the conflict. This was also true in Yugoslavia, where many villages, especially in Bosnia, contained members of two or more religious and ethnic groups. Although they may have tended to cluster in different parts of the village, communal life would bring them into frequent contact with each other. Compared to Spain and Yugoslavia, the Ottoman Turkish genocide against the Armenian Christians was much more concentrated in specific geographic regions than was the case in either Yugoslavia or Spain. The large-scale killing took place in the far east, although the urban Armenian population was also killed in large numbers.[20]

Even in the case of Spain, Yugoslavia, and Turkey, where there are significant victim populations within the society, these groups often found it very difficult to organize themselves. As we will see in the individual case studies, although each of these countries experienced extended periods of authoritarian rule, there were limited possibilities for victimized groups to organize and to protest for recognition of their suffering. This was most apparent for the Serbian victims of the Croatian genocide against Serbs during World War II. The Jasenovac extermination camp came to serve as a core symbol of the genocide, similar to the role that Auschwitz plays in the German genocide against the Jews. The ability of victimized groups to organize was much weaker in Spain and Turkey, where Republican voices and Armenian concerns remained largely silenced during the authoritarian periods. While Spain has changed significantly since the turn toward democracy after Franco's death in 1975, Turkey has remained more trapped in patterns of authoritarian rule, although civil society groups have become far more active over the past two decades. In each of these cases, external pressures came to play an important role. Members of the victimized groups living in exile sought to influence affairs back in the home country. Exiled groups have sought to influence discussions in the home country through interaction between members of the civil societies as well as pressuring their new home states to intervene on their behalf and to demand recognition of their past suffering.

### *Internal Politics: Regime Type and State-Society Relations*

Along the political vector, it will be useful to divide our discussion about democracy and authoritarianism into two separate but interrelated components—those of the state and the society. Another important factor to recognize within the field of politics is that the push for deeper and self-critical engagement with a country's difficult history has almost always come, in the first instance, from the civil society and not from the state. The state may come to play a positive role in this process, but the initial push for self-critical engagement comes from actors within the civil society. Democratic and authoritarian states both clearly try to shape a positive, national narrative, but they are less likely, at first, to engage in a self-critical analysis of the national history. While talking about the political vector, we will want to keep state-society relationships in mind.

The cases selected for this study provide a great deal of diversity along both of these vectors, as each of the cases has varied significantly along the democratic-authoritarian continuum with the passage of time. Japan and West Germany both began the period after World War II as democracies with regard to formal, constitutional institutions and evolved into more democratic societies. East Germany (1949–1990) remained an authoritarian state throughout, although the level of state repression did not remain constant. In 1990, the East German state was dissolved and incorporated into the constitutional democracy of West Germany. Spain, Yugoslavia, and Turkey have moved backward and forward along the democratic-authoritarian continuum over time. Turkey has become a more democratic state and society over the past two decades, compared to the first several decades of the republic, although the events of the past two years have seen a strong swing back in a more authoritarian direction. Spain made a formal transition to democracy after Franco's death in 1975. And Yugoslavia, although failing in its attempt to adopt formal democratic institutions as a unified country, also had periods of more or less freedom with regard to discussing its difficult history.

An important part of our model involves individuals encountering cultural expressions that bring them into dialogue with others regarding the meaning of the past. As these cultural expressions change, with more or less discussion of the difficult history, the conversations between individuals will also be pushed and pulled in different directions. But it is essential to realize that the meaning is generated in the social interaction; the meaning is never *in* the cultural expression. Therefore, a great deal depends on the types of narratives that are being made and the autonomy that individuals have to discuss them.

I proposed the concept of the *memory-market dictum* in my earlier research on East and West Germany as a way of thinking about the production and consumption of cultural expressions in a society, and how they might differ in democratic and authoritarian societies. In its original formulation, the memory-market dictum recognizes that "memory makers need access to 'capital' to take their products to market, and the more capital intensive a product is, the more sensitive the producer will be to prevailing attitudes either in the population at large (democratic regime) or in state ideology (authoritarian regime)."[21] I came to this realization when I was struck by the radical difference that existed in the postwar West German cinema compared to what was available on West German public television stations. The public television stations were taking far greater risks in offending their German audiences with challenging narratives about the war and the Holocaust decades before such narratives became more prevalent in West German cinemas. The same was also true for theater plays and novels, compared to the mainstream cinema. The playwrights and novelists were able to provide more challenging, more self-critical narratives about the past than was the case in the cinema, which was far more capital intensive. The current comparative research provides still more evidence in support of the memory-market dictum. For example, when authoritarian states began to loosen their control over cultural production, the first challenging and self-critical narratives about the national past began to appear in novels and theater plays, and then only later and less frequently in the cinemas.

Thus, a democratic state and society coupled with a capitalist market economy certainly offers more freedom and plurality in terms of allowing for the generation of self-critical narratives about the past. But that same capitalist economy can act as a severe break on these types of discussions in the more expensive visual formats of television and movies that reach vastly larger audiences if producers view certain themes as too alienating and upsetting. The West German encounter with the difficult history of the war and the Holocaust would have been very different if the public television stations had not been so prominent and far more willing to take risks. The growing role of capital interests and the declining role for the state in all of these countries is not necessarily a change that will aid the development of self-critical narratives about the past. These changes certainly weaken the oppressive force of the authoritarian state, but mainstream mass attitudes may remain very hostile to self-critical narratives about the past. This can also have a censoring-like effect, as producers shy away from difficult material because they fear the market for such stories is too small. To the extent that democratic states wish to support and subsidize difficult, self-critical discussions about the past, they are now in a far weaker position today than was the case with West Germany in the postwar years, where public television was the only game in town. The memory-market dictum encourages us to think about the relationship between the production and consumption of material related to the difficult histories in each of our cases in this study.

### *External Politics: International Relations*

Successful engagement with a difficult national history, when it has occurred, has come about primarily as a result of internal political and social-cultural struggle, rather than something that has been successfully imposed and pushed for from outside the country. The legacy of war crimes trials managed by the victors of World War II in Japan has been largely negative and ambiguous in Germany. As with the Nuremberg trials in postwar Germany, the International Criminal Tribunal for the former Yugoslavia has not been well received by the local populations, which rally in support of "their" people when they are on trial. In general, people do not like outsiders telling them what to think about their most recent and violent histories.[22]

The ethnocentrism of death tends to shut down these sorts of discussions that outsiders try to promote. It may lead to official gestures of reconciliation and play a role in elite and state-to-state relations, but the local populations often remain hostile or indifferent. Drawing on *Antigone* for understanding, all populations tend to behave more like Creon than Antigone. We want to bury our dead with dignity while denying this possibility to our enemies. This dynamic in the present tends to generate the same negative and tragic consequences that Sophocles warns about in his play. The Furies of ancient Greece remain loose, threatening future violence.

In all the cases, the primary force for change has come eventually from inside the country itself. At the same time, there has been agitation from outside the country for engaging the difficult historical legacy. The external forces are not negligible, but they have never been the primary force for change. It has only been when those advocating for change from outside the country have found internal allies that change has come about.

The effectiveness of the external agitation for engaging a difficult history varies significantly between democratic and authoritarian societies and between Western and non-Western countries. On the political side, democratic states and societies are far more open to exchanges with other societies in terms of the movement of people and ideas. Furthermore, there has been a growing international consensus and set of norms over the course of the twentieth century that states and societies need to take responsibility for their difficult histories, especially coming out of World War II and the legacy of the Holocaust. Authoritarian states have always placed more restrictions on internal debates about the past and have been far more closed to external pressure than democracies, although the extent of this closure has varied over time. As we will see with the cases of Spain, Turkey, and Yugoslavia, when the authoritarian regimes opened up toward the Western democracies, the flow of people and ideas began to work toward internal changes.

At the same time an international consensus has been building, there has been a marked difference in how Western and non-Western states and societies have reacted to external pressures. It is not only the political authoritarianism that has been a restrictive force but also certain aspects of non-Western cultural traditions that have limited self-critical discussions. First, part of the problem grows out of the fact that, at least with the cases of Japan and Turkey, these countries are caught in a bind. They long to be considered part of the West or, at least, the modern era, and they desire to be recognized as such by the Western democracies. But they also resent this desire and dependency and often feel judged or stigmatized by the Western states and societies.[23] I will return to this point below in the section on culture, but one key point is to realize that whereas the Western tradition, especially since the Enlightenment, embraces self-critical reflection, this is not something that tends to be valued in societies that are more collectivist and non-Western in their orientation. Internal critics are often dismissed as agents of the West and the West's attempts to stigmatize and undermine the native culture. It is a mistake to transpose a growing consensus among Western societies to the world as a whole.

While non-Western states and societies may resent pressure from the Western democracies, they are even more closed to pressure from other non-Western states and societies, from which they wish to distinguish themselves. In a recent study that focused on the challenges of dealing with the legacy of war and imperialism among the East Asian countries of Korea, China, and Japan, one of the problems that the authors pointed to was that ordinary citizens and scholars tend to be extremely positivistic in their attitudes toward history, thus closing the possibility of recognizing that there can be different and legitimate interpretations of the past.[24] Furthermore, apologies work differently in East Asian cultural traditions compared to the Western cultural tradition, as they seek to restore harmony but are not necessarily driven by a sincere feeling of remorse. Rather, apologies function primarily as a social practice to restore harmony within one's own group rather than between national groups. The Western trend of issuing official apologies for past crimes will not work the same sort of magic, a point that we will need to return to later in the next section on culture and in the individual case studies. In summary, external forces will have a greater effect in the Western democracies than in the non-Western countries, democratic or not.

### *The Cultural Matrix: Differences between Western and Non-Western Cultural Traditions*

In terms of culture, there is clear evidence that the Western and more individualistic societies in Germany, Spain, and Yugoslavia engaged their difficult histories in ways that are markedly different from those in Japan and Turkey, which have a more collectivist cultural orientation. While one can certainly point to numerous ways in which Japanese and Turkish societies have become more Westernized and individualistic over the course of the twentieth century, there remain very stark contrasts between more individualistic Western societies and more collectivist non-Western societies.[25] Westernization or modernization in terms of technological progress and economic development has not necessarily led to the same pace of change in terms of other cultural values.

Whereas the proposition that democratic states and societies are more open and willing to engage in self-critical discussions about the national past may appear self-evident and uncontroversial, it is anything but obvious that there might be a difference between Western and non-Western societies. Some may wish to maintain that everything in this discussion should be reduced to a discussion of politics and that cultural differences are not a useful or appropriate level of the analysis. This is a profoundly mistaken proposition but one that is a widespread assumption in the literature, if more implicit than explicit, because cultural differences are often hardly discussed at all, even in comparisons of Germany and Japan.[26]

For example, Lind does not see the cultural differences between Germany and Japan as playing any significant role in terms of how apologies can function in international relations and diplomacy. She notes that social psychologists argue that the basics of an effective apology "transcend cultures."[27] Perhaps the basics transcend cultures at the level of diplomatic relations governed by Western norms and expectations, but that does not mean that there are not very significant cultural differences. In order for apologies to be effective and make sense to both sides, they may need to pay careful attention to culturally specific traditions.[28] For example, when it became known that the student responsible for the Virginia Tech University massacre in the United States was Korean born, the South Korean ambassador to the United States called on Korean Americans to "repent" and fast for thirty-two days to atone for each victim.[29] Obviously, this makes little cultural sense to those steeped in Western individualism, but it does make cultural sense within Korea's more collectivist culture. Indeed, as we will see in a moment, the content and form of apologies are filled with cultural assumptions that differ significantly from one cultural context to the next.

Consider one additional example at this point, the fact that within Christianity, Judaism, and Islam there has been historically a great deal of interest about the ethics of what constitutes a just war. In contrast, these debates are almost wholly absent within the East Asian contexts of China and Japan, where the justice of a war has been simply defined by the fact that the sovereign acted to initiate warfare.[30] Historically, there was no clear moral or ethical universe against which to judge the actions of the sovereign, a point that Masao Maruyama made while trying to explain the extreme barbarism of Japanese soldiers during World War II.[31] If a society lacks a sense of a "just war thesis," then it can be difficult to apologize for something for which one feels no sense of moral responsibility. The question of whether or not a war is "just" may simply exist outside the realm of reasonable discourse. Once one appreciates this cultural fact along with how individualist and collectivist notions of apologies differ, one can understand why Japan's numerous apologies for World War II in East Asia have not brought about the desired reconciliation. This is true even between the two democracies of Japan and South Korea. Obviously, politics and international relations alone cannot explain these difficulties.

The point about cultural differences and the ethics of just wars is significant in another way as well in that Turkey, as a predominately Muslim country, is clearly different from Japan in this context. Although I group Japan and Turkey together as non-Western in the context of this work, this does not mean that the two cases are themselves at all that similar. Rather, they are similar primarily in so far as they are both significantly different from the Western norm in a couple of key ways, which I turn to next.

Some readers will undoubtedly feel uncomfortable with my choice of using the categories of "Western" and "non-Western" as part of my analysis. Indeed, some parts of the academy have become extremely hostile to such discussions, but this is largely for political reasons and not because the categories themselves lack any analytic utility. For myself, while I began this project with the intention of giving equal attention to politics and culture, as I have done with my previous work, the categories of "the West" and "non-West" were far from my thoughts. It was only over the course of conducting this research that I came to see some utility in using these categories. It will also be useful to think of these categories as end points on a continuum and not to treat them as rigid binary categories. Furthermore, we should not treat the different cases as firmly fixed in one category or the other.

Whereas the Axial Age opened up new possibilities for the spread of human empathy, compassion, and understanding, the European Enlightenment was a far more recent event, the effects of which were at first more limited to the European continent and then gained some global prominence as a result of European colonial expansion and now the ongoing process of globalization. The many negative consequences of European colonization for much of the world's population and especially the indigenous populations of North America, Latin America, Australia, and New Zealand are one reason why discussion of the West has become politically heated. Despite the process of globalization, there remain some very persistent differences between certain Western cultural values and beliefs and those of the non-Western or less Western.[32] As with all discussion of cultural matters in this book, the following must be kept in mind: (1) all human societies are dynamic and changing, and (2) they embody a great deal of diversity within themselves. To be clear, I am making the claim that these large categories are of analytic value and that the alternative of extreme cultural relativism and a focus on cultural specificity leaves us blind to important macrolevel observations.

There are several aspects of the Western cultural tradition, especially since the European Enlightenment, that leave Westernized societies more open to engaging their difficult histories than non-Westernized societies. By working through these differences, I hope to awaken the reader to the profound role that cultural differences can play in terms of how societies come to deal with their difficult histories. It is only by drawing comparisons that such differences become manifest, as the examples below will illustrate.

### *The Cultural Matrix: Educational Values*

Let's begin with educational values, as I give specific attention to the role of schools in teaching the difficult history of the nation in each of the case studies. Jin Li is a scholar of education who grew up in China and then continued her formal training in education at American universities. Even given this personal experience of East and West, Li confesses at the opening of her book that she had been "blind to culture" in terms of appreciating Eastern and Western differences: "Finally and inevitably, I encountered culture as a developmental concept. As I delved deeper into my studies, I realized—this time, to my personal astonishment—that I had been blind to culture."[33] What Li uncovered were some profound differences in terms of Western and East Asian educational values. The Western educational model is mind-oriented learning directed toward understanding and gaining mastery over the world. It is directed outward from the individual toward the broader world. The central values are (1) critical thinking, (2) active engagement, (3) exploration and inquiry, and (4) self-expression and communication. In contrast, the East Asian educational process is virtue-oriented learning in which one strives for self-perfection and self-mastery. East Asian educational values include (1) earnestness and sincerity, (2) diligence and self-exertion, (3) concentration, (4) endurance of hardship, and (5) perseverance.[34] In a survey of Western and East Asian students, Li shows that both groups of students appreciate some of the values of the other cultural tradition, but both show a clear preference for their own cultural tradition, with Westerners being even more committed to their value set than East Asians.[35]

These different educational values between Westerners and East Asians have some clear implications for the likelihood that a society is going to launch into a self-critical evaluation of the national history. Whereas the Western tradition embodies within itself the process of critical thinking and self-critical reflection and makes this a core value, the East Asian educational values place the mastery of received knowledge from the teacher at the core. What the European Enlightenment unleashed has been a constant reevaluation of all human knowledge, a restless contentiousness, a sense that progress is possible.[36] This sense of progress has such a taken-for-granted feeling to it in the modern Western world that we forget that this was not always the case. The European intellectuals during the Enlightenment struggled with the idea of progress and what the proper place of the ancients was in their present-day world. In the end, the broader consensus settled on the position that progress meant questioning all previous generations and their knowledge; nothing was sacred. In contrast, the East Asian educational values are geared toward the maintenance of existing tradition. This does *not* mean that Westerners have no attachment to tradition or that East Asians are frozen in the past; rather, in comparison to each other, the Western educational values set up a more dynamic process that is more open to new information and flexible. Most importantly, Westerners value critique and confrontation as an expression of individualism.

Akiko Hashimoto has done more than any other scholar to bring the importance of cultural analysis to the discussion of Japan and its difficult encounter with its violent history. In an occasional paper for the Reischauer Institute of Japanese Studies back in 1999, Hashimoto drew attention to the cultural resources that individuals could use as part of a project of what she called moral recovery, or regaining a moral stature of being good in the face of highly damaging actions in the past. In Germany and the West, individuals can engage in a courageous self-investigation of past failings and, in the process, gain the respect of others. Hashimoto writes,

"The painful work of introspection then puts one in a category of people who are morally responsible. In this sense, confronting the past—in itself—adds significantly to one's symbolic capital." Hashimoto continues, "For the Japanese, this cultural resource does not exist. In Japan, confronting the past does not necessarily connote a person of dignity, honor, and learning. . . . The notion that the unexamined life is not worth living is a Western construct; as such, it carries no *cultural legitimacy* in Japan, or, for that matter, in many other parts of the world."[37] As we will see later in the chapter on Japan, the Japanese have had to find a different route toward what Hashimoto calls moral recovery, because the Western style of a self-critical investigation is largely closed off to them.

As we will see in the chapter on Turkey, the core Western educational values are also far weaker in Turkish schools. Indeed, recent attempts to Westernize Turkish educational institutions since 2004, as part of Turkey's process of trying to join the European Union and to address Turkey's very low rankings in the Programme for International Student Assessment (PISA), a cross-national educational rankings report, have almost completely collapsed as they ran into deeply embedded cultural norms that seek to maintain the teacher as an absolute authority in the classroom. The European Enlightenment value of self-critical engagement and self-expression is not one that is universally practiced and with equal enthusiasm everywhere, even within Western countries. This should remind us again not to treat these categories as homogeneous or strict binaries. As we will see in the chapter on Japan, there are educational institutions geared toward the development of these Western values, and one can certainly think of many educational institutions in the Western world that are far more conservative. The point is that the broad distribution of one set of values or the other in a society has significant consequences for how that country will confront its difficult national history.

### *The Cultural Matrix: Patterns in Moral Reasoning*

The divergence in educational values between Western and non-Western societies also has consequences for broader patterns of moral reasoning and argumentation in societies. When Lawrence Kohlberg first articulated his six stages of moral development, he thought he had discovered a universal truth for human development, not one that was limited to the Western world, although this is where he had at first conducted all of his experiments.[38] However, once he began to look for the same six stages in non-Western societies, he began to discover some surprising results. In the non-Western societies, the final two stages, what Kohlberg saw as the highest stages and the goal of a good education, appeared to often be very weak or missing all together.

In the first two stages, children focus on obedience, avoiding punishment and serving their own needs. Kohlberg called these first two stages the preconventional level of moral reasoning. Next, as children mature and develop a conventional level of moral reasoning, in the next two stages, they begin to consider the needs of others and draw on the standards of the group, which help to maintain social order. Finally, in the last two stages, Kohlberg then argues that some, but not all, will begin to develop a postconventional level of moral reasoning where they begin to reason from abstract ethical principles such as justice, individual rights, and human dignity. What is important about the postconventional level is that individuals can appeal to these higher principles that exist beyond the group and may even put them in conflict with the group. These principles serve as a moral basis to challenge existing authority, as constituted by the social group and its leaders, and to offer a rational basis for promoting justice, which the current order impedes.

When Kohlberg first established his three different levels of moral reasoning (preconventional, conventional, postconventional), each composed of two stages, he argued vigorously and provided evidence suggesting that postconventional moral reasoning would develop everywhere with the advancement of education and urbanization. In one study, he carried out a cross-cultural comparison of the United States, Mexico, Yucatán, Taiwan, and Turkey and argued that the evidence supported his claim for the universality of the stages.[39] Indeed, there is clear evidence that as an age cohort goes from ten to sixteen years old that stage 1 and 2 (preconventional) moral reasoning drops quickly in all cases, and stage 3 and 4 (conventional) moral reasoning begins to increase in all five cases. But what is striking, despite Kohlberg's claim for universality, is that there is basically no evidence of stage 5 and 6 (postconventional) moral reasoning in Turkey and the Yucatán even by sixteen years old. In Taiwan, there is evidence of stage 5 moral reasoning but almost no development of stage 6. In the end, the United States looks distinctly different from the other cases. In a later and longer-term study focused just on Turkey with a split between village and city dwellers, Kohlberg began to trim his claims to universality noting, "The universality claim allows for the possibility of differences in the rate and end point of development. Such differences are indeed revealed in our study."[40] What is striking is that even by nineteen-plus years old, only one out of twenty city dwellers had achieved something between stage 4 or 5 moral reasoning. All other city dwellers at nineteen-plus years old were still grouped between stages 2 and 3/4. None of them had fully achieved even stage 4 moral reasoning. In short, by nineteen-plus years old, not a single city dweller had reached a postconventional stage of moral reasoning. Urbanization and "modernization" did not appear to have the hoped-for effect.

Kohlberg placed a great deal of faith in the power of education and urbanization, and in this sense, he fit his times when there was widespread belief in the academy that something called "modernization" was reshaping all global societies along the path of Western secular development. Thus, like many of his contemporaries, he overestimated the power of education and urbanization as modernizing forces and seriously underestimated the power of cultural traditions that worked against the development of postconventional moral reasoning. Most significantly, he did not take into consideration any of the differences that might exist in educational norms, which Li discovered later. Hisham Sharabi has documented how the processes of modernization have reshaped much of the outward appearances in the Arab Middle East, while producing very little in terms of a change of consciousness, a phenomenon he called neopatriarchy.[41] We will return to Sharabi's observations in a moment and see that many of his observations apply to Turkey as well.

In a recent study that has challenged many assumptions about human psychology that were once taken to be more or less universal, the authors note that cross-cultural comparisons and research since Kohlberg's work has revealed that postconventional moral reasoning is very common among Western populations in North America and Europe but very rare or nonexistent outside this population group.[42] Other researchers have suggested that while the ethic of autonomy dominates Western discussions of moral reasoning, which focuses on the autonomy of the individual and questions of avoiding harm, non-Western cultures and Western religious conservatives focus much more on the ethic of community and an ethic of divinity, which limits the autonomy that an individual can exercise because they are part of a divine order that they should not pollute. It is useful to see that Western religious conservatives share some similarities with non-Western cultures to remind us that our categories of Western and non-Western must not be treated as homogeneous wholes or clear geographical designations. By recognizing that individualism and collectivism are traits spread around in all populations, and that individuals may change their orientation based on a given context, we avoid an essentialist argument about culture, while also recognizing that there are significant differences between societies in terms of the concentration of these traits in the population at large.[43]

More recently, economic historians have begun to turn toward culturally rooted explanations for the radically different economic trajectories of Europe, on the one hand, and China[44] and the Islamic world of the Middle East,[45] on the other hand, since the sixteenth century and the European Enlightenment. Of greatest interest for us here is the argument put forward by Avner Greif and Guido Tabellini that from the tenth century onward, Europe saw the slow decline in kinship-based forms of cooperation in favor of more impersonal institutions of the corporation, whereas Chinese society became more deeply rooted in the maintenance of kinship-based forms of cooperation. Within the Chinese model, morality becomes deeply rooted in the personal relationships specific to one's own group, a "limited" form of morality, whereas the growth nonkinship forms of cooperation in Europe began to generate a "generalized" form of morality, which was not limited or specific to the kinship group but rather reached outward toward others as well.[46] They find these different moral patterns reflected in the core religious beliefs in each civilization, the legal codes, and the patterns of charitable giving.

By working on two completely different problems and in literatures that make no reference to each other, we can see how the generalized morality that Greif and Tabellini have identified in Europe can lead to concepts such as individual human rights and the openness to postconventional moral reasoning, as identified by Kohlberg. At the same time, one can see how the moral universes of the Chinese kinship clans remain limited to one's own members and thus more closed off to such discussions as "universal human rights" or abstract principles that can be used to critique the morality of the group. The same is true in the Muslim Middle East, where understandings of "justice" are tied to the person, their relationships with others, and a specific context rather than abstract principles. As Lawrence Rosen observes of the Muslim Middle East, "Indeed, since justice is an aspect of the person and not a disembodied isolate, only a full knowledge of the contexts of a person's attachments can give one a sense of the qualities of justice that may cohere in that individual."[47] What Kohlberg had discovered, without realizing it, is that the moral universes of human societies are not universal. It is not that non-Western societies so much "lack" postconventional reasoning but rather that they have a significantly different moral universe altogether. As we will see throughout this work, these different moral universes have a significant impact on how diverse societies and cultures approach their difficult histories.

### *Cultural Differences: Family, Filial Piety, and Patriarchal Authority*

We can see how the educational values in Western and non-Western societies help to shape attitudes toward established authorities. Whereas the Western educational system is geared toward critical thinking and the evaluation of new information against existing knowledge, the non-Western educational values place a greater weight on existing patterns of authority. The educational system marks a significant transition for the child from the intimate sphere of the family out into the broader society. Obviously, the values that the child has learned within the family will also shape the child's attitudes toward established authority figures.

Thus, we need to understand more about the role that filial piety plays in families, and how these lessons about obedience and authority are then transferred to other relationships in the society. Whereas filial piety has long been the principle that has dominated in East Asia, the relationship between the master and the disciple, or father and son, has played a central role in the Middle Eastern and Muslim societies.[48] Rosen writes that the Middle Eastern Muslim submerges the self in such relationships: "It is evident in the master-disciple, father-son relationship when the acolyte or offspring at least initially, lacks a social personality of his own."[49] I will first discuss patterns within Japanese and Turkish families and then contrast this with patterns in the West. The argument here is not that Japan and Turkey are very similar to each other but rather that they differ from the Western cases in a similar manner.

Hashimoto has written and published extensively on the Japanese family, which gives her excellent insight into how dynamics in individual families can have broader social consequences. While it is true that confrontation between the generation of "perpetrators" and the postwar generation in West Germany was difficult and something to still be avoided within families, if not also in public, such confrontations did occur.[50] In Japan, by contrast, these confrontations hardly materialized inside Japanese families or in the general public. Curiously, almost all of the existing literature on Japan is silent on the reasons for this lack of intergenerational conflict in Japan.

The one central exception is Hashimoto's work. The reason for this lack of intergenerational conflict, Hashimoto notes, is that the *generational proximity* and dependence is significantly different in Japan compared to Western norms. Patriarchy, age hierarchies, gender norms, and filial obedience made any criticism of parental authority "anathema."[51] All of these factors have tended to shut down difficult discussions about the wartime past, especially with regard to perpetrator narratives, and to focus attention instead on a pervasive sense of powerlessness of those living through the war. Postwar Japanese children came to abhor war, and today pacifism is a widely held value in Japan, thus fulfilling the promise of future peace as a pathway to moral recovery. But in this process, the postwar Japanese generations came to view their parents as the powerless victims of war and militarism. As a consequence, the younger generations have not developed a sense of efficacious behavior, a way to justify resistance and rebellion against unjust state authority. In Kohlberg's terminology, they are not developing patterns of postconventional reasoning in the same way that postwar Germans did.

Let me quote Hashimoto at length on this point, because her observations go to the heart of how our interpretation of the past can have a profound impact on present-day politics:

> A pervasive sense of inefficacy, shaped by accounts of defeat, is part of what forms the narrow apolitical vision of the postwar generation. . . . This problem of inefficacy also makes sense when we realize that postwar pacifism failed to train postwar citizens to think about, or even imagine, the legitimate means of resistance to a military machine at war. . . . This prescription to delegitimize aggression and belligerence declawed the citizens, and also deprived them of the legitimate means to act *against* authority when needed.[52]

The roots of this go back further in Japanese history, even in its liberal tradition. Maruyama, one of Japan's best-known political scientists, brought attention to the problem of filial piety in his attempts to understand Japanese acceptance of the militarists and their wartime behavior. In an essay titled, "Theory and Psychology of Ultra-Nationalism," Maruyama tries to help the Western reader understand the implications of filial piety for what happened in wartime Japan, as well as the postwar developments and problems with democratization. The Japanese people's rights movement at the end of the nineteenth century and the beginning of the twentieth century was not, as Maruyama notes, "concerned primarily with the right of ultimate judgment on such *internal* values as truth and morality."[53] Remember that the internal life of the individual and its cultivation has been primarily a Western development, especially since the Enlightenment. He quotes Kono Hironaka, the Liberal Party leader at the turn of the twentieth century, about his democratic epiphany:

> I was riding on horseback when I first read this work [*On Liberty*]. In a flash my entire way of thinking was revolutionized. Until then I had been under the influence of the Chinese Confucianists and of the Japanese classical scholars, and I had even been inclined to advocate an "expel the barbarian" policy. Now all these earlier thoughts of mine, *excepting those concerned with loyalty and filial piety*, were smashed to smithereens. At the same moment I knew that it was human freedom and human rights that I must henceforth cherish above all else.[54]

But as Maruyama points out, how is one to secure human freedom, human rights, and secure the integrity of the individual unless one relaxes the principles of loyalty and filial piety? One of Japan's leading liberal thinkers at the turn of the last century saw no contradiction. These same sorts of attitudes had persisted into the European Enlightenment as well, although the key difference is that they did not survive into the eighteenth century. In 1680, the Royalists in England drew on the work of Sir Robert Filmer in an attempt to defend the divine right of kings, but this had become too extreme a position for late-seventeenth-century England. The result was the Glorious Revolution of 1688 and the placing of constitutional constraints on the monarchy.[55]

To note, as Maruyama does, the persistence of these values of loyalty and filial piety is not to make them an essentialist and unchanging characteristic of the Japanese. Obviously, a great deal has changed in Japan since Hironaka read *On Liberty* while riding his horse, but the strength of Confucian values of obedience and filial piety continue to shape East Asian societies in ways that keeps them distinct from Western societies. Despite significant changes in Japanese society since the end of World War II, Hashimoto argues that the practice of filial piety remains a powerful force in Japanese families and society, with serious and negative consequences for Japanese youth.[56] Before Japanese children can pick up *On Liberty* or *Antigone*, they have been pressed through a family and social system that creates an interdependent understanding of the self with moral reasoning based on the maintenance of social relationships, the fulfillment of preexisting obligations, the importance of obedience, and the avoidance of conflict. Hashimoto notes of the child's experience in preschool that "Teachers may therefore co-opt the child—without force—to the point that the child comes to understand that rebellion is useless, that it results in defeat, and that she/he is powerless to do otherwise than acquiesce."[57] In terms of one's ability to find a ground on which to challenge existing authority, the conditions in Japan are actually more difficult than in China,[58] thus reminding us of the diversity that exists in the non-Western and Western cultural traditions, although filial piety remains a potent force in China and Korea as well.

But the contrasts between non-Western and Western are significant and important, because the goal in the two cultural traditions is to create two different senses of the self, two different conceptions of the good child. In the non-Western context defined more by collectivism rather than individualism, the good child is an obedient child who respects and comes to understand him-/herself primarily in relationship to others, an interdependent sense of self. In the Western context, the child is encouraged to develop an independent sense of self in which he/she develops an internal moral narrative about the self and determines for him-/herself what is good, and is prepared to argue in defense of his/her position.[59]

This obviously does not mean that there is no conflict in the non-Western cultural tradition and that there is perfect harmony. But it is the social ideal, toward which one should strive. Therefore, what happens in Japan when the tension between *ninjo*, one's own internal desires, become too great and it becomes impossible to continue submission to *giri*, one's social duty? Scholars point to two common strategies of resistance in Japan: retreatism and ritualism.[60] In retreatism, the subordinate tries to remove him-/herself from the relationship to the greatest extent possible. With ritualism, one strives for the outward appearance of compliance while maintaining an inward resistance. Both strategies can lead to extensive attempts to sabotage the will of the superior in the relationship. But as Hashimoto notes, the weakness of these strategies is that they fail to change the nature of the relationship with the superior, and this leads to psychological distress on the part of the subordinate.[61] The lessons learned in the family, the preschool, and in the literary traditions of Japan that rebellion always leads to defeat have been well learned.

It is worth noting that these two forms of dealing with an abusive authority are exactly the strategies most commonly followed by those who did offer wartime resistance. In Saburo Ienaga's words, some opted for "perfect silence"; they withdrew from professional work that would involve them in the war effort. The advantage of these passive strategies of resistance is that they are nearly impossible to detect, but it also leaves the rebellious individuals almost completely isolated as they fail to connect with others who are also unhappy, because the other rebels also continue to maintain an outward face of compliance. This is exactly how Masaki Kobayashi's hero behaves in *Samurai Rebellion* (*Joiuchi*) (1967), a dramatic example I use in the next section to illustrate some of these points. First, Kobayashi's samurai maintains the ritualism of outward compliance; then he tries to retreat from his relationship with his feudal lord. Finally, he erupts in open rebellion and is destroyed and forgotten.

And there is yet another layer to filial piety that is not immediately easy for a Western observer to grasp, and that is the position and role of the ancestors in the Japanese cultural tradition. The patterns of ancestor worship and the protection of family honor vary across the East Asian world, but they are significant for our concerns here because they consistently place the living in a far closer relationship with the dead than is often the case in the modern Western cultural tradition.[62] Returning to Hashimoto's arguments in *The Long Defeat*, one reason why Japanese families have done even more than German families to subvert difficult discussions about the past is that the generational proximity is far closer and the dependence of the family members on each other is far higher than in the West. As a result, criticism of parental authority has remained extremely difficult, even as many other aspects of postwar Japanese society have changed. Furthermore, this bond does not necessarily lose its potency when the wartime generation dies, because the obligations can remain the same in death as in life. This means that generational turnover, which can spur a more open confrontation with the past in the West, is less likely to have an impact in East Asian societies. Although she does not talk about this as explicitly in *The Long Defeat*, Hashimoto has written elsewhere, "The imagined connection to ancestors—especially identifiable ancestors—has profound implications for parent-child relations in the Confucian cognitive understanding. It means that the filial tie is in effect prolonged beyond death, and the parent-child tie never ceases. Therefore, the relation of domination never ceases and as a result the status differentials are permanent."[63]

Turkey today clearly combines elements common in the Western world with those more associated with non-Western traditions. But in terms of the individualist and collectivist continuum, Turkey tends toward greater collectivism. The patterns of authority in Turkish families and the understanding of the individual as an interdependent self rather than an independent self continue to play an important role in how Turkish society deals with its difficult history of the Armenian genocide and the other instances of minority repression that continued into the period of the republic founded by Atatürk. Turkish society remains more on the collectivist end of the spectrum rather than the Western and individualist. Although Sharabi was writing about Middle Eastern Arab societies in his work *Neopatriarchy*, many of his observations of how outward signs of modernization in the Arab world have masked a more traditional consciousness, a neopatriarchal consciousness, hold true for Turkey as well.[64] Just as Hashimoto has noted that Japan lacks a tradition of a self-critical reflection, Sharabi writes of the Arab world, "Criticism is not a luxury but rather a matter of vital need, not just for instituting a 'careful and critical discourse' that can yield fresh, self-critical consciousness, but also for deconstructing and transcending the prevailing neopatriarchal consciousness that has bounded and immobilized thought and practice for over a century."[65] Timur Kuran finds this lack of open public discussion in the Middle East, including Turkey, as one of the key elements for understanding the lack of economic development in the region.[66] The problem is not so much any specific teaching in Islam but rather the collectivist society that limits individualistic heterodoxy and a challenge of existing authority.

In looking around for a force that might begin to create more cracks in this "neopatriarchal consciousness," Sharabi points to the women's movement. "Even in the short term, the women's movement is the detonator which will explode neopatriarchal society from within. If allowed to grow and come into its own, it will become the permanent shield against patriarchal regression, the cornerstone of future modernity."[67] *If* traditional patterns of male authority are challenged, transformed, and broken, this means that authority can be challenged and reasoned with, that principles of human dignity and human rights must be considered, rather than just preexisting power hierarchies. As we will see in the chapter on Turkey, some of the most important cultural figures that are pushing Turkish society to recognize its past and current crimes against minorities are indeed women. This is not incidental or without consequence. While Turkey is not an Arab society, it does remain patriarchal in ways similar to what Sharabi highlights in the Arab world. And as we will see, Turkish intellectuals are aware of the problems that continued patriarchal authority pose for the further Westernization of the country.

While there are obviously numerous differences that one could point to in terms of how Japanese and Turkish families operate, they also share some important similarities, which are bound up with the more collectivist cultures that predominate in both countries. As with Sharabi's discussion, Güler Okman Fişek notes that Turkish families continue to be "traditional, authoritarian and patriarchal."[68] In a summary, she writes, "Regarding the implication of personality development of the above, most authors agree that the traditional Turkish family dynamics would foster the development of a passive, dependent, constricted and somewhat frustrated person without a sense of autonomy and with a reliance on external sources of control and reinforcement."[69] Orhan M. Öztürk and Vamik Volkan come to a similar conclusion, that "autonomous will and autonomous activity are discouraged. The child is preferred and rewarded if he behaves as an extension of his parents."[70] Öztürk and Volkan are careful to point out that this is *not* pathological but rather a different cultural adaptation. In terms of educational norms outlined by Li, we can see that the Western cultural norms of open inquiry, outward-directed engagement, and critical thinking are, in general, not encouraged.

In fact, we can see these patterns replicated outside the family as well, most importantly in schools.[71] Teachers tend to replicate the patriarchal authority in the broader society by maintaining themselves as the sole authority in the classroom and not engaging students in dialogic learning. These cultural patterns mitigate but do not prevent challenges to existing patterns of authority. It should also be obvious that these same patterns once tended to dominate in Western societies, as any reader of nineteenth-century British and American literature will be well aware. Indeed, Michael Haneke gives a vibrant portrayal of how repressive patriarchal authority in pre–World War II Germany helped to drive the violence that would later consume Germany and Europe in his film *Das weiße Band* (*The White Ribbon*) (2009). And, indeed, we can continue to find many subgroups in Western societies that maintain these patterns. The argument here is that the extent to which any given society orientates itself around Western educational and cultural values has consequences for how that same society deals with the legacy of violence.

Cross-cultural psychological studies of families confirm many of the observations above while also reminding us that families and cultural norms change over time. Changes in socioeconomic development have increased global trends toward greater emphasis on individualism rather than collectivism, especially with the movement away from largely agrarian and rural societies. Nonetheless, while hierarchical role values for fathers and mothers have shifted a great deal with increasing affluence, this overall trend is blunted in East Asia.[72] Moreover, support for patriarchy also varies by the dominant religion in a country, from the highest levels in Muslim countries and then decreasing through Christian Orthodoxy, Catholicism, and then Protestantism.[73] In his comparative work on families and respect for gender-based hierarchies within the families, James Georgas found that Japan and Turkey were more similar to each other than Germany and Spain, while these differences were even sharper in Hong Kong, Korea, and Saudi Arabia.

The literature on families and how they have dealt with violent national histories is most fully developed in Germany and Austria and among Jewish survivors of the Holocaust. But before we draw on this literature, it is worth considering some more universal reasons why family members might be extremely protective of each other. The psychiatrist Antonio Ferreira was struggling in the 1960s to understand why family members constantly worked against his efforts to try and help a family member, who clearly was suffering from a mental illness. He wrote at the time,

> Like any other homeostatic mechanism, the myth prevents the family system from damaging, perhaps destroying, itself. It has therefore the qualities of any "safety valve," that is, *a survival* value. This is undoubtedly an enormously important function of the family myth and one which must not be overlooked in the course of any form of psychotherapeutic intrusion. For *the family myth is to the relationship what the defense is to the individual*. The myth, like the defense, protects the system against the threat of disintegration and chaos.[74]

There is probably a powerful, universal bias to defend the family, not only from physical harm but also in terms of reputation and status.

The literature that we have on German, Austrian, and Jewish families allows us to draw some tentative general conclusions about how dynamics within families may shape broader societal discussions about a difficult and violent past.[75] First, whereas there is a broad social recognition of the vast crimes in German and Austrian history and a norm for public pronouncements of needing to take responsibility for that past, this same sense of engagement is largely absent within German and Austrian families themselves. While there is a social and public recognition of "Nazi" crimes, families are extremely vigilant in making sure that no one in the family can be placed in this perpetrator category. The perpetrator vanishes into the abstraction of Nazi evil; the perpetrator is externalized symbolically from the community of the good. Gabriele Rosenthal writes in her study of family dialogues,

> However, even when such intimations and hints [of Nazi crimes] are quite clear, there is very little risk of further exposure in inter- and intragenerational dialogue in Germany, as intimations of involvement in Nazi crimes are often passed over or blocked out by the listeners because of their own fears. That we ourselves as non-Jewish German interviewers are not free from this is something my colleagues and I experience time and again, even though in our conscious judgment we are so interested in exposing implications of this kind. We, too, are members of the children's and grandchildren's generation and have vague fears about exposing the past of people we encounter who despite their pleasant personalities may have done terrible things. We were socialized in our families and in German daily life in milieux where taboos about addressing certain themes, prohibitions against asking further questions and certain exonerating depictions were and continue to be operative.[76]

The phenomenon that Rosenthal is writing about here is an example of what we identified above as SS-RIF. As a result of SS-RIF, just when German and Austrian societies have vastly increased their storehouse of readily available information about the crimes of National Socialism, the direct relationship of this history to one's own family remains obscured and pushed further into the realm of the forgotten.

As discussions about the Holocaust and the war crimes of Germany in World War II became far more prevalent in West German society in the 1980s and later in Austria, the processes of social contagion and reinforcement put more pressure on individual family members to recognize that their parents and grandparents *may have been* directly or indirectly involved in those crimes. This increased the likelihood of conflict within families. Nonetheless, while some family members may defect from the family or try to force a confrontation with other family members, this is far less common than demonstrations of disinterest in the past, defending the family, or engaging the difficult history in the broader society while remaining silent within the family.[77]

In summary, as we can see, there are probably universal aspects of family life that mitigate against the family becoming a site of contestation and self-critical reflection regarding the national past. The differences between Western and non-Western families is one of degree. Families that demand greater respect for the ancestors, the principle of filial piety, patriarchy, and family honor will tend to restrict critical discussions of the national history and the legacy of mass violence at the microlevel. Whereas Hashimoto writes that challenging parental authority in Japan is "anathema," we can recognize that it is still very difficult in the Western context as well but not as severe. Moreover, the independent sense of the self in the Western context will push some individuals further to recognize the contradiction of their condemnation of past crimes while failing to address those same issues in their personal lives. While they may decide not to do this, they may recognize this as a good they probably should pursue. In contrast, as Hashimoto has noted, this is frequently not even seen as a good goal in Japan and other more collectivist societies with interdependent understandings of the self, where the maintenance of these relationships is more important than adherence to abstract, external values. In Japan, the maintenance of personal relationships, especially within the family, are even more important than in the Western cultural context. Perhaps the most important categorical difference between the Western and non-Western contexts are those individuals who take their unease with the family's relationship with the national past and pour their energies into engaging that difficult history in the broader society while trying to maintain the peace at home. It is far easier to employ the self-critical engagement with a difficult history outside the setting of the family.

### *Cultural Differences—A Literary Discussion and Example*

To aid our discussion of cultural differences, let me offer an incongruous and anachronistic comparison of Sophocles's (497 BCE–406 BCE) tragedy *Antigone* and Masaki Kobayashi's film *Samurai Rebellion* from 1967. Both dramatic tales pit individuals against the power of the state, and both individuals rebel against the state out of respect for bonds of love toward family members. In *Antigone*, the eponymous main character challenges the authority of the state represented by King Creon, who orders that no one should bury the body of Polyneices, Antigone's brother, because he is a traitor of the city. In *Samurai Rebellion*, Isaburo Sasahara, the main character and samurai, rebels against his feudal lord because of the repeated insults that are leveled against his family and its integrity. Antigone rebels against state authority, buries her brother, and is herself entombed alive on Creon's orders, where she commits suicide. In *Samurai Rebellion*, Isaburo launches a violent, hopeless, one-man rebellion against his feudal lord and is eventually killed. Both dramatic narratives share many important aspects. Both suggest to the audience that individual rebellion against state authority in defense of the family and love is justified, although dangerous. But there are also important, critical differences.

Antigone does not simply throw herself into rebellion against the state. First, she seeks to enlist the aid of her sister and discusses the reasons for her rebellion with another, appealing to the principle of equality, that all the dead should be buried with dignity, no matter which side they have fought on, noting how the birds of prey will feed on Polyneices's corpse.[78] When her rebellion is discovered, she argues with Creon and offers reasons why he is wrong to act as he does. She makes appeals to ancient traditions regarding the proper behavior toward the dead as decreed by the gods: "It wasn't Zeus who issued that decree. The justice that resides with gods below has never sanctioned practices like yours. I didn't think a mortal man's decrees possessed sufficient strength to nullify the deities' secure, unwritten laws."[79] She makes a direct appeal to a power and authority beyond that of the state. And she does not challenge Creon one-on-one but in front of the chorus; she makes an appeal to the broader public. Creon dismisses all of her arguments and makes his own reasoned statements about the importance of the state and the legal order.

In contrast, Isaburo in *Samurai Rebellion* accepts, outwardly, insult after insult from his feudal lord. The samurai demands that his family continue to show respect toward their feudal lord. He does not seek to enlist the aid of anyone else in his rebellion and acts completely alone. Eventually, the humiliations and threats to his family are more than he can bare, and he launches himself into violent rebellion against the feudal authority but without argument or justification. Violence erupts in a spectacular form and is crushed.

Although separated by more than two thousand years of human history, the contrast of *Antigone* and *Samurai Rebellion* is very instructive and helps to highlight some key differences between Western and Japanese cultural traditions. In pursuing this discussion, it is critical not to treat culture in an essentialist manner with deterministic outcomes. Cultures are dynamic and change over time.[80] Western notions of individualism and rational debate changed dramatically from the sixteenth century of the Enlightenment until the present day.[81] Notions of individual love,[82] sincerity, and authenticity[83] developed during this time, as well as an increasing weight for reasoned argumentation and evidence against the weight of tradition.[84] And there is no shortage of exceptions in both the Western and non-Western contexts. But at the same time, there are persistent differences of which we must take account if we are to better understand how collective memory formation and dealing with difficult histories takes shape in different cultures, societies, and nations.

The *Antigone* narrative was not only celebrated in ancient Greece but also throughout Western literature, drama, and modern-day cinema. In ancient Greece, the individual was celebrated as the location of power and efficacy in the society, and public debate in the agora was encouraged. Individuals were encouraged to cultivate an *independent sense of the self*; this is what a good person does. In contrast, the Chinese and Confucian orientation is focused much more on the cultivation of an *interdependent sense of the self*, so that fulfilling obligations toward others is what a good person strives to achieve.[85] Whereas debate, argument, and conflict, within limits, was encouraged in the context of ancient Greece, in ancient China, by contrast, the focus was on avoiding disagreement and debate while working toward conciliation and maintaining harmony.

Antigone not only argues with the king, but she also presents a well-reasoned argument for why he is wrong and should change his position. In fact, the entire play is filled with debates as characters seek to reason and argue with each other. Haemon, Creon's son, argues with his father and tries to change his mind about Antigone's fate, cautioning Creon at one point, "Step back from anger. Let your feelings change."[86] One of the most important parts of Antigone's argument is that in trying to justify her open rebellion against state authority, she appeals to an authority beyond that of the state, to tradition and the ancient rule of the gods, which states that all the dead should be buried, no matter which side they have fought on. This appeal to a higher, external, and transcendental authority and the principle of human dignity can appear so natural to a Western audience as to hardly justify any particular note.

When Antigone appeals to the rule of the gods, she is reaching for a type of postconventional reasoning in the sense that it is a moral principle that transcends and trumps any rules that a sovereign ruler may develop. She is, in this sense, making an appeal to an individual human right based on dignity, which no king can violate. And she uses this argument to justify her rebellion.

Kobayashi's hero in *Samurai Rebellion* presents no reasoned argument to his feudal lord; there is no effort made toward a postconventional level of moral reasoning. In fact, in his moral universe of feudal Japan, there is no transcendental authority that he can appeal to as a source of justification for his rebellion. In this manner, Kobayashi's hero is anything but an exception in Japanese dramas. And in making a *jidaigeki* or period drama, Kobayashi was not seeking to offer a history lesson about the Edo period for his present-day Japanese audience but rather to provoke critical reflection on their part as to how similar their modern-day society remains to that of the samurai hero in Edo Japan.[87] But the fact that Kobayashi's hero can offer no solution to the problem is not unique to this film. As the Japanese film scholar Donald Richie notes, "Perhaps this is because the films, which like kabuki itself find fault with authority, can only advise traditional remedies: *shikata ga nai* (can't be helped), *gambaranakucha* (you just got to put up with it). They do not offer solutions."[88] We will return to the problem of formulating a reason for resistance as well as the dilemma of taking action in the chapter on Japan.

Let's return to our discussion of *Antigone* and *Samurai Rebellion* to help illustrate the implications of this realization. For a Western audience, the behavior of Kobayashi's hero is somewhat intelligible in that the indignities forced on his family by the feudal lord would strike a Western audience as unjust. But a Japanese audience will have a very different relationship with this hero and the final outcome of the film, because it conforms to some of the traditions in Japanese kabuki stage dramas and their expectations of where rebellion ultimately leads, which is the defeat of the hero without any social transformation.

First, it is important to understand a fundamental tension that drives Japanese drama: the conflicting demands of *ninjo* and *giri*. *Ninjo* refers to personal inclination, whereas *giri* refers to duty and obligation toward others. These tensions themselves are hardly something that will appear strange to a Western audience, as more than one romantic story has been told about young lovers struggling to overcome the opposition to their union by their families. But Japanese characters and their Japanese audience have a different sense of this conflict because the pressures of *giri* are far more intense in a society based on interdependent understandings of the self, compared to those based on individual understandings of the self. Whereas the Western imperative is to remain true to oneself, sincere, and authentic, the Japanese imperative is to achieve maturity by maintaining harmonious relationships with others, avoiding conflict, and respecting one's duties and obligations toward others, even when these come into conflict with one's own human sentiments.

In his excellent discussion of Japanese popular culture and dramaturgy, Ian Buruma made the following observation, which is worth quoting at length because it helps the Western reader to understand Kobayashi's samurai hero and how a Japanese audience might react to the story:

> It is, however, private inclination [*ninjo*] restrained to bursting point that provides the real tension in Japanese drama. The consummate Japanese hero, admired even more than the honest hot-heads, never breaks out wildly immediately. . . . Heroes, especially on the Kabuki stage, are a little like hissing and puffing pressure cookers, and it is at the final breaking point, when they simply cannot take it any more [*sic*], that the audience applauds. It is the period of enduring the unendurable that makes the final act of revenge so cathartic.[89]

Kobayashi viewed his filmmaking as important because it showed the struggle of the individual against the society and its feudal order, which Kobayashi and other Japanese intellectuals considered as continuing well into the postwar era. Kobayashi said of his work, "In *Seppuku* [*Hara Kiri*] the theme is similar [to the one in *The Human Condition*]. It ends in tragedy. But my underlying theme transcends that. I try to express the possibility that human beings can overcome the tragic events of the world. I intend to be humanistic. In *Seppuku* the tragedy was triggered by authoritarian pressure which smothered individuals. In this film, human evil takes the form of an oppressive feudal power structure. I was fascinated by the tenacious human resilience which continued to defy this extreme pressure."[90]

But what is also essential to understand, from the Japanese perspective, is that rebellion has no hope of changing anything. While the explosion of rebellious violence against injustices offers a cathartic release of emotion, the hero is destroyed by the existing social order and the audience is reminded that nothing has changed. As Kobayashi also emphasized in his work, the memory of the rebellion is also lost, failing to provide any hope for others. There is a powerful real-life parallel in that the little resistance that some Japanese offered to the rise of militarism is largely forgotten and remains uncelebrated in Japan today. We will return to this real-life resistance in a moment when we discuss the work of Ienaga. Although Kobayashi wants to critique the continued existence of a "feudal" order in postwar Japan, he still remains very much in the Japanese cultural framework within which postconventional moral reasoning plays no role.

Here, again, Buruma commenting on and quoting Richie, the American scholar of Japanese cinema, offers some very useful insights. In a largely closed society, the fact that the rebellious hero is destroyed "is reassuring as well as tragic. It is reassuring because, as Donald Richie, the film critic put it, 'it so clearly defines one's choice. This seems especially comforting on the stage, or the screen, because this simplification can suggest that there is nothing more than this to life. . . .' It is tragic because any attempt to break loose inevitably—in drama, if not always in life—leads to disaster."[91]

Whereas Western and especially American dramatic culture celebrates and certainly exaggerates the ability of the hero to transform the world, the Japanese dramatic arc is in the opposite direction. Obviously, Kobayashi sought to provoke his Japanese audience to reflect on the consequences of dwelling on their sense of powerlessness, which Hashimoto has also pointed to in her work. But at the same time, this most rebellious of Japanese filmmakers also reconfirms existing cultural sentiments about rebellion and resistance. Where Kobayashi did set himself apart from others is that he emphasized in both *Samurai Rebellion* and *Hara-Kiri* (*Seppuku*) (1962) that these are lost histories that no one knows about, which is obviously paradoxical because the audience is now learning about these lost stories. In this way, he is suggesting to his audience that there may be other lost histories of rebellion and resistance in Japanese history of which they should avail themselves. Kobayashi had the following to say about his films: "I try to express the possibility that human beings can overcome the tragic events of the world. . . . In any era, I am critical of authoritarian power. In *Ningen no joken* it took the form of militaristic power, in *Seppuku* it was feudalism. They pose the same moral conflict in terms of the struggle of the individual against society. These struggles are the main drama of all my films."[92] While Kobayashi clearly wishes to spark a willingness for the individual to stand against society, his film narratives do conform to the Japanese norm of showing that the individual rebel will be beaten down by the existing authority. As Buruma observes, this is in some ways comforting: "The certainty that non-conformity will ultimately be punished, that the stubborn nail will be knocked back in, is in a way reassuring. It lends a fixed contour to the lives of people who are terrified of the amorphous. It enables them to see the precise limits of their existence."[93]

The Western dramatic and heroic narrative tends to favor the transformative narrative, even if the hero dies, whereas the Japanese narrative tends to focus on the uselessness of resistance, although it feels good to see someone else explode on stage. The Japanese will celebrate the hero for his willingness to sacrifice himself for a pure cause, but they tend not to expect anything to change as a result.[94] We can see this contrast again with our comparison of *Antigone* and *Samurai Rebellion*. While *Antigone* ends with the death of the heroine, we are clearly warned by the Greek chorus that we should be on guard against hubris, which spins the tragic human tale forward. The promise is held out that through the instruction of the play and the self-critical examination of one's own behavior in relationship to the narrative of the play, that cycles of tragedy can be reduced in the future. As a Greek tragedy, fate plays a significant role, but there is also a strong sense that *if* the individuals in the story had chosen differently, a better outcome, a transformative outcome, would result.

Western and non-Western relationships with power and authority differ significantly, and this has deep implications for the process of collective memory formation and engaging a difficult national history. Engaging a difficult history means confronting the fathers in the family and the fathers of the nation. If something went wrong in the past, someone has to be responsible for that, and they need to be held accountable. But this is far from an easy task. And as Hashimoto has noted above, those in the Western cultural tradition have different cultural resources that they can draw on in this struggle than those living in the non-Western cultural tradition. While such a critical self-examination can lead to moral repair in the Western context, this is not necessarily something that is valued in the non-Western cultural context.

Ienaga was a Japanese intellectual and historian who sought to model himself and his scholarship on the Western ideals of self-critical reflection, demonstrating that such efforts are not absent in Japan. In addition to his work as a historian, he spent his lifetime taking the Japanese Ministry of Education to court over the portrayal of World War II in the state-approved history textbooks, which he felt minimized Japanese aggression and atrocities. His work helped to open up public discussion and recognition of Japan as the aggressor in the war and highlighted Japan's role as a perpetrator of war crimes. Part of what motivated Ienaga was his own passivity during the war years. At the same time that he was involved in pushing for the moral renewal of his country, he was engaged in his own personal moral renewal and atonement for what he felt he had done wrong during the war.

In his classic work, *The Pacific War, 1931–1945*, Ienaga gives a highly critical account of the Japanese leadership and the general Japanese public. But he does dedicate one chapter in the book to those who resisted Japanese militarism. He writes at the opening of this chapter, "The existence of these intrepid individuals enables us to find even in this disgraceful period accomplishments worthy of Japan's best tradition. These persons kept the flame of conscience burning during the mad storm of tyranny and aggression. They added a distinguished chapter to Japan's long history; they have bequeathed a valuable legacy to later generations. . . . They also suggest that an individual or a society's choices are not predetermined."[95] One can hear in his voice that of a Western intellectual.

The problem is that this is not a voice that has resonated very well in Japan. The conscience that Ienaga calls on is not fully part of the Japanese cultural tradition. He is asking for his compatriots to draw on a style of moral reasoning that is not readily available to them; he is asking them to draw on, in Kohlberg's phrasing, post-conventional moral reasoning, as Antigone did in challenging Creon. But this is not a cultural resource that this readily available to the Japanese. In a society defined by obligations to others, it becomes very difficult to exercise that type of autonomy and to call on a transcendent source of authority.[96]

It is very significant that the two primary sources of resistance that Ienaga identifies in his chapter came from Communists and Christians, those who had reached outside of their own cultural tradition for a set of values and a basis for action, as Ienaga notes, perhaps unfairly, "Buddhism had always lacked the capacity to challenge the state."[97] But even for Communists and Christians, the commitments did not necessarily run that deep. The Communists were guided by an ideology that provided a narrative of following the natural, organic unfolding of history. By being a Japanese Communist, one placed oneself in harmony with the natural path of history. It was not a movement dominated by ideas of individual autonomy, action, and values. In contrast, some Christians, although not many, were better able to articulate a clearer voice of resistance in that their Christian God forbade murder, and war was murder. Otherwise, the resistance that Ienaga identified was largely that of people who were unhappy because the war was going poorly, and they were suffering.[98] In this sense, their rebellious spirit was no different than that of any peasant rebellion in which the masses were moved by the misery of their circumstances. What is important to realize is that such a rebellion against deprivation is not a rights-based movement with a transcendent vision. It is a rebellion designed simply to rebalance the given order that has gotten out of hand between the ruler and the ruled, not to transcend the order itself.[99] The rebellion is designed to restore harmony within the existing order.

There is no question that Ienaga's life and work played a significant role in pushing Japanese society to deal with its difficult past. But in terms of that society coming to see the wartime resistance as heroic and something to be emulated, this simply has not happened. Whereas Ienaga and the Western cultural tradition would want to read those who resisted Japanese militarism as examples like that of *Antigone*, wherein the audience, once enlightened about Antigone's struggle and her suffering can be spurred to critical self-reflection, the Japanese have handled the wartime resistance much more in the manner suggested by Kobayashi's films *Hara-Kiri* and *Samurai Rebellion*. Not only was the resistance futile, but we do not even know that it happened. Remember that another part of Kobayashi's storytelling is that he is revealing histories that have been lost to everyone because no one who survived the two rebellions in the films ever talked about them again—it is *as if* they never happened.

Here, we come to a puzzle and paradox. Why is it that Germans eventually came to accept the anti-Hitler resistance in exactly the manner that Ienaga hoped that the Japanese would embrace their own resistance during the war? In pondering this question, it is worthwhile to remember that postwar West German society was very divided over the meaning of the wartime resistance against Hitler, with a plurality in the early postwar years viewing them as traitors. It was only with time, when the extent of German wartime barbarism became clearer, that Germans began to view the resistance in a more positive light.[100] In East Germany, the Communist resistance was celebrated from the beginning, while the so-called bourgeois resistance was at first rejected. But eventually, Germans came to embrace the wartime resistance in exactly the way that Ienaga outlined: as examples of the best in Germany's history; as a sign of conscious in dark times; as noble gesture and a model for inspiration for future generations. And within a Christian cultural context, the resistance could redeem the nation through their blood sacrifice.

Table 2 Key Differences between Western and Non-Western Cultural Traditions

| | *Western* | *Non-Western* |
|---|---|---|
| Sense of Self | Independent Sense of Self | Interdependent Sense of Self |
| | Individualism | Collectivism |
| Family and Authority | Weaker Patriarchy, Weaker Connection to Ancestors | Stronger Patriarchy, Stronger Connection to Ancestors |
| Education | Critical Thinking, Self-Expression, Outward Exploration | Earnestness, Diligence, Concentration, Perseverance |
| Moral Reasoning | Post-Conventional, Self-Critique, Generalized, Universal | Group Oriented, Limited, Restricted Self-Critique |
| Role of Apology | Sincere reconciliation based on a changed sense of self, expression of regret | Restoration of social harmony, no assumption of inner conversion or regret |

In her broad survey of Japanese popular culture, official culture, and school textbooks, Hashimoto not once mentions the Japanese wartime resistance because it simply does not exist in the Japanese discussions about the past. The wartime resistance is not even discussed in Japanese peace museums. The potential moral renewal offered by the resistance is not available or recognized in the Japanese cultural context. The near complete absence of this discussion is really very striking, until one begins again to understand the difference of the Japanese and Western cultural traditions. Hashimoto shares Ienaga's frustration with the passivity of the Japanese and Japanese youth. What one might call the master narrative arising from Hashimoto's work is that the wartime Japanese population was powerless to change anything; and this sense of powerlessness has continued into the present-day political setting. The wartime resistance narrative runs counter to this sense of powerlessness—it contradicts it. *If* some individuals did manage to resist and challenge the wartime regime, as brutal and threatening as it was, it means that this was possible, that rebellion was possible. If this is true, then perhaps one's parents were not as powerless as one has been led to believe. But this is an uncomfortable place to go.

Table 2 helps to summarize the preceding discussion by outlining some of the key differences that help to distinguish the Western cultural tradition from those of non-Western cultural traditions. It will be useful to think about these two categories as ideal types, which help to clarify some of the differences, while not making the categories themselves essentialist, fixed, or unchanging. All of the societies under consideration here are dynamic and are far from homogeneous. Nonetheless, the predominance of Western characteristics in any society will tend to leave that society more open to a critical reevaluation of the national history, compared to a society where these same characteristics are weaker.

## Conclusion

We can now use this general model of collective memory formation as a guide to understand and explain the different ways in which five countries have engaged their difficult and violent histories. In doing so, we must give attention to both politics and culture. Each of these factors is dynamic and change over time. In the area of politics, we need to give specific attention to the formal political institutions of the state, as either more democratic or more authoritarian, as well as the society as a whole, which may be more open or closed to pluralism. Democratic states and pluralistic societies help to foster self-critical discussions about the national past. Authoritarian states and antipluralist societies are more closed and tend to shut down such discussions.

In the realm of culture, it will be useful to think of each case as belonging either more to the non-Western cultural tradition, collectivism, and interdependent understandings of the self, or the Western cultural traditions of individualism and an independent understanding of the self. In talking about these cultural traditions, it is important not to treat them as unchanging and unchangeable. What we commonly refer to as the Western world had for most of its history a tradition-bound culture that minimized individual autonomy and the questioning of authority. It is only with the rise of modernity in the European continent at the time of the Enlightenment that a decisive move was made to free the individual from traditions that could not be questioned.[101] Although the possibility for this realization has deep roots in the Western cultural tradition, as the ancient Greek play of *Antigone* demonstrates, it took many centuries before this became more of the norm.

The non-Western world has also undergone significant transformation, especially as a result of its encounter with the Western world through colonialism and imperialism. This violent history of oppression and subjugation leaves many in the non-Western world today with a sense of ambivalence toward the idea of the West and its claims of universal human rights, individual autonomy, and self-critical reflection. While there is a strong desire for the material wealth that the Western world has accumulated for itself, there is a sense of resentment regarding the colonial and imperialist past and an ambivalence that grows out of feeling judged by the West. This has led to some forms of modernization in terms of formal institutions and some accommodation of human rights as with, for example, women. But at the same time, collectivism, filial piety, and interdependent understandings of the self lead to different patterns of social behavior. This continues to result in a greater resistance within the non-Western cultural world for a self-critical investigation into the legacy of violence in the national history.

There are also more universal social-psychological processes that will play a critical role in each of the cases. At specific points in time, social contagion and reinforcement effects may begin to create a rapid change in how a society views its relationship with its history. At the same time, SS-RIF will act as a break on discussions of difficult histories. The way in which these social-psychological processes function in each case will be shaped by the political and cultural context. Furthermore, the ethnocentrism of death and the externalization of blame combine with SS-RIF to close down difficult discussions about the past and to limit the spread of countermemory narratives.

By keeping a balanced focus on politics, culture, and social-psychological processes, we can begin to identify patterns in how societies deal with their difficult histories of war and genocide. This can help us to anticipate how things might unfold in countries that are recently emerging from a period of extreme violence and also what role outside intervention might be able to play. But in many ways, we are left with the multiple ghosts of Antigone and her tragic tale. Perhaps we have made some progress that allows us to break free of the tragic cycle that Sophocles clearly articulated in his play so very long ago. What remains clear is that until all of the war dead are buried with dignity by their loved ones, the threat of future violence remains very real. *Antigone*'s multiple ghosts continue to haunt us today.

# 1 Germany

*The shores of Salamis and nearby lands*
*are heaped with bodies of the ill-fated dead.*
—Messenger in *Persians*[1]

## Introduction

Germany under the leadership of Hitler and the National Socialists took the country into a disastrous war of mass atrocities and the genocide of six million of Europe's Jews, in which they were frequently aided by local collaborators. They were also opposed by anti-fascist forces throughout Europe, including Yugoslavia. The outcome of the war was the occupation of the country by the Western allies of the United States, the United Kingdom, and France, which took over collectively three zones of occupation that were to become West Germany. The Soviet Union's eastern zone of occupation became East Germany. The Federal Republic of Germany, also known as West Germany, was established in 1949, as was the German Democratic Republic (GDR), also known as East Germany. The country was reunified in October 1990 as a result of the collapse of the Soviet Empire in Europe. In the context of this study, the two German cases most closely resemble that of Japan in that the country had carried out primarily a war of external, imperialistic expansion, although there was no shortage of domestic victims, which stretched beyond the genocide against the Jews. Still, the conflict never took on the characteristics of a civil war, along the lines of what was experienced in Spain, Yugoslavia, or Turkey. Most of the regime's victims lived outside the country, and at the conclusion of the war, most of the survivors lived outside the country as well.

Unlike in Japan, there was a significant German prewar and wartime resistance against the Nazi regime. The resistance involved lone wolf individuals, small groups of social democrats and communists, and conservative elites. The communist resistance was celebrated in the Soviet zone of occupation and then in East Germany as a source of legitimacy for the new regime. In the West, the different forms of resistance against the Nazi regime were initially viewed with a great deal of skepticism by the general public. Willy Brandt, who would go on to become the mayor of Berlin and later the chancellor of West Germany from 1969 to 1973, had been active in the social democratic resistance to the National Socialist regime, first inside Germany and then from exile. This led some to view him as a traitor to the nation, a theme that his conservative Christian Democratic rivals never failed to use against him in political campaigns.

Nevertheless, the prewar and wartime resistance to the National Socialists and Hitler became an important legacy for both East and West Germany and a positive model for resistance against the illegitimate exercise of power. Although the legitimacy of the resistance and its different forms remained debated for many decades, the fact that Germans were willing to formulate arguments about what forms of resistance could be justified against the exercise of illegitimate power became an important legacy for the democratization of West Germany and reunified Germany after 1990. As I have identified above in the introduction, the absence of these debates in postwar Japan remains a lingering problem that the Japanese have in debating the legitimate excise of authority and how one might be justified in opposing the illegitimate exercise of power.

## Psychological and Social-Psychological Processes

As with the other cases in this research, the *externalization of blame* has played a significant role in the development of postwar culture in both East and West Germany, although this has changed significantly in the most recent decades. In the earliest postwar decades, the roots of war and genocide tended to find their explanations in abstractions and external forces. The domestic roots of National Socialism tended to be ignored, and there was a great sense of Germans having been the primary victims of the regime that had arisen in their own society, while ignoring the popularity of the regime and the widespread social participation in supporting the regime and its goals. Both the East and West German regimes were anxious to shift as much of the blame for what had happened on to the Nazi elites, while sparing the broader society a more honest investigation of the role that many others had played in the rise of the regime as well as the crimes that it committed. This became part of the mixed legacy of the Nuremberg trials, which were widely viewed in Germany as an example of victor's justice.[2]

The *ethnocentrism of death* also played a critical role in both East and West Germany. Contrary to more recent claims by some in Germany that Germans have been denied the right to mourn their own losses and suffering, the early postwar decades were almost entirely focused on German victims. This meant that Jewish victimhood, to the extent that it was acknowledged at all, tended to be subsumed under a broader label of the entire population having been a victim of the fascist violence. It was only over the course of the 1970s and especially the 1980s that Jewish victims in the Holocaust gained a separate status from that of the Germans in general.

This was true primarily in West German and almost wholly absent in East Germany. When East and West Germans were asked if there was something that made German history different from that of other countries, in an open-ended survey, West Germans were far more likely to mention the Nazi persecution of the Jews than East Germans. When asked this question in 1989–1990, 13 percent of West

Germans mentioned the Nazi persecution of the Jews compared to only 1 percent of East Germans. When the same question was asked again in 1996, 20 percent of West Germans mentioned the Nazi persecution of the Jews, while only 4 percent of East Germans did the same.[3] Clearly, the division of the country for forty years had created two very different memory communities when it came to reflecting on the legacy of the war and genocide.

One of the most important developments in West Germany, which was largely absent from East Germany, was the creation of the broad social narrative of the Holocaust in the 1970s and into the 1980s. Despite the war crimes trials at Nuremberg, the Frankfurt Auschwitz trial (1963–1965), and the Majdanek trial (1975–1981), the Nazi genocide against Europe's Jews, remained a poorly defined event in general public discussions about the war. This lack of clarity about the nature and extent of the genocide helped to maintain a residual legitimacy for National Socialism and Hitler. Although a plurality of Germans continued to reject the proposition that Hitler would have been one of Germany's greatest leaders if not for the war (but not the Holocaust), a growing percentage of Germans were willing to grant him this status between 1965 and 1975, ranging between 30–40 percent. Roughly 30 percent of Germans also continued to defend the National Socialist regime, claiming that one could not say that the regime itself had been "fundamentally unjust." It was only the arrival of widespread public discussion of the Nazi persecution of the Jews and the Holocaust in the mid-1970s and throughout the 1980s that finally smashed most of the residual legitimacy that Hitler and the National Socialists continued to hold.[4] In terms of reshaping widespread attitudes toward National Socialism, popular culture played a far greater role than debates among intellectuals, known as the *Historikerstreit* or "historian argument," which only really took off in 1986 and was largely confined to those born before 1945.[5]

What can account for this change in West German attitudes toward their history that is largely absent in East Germans at the point of reunification? Here, we can see the significant impact that the processes of *social contagion* and *reinforcement* can have on broad social attitudes and memories of the past. While discussion of the Nazi persecution of the Jews was never absent from East Germany, it never took on the dimensions that it did in West Germany, especially in the context of the 1970s and 1980s. What we can see in West Germany from the mid-1970s and through the entire decade of the 1980s is a sharp rise in the amount of material that the society was generating about the Nazi persecution of the Jews and the Holocaust. This is true across all major media outlets, public and private. For the commercial cinema, there were more films made dealing with Jewish persecution in Germany in the 1980s than in all previous decades combined. The same can be seen in radio programs and the coverage and discussion of the *Kristallnacht* (Night of Broken Glass) memorial dates in the 1970s and 1980s compared to previous decades.[6] We can see significant social contagion and reinforcement effects in all these data.[7]

In East Germany, the production of television programs dealing with the Nazi persecution of the Jews actually reached a peak in the 1960s and then declined in the following decades.[8] In terms of domestically produced films, there was never more than a single film produced in any single year, and there were five films made in the 1960s compared to a total of three during the next two decades.[9] And these are only the numbers. When we compare the actual content of many of these programs, the East German productions contain a great deal of material that may include some historical analysis. However, they are primarily focused on how anti-Semitism has been overcome in East Germany, whereas it remains a problem in the "capitalist-fascist" West Germany. Not only was there significantly less material about the history of anti-Semitism in Germany and the Nazi persecution of the Jews, but East Germans were encouraged to view this as a problem that had been overcome through the socialist development of the East German state.

## Politics

### *East Germany: 1949–1989*

In contrast to Yugoslavia, East Germany was a far more repressive and closed society. After the uprisings of June 17, 1953, the East German government accelerated the development of an extensive police state apparatus, which turned the entire society into a system of informers and surveillance, the extent of which only became known gradually after the collapse of the regime in 1989. The East German regime developed far more in the direction of a totalitarian regime than was the case in Spain or Yugoslavia.

Travel outside the country was extremely restricted and the consumption of foreign goods far more limited. The interchange across borders was tightly controlled. Although there was more or less free movement across the East-West border within the city of Berlin prior to the building of the Berlin Wall in August 1961, all other movement within East German and across its borders was tightly controlled. With the closing of the border in Berlin, which the regime carried out in a desperate attempt to prevent further loss of its younger population, all movement outside the country and interaction with the West was closed off. Whereas Turks and Yugoslavs began to move to Western countries in the 1960s to deal with labor shortages in the West and the lack of employment opportunities at home, East Germans remained, by and large, enclosed within their state borders.

Furthermore, the movement of other people into East Germany through a tourism industry was never encouraged by the regime, except for visits to East Berlin from the West, which helped to bring in some much-needed foreign currency. By setting an artificially high exchange rate and setting compulsory exchange requirements, the regime sought to maximize what little tourism traffic flowed from West to East in Berlin. Tourism was effectively limited to East Berlin. Whereas tourism played a positive role in the democratization process in Spain and helped Yugoslavia to remain in contact with Western ideas and values, these external forces were extremely restricted in the case of East Germany. What did remain was the contact between family members on both sides of the border thanks to Willy Brandt's *Ostpolitik*, which accepted the division of the country as a practical matter that needed to be dealt with for the foreseeable future. But compared to Spain and Yugoslavia, the external pressure for change or the flow of ideas and people across the state border was very minimal.

The flow of information across the German-German border was far more difficult to control, as almost the entire East German population lived in areas where they could receive West German television and radio broadcasts. East Germans had ample opportunity to learn about life in the West, although there were frequent propaganda efforts by the government to frame the negative aspects of life in the West in terms of criminality, prostitution, and drug addiction, as well as unemployment and other forms of social insecurity. Although the consumption of West German broadcasts was a criminal offense for the first several decades, and there were even teams of East German security officials that would storm the rooftops to check the positioning of aerial antennas, there was a shift in the early 1970s under Erich Honecker's government to accept the fact that East Germans were going to listen to and watch West German broadcasts. The regime even came to see this as a positive development, as it helped to keep the population entertained and content. And the East German television service did a good job of generating its own popular broadcast programs such as *Polizeiruf 110* (*Police Call 110*) and *Der Staatsanwalt hat das Wort* (*The Prosecuting Attorney Takes the Floor*), both of which sometimes captured 50 percent of the viewing audience in prime time. These police procedural programs gave the state a positive way to portray East German life and the security that the state was able to provide for its citizens, while also providing a source of entertainment.[10] And sporting events were always very popular. Through competition with West Germany and other Western countries in athletics, the state was able to generate a certain level of East German patriotism and pride.

The level of state control, censorship, and surveillance increased dramatically after the events of June 17, 1953, after which state officials always viewed their population with far greater suspicion. This high level of surveillance lasted until the very end of the regime in 1989. It was a closed regime that limited one's freedom of thought and movement and blunted the potential impact of information coming from West Germany. East German narratives about the past developed very much in line with state doctrine. When we look at the memory-market dictum, state ideology set the terms of the debate from the beginning to the end with very little variation.

### *West Germany: 1949–1989*

West Germany was quickly set on the path toward democracy and capitalism after the end of World War II. The basic democratic institutions were laid out in the 1949 Basic Law or constitution, and they remain in place today. Social-democratic market–based capitalism was also embraced from the beginning, with a general agreement between the more conservative Christian Democrats and the more left-of-center Social Democrats about the general outlines of a welfare state.

In terms of the memory-market dictum, the production and consumption of narratives related to the past occurred largely without interference from political forces. As a democratic country, West Germany never developed a system of censorship, although this did not mean that political forces did not exercise some influence over the types of programs generated for public television or the films that were shown in the cinemas. Public television dominated all the way into the 1980s, with private broadcasters having a significant role beginning only in the 1990s. The print media was always owned by private investors. West Germany was a federal state, and cultural policy was considered an area for the *Länder*, with each *Land* or provincial government setting its own policies, as long as they respected the Basic Law.

Public radio and television broadcasters played a very important role in the West German process of dealing with the war and the Holocaust. The public broadcasters in each *Land* are governed by councils made up of "socially significant groups." This has meant that it was the responsibility of each *Land* government to appoint appropriate members to the councils to oversee the production and purchasing of programming for public radio and television, which obviously gave regional governments an opportunity to exercise some political control. And indeed, the public broadcasters in *Länder* controlled by the Social Democrats had a different tilt to their programming compared to those that were controlled by the Christian Democrats. One could see this in some programming around the war and the persecution of the Jews.

From 1949 until 1966, the federal government was dominated by the more conservative Christian Democrats and Chancellor Adenauer, who frequently governed in coalition with the more centrist Free Democrats. But the Social Democrats controlled a number of the *Land* governments, especially where union membership in the heavy industries was high. The 1950s were marked by a fierce competition between Chancellor Adenauer and what he called the "Red" Nordwestdeutscher Rundfunk (Northwest German Broadcasting) and some of the other members of the ARD, the Arbeitsgemeinschaft der Rundfunkanstalten Deutschlands (Consortium of Public Broadcasters in Germany), which served as a representative body for all of the regional broadcasters. The ARD produced the more expensive programming, which was then shared among the regional stations, such as the national nightly news broadcast. The outcome of the political and legal battles in the 1950s was a defeat for Adenauer, as the courts continued to recognize *Land* control over cultural issues and public broadcasting. What did emerge from these battles was a second federal broadcaster, the Zweites Deutsches Fernsehen (Second German Television) or ZDF in 1961. This meant that most Germans had access to two federation-wide networks, the ARD and ZDF, as well as their regional programming, which remained part of the ARD network.

I formulated the memory-market dictum as a result of my previous work on East and West Germany because of not only the content differences that I noticed between the different public broadcasters in West Germany but also, even more so, the differences between the public broadcasters and the commercial cinema. While it is certainly the case that one can find material dealing with the war and the persecution of the Jews from the beginning of West Germany in 1949 all the way to the present, the programming provided by the public broadcasters tended to be more self-critical, challenging, and perhaps uncomfortable for more viewers. Eventually, by the 1980s, when discussion of the Holocaust entered the mainstream, the commercial cinema industry began producing more films on the topic. However, prior to that, there were clear differences between commercial cinema and the public broadcasters.

What one can see in the public television viewer surveys of the 1960s, which are rich in terms of both qualitative and quantitative data, is that public television producers knew that they were going to anger a good portion of their audience, perhaps between 20 percent to 30 percent, by producing programming that dealt with Jews in Germany or the persecution of Jews during the Nazi regime. However, they felt committed to challenging their audiences with this material as part of their public service mandate. In contrast, commercial film producers and distributors were far more reluctant to handle such material. They lacked the state subsidy that flowed to the public broadcasters, so they were far more inclined to try and capture as big an audience as possible. This did not mean by any measure that they completely avoided the topics of the war and the persecution of the Jews, but it did shape the types of narratives that made it into films.

One way to illustrate this point is to look at the fate of Kurt Hoffmann's film, *Das Haus in der Karpfengasse* (*The House in the Karpfengasse*) (1964). Hoffmann was one of West Germany's most successful filmmakers of the 1960s, whose previous work had not necessarily been focused on dealing with the difficult legacy of the Nazi regime in the country. M. Y. Ben-Gavriel was a former school friend of Hoffmann's, and he sent him a copy of his book that he had published in 1957 with the same title. Hoffmann was deeply moved by the story, and he had a movie script prepared based on the novel by 1959. Because the story is set in Prague, Czechoslovakia, Hoffmann was determined to film on location in the city. The story deals with the different lives of a number of tenants who live in the same building in the Karpfengasse or Carp Street. The film shows the persecution of the Jewish family and brutal occupation of the country by the German army, which shoots into a crowd of young demonstrators at one point. And, unlike many other German films that dealt with similar subject matter, there was not a particularly sympathetic German character with which the audience could easily identify. Furthermore, the film adopted a perspective that helped to show the Jewish perspective of these events rather than a sympathetic German perspective. Although Jewish characters did appear in German television dramas and films, their perspective on the events tended to be marginalized or ignored. They were more often stock figures in need of help, which the good German in the story could try to provide in some way. *Karpfengasse* took more of a Jewish or non-German perspective, and it was a difficult one for many Germans to see and hear.

Hoffmann started to receive negative press even while working on the film, with the *Neue Zürcher Zeitung* (Zurich) commenting, "How honest can this film be against tyranny when the tyrants want to help make it?," with reference to Hoffmann shooting the film in Prague.[11] By the time the film was completed, he was unable to find a distributor for his film, which was quite surprising given the prominence of Hoffmann in the film industry at the time. Furthermore, the organizers of the Cannes Film Festival, where the film was to be premiered, had the film withdrawn for "technical-aesthetic" considerations, although they were actually reacting to direct pressure from the German Foreign Ministry.[12]

In the end, the film was saved by the Westdeutscher Rundfunk (West German Broadcasting; WDR) public television station, which picked the film for a television broadcast during the Week of Brotherhood. While the commercial distributors and cinema houses had rejected the film, the more liberal WDR was willing to show it. As a result of the television broadcast and the positive public response, a small film distributor did take up the film, and it was shown to a limited audience. The film even won a series of film awards, and Hoffmann was given the Deutschen Filmpreis (German Film Prize) for best director. But it never reached a large audience, and by the end of 1965, it had not even cracked the top 190 films shown that year in terms of audience numbers.[13]

The story of Hoffmann's film helps us to understand how narratives dealing with difficult themes from Germany's recent past were dealt with in the society. It gives an example of how even in an open and democratic society, difficult material can fail to find a broader public not because a public for the material does not exist, but because producers are concerned that they may alienate some consumers. As the memory-market dictum suggests, an open marketplace can have its own censoring effect. Ben-Gavriel's book had found a publisher and certainly a small but willing readership. However, as Hoffmann attempted to adapt the book into a film, where far more money was at stake, he ran into numerous difficulties. It was only Hoffmann's well-established reputation in the industry that even allowed him to make the film in the first place. At the same time, this example shows us the positive role that public television played in the postwar years. Public television producers and executives could take chances with annoying a certain segment of their audience because of their subsidization by the state, and in the case of West Germany, by *Länder* governments, which were sometimes more sympathetic to a more direct confrontation with the Nazi legacy in Germany.

### *Reunified Germany 1990 to the Present*

Reunified Germany today is a strong example of an open, pluralistic, democratic country that has probably done more than any other country to confront its difficult historical legacy. With time and the passing of the wartime generation, the state and society have shown an increasing willingness to move into more and more difficult territory in terms of dealing with the legacy of National Socialism, the war, and the Holocaust. While in previous decades there had been a tendency to avoid discussions of anti-Semitism in German society, which the Nazis had been able to manipulate and exploit, these are now a regular part of public discussions.

This does not mean that the history of war and genocide has been mastered or fully normalized. Pockets of deep emotional difficulty remain, which can help us understand where other countries are in comparison to Germany and also to appreciate how long it may take to deal with the long legacy of war and genocide.

For example, given the amount that National Socialism, the war, and the Holocaust had been discussed for nearly two decades, one might have assumed that by 1995 the topic had been exhausted, and Germans were ready to move on, now that this history had been fully incorporated into public and private life. But it turns out that this had not yet happened. In public life, it would be difficult to argue that the history has not been fully integrated into state ritual, ceremonies, and state-sponsored institutions. In the private realm, however, it appears that there is still a great deal of turmoil and discomfort with these topics.

In March 1995, the Hamburg Institute for Social Research opened a photography exhibit in Hamburg titled, *Vernichtungskrieg: Verbrechen der Wehrmacht 1941 bis 1944* (*War of Extermination: Crimes of the Wehrmacht 1941 to 1944*). In one sense, the information contained in the exhibit was nothing new. The exhibit did not plow any new historiographical ground. What it did do was bring together into a public forum a very personal perspective of the criminal acts that members of the Wehrmacht engaged in directly or facilitated. The photographs in the exhibit came from ordinary German soldiers who photographed the atrocities that they had participated in on the Eastern Front and in Yugoslavia. At first, the exhibit did not attract any national attention, as such small-scale exhibits had become a regular part of the landscape of German cities, especially after the upheavals of the 1980s.

But this exhibit was challenging one of the postwar myths that still held a strong influence over German thinking about the war and the genocide: that the perpetrators had been confined to a group that were carefully marked off as "Nazis" and that ordinary Germans had had very little to do with these crimes; ordinary German soldiers had served Germany and not Hitler. Although this statement makes little empirical sense, it was absolutely essential in German narratives about the war and the Holocaust to build a thick rhetorical wall between Germans and Nazis. One could watch documentaries about the war, produced by public television, in which the audience would be comforted by the fact that the soldiers had died for Germany and not Hitler, as if the war effort could easily be separated from National Socialism.

What the Wehrmacht exhibit did was to help move the perpetrators out of the shadows and into the public imagination in a way that fictional narratives and documentaries tended to avoid. In fictional narrative accounts dealing with the war and genocide, one could certainly portray criminal acts, but they were always perpetrated by characters that were clearly identified as being "Nazis" or deviants in other ways. The ordinary soldiers and Germans rarely, if ever, disappointed the audiences. They were provided chances to save Jews, show compassion for occupied populations, or committed other acts that maintained their humanity. The Wehrmacht exhibit shattered these conventions of talking about Germany's difficult history with documentary evidence provided by the soldiers themselves.

We can see some striking similarities among the cases in the present study. To the extent that societies begin to overcome the obstacles created by the tendency to externalize blame and to focus on one's own suffering through the ethnocentrism of death, they may begin to grope toward some identification with certain classifications of victims. But the perpetrators tend to remain in the shadows, abstracted and less clearly identified. While the society may eventually identify and denounce a criminal leadership, the role that others in the society played will continue to remain largely hidden.

Even while societies may move toward a greater confrontation with a difficult history in the public realm, there is a great deal of reluctance and fear of doing so within the family and the private sphere. As we have already discussed in the introduction, this probably is a universal human pattern of behavior that can become more pronounced in some cultures than in others.

The Wehrmacht exhibit went on to have a dramatic impact on discussions in Germany about the identity of the perpetrators; it weakened the rhetorical barrier that had been built up over decades between ordinary Germans and "the Nazis." Almost two years after the exhibit had opened in Hamburg, it arrived in Munich in 1997. By this time, it had become widely discussed and known throughout Germany. Germans lined up for hours to view the exhibit, many of them curious, and fearful, that they might recognize some of the German soldiers in the photographs. Politicians also began to stake out positions on the exhibit, with conservative politicians denouncing the exhibit as creating a collective guilt or blame for all Wehrmacht soldiers, who did their duty during wartime. By fall 1999, the exhibit had visited thirty-three cities in Germany and Austria and been visited by approximately 860,000 visitors.[14] In the fall of that year, a Polish historian had identified approximately ten photographs out of the hundreds on display as having been improperly labeled. In these ten photographs, the Soviet People's Commissariat for Internal Affairs (NKVD) was responsible for the killings and not the Wehrmacht. The exhibit's creators were too slow in responding to these criticisms, and the conservative media in Germany, especially the *Frankfurter Allgemeine* newspaper, began a relentless attack on the exhibit as a propaganda project of the far left. Eventually, the organizers closed the exhibit, and they brought in historical experts to evaluate the photographs and to make sure that all of the labels were correct. In the end, while additional changes were ultimately made, the primary narrative of the exhibit remained unchallenged and additional material had been collected as Germans turned over more photographs from their grandfathers and fathers, who had served in the Wehrmacht, to the Hamburger Institute for Social Research so that material might also become part of the exhibit.

To close our discussion of political developments in reunified Germany, the country today is a well-established democracy with an open commitment to pluralism and diversity. However, while there is a broad commitment to remaining engaged with Germany's difficult history and to keep it incorporated in official state ceremonies, there remains some reluctance to incorporate this history into the realm of private lives. Many Germans continue to avoid looking too closely at the past for fear of what they might find there, especially as this comes close to family relationships.

## Culture

The family is a central site of collective memory formation and one that differs significantly from one case and cultural context to the next. A core hypothesis of this research is that the level of family solidarity differs from one social and cultural context to the next, although there is always a high level of bias toward protecting the family unit against outside threats. First, to rearticulate a point made in the introduction, there is probably a near universal human bias toward the defense of the family from threats both internal and external. The psychiatrist Antonio Ferreira wrote the following while puzzling over how family members can actually work to block the treatment of a mentally ill family member:

> Like any other homeostatic mechanism, the myth prevents the family system from damage, perhaps destroying, itself. It has therefore the qualities of any "safety valve," that is *a survival* value. This is undoubtedly an enormously important function of the family myth and one which must not be overlooked in the course of any form of psychotherapeutic intrusion. For *the family myth is to the relationship what the defense is to the individual.* The myth, like the defense, protects the system against the threat of disintegration and chaos.[15]

The bias in each family is to ignore or reinterpret any information that could threaten the solidarity of the family and the maintenance of familial relationships. While this defense of the family probably is highly generalizable to most human communities, at least in modern societies, there can also be a fair amount of variability from one society and culture to the next. The principle of filial piety and the generational proximity that Hashimoto writes about in Japan shows an even higher level of defensive strategies that are used to protect family members, both alive and dead. The same can be seen in Turkey as well.

East and West Germany clearly fall within the Western cultural tradition, in terms of this research, although as with Spain and Yugoslavia, this is not so much a definitive state but rather part of an ongoing transition. Each of these countries have become more Western over the course of the twentieth century at the same time that they have helped to define what it means to be Western and modern. As we can see in the chapter on Spain, the longing of Spaniards to join Western Europe and the project of modernity led to significant changes in Spanish society over the course of the past century. Familial relationships in each of these countries have become more open, modern, and democratic over the course of the twentieth century. This means that while the strong bias toward one's own family remains, as described by Ferreira, there is an increasing willingness to challenge both the generation of one's parents as well as one's own parents.

The intergenerational transfer of information about the history of one's family and that of the broader society plays a central role in the process of collective memory formation for the entire society. Families can either be more open or closed to discussions about a difficult national history and the position of the family in that history. Cultural norms as well as the broader social and political context within which the family exists will play an important role in this process. The repressive authoritarianism in Spain, Yugoslavia, Turkey, and East Germany all worked to suppress discussions within families. In terms of the comparative cases within this research project, West German families were the freest to engage the difficult legacy of the war and genocide. The Western cultural norms and democratic society provided the best possible conditions within which such discussions could develop. The openness of West German society also meant that it was the most fertile ground for research by social scientists and historians over an extended period.

We now have a fairly extensive body of research that looks at how discussions within German and Austrian families have developed regarding the legacy of National Socialism and the Holocaust.[16] One of the most important conclusions of this body of literature is to realize just how strong the mechanism of family myths, as first identified by Ferreira, is. Given the amount of information there is about the National Socialist past in both Germany and Austria, especially since the 1980s when the social contagion and reinforcement effects were the strongest, one might assume that this information would have forced a reevaluation of the family's position in the national history. Although there is clearly a variation among families, a point that we will turn to in a moment, the overwhelming response is summarized in the title of a book by a group of German researchers, *"Opa war kein Nazi"* (*"Grandpa Was Not a Nazi"*).[17] While there has been widespread social recognition of a perpetrator group known as "the Nazis," families have been extremely resilient in defending their own family members from the charge of having been "a Nazi" despite having worked for the party, been a member of the Schutzstaffel (SS), or participated in the National Socialist program in some manner. While there has been a surge in identification with the innocent Jewish victims, the "vanishing perpetrator" or the "shadow perpetrator" phenomenon remains widespread. Gabriele Rosenthal's research, quoted at length in the introduction, demonstrates how social conventions push listeners to block or ignore potentially damaging information related to National Socialist crimes, and provides further evidence of *socially shared retrieval-induced forgetting* (SS-RIF).[18] I have observed exactly this dynamic at play in the archived interviews with which I have worked.[19]

In her investigation of how Austrian families have dealt with the history of the war and genocide, Margit Reiter found six different responses, which give us a sense of the range of responses that can exist when children learn uncomfortable information about the national past and the family's relationship with that history: (1) the children display indifference toward the topic, (2) the children become defensive and seek to protect the family, (3) the children become enraged and leave the family, (4) the children turn the family into a history project to find out more while remaining emotionally disengaged, (5) the children engage in political activities in the present to fight against what their parents have done in the past while remaining emotionally connected to the family, and (6) the children create a new distance between themselves and the family while not completely leaving, but also come to see themselves as a new victim of National Socialism.[20] Reiter's research is highly qualitative in nature and cannot provide us with any statistical measurements of these different categories, but her impression is that the third category (rage and separation) is the smallest, and the first category (indifference) is the largest. Reiter's conclusions reinforce Ferreira's observations about the resilience and maintenance of family myths to protect the solidarity of the family. Of the six responses, only one involves a complete breakdown in the family, and Reiter finds this only in rare cases. All other responses involve ways to try and maintain the solidarity of the family.

There is some evidence to suggest that with the passing of the wartime generation that the broader society may be more willing to engage the difficult history of the community. This will probably again vary from one society and culture to the next. As we can see in the case of Japan, the principle of filial piety extends not only to the living but also to all the dead generations. The ancestors weigh more heavily on the Japanese than is the case in Western societies. This is not to say that respect for the dead is absent in Western societies, as this is clearly not the case, but there is a greater temporal and emotional distance that opens in Western societies as the wartime generations pass from the scene.

## Chronological Development

### *East Germany*

The East German regime exercised strong ideological control over the development of discussions of the war and Holocaust with a high level of consistency from the beginning in the Soviet Union zone of occupation, through to the founding of the GDR in 1949 to its collapse in 1989. There were some minor variations in these narratives, but they always reflected regime preferences rather than those of the general population. Thus, using the memory-market dictum, the patterns of production reflect regime preferences far more than the preferences of the general population. While the preferences of the general population are somewhat difficult to discern, the state's propaganda efforts were not without an effect on the general population.

In terms of the regime's interpretation of the Holocaust and its representation, this was always constructed through the lens of Marxist-Leninism, which reduced all causation to the economic sphere. This meant that Nazi anti-Semitism was instrumental and rational in nature, and rooted in capitalism and fascism. The Nazis used anti-Semitism to distract workers from the real source of their plight, which was capitalism itself. In this way, German communists argued that National Socialism instrumentalized anti-Semitism as a way to weaken the class solidarity of the workers.

In the period between 1945 and 1948, there was a fair amount of fluidity in terms of how the international communist movement analyzed the Nazi persecution of the Jews and the status of Jews as, perhaps, a unique victim category. Paul Merker and Leo Zuckermann were leading communist intellectuals who returned to the Soviet Zone after the end of the war. Merker had advocated for the special recognition of Jewish suffering under the National Socialists while in exile and continued to advocate for the unique recognition of Jewish suffering upon his return to the Soviet Zone, while writing for *Neues Deutschland*, the official newspaper of the German communist party. On the tenth anniversary of Kristallnacht, Merker wrote in *Neues Deutschland* about the Nazi persecution of the Jews: "In reality, however, the Nazi racial hatred did not spring up from irrationality but rather a cold contemplativeness. The stepwise increase of the terror until mass murder, in agreement with the realization of specific political goals proves this."[21] While the Nazis clearly did use anti-Semitism in an instrumental fashion, what was lacking from the Marxist-Leninist interpretation was a cultural analysis of anti-Semitism and its roots in German culture.

It was also during this initial period that the German communist party and the DEFA film company supported the production of three films that dealt with the persecution of the Jews during the Nazi regime. Wolfgang Staudte's *Die Mörder sind unter uns* (*The Murderers Are among Us*) (1946) was DEFA's first film, and one of the first to address directly the crimes of the Nazi regime along with an allusion to the fact that many had been Jews. Staudte had originally taken the film script to the French and the Americans, but neither one was willing to grant him permission to make the film. The brutality of the German military occupation is clearly shown in the film, without an attempt to clearly mark the war criminals as "Nazis." Furthermore, we learn that one of the characters in the film living in postwar Berlin in the present is a former military officer, who ordered the mass shooting of women and children on Christmas Eve in a Polish village in retaliation for partisan attacks. Although none of the victims are specifically named as being Jewish, Staudte clearly wished to bring this association into the mind of his audience. For example, when the former German officer unwraps his lunch in a piece of newspaper, we can see the headline reading, "2,000,000 People Gassed." Given the level of anti-Semitism in postwar Germany, Staudte was perhaps wise to keep any direct references to Jews out of his film in hopes of encouraging Germans to investigate what had happened during the war. The film was extremely successful, attracting five million viewers by 1951.[22]

DEFA supported two other films that dealt directly with the Nazi persecution of the Jews: *Ehe im Schatten (Marriage in the Shadows)* (1947) by Kurt Maetzig, who would go on to have a long career with DEFA, and *Die Affäre Blum (The Blum Affair)* (1948) by Erich Engel. *Ehe im Schatten* is based on a true story of a German actor who poisons his Jewish wife and then himself rather than submit to the Nazi demand that he leave his wife. *Die Affäre Blum* explores the anti-Semitism during the Weimar Republic when Jakob Blum, a Jewish industrialist, is wrongly accused of a murder, with clear anti-Semitic intent on the part of the police.

After 1948, these initial openings in discussing the persecution of the Jews in Germany both before and during the National Socialist regime ended. The reasons for this lay entirely in the realm of international relations and Stalin's decision to turn against the founding of the State of Israel in 1948. This led to a new wave of anti-Semitism within the Soviet Empire and what became known as the anticosmopolitan purges. Paul Merker and Leo Zuckermann, along with many others who had argued for the special recognition of Jewish suffering during the National Socialist regime, quickly found themselves on the wrong side of the new ideological line.

DEFA did produce other films dealing with anti-Semitism in the 1950s and 1960s, but the tendency was to focus on the relationship between "capitalist-fascism" and to show that anti-Semitism remained a problem in West Germany. The implication was always that the problem of anti-Semitism had been solved in socialist East Germany. However, there were also other films that dealt in a more honest manner with the Nazi persecution of the Jews. Konrad Wolf, who was the best known DEFA director until his death in 1982, made *Sterne* (Stars) (1959) and *Professor Mamlock* (1961), and Frank Beyer made *Nackt unter Wölfen (Naked among Wolves)* (1963) and *Jakob der Lüger (Jakob the Liar)* (1975), which became the only East German film ever nominated for an Academy Award. *Nackt unter Wölfen* first appeared as a novel by Bruno Apitz in 1955 and was then filmed and broadcast on East German television in 1960, followed by a cinematic release. The story came to play a role similar to the *Diary of Anne Frank* in West Germany in that it was used on a regular basis in the classroom as a literary text to engage young students in the history of the Holocaust. It was also the first German film, in either East or West Germany, to take place in a concentration camp, although it was the Buchenwald camp in Germany, which was primarily for political prisoners, rather than one of the extermination camps in the east. In the story, the communist inmates band together to protect a young Jewish boy, although he is referred to as "the Polish child" in the film. They protect the innocent life of the boy, while also organizing to liberate the camp and continue the resistance against the fascists.

Beyer's film *Jakob der Lüger* is a remarkable East German film for its lack of ideological agenda and suggests that the regime was easing some of its control over cultural production in the later years. Indeed, there is no reason to believe that the film had not been made in West Germany, and the American comedian Robin Williams remade the film in 1999 as *Jakob the Liar*. The film is set in a Polish-Jewish ghetto. From the beginning, we are completely immersed in the Jewish perspective, without the aid of a "good German" to balance out the narrative and give the audience an easy figure with whom to identify. Jakob tells his first lie to try and dissuade a fellow prisoner from trying to escape, which would have certainly led to his death. Jakob tells him that the Russians are probably not that far away and that the ghetto will soon be liberated. Jakob continues to tell "lies" when he sees that this brings hope to those around him who are hopeless. Most touching are Jakob's efforts to provide hope and entertainment for a little girl. But in the end, Jakob, the little girl, and all the other Jews are loaded onto a cattle car and taken away, with the train entering a tunnel and the screen going black but with the sharp pierce of the train whistle in our ears. Nothing emerges from the darkness.

We can see a similar weakening of the regime's ideological rigidity in terms of how the German anti-Nazi resistance was portrayed over time, although the changes came at the very end of the regime. From the beginning, the East German regime celebrated the communist anti-fascist resistance to the Nazis along with the National Committee for Free Germany (NKFD), which was established by German officers in Soviet prisoner of war (POW) camps.[23] These figures of heroic resistance and action are contrasted with the weak and ineffective bourgeoisie or conservative resistance figures, such as Claus von Stauffenberg, who led the July 20, 1944, assassination attempt against Hitler, and Carl Goerdeler, a key figure in the conservative resistance. There was a steady production of anti-fascist films during the entire existence of the regime, averaging about three per year, so the celebration of the communist resistance did not wane with time.[24] What did change was the attitude toward Stauffenberg's assassination attempt, which became accepted as part of the all-German resistance against Hitler. For example, in 1984, the East German television broadcast a short documentary called *Wir haben nichts zu bereuen* (*We Have Nothing to Regret*), which lacked almost any signs of partisanship. The documentary includes interviews with three widows of those murdered by the Nazis from the Kreisauer Circle, which was a group of aristocrats that came together to talk about the need to transform Germany after the war.

The movement in the East to embrace the noncommunist resistance was being mirrored by changes in West Germany as well, where Peter Steinbach struggled between 1983 and 1989 to include the communist and NKFD resistance in a new exhibit at the Bendlerblock, which is the site where Stauffenberg and other members of the assassination attempt were executed by the Nazis. We will return to the West German case in a moment, so we only need to note here that many West Germans and the conservative federal government headed by Helmut Kohl were opposed to recognizing the communists and the NKFD as part of the legitimate resistance against the Nazis. West Germans struggled more to accept the different aspects of German resistance against the Nazi regime, especially in the context of the war. Wartime resistance was long viewed by many as traitorous.

Konrad Wolf dealt with his own sense and fear of having been a traitor when he made an autobiographical film in 1968 called *Ich war neunzehn* (*I Was Nineteen*). Through the character of Gregor, he tells his own story of returning to Germany with the Soviet army during the war. In the film, Gregor is accompanying Russian soldiers but not shooting at German soldiers, until the very end of the film. German-on-German violence remained a largely taboo subject in both East and West German narratives about the past. This is one reason why the NKFD was particularly hated in West Germany, because they had aided the Soviet Union during the war. In Wolf's film, Gregor only picks up a gun and shoots at some SS soldiers, in the distance, after they shoot his friend. This is one of the very few scenes in postwar German cinema where a German soldier shoots at another German, even though he is shooting at the SS. Part of what Wolf wrestles with in the film is Gregor's sense that he may very well be a traitor, and he fantasizes about his own execution as such. The film was apparently very popular with 1.7 million viewers in just three months. In an interview, Wolf was asked whether or not he could have made the film ten years earlier, and he said probably not because the audience would have seen Gregor as a traitor rather than a hero.[25] Throughout the film, Gregor has avoided identifying himself as a German, even when encountering other Germans as the Red Army advances. But by the end of the film, we hear him say, in a disembodied voice, "I am German. I was nineteen."

Wolf's film also reflects the way that the regime wanted its population to view the Soviet Union, in both the context of the war and in the postwar setting. While it most certainly was the case that East Germans held ambivalent views of the Soviet Union, especially those who experienced the brutality, revenge, and mass rapes that occurred as the Red Army advanced toward Germany, the younger, postwar generation appears to have somewhat accepted that "liberation" narrative. The East German regime knew they had to work hard to overcome negative attitudes toward the Russians, given what had happened at the end of the war. In Wolf's film, when a former concentration camp survivor suggests taking revenge against the Germans, a Russian officer comments, "Revenge is a poor preparation for the future." As the Russians advance in the film, they are always seen distributing food to those in desperate need. This image of the Russians feeding the starving German populations was a frequent feature of the photographs printed in *Neues Deutschland* in the postwar years for the annual celebrations around May 8, which marked the end of the war.

While there was some movement within the narrative framework about the Holocaust and the nature of the German resistance toward the end of the regime, there was never any ideological movement on East Germany's interpretation of the end of the war as a liberation, and one that was brought about through the

Soviet Union. The slogan that frequently appeared in *Neues Deutschland* toward the annual celebrations around the end of the war was, "Long Live the Weapon Brotherhood with the Glorious Soviet Army!" Although the big celebrations were focused around May 8, the preparations for the celebrations and notices in the newspapers and television program guides could begin as early as March.

We can clearly see the effects of the social contagion and reinforcement of this material year after year in East Germany. When East and West Germans were polled in 1995 and asked whether Russia or the United States had played the most significant role in the defeat of Nazi Germany, 87 percent of East Germans identified Russia and only 23 percent the United States. The relationship was exactly inverted for West Germans, with only 24 percent naming Russia and 69 percent naming the United States.[26]

But this does not necessarily mean that East Germans had favorable views of the Soviet Union and its role in the war and their country after the war. Given the brutality of the initial occupation and the suppression of the workers' uprising in East Germany on June 17, 1953, we might be surprised to find any support at all for the Soviet Union among East Germans. Indeed, when they were asked their views about the Soviet Union in 1994, a plurality of East Germans identified them "more as an occupation force" at 42 percent. But 32 percent of East Germans viewed them "more as friends and allies" or remained "undecided" at 26 percent.[27] Clearly, the efforts of the regime to create a more positive view of the Soviet Union had not been without some effect.

Although we lack significant polling data on these issues during the existence of the regime itself, we can gain some insight into East German thinking about the Soviet Union based on their responses to detailed television viewer surveys, which were conducted on a regular basis by the television service beginning at the end of the 1960s and continuing to the end of the regime. I have provided a lengthy discussion of the validity of these data elsewhere.[28] In early May 1980, the East German television service broadcast a Soviet film, *Blokada* (*Blockade*), which was shown in four parts. The film tells the story of the three-year German siege of Leningrad and the struggle of the Russians to break the siege. The focus is on the heroic struggle for survival in the city, which obviously put the Germans in a bad light. We have the television viewer data for only the final two days of the film with a 20 percent viewership for part 3 and an 18 percent viewership for part 4. These viewership numbers for East German television in 1980 would have been considered good; some people were at least tuning in. But what did they think of the film? Here, we can benefit from some of the detailed information in the viewership survey, which broke the data down along different segments of the society. Viewers were regularly asked for their opinion about programs, rating them with 1 for best and 5 for worst. For *Blokada*, members of the intelligentsia gave the film the highest marks of 1.06 and 1.00 for parts 3 and 4. Students gave part 4 a 1.54 rating. Clearly, the regime was successful in socializing key segments of the population to a more positive view of the

Soviet Union. These positive views of the program contrast starkly with those over the age of sixty-five, who gave both parts of the film the worst possible rating of 5.00.[29] Those with lived experiences of the Soviet occupation at the end of the war or who may have fought in the war were far less inclined to accept the regime's perspective.

In conclusion, the ideological goals of the East German regime in terms of shaping the population's perceptions of the past had some effect. First, East Germans were far less likely to identify the Nazi persecution of the Jews as a part of their history, compared to West Germans. This can be traced back to the regime's general reluctance to deal with the subject of German anti-Semitism outside of a Marxist framework, or to encourage the production of narratives about the Holocaust. The wave of Holocaust material that swept over West Germany in the 1980s was completely absent in East Germany. What is curious is that even with a regular consumption of West German radio and television broadcasts, East Germans appear not to have been greatly affected by these changes in the West. Second, East Germans were encouraged to identify with the anti-fascist resistance and to reject the legitimacy of the resistance that came from a few members of the bourgeois class. Last, the regime had limited success in socializing the population to some acceptance of the Soviet Union as a liberator of the country and a postwar partner for peace and stability.

### *West Germany*

In comparison to East Germany, West German society was far more dynamic and diverse in terms of how the history of the war and Holocaust was processed over the postwar decades. The obvious reason for this is simply that a freer, democratic society promotes pluralism and diversity. But as we have seen above with the example of the TV broadcast of the Soviet film *Blokada* in East Germany, there was also a great deal of diversity and pluralism there as well, if hidden and submerged. The crucial difference is that this pluralism was able to express itself in the West, whereas in the East, such social divisions regarding the interpretation of the nation's difficult history was always suppressed to a significant degree. One can imagine that at the microlevel of day-to-day interactions, this diversity probably found some expression, but as it was blocked from gaining a broader social expression, the ability for the processes of social contagion and reinforcement were kept to a minimum. We can see a similar dynamic in both Franco's Spain and in Tito's Yugoslavia, although both of these other cases allowed for greater pluralism than was the case in East Germany. Only the very strict censorship regime in Turkey is comparable to the control that was exercised in East Germany.

One way we can think about this is to realize that there is always some level of pluralism in a society, but that the ability of these diverse views to find a broader social expression are frequently limited. This again is emphasized in the memory-market dictum, which reminds us that market capitalism can have its own censoring effect, as narratives that are perceived to be too difficult for mainstream audiences will be marginalized to media that are less expensive to produce, such as books compared to cinematic films. Nonetheless, pluralism exists and is far more likely to be expressed.

A good example of this is the production of the film *Lang ist der Weg* (*Long Is the Way*) by a group of Jewish producers, directors, and actors in 1947. The film was made in hopes that by sharing the Jewish perspective of the war and genocide, the survivors could begin to develop a new life and shared understanding of the past with the broader German public. The film is remarkable for a number of different reasons, and the fact that the film was a commercial failure reminds us that we need to look for both that which is popular and that which is rejected. By comparing popular works with ones that are commercial failures, we can begin to theorize about what audiences find acceptable and less acceptable.

As a commercial enterprise or an effort by a group of Jews to engage a German audience, the film was a failure. Completed in 1947, the film received its premiere at the West Berlin Marmorhaus in September 1948 on the famous commercial shopping street of the Kurfürstendamm. This was a big, central theater in which to premiere a film in hopes of finding a distributor. Things did not go well. Herbert B. Fredersdorf, one of the film's two directors, complained to a journalist at the Berlin *Der Kurier* that he had little hope of being able to find a distributor for the film when "the Auschwitz crematorium is greeted with applause and catcalls of 'There weren't enough that went in!'"[30] The film never found an audience in Germany, although the film also opened in Paris, Vienna, and New York in December of that year. The film then quickly disappeared and has only recently been rediscovered by audiences when it appeared at a New York Jewish Film Festival in 1996. Film scholars of Jewish films and the Holocaust have also neglected the film, probably because very few even knew it existed. But it is exactly the failures and historical narratives on the margins that we need to give special attention to. By contrasting the popular with the unpopular, we can begin to understand more about public attitudes at the time.

There are a number of aspects of the film that made it so unpopular in the immediate postwar years. In some ways, the naïveté of the directors, producers, and actors is endearing at the same time it probably should serve as a warning to postconflict interventions in today's world. Given the heavy involvement of Jews in the project, it is hardly surprising that the film takes a Jewish perspective on the events and encourages the audience to identify with David, the central character in the story. German cinema would not see another central Jewish character of this type until 1978 with the film *David* by Peter Lilienthal, a German-Jewish director whose family fled to Uruguay in 1939, when he was only ten years old. For most of the postwar period, Jews were peripheral characters in German films, whose perspectives and thoughts remained distant and unknown to the audience.

*Lang ist der Weg* is remarkable in a number of other ways, given what was to follow in the coming decades. There is an explicit and unambiguous reference to the Holocaust when we see David's elderly father's image superimposed over the smoke stacks of the crematorium at Auschwitz. The film does not provide any images or story about the brutality in the camp, but West German films avoided any direct confrontation with the camps for decades, and here was a clear reference to the death camps in 1948.

Perhaps the most explosive scene in the film is when David escapes from a deportation train and joins the Polish partisans to fight against the German army. While this makes perfect sense for the story, one wonders from today's perspective if the film's producers had any idea how explosive this material was. Not only was the German audience being invited to share in a Jewish perspective on the most recent history, but the central character was taking on a role that most Germans at the time probably still labeled as traitorous. In 1948, Germans were still highly ambivalent about the justification of the Stauffenberg group's attempt to assassinate Hitler, let alone a Polish Jew joining the Polish partisans to fight against their German men in the field. As I suggested above with Konrad Wolf's film, *Ich war neunzehn*, German-on-German violence was a taboo subject in postwar East and West Germany. Only once someone had been clearly marked as "a Nazi" or a fanatic officer could German-on-German violence be sanctioned—and even this was extremely rare. In *Lang ist der Weg*, we not only learn that David has joined the Polish partisans, but as an act of initiation, he must kill a German soldier with a pistol and then take his weapon. The directors probably had some sense that this might not go down well with the audience because we see David taking the pistol, but the killing of the German soldier is off-screen. We only hear the shot. The rest of David's partisan activities are only hinted at in the narrative of the film.

It is sometimes claimed that there was a silence about the Holocaust in postwar West Germany until the showing of the American TV series *Holocaust* in January 1979, but this is not exactly correct. As *Lang ist der Weg* in the West and DEFA's *Die Mörder sind unter uns* have shown us, the crimes of the Nazi regime were part of German cinema from the very beginning. But as the popularity of *Die Mörder sind unter uns* compared to the commercial failure of *Lang ist der Weg* demonstrates, one could talk about the criminal nature of the regime, but it would be best, from a financial standpoint, to avoid too much direct discussion of the Jewish victims or to take a Jewish perspective. Jewish characters would continue to appear in German cinema on a regular basis up to the 1980s, when there was a seismic shift, but they were almost always on the edge of the story. We would learn that they were in trouble, that some great evil threatened them, but it was almost always an individual Jewish character that was in danger, and someone whom the good German in the film could try to help in some way—or perhaps fail to help. But the scale of the genocide always remained hidden, not openly discussed.

When films like Hoffmann's *Das Haus in der Karpfengasse* moved away from the German perspective and adopted more of a Jewish or outsider view, the popular reaction was harsh. The forms of resistance against these narratives could take many different forms. As already noted above, the German Foreign Ministry asked that the film be removed from the Cannes Film Festival, so even in a democracy, pressure can come from the state, although these attempts are hidden from public view. Another example of this, as we will see in the chapter on Turkey, is the pressure the US government put on the MGM film studio to drop the production of *Musa Dagh*, which dealt with the Armenian genocide. At other times, the pressure against the presentation of such material can take many small forms, which will remain hidden from public view, as they take place in private conversations or are discussed in abstract ways in committee meetings. Sometimes one can even find evidence of such resistance. While working in the Landesbildarchiv (State Picture Archive) for Berlin, I found a scrap of paper that an archivist had decided to put in a folder related to Hoffmann's film. It showed the vote by the Filmgutachtungskommission für Jugend und Schule (The Film Expert Commission for Youth and Schools) in Berlin on whether or not to recommend the use of the film in the education programs in the city. The vote went five to two against a recommendation based on "artistic shortcomings," a clear reminder of how the exercise of power within bureaucracies is often cloaked and hidden.[31] What might have been the artistic shortcomings of the film identified by some of the committee members?

But the story about Hoffmann's film also reminds us of the important role that West German public television played in helping the society come to terms with the legacy of the war and genocide. During the 1960s, the public television stations conducted detailed viewer surveys of their programing, which included more information than simply the viewership numbers. Viewers were also asked questions about their reaction to the program or specific characters. In my research into the presentation of material related to the Holocaust and the Nazi persecution of the Jews on West German public television, there was a fairly consistent pattern of reactions to programs that dealt with this subject. Programs that dealt with the legacy of the war would draw divided reactions, with some wanting to leave the past alone while others saw it as a useful warning for the youth of today. But the negative reactions would often intensify when the subject focused specifically on Jews and the Nazi persecution. About 10 percent to 20 percent of the audience would make very specific and negative comments about such programs, although there was usually a more positive than negative response. This demonstrates that there was a latent willingness on the part of a significant portion of the public to engage this difficult material. But this appears to again be tempered by the perspective that was taken.

For example, in 1963 the ZDF, during its first year of broadcasting, made an effort to present a number of programs related to the Holocaust by marking the twenty-fifth anniversary of Kristallnacht. One of the programs was *Bilanz eines Verlustes* (*Balance of a Loss*), which attracted a smaller than usual audience and drew negative reactions from 50 percent of the audience. The subtitle for the program was, "Jewish Fellow Citizens in Germany—Yesterday and Today." What made this program more difficult than some of the others? The reaction was far more negative than usual. It may have been again that an explicit Jewish perspective was brought into focus by having Jews living in Germany talking directly to the audience about their experiences during and after the war. Whenever confronted directly with Jewish perspectives, the defensiveness of the audience appears to have risen quickly. Although, at the same time, we should remember that the other 50 percent of the viewers responded quite positively to the program and thought it was something particularly important for the German youth today to engage with.[32] Nonetheless, the defensive reaction in the audience is quite telling.

Thus, we can see that there was never a silence about the Nazi persecution of the Jews in postwar West Germany but that the manner in which it was confronted was sometimes circumspect or muted. And here, we come to one of the most important points to take away from this research, a point that will be emphasized in each of the cases: the ethnocentrism of death and the externalization of blame. At the same time that West German audiences were being pushed, slowly, toward a recognition of the Holocaust, they were also mourning the loss of their own family members and other losses that they suffered as a result of the war. Tens of thousands of German families waited years after the end of the war for their husbands and sons to return from POW camps. It was only a full decade after the end of the war that the last ten thousand POWs were returned from the Soviet Union in winter 1955–1956. The continued suffering of German men after the end of the war helped to encourage a sense of victimization among the German population.[33] The externalization of blame for the Holocaust onto "the Nazis" also remained extremely important, because the sacrifice and suffering of the German nation in the war had to remain symbolically separated from the crimes of the Nazi regime. Although there were other challenges to this symbolic separation over the years, the Wehrmacht exhibit played a significant role in breaking down this division. The realization that all of the suffering, death, and destruction of the war had aided a criminal regime was a very difficult one to make. This, in large part, explains the reluctance that many Germans experienced when trying to deal with the Holocaust. This sense of betrayal—that the losses suffered in the war had been for an unjust cause—can be extremely explosive. We will see this in the Yugoslav case as well, especially in the context of the 1980s.

One reason that increasing public information about the criminal nature of the Nazi regime was difficult to process was that it started to open up questions about resistance against the regime and what forms of resistance were legitimate. How did one best serve Germany, the "true" Germany? How did one rehabilitate the community of the good after the terrible conflagration of World War II?

One answer to this question was to celebrate the German resistance against the Nazi regime, especially the bourgeois resistance, or conservative resistance, rather than the communist, anti-fascist resistance. The communist resistance was almost universally denounced in West Germany as having led to a new form of totalitarianism within the Soviet Empire and was blamed for the division of the country after 1949. By celebrating the "proper" form of German resistance against the Nazis, there was an attempt to identify with the resistance as the "true German nation," in contrast to the corrupt and polluted National Socialists.

This discussion about the German resistance was clearly driven by conservative elites in West Germany, although there was some resonance within the general population as well. The first clear attempt to celebrate the German resistance presented itself in 1954, ten years after the Stauffenberg assassination attempt. Although the commemoration date for the resistance was set on July 20, the date of the Stauffenberg assassination attempt, the first ten-year anniversary was heavily weighted in favor of the conservative resistance around Goerdeler rather than Stauffenberg. Although the conservative resistance around Goerdeler was not particularly clear in their dedication to the restoration of democratic institutions in Germany after the anticipated Nazi defeat, they were celebrated as the "true" Germany that had continued to exist in the nation's darkest hour. West German public opinion after the war was divided on the question of whether or not the resistance had been justified. In a June 1951 survey, 30 percent of Germans rejected the legitimacy of Stauffenberg's assassination attempt, while a clearer 59 percent of former career officers rejected it as a traitorous act.[34]

In the years that followed, there was a shift from a focus on Goerdeler and the conservatives toward Stauffenberg's assassination attempt, and a growing acceptance of the act as a legitimate blow against a criminal regime, which was somewhat helped by the fact that the act was focused on the person of Hitler. Newspaper commentators used the assassination attempt to try and remove the stigma of "collective guilt," which many felt had been placed on the entire nation as a result of the Nuremberg trials. Although the Nuremberg trials are often celebrated in American memory as having helped Germans come to terms with the war and genocide, the postwar reality was far more bitter and rejectionist.[35] In 1959, Marion Gräfin Dönhoff wrote in the elite weekly *Die Zeit* (Hamburg), "They [the men of the July plot] are the most distinguished witnesses against the collective guilt of the German nation, their spirit and behavior are examples for us." She continued, "They [the judges at the Nuremberg trials] portrayed everyone who had not deserted [the German army] as a cad and stamped each who had stood up to the enemy [the allies] a moral coward. How incomprehensible must that have been for all those who had endured and believed they had only done their duty."[36] In contrast to Dönhoff's exculpatory reading of the assassination attempt, Helmut Krausnick wrote in the same year about the relationship between the army and the regime. He not only acknowledged the part that the elite killing squads had played but also the role of the Wehrmacht itself. They had not only passively enabled the killings; they had also actively participated in them. Krausnick was a historian and a recently appointed director of the Institute for Contemporary History in Munich. His 1959 essay demonstrates an attempt to weaken the symbolic division that existed in the broader popular culture that sought to keep the German nation and Hitler separate, to keep the Wehrmacht at a distance from the worst crimes of the regime. Although the historiographical knowledge was already there, the broader popular culture fought against this realization for decades to come, as one never saw a German soldier committing a war crime in any of the war films. It took until 1995 for this symbolic barrier to be breached.

There were different segments and types of resistance that were celebrated in West Germany. Christian resistance against the Nazis was celebrated in television dramas, such as the ZDF's *Bernhard Lichtenberg*, which was shown as part of the station's marking of the July 20 anniversary in 1965 and celebrated the resistance of a Catholic priest. Earlier in 1960, the NDR had broadcast *Waldhausstr. 20* (*Tree House Street 20*), which featured a Pastor Tornqvist and his attempt to save Jewish lives by helping them escape to Sweden. Christian suffering and martyrdom played an important part in helping to appeal to the redemptive theme embedded in the resistance narrative. Tornqvist hears the dogs of his Nazi pursuers as he watches the ship safely take the Jews he has helped to Sweden; he then turns to face his tormentors.

There are also several more-problematic examples of those within the regime engaging in resistance, although they were deeply implicated in some of its worst crimes. This did not prevent them from being extremely popular figures in the 1950s. The 1954 film *Canaris* claims to tell the tale of Wilhelm Canaris's resistance against the regime while head of military intelligence. He did become involved in the July 20 plot but only after having played a key role in the regime for many years. The film was extremely popular. Harald Reinl made a series of films that appeared to be openly sympathetic to a fascist perspective, and his film *U47—Kapitänleutnant Prien* (*U47—Lieutenant-Commander Prien*) (1958) celebrated a wartime hero, something that was common in the 1950s. Before films were released in Germany, they had to be passed by the Freiwillige Selbstkontrolle der Filmwirtschaft (Self-Regulatory Body of the Movie Industry; FSK) for a rating, and Reinl's film was criticized for glorification of the war for which the FSK demanded certain changes.[37] The celebration of military war heroes was common in the commercial cinemas and the illustrated presses of the 1950s, where "ambivalent" elite Nazis are shown fighting a good war while also questioning the intelligence of the upper leadership.

Such material tended not to appear on the public television stations, which were more inclined to produce programming directed toward a confrontation with the difficult past rather than exculpatory narratives. But in 1964, the ZDF broadcast a two-part docudrama about Arthur Nebe called *Der Fall Nebe* (*The Nebe Case*). According to a broad survey of German television and material related to National Socialism from 1955 to 1965, this was the only program during this decade to celebrate an elite Nazi figure as a member of the resistance.[38] Although clearly an exception, it is a troubling exception given that very little is known about Nebe's resistance efforts, while his direct involvement in some of the worst crimes of the regime are well documented, such as his command of Einsatzgruppe B, an extermination group on the Eastern Front, from June to November in 1941, which was responsible for killing 45,000 people during those five months. The ZDF's own promotional material for the program is extremely problematic, writing that because of his nationalist worldview, Nebe "succumbed very soon to the seduction of the National Socialist movement." The ZDF's material continues: "Arthur Nebe . . . saw himself in war year 1944 entangled in the guilt of the regime, in whose service he had, like numerous other Germans, placed himself as a professional."[39]

As with any cultural product, the reaction to *Der Fall Nebe* varied, but it clearly stirred a great deal of debate, perhaps encouraged by the fact that it was broadcast against the background of the ongoing Frankfurt Auschwitz trial, which ran from late 1963 through 1965. The television viewer survey demonstrated that people not only watched the show but also discussed it with others. One viewer commented that it was widely discussed at his place of business. While some viewers simply did not like the program because it dealt with National Socialism, there were those who were open to the rehabilitation of a key Nazi figure who had been responsible for the deaths of thousands. One viewer commented, "One learns that the leading people at the time indeed had a conscience." Another one said, "It is good that in those times there were still such individuals, who had a heart, even when they were not able to push through their opinion."[40] Others commented about the "objectivity" and "reality" of the program or the fact that a facade had been removed. They could see things as they really had been. Rather than showing how things "really had been," the response to the show demonstrates a deep wish fulfillment on the part of many viewers to believe this was indeed the case. Narratives like *Nebe* helped to exculpate the National Socialist movement and those who had once supported it.

One last example to consider from the resistance theme in West Germany is Carl Zuckmayer's theater piece, *Des Teufels General* (*The Devil's General*), which premiered in Zurich in 1946. The theater piece was adopted for film in 1954. In the play, Zuckmayer confronts directly the dilemma of providing resistance against a criminal regime in the context of a war. One's efforts to resist the war and the regime are going to result in the death of one's own fellow soldiers, who are no more guilty or innocent than oneself. In the play, the character of Oderbruch embodies this moral dilemma when he sabotages war planes that are going to be sent into combat. In the film version, this act of resistance is softened by having the test pilots of the sabotaged planes parachuting to safety. The way in which the central moral dilemma was softened in the film adaptation of Zuckmayer's play gives us an example of the memory-market dictum, which suggests that large-scale capital-intensive narratives will tend to be less confrontational and seek to accommodate the expectations of the audience.

Whereas the official interpretation of the end of the war was always treated as a liberation in East Germany, the response to events marking the end of the war in West Germany were far more ambivalent. With the passage of time, the narrative shifted from one of bitterness and capitulation to one of liberation and a celebration of a new beginning for German democracy. Whereas Europe's Jews could celebrate the war as a definitive liberation from the terror of German fascism, the German public was far more ambivalent. One can readily assume that the ambivalence felt and expressed in the West was also felt in the East, although there it could not be openly expressed given the views of the regime. The West German state was uncertain with how to handle the ten-year anniversary of the end of the war, and there were not any notable state ceremonies to mark the date. Nonetheless, there were three narrative threads that emerged from the newspaper commentaries, which would continue in the following decades. First, there were detailed, historiographical essays about the events leading to the capitulation of the German forces. While much of this was written in a neutral tone, some authors used their May 8 essays to criticize the Western allies for their unfair treatment of Germans. A second narrative thread focused on German victimhood and suffering, while the third narrative thread asked Germans to take pride in their ability to overcome adversity and thrive in their new democratic state. It is this third narrative thread that gained the most ground in the following decades. While the end of the war clearly marked a liberation for Germany's and Europe's Jews, this was not the immediate sentiment among the German population. This led to a clear narrative and memory divide between Jews and Germans in the following years, although eventually they found a common ground in celebrating the end of the war as a new beginning for the country.

Over time, a partisan division developed between conservative Christian Democrats and more liberal Social Democrats. In 1975, Federal President Scheel gave a speech at the church at the University of Bonn in which he emphasized the theme of liberation but a liberation that had largely come from outside the country. Germans, he noted, had not liberated themselves from the National Socialist regime. Of even greater significance, Scheel began to turn a more critical eye on German society as a whole, moving away from the ethnocentrism of death and toward a more self-critical evaluation. He said, "He [Hitler] had changed our land into a gigantic war machine and each of us was a wheel in that machine. This was recognizable. But we closed our ears and eyes, hopeful, that it might be otherwise."[41] Scheel was detested by conservative members of the federal parliament, and many decided not to attend the speech. Jews tended not to be included in the ceremonies marking May 8, but in West Berlin, which had Germany's largest surviving Jewish community, Heinz Galinski was invited by Berlin's mayor to speak at the ceremonies in 1975 and 1980.

The 1980s marked a crucial juncture for West Germany's encounter with its difficult past. As I have previously noted, there was an explosion of activity and narratives about the Jewish Holocaust, which had not been absent in the previous decades but had never been as sustained as it was during this decade. The social contagion and reinforcement effects made it impossible, perhaps for the first time, for West Germans to avoid the topic of the Holocaust and a clearer understanding of its dimensions and scale. There were more films made dealing with Jewish persecution in the 1980s than all previous decades combined, and there was a sustained amount of reporting on the radio that addressed the Nazi crimes against the Jews.

If we think about the different narrative threads that had existed in postwar West Germany, what happened with the arrival of the widespread discussion of the Holocaust in the 1980s is that it forced everyone to relate what they had thought previously about their experience of the war to the Jewish experience as well. Clearly, not everyone was open to a reevaluation of what they had thought before, but they now had to take the Jewish perspective into consideration. Conservatives began to lose control of their preferred interpretations. A good example of this is the Christian Democratic chancellor Helmut Kohl and his attempts to try and reestablish conservative interpretations of the past in the context of the 1980s. Whereas his symbolic gestures would have been accepted in the West Germany of the 1950s, 1960s, and in part in the 1970s, by the 1980s they were very open to challenge. One clear example of this was Kohl's attempt to organize a visit to the Bitburg cemetery when US president Ronald Reagan visited. The goal was to try and strike a reconciliatory tone with one of West Germany's closest postwar allies, but the fact that the cemetery included the graves of members of the Waffen-SS caused protests to erupt. Kohl refused to back down from the Bitburg visit, but there was an attempt to rebalance the symbolism by also including a visit to the Bergen-Belsen concentration camp. Although Richard von Weizsäcker's speech in 1985 has become by far one of the best-known speeches by a federal president, many of the key points that he touched on were those that Federal President Scheel had made a decade earlier in 1975, and which had been rejected by Germany's conservative political class. Weizsäcker, like Scheel, reminded Germans that they could not separate 1945 and the end of a disastrous war from 1933, when many Germans had embraced the National Socialists and Hitler as saviors of the nation. He encouraged Germans to engage in a more self-critical reflection on the role that they had played in the past.

## Conclusion

The German cases provide a rare natural experiment that allows for a comparison of a nation split in two and governed by two different political regimes. First, it is abundantly clear that the democratic example of West Germany fared far better than the authoritarian example of East Germany in terms of engaging the difficult history of the war and genocide. With time, West Germany was able to repair its relationships with its neighbors through official diplomacy, while also finding a way to recognize the suffering of the Jewish victims in the Holocaust. Both of these external and internal processes took many decades, and they took place in near ideal conditions of stable economic growth and the deepening of democratic institutions. The West German case and that of democratizing Spain help to underline the importance of democratic institutions and an open, pluralistic society for the process of dealing with the long legacy of war and genocide.

At the same time, it is important to emphasize how long this process has taken, as the current literature on transitional justice, reconciliation, and historical dialogues tends to expect far too much in far too short a time. The ethnocentrism of death and the tendency to externalize blame are powerful processes that blunt the willingness of individuals and groups to engage in self-critical reflection. Before individuals and societies can begin to broaden their empathetic identification with others, they first need time to mourn their own losses. It is quite natural for outsiders and the victims of violence to demand an immediate accounting of what they have suffered, but it also does little good to tell someone that they have no right to grieve their own losses. To deny this to someone is most likely to result in bitterness, rage, and a desire for revenge, as we see in *Antigone*. These emotions are rarely in short supply after a period of mass violence.

The natural human tendency is to focus on our own suffering and losses, which traps us. By focusing on ourselves, we risk blinding ourselves to the suffering we may have caused others, to deny them the right to mourn their own losses. This is a very difficult position to work our way out of emotionally, and it may well take a great deal of time. If we realize that West Germany went through this process under near ideal conditions of relative prosperity and a stable democracy, we should recognize that things may turn out radically different in more difficult settings. The ethnocentrism of death and suffering is a difficult position to escape.

The ethnocentrism of death and the externalization of blame combine to create a very powerful resistance to engaging a difficult history. We can see how the externalization of blame continues to play a key role in Germany, even today, in that the perpetrators remain largely in the shadows. The externalization of blame is a mechanism that allows a society to reconstitute itself as a community of the good. The ethnocentrism of death then compounds the problem as we tend to turn inward and to focus on our own sense of suffering and loss, while shutting out how we have harmed others.

Very few Germans are willing today to defend National Socialism or Nazis, but it remains extremely difficult, several generations later, to reconcile what the earlier generations did during those years. While the broader society and the state today is open in its condemnation of National Socialism at the macrolevel, it still remains extremely difficult to integrate that history into one's own family or personal relationships at the microlevel. SS-RIF continues to block everyday conversations from turning too far in the direction of an uncomfortable past. Families continue to remain very protective of their members and seek to construct narratives about the family's relationship to the national history in such a way as to protect the status of family.

The West German case also helps to highlight how change, when it comes, can happen fairly rapidly. The period from roughly 1975 to 1989 represented a time during which the processes of social contagion and reinforcement worked to finally crush some of the lingering attachment to Hitler and National Socialism that remained in West Germany. The widespread macrolevel discussion about the Holocaust and the war during this period created a significant shift in public attitudes toward the past so that there was a growing willingness to identify with the plight of Germany's and Europe's Jews. This identification with the victims, however, did not lead to a similar investigation into the identity of the perpetrators, as we can see with the reaction to the Wehrmacht exhibit, which opened in 1995. We will see that this remains a problem in the other cases as well.

# 2 Japan

*Plataea's land will see a blood-soaked slush*
*of clotted gore, caused by a Dorian spear;*
*the heaps of corpses there will wordless show*
*to eyes of men, for two more generations,*
*that mortals must not cast their thoughts too high.*
—Ghost of Darius in *Persians*[1]

## Introduction

Japan provides an instructive contrast with that of the German cases in that both countries fought aggressive, imperialistic wars. This meant that most of the victims of Japanese violence lived outside the country in the postwar period. Furthermore, both West Germany and Japan quickly adopted formal constitutional democracies soon after the end of the war. While both countries were integrated into the security sphere created by the United States in the context of the cold war, thus putting each country into a close partnership with one of the powers that had defeated it in war, West Germany began the process of regional integration with the other West European countries, while Japan remained far more isolated from Communist China and authoritarian South Korea until the 1970s and 1980s. The last significant difference between the two cases is that Japan clearly finds itself rooted more in the Eastern cultural tradition and collectivism, while West Germany and then East Germany were more rooted in the Western cultural tradition and individualism.

By weighing these different factors of politics and culture, we can come to a better appreciation of how Japanese society has dealt with the difficult legacy of imperial Japanese expansion in East and Southeast Asia both before and during World War II. This chapter will examine each of these factors in turn, beginning with the psychological and social-psychological processes, followed by a discussion of politics, culture, and a synthesis of all these different factors in a chronological discussion of how the Japanese narrative about its difficult past has evolved over the course of the twentieth century.

## Psychological and Social-Psychological Processes

As we have seen in the German cases, there was an extended period during which Germans focused on their own suffering in the war, which tended to limit discussion of what Germans had done to other people. The *ethnocentrism of death* is clearly apparent in the Japanese case as well, where the immediate postconflict discussions were almost wholly centered on the suffering of the ordinary people in a terrible war that had been led by the militarists. What was quickly forgotten in these critiques of the militarists were all the actions that the ordinary people had taken during the years of imperial expansion and the war to aid the militarist cause,[2] and how weak to nonexistent the internal opposition or resistance had been.[3] One important contrast between the Japanese and German cases is that the Japanese have never come to recognize the wartime resistance, as weak as it was, as a positive part of the national history. It has simply been erased from the discussion, perhaps through the process of *socially shared retrieval-induced forgetting* (SS-RIF). We will discuss some additional reasons why the Japanese probably have avoided discussion of the wartime resistance in the section on culture below.

Scholars writing about the Japanese case have frequently pointed to the sense of victim consciousness, which they take to be prevalent in Japanese society. Again, the ethnocentrism of death means that victim consciousness is going to be prevalent in most cases. Is the level of victim consciousness higher in Japan than other cases? Perhaps. Although the term *victim consciousness* has not been applied to the German cases, there is no question that during the first couple of decades after the war that Germans were primarily focused on their own suffering. What perhaps makes the Japanese appear more focused on their own suffering is that explicit discussion of the Japanese as perpetrators in the war has been more muted for a longer time than was the case in West Germany, although this has changed significantly since the 1980s.

One factor that can help to account for these differences between Germany and Japan are two central events in the history of the two countries: (1) the Holocaust in the case of Germany and (2) the atomic bombings of the Japanese cities of Hiroshima and Nagasaki by the Americans at the end of the war. The Holocaust, while not a single event, is now seen as a single historical narrative, as distinct from "the war." This means that a massive genocide now sits at the center of the German understanding of that period, although this was not the case in the earliest postwar years. There is no comparable single event of German suffering to balance against this, although the firebombing of German cities, the expulsion of Germans from the east, and the mass rapes by the Russian army have competed for this status, briefly, in recent years.

In the case of Japan, while the massive scale of the destruction unleashed by the Japanese imperial conquest in Asia reached similar proportions to that of Germany in Europe, there was no single event that came to symbolize the Japanese barbarism in the same way as the Holocaust did for Germany. The primary symbolic markers of Japanese barbarism have always been of a smaller scale and less clearly defined. The only atrocity that begins to compete with a Holocaust like narrative is the "rape of Nanking," although even this does not begin to compare. In the end, Japanese wartime violence simply had a more dispersed characteristic, whereas Japanese victimhood became highly concentrated in the American atomic bombings of Hiroshima and Nagasaki.[4] We need to avoid the naturalistic fallacy when talking about collective trauma, which mistakenly locates the trauma in the event rather than the sociological experience.[5] It was not a given that the atomic bombings, which were not well understood in Japan immediately after the war or during the US occupation, due to US censorship, would take on the dimensions that they have. But as a result of the *Lucky Dragon* incident in 1954, which I will discuss below, the Japanese sense of victimhood came to crystallize around the atomic bombings.

The *externalization of blame* has also played an important role for conservatives and nationalists in the postwar era, although interestingly enough, much less so for progressives and liberals. Conservatives and nationalist narratives of the war have long maintained that Japan had no other option than to fight the war, which they also deny was an aggressive war. The cause of the war exists elsewhere, in the fateful unfolding of history. In contrast, progressives and liberals have been far more direct in placing the blame on the Japanese state, the "militarists," and sometimes the emperor himself. But this left, liberal, progressive critique of the Japanese state has had a specific Japanese inflection in that it focused almost solely on how the Japanese themselves had been the primary victims of that militarist state. Here, we can see one way in which the victim consciousness in Japan was stronger than the case in Germany.

In this manner, the Japanese encounter with World War II tends to become something along the lines of a civil war in which the state victimized the domestic population, while blending out the massive suffering that the Japanese had caused elsewhere. But there is another component to this, which Akiko Hashimoto has done so much to highlight. Although criticism of the wartime dead has remained a painful and ambivalent position in Germany, as can be seen with our discussion of the Wehrmacht (Armed Forces) exhibit and the careful mythological barrier that Germans constructed between Germans and Nazis, the Japanese relationship to the older generation and between the living and the dead is even more intense, thus making any criticism of the older generation or the ancestors "anathema."[6] I will return to the reasons for this, which require a much longer discussion, in the culture section below. For the moment, it is simply important to note that while progressives and leftists could criticize the abstractions of the state and the militarists, they absolutely had to avoid any direct criticism of the soldiers themselves. This led to what some authors have identified as the "fortunate fall" myth—that the soldiers carried out a noble sacrifice in the war, which then led to the collapse of militarist Japan and the rebirth of the peaceful and progressive Japan after the war.[7] This may be a clear example of how hindsight bias might differ between East Asian and Western cultural contexts.

What if hindsight bias in East Asian cultures is stronger than in Western cultures, leading the individual in the present to feel that the way things have unfolded in the past is the only way that they could have happened? Richard Nisbett and his coauthors have observed, "In contrast [to the West], if Eastern theories about the world are less focused, and a wide range of factors are presumed to be potentially relevant to any given outcome, it may be harder to recognize that a particular outcome could not have been predicted. Hindsight bias (Fischhoff 1975), or the tendency to assume that one knew all along that a given outcome was likely, might therefore be greater for Easterners."[8] It had to be; it was fated to be so. Therefore, it makes little sense to engage in arguments such as, "What if the Japanese people had resisted? What if the Communist movement had been stronger?" If one is not inclined to engage in counterfactual reasoning, these questions make little sense. If one's view of the past is dominated by a sense of hindsight bias, if things *had to* and *only could* unfold as they have, then the logic of the "fortunate fall" myth makes perfect sense. It is a logical manner in which to interpret the past. More importantly, for this study, it means that researchers of memory need to be far more sensitive to cultural differences than they have been thus far. The soldiers had to fight a tragic war in order for Japan to be reborn as the peaceful country that it is today. Only by this happening could Japan be what it is today.

Nisbett et al. argue that all of this is embedded in an even larger difference between East Asian and Western ways of reasoning and analyzing outcomes. East Asians tend to be more holistic in their observations and reasoning about why something has happened; they give far more attention to the entire scope of an event. In contrast, Westerners are far more analytic in their approach, giving more attention to specific objects in the field or scope of an event, and develop rules and formal logic to explain outcomes.[9] To ask, "What if the Japanese people had resisted the movement toward militarism?" is to put an analytic question, to focus on the object of the potential for Japanese resistance while pushing the context toward the background; it is a very Western question. Therefore, it becomes difficult to classify the "fortunate fall" myth as *poorly reasoned*; rather, it is reasoned from a different cultural perspective, a non-Western perspective. These matters are not settled in the scholarship, and there is an extended debate about the extent and manner of counterfactual reasoning in Eastern cultures compared to Western cultures.[10] Hazel Rose Markus and Shinobu Kitayama suggest through their contrast of independent selves (Western) and interdependent selves (Eastern) that Westerners may be more inclined to think abstractly about counterfactual proposals, while Eastern cultures will give more attention to the personal relationships at stake in the counterfactual reasoning.

There are also ways in which Western reasoning can also face the charge of "poor reasoning" in that Westerners suffer more from the fundamental attribution error.[11] Westerners sometimes focus on the cause in the object or individual to such an extent that they can almost wholly ignore the context. Westerners tend to exaggerate the supposed character or personality traits of an individual, while minimizing or ignoring the context within which the individual has done something. For example, in an experimental setting, Americans still insisted on assigning responsibility to an individual for statements that he made *even after* they were told that the individual had been put in a "no choice" situation. For Americans, with a heightened sense of individualism and an ethos that demands that one "always has a choice," the idea of a "no choice" situation does not seem all that realistic. In contrast, Korean and Japanese participants in the same exercise gave far more weight to the "no choice" condition that the individual found himself in. One reason for this is that Koreans and Japanese are far more sensitive to the "no choice" position, which is a daily one for them to find themselves in, given the obligations placed on them by their more collectivist cultures and an interdependent understanding of the self. For them, the right action often depends far more on their relationships with others and the context (*giri*) rather than their own personal preferences (*ninjo*).

It should not surprise us, then, to discover that these patterns of thought, holistic versus analytic, are replicated throughout the culture. In his masterful work on Japanese cinema, Donald Richie notes the following: "While Western plot stresses occurrence, causality, and responsibility, Japan's traditional narrative means, the *suji*, emphasizes sequential flow, connection, association. The presumed Japaneseness of Ozu's approach—his emphasis upon effect rather than cause, upon emotion rather than intellect—coupled with his ability to metamorphose Japanese aesthetics into terms and images visible on film—is what makes him, as is so often said, 'the most Japanese of all directors.'"[12] There are very deep and serious implications for these different patterns of thought and reasoning for how the Japanese set about dealing with their difficult history in comparison to the Germans and other Western societies.

## Politics

### *State-Society Relations*

From the end of the war in August 1945 until the present, Japan has continued to develop as a democratic state and society. The open, capitalist economy coupled with a state that generally has been very respectful of civil liberties has permitted the production of a vast array of cultural products that have approached the questions of Japan's wartime responsibility from a wide variety of perspectives. Masaki Kobayashi's film adaptation of *The Human Condition* (*Ningen no joken*) (1959) was made in exactly the period when many other aspects of Japanese society suggested increasing conservatism, especially with regard to questions of wartime responsibility. At the same time, conservative and nationalistic narratives have also been published and produced and found significant audiences. There has been throughout Japan's postwar history a great deal of pluralism in terms of how the past has been discussed. The most significant turn against pluralism in Japanese society occurred during the US occupation period (1945–1952) and especially the anti-communist purges of 1946 and 1947.

The vast majority of Japan's citizens are ethnic Japanese. There are very small Chinese and Korean minorities. This is significant because it means that there has never been a very strong basis for non-Japanese harmed by Japanese imperialism to advocate for recognition of their suffering from within the country. As we will see in the next section, the fact that Japan was cut off from the countries that it invaded during the war has also limited pressure from outside the country until the 1980s. Whereas Jews in West Germany were able to organize and advocate their versions of German wartime atrocities and the Holocaust, the non-Japanese groups in Japan have never been as successful. This has meant that pressure for recognizing wartime crimes has had to come domestically from the Japanese themselves or from outside the country. This is not to say that the domestic Chinese and Korean populations have been without any influence at all. But when compared to the role that Jews played in West Germany's confrontation with its wartime past, the role of Japan's ethnic minorities has been far more muted. Philip Seaton notes that the municipal museums in Osaka and Kawasaki, in contrast to the national museums, are far more open to talking about Japanese aggression in the war.[13] This may be because there are larger populations of non-Japanese minorities in these two cities.

### *International Relations*

Although West Germany and Japan were both integrated into the West during the cold war, West Germany developed far closer relationships with countries it had invaded and occupied during the war. We have seen the impact that the cold war had on West and East Germany in the previous chapter. In contrast to West Germany's close integration with former wartime enemies, Japan remained almost wholly isolated from the countries that it occupied during its imperial project and far more dependent on the United States, because of the official renunciation of war as a tool of state policy in the postwar constitution. Scholars have long recognized this as one reason that Japan has been slower, compared to West Germany, in coming to a more critical perspective of its wartime history and role as an aggressor and perpetrator.[14]

In terms of formal state-to-state relations, Japan restored formal diplomatic relations with South Korea in 1965 along with an official apology.[15] In 1972, Japan began to normalize relations with China. But in both cases, the suppression of civil society forces in South Korea and China meant that any reconciliation and offering of apologies was limited to the official or elite level. Internal changes in China and Korea in the 1980s resulted in increasing discussions within their respective civil societies about the consequences of the war and Japan's success or failure in addressing these issues.[16]

At the level of exchanges between civil society organizations, this has also been slower to develop than was the case of West Germany in the European context. West Germany was bordered by the restored democracies of Western Europe, which promoted free, open, and pluralistic societies. For example, foreign films with different narratives about the wartime history quickly began to move back and forth across national borders, thus forcing Germans to confront the reality of the war from the perspective of those they had invaded and harmed. In Japan, this has been a far slower process, as China was and remains a more authoritarian society, although far more open in the past three decades than was the case in the immediate postwar years. However, the Communist Party in China has demonstrated a new willingness to exercise rigid ideological control over the society during the past five years. The future for pluralism in China is far less certain today. In contrast, South Korea has also democratized significantly since the 1980s, thus freeing up forces in the civil society to wrestle with the legacy of the Japanese colonization and occupation of the country. During the past several decades, Japanese audiences have been confronted with more narratives about the wartime past from Chinese and Korean perspectives.

## Culture

The institution of the Japanese emperor clearly shows the difficulty of trying to maintain an analytic distinction between the realm of political power and cultural power. Robert Bellah has called Japan a nonaxial society, meaning that the transformations that took place during the Axial Age in the ancient world between 800 and 200 BCE have not had the same transformative effect in Japan.[17] Writing about the Meiji period, Bellah notes,

> But by speaking of "opening up" we can consider not only open hostility to the regime, which was quite rare, but all those tendencies that called into question the fusion of divinity, state, society, and self in the pattern that I am calling "nonaxial." Thus any tendency to assert an ultimate principle higher than the emperor, any effort to affirm the independence of society from the state or the responsibility of the government to the people and not just to the emperor, and any tendency to affirm an autonomous individual self, would be signs of opening up even if involving nothing obviously radical or rebellious.[18]

The societies that experienced the axial transformation in human consciousness began to gain a perspective on their social world that allowed them to question existing social institutions and patterns of authority.[19] This transformation, however, did not affect Japan in the same way. Although there are numerous examples of individuals and groups in Japan that have tried to open up an axial and transcendent perspective on Japanese culture and society, they have, for the most part, not had much success.

### *The Japanese Father Figure: The Emperor*

What responsibility did the Japanese emperor bear for the catastrophic rise of militarism in Japan, the war, and the wartime atrocities? The decision by the American occupation officials not to hold the emperor responsible, in any manner, was a fateful one, with long-term consequences. The most critical, anti-emperor voices came from communists, such as in Fumio Kamei and his 1946 film *Nihon no higeki* (*A Japanese Tragedy*), which was first permitted and then banned by the US occupation authority.[20] The sudden swing in US policy against the communists in 1946 resulted in a stifling of anti-emperor intellectuals in Japan. Whatever his actual decision-making capacity, he was the symbolic head of the state that had led the Japanese people into a disastrous program of imperial expansion, wartime aggression, and massive wartime crimes. If the emperor could not be held responsible for what had happened, it quickly became difficult to hold others responsible.[21]

In the immediate postwar years, the Japanese themselves were divided about the appropriate fate for the emperor and the imperial institution. But as the more conservative forces began to regain control of the Japanese state, after the end of the US occupation in 1952, they started to rebuild support for the emperor and State Shintoism. While critical voices would remain audible in postwar Japanese society, a broad social acceptance of the person and the institution was reestablished.

There is nothing in particular that the emperor did after the war that limited discussion of Japan's difficult history. The mere existence of his person and the institution was enough to limit discussion about the wartime past. The institution represented a continuity in Japanese life and tended again to remind the Japanese of the "unchanging nature" of what is essentially Japanese.[22] As we will see throughout this chapter, there was never an absolute silence in Japan about wartime atrocities. Indeed, each postwar decade is marked by significant events of countermemory, where there was an active attempt by different groups and individuals to engage the difficult wartime past.

Nonetheless, the emperor served to set some limits to this discussion. This became clear, as there was a marked increase in discussions about the wartime past with his death in 1989. During the emperor's extended illness from September 1988 to his death on January 7, 1989, the entire Japanese society was asked to demonstrate "self-restraint" out of concern for the emperor's health. Couples were to delay their weddings; festivals were to be postponed. When Hitoshi Motoshima, an elderly Liberal Democratic Party mayor for Nagasaki, suggested that it may have been better if the emperor had ended the war earlier, thus having avoided the atomic bombings of Hiroshima and Nagasaki, he was attacked in the national press, expelled from his party, had his building surrounded by right-wing extremists, and was denounced as "not really being Japanese" or "not really understanding Japanese culture." A year later, he was shot and wounded by a right-wing extremist. All of this occurred with very little public defense from Japanese intellectuals. But when the Christian Meiji Gakuin University decided not to demonstrate any "self-restraint" and held symposia on the nature of the emperor system, they received some support from the liberal *Asahi Shimbun* newspaper and those who wrote to the newspaper. As Bellah observed, "This would suggest that apparent conformity to the pressure of self-restraint obscured more than a little private dissent, a not unusual situation in

Japan."[23] But that apparent conformity does stifle open public dissent and discussion, thus further silencing those who have a different opinion. In behaving *as if* the emperor deserved this respect, whether this was a deeply felt sentiment or not, this added to the aura of the imperial household as the symbol of all Japanese.[24] There is no question that after the emperor's death that something fundamental changed and the *as if* self-restraint quickly fell away. Franziska Seraphim marks the period from the beginning of 1989 through a peek in 1991 "as the lifting of the 'Chrysanthemum taboo.'"[25]

There is a near consensus in the literature that the 1980s were an important turning point in terms of the Japanese engagement with their difficult past, but also that the death of the emperor furthered developments in this direction. Carol Gluck refers to the emperor as a special ghost that limited discussion in Japan for decades.[26] But since the death of the Showa emperor in 1989 and some time before this, the aura of the imperial household had weakened significantly.[27] One can see evidence of this in the popular culture as well. In the most recent Japanese war films, the soldiers are prepared to fight and die for their loved ones, not the emperor, as had been the case in the past. Their motivations for fighting have shifted away from the imperial household in an anachronistic manner.[28] This increasing individualism is also reflected in the mass abandonment by the younger postwar generations of arranged marriages in favor of personal, love relationships. In some areas of Japanese life, *ninjo*, personal preference, has begun to trump *giri*, social duty.

While the decision-making capacity of the emperor in the development of the imperial project and the war remains unclear, he was either given or took a decisive step to end the war, a moment that Japanese popular culture returns to again and again. The emperor's announcement that Japan was ending the war, which was broadcast to the Japanese population, is often portrayed in Japanese films. And in the statement, he suggests that Japan is taking a noble step for all of humanity, not just for Japan, in bringing the war to an end, because of the immense destructive capacity of the atomic bombs. As Yoshikuni Igarashi has noted, the emperor was able to take the military necessity of ending the war, which Japan could not win, and turn it into a concern for humanity at large.[29]

When we compare the Japanese emperor to the other father figures in this study, we can see that each of them has played a role in limiting discussion about their respective country's difficult past. In the case of Japan, the emperor had this effect not because of any institutionalized political power—indeed he had none—but rather as a symbol of Japanese continuity. As we saw in the chapter on Germany, Hitler was dead at the end of the war but also existed as a ghostlike figure in postwar Germany in which the love that many Germans had once invested in him was not gone. Indeed, a plurality of Germans thought him to have been one of Germany's greatest statesmen in 1955, and his popularity increased between 1965 and 1975.[30] Franco exercised institutional political power until his death in 1975, but he failed to cast much of a shadow over events after his death, unlike the immortality that Atatürk has attained in Turkey. In Yugoslavia, Tito's death marked a new period of crisis for the Yugoslav state, and with the complete collapse of that state after 1992, he has faded from the scene. As we will see in the chapter on Yugoslavia, the unifying mythology of the partisan struggle was very weak by the time of Tito's death.

### *Filial Piety and Ancestor Worship*

The comparative research in this project has helped to highlight the differences that exist in societies with regard to the sense that the past is something open to reinterpretation and investigation. There is a strong contrast between the countries located primarily in the Western cultural tradition, in Germany, Spain, and Yugoslavia, on the one hand, and in the Eastern cultural tradition, in Japan and Turkey, on the other hand. Societies that are anchored more in the Eastern cultural tradition have stronger bonds between the younger and older generations within families and between the living and the dead. Not all cultures share the same sense of obligation between the living and the dead. When the bonds among the living generations are tighter, as with filial piety, and when the bonds between the living and the dead are closer, as with ancestor worship, it becomes increasingly difficult for members in these societies to engage in self-critical reflection on the past, as these close relationships are potentially put at risk. In collectivist societies with a focus on the interdependent sense of the self, which places a premium on the maintenance of relationships above the defense of abstract values, we can expect greater defensiveness when questions are raised about the behavior of the previous generations.

As has already been outlined in the introduction, one should not imagine that those societies anchored more in the Western tradition are somehow freed from these same bonds, as they clearly are not. There was no shortage of criticism leveled against West Germans who "dirtied their own nests" through their self-critical reflections on National Socialism, the war, and the Holocaust. What we are dealing with is a difference in degree, not a difference in kind. There is without a doubt a sense that ancestors and founding fathers also deserve respect in Western societies, but unlike the case in the more Eastern societies, self-critical reflections on the older generation and the ancestors is not nearly as fraught and taboo. For example, in her survey of Japanese postwar literature, Irmela Hijiya-Kirschnereit notes that she can find no examples of authors born after the war who had their postwar generation characters questioning the decisions of the older generation during the war.[31] There is no Japanese equivalent of the *Vaterliteratur* or "father literature" that appeared in postwar West Germany, where the younger, postwar generation took their father's generation to task for what happened during the National Socialist years. As with Hijiya-Kirschnereit's study of literature, Richie observed a similar disinterest in the filmmakers born after the war.[32] We can see this cultural value of respecting the ancestors reflected in the popular culture.

Hashimoto coined the term *generational proximity* as a way to express this relationship between the generations. Other scholars have placed even more emphasis on the reciprocal nature of the relationship between the living and the dead in which the living continue to demonstrate care for the dead, and the dead, in turn, bestow good fortune on the living.[33] Indeed, it is the disruption of this reciprocal relationship in a massive natural disaster such as the March 2011 earthquake and tsunami that may help to explain the frequent reporting of ghosts in the days, weeks, and months following the disaster.[34] The closer the proximity between the generations and between the living and the dead, the harder it will be for the younger generations to gain some emotional and ethical distance from the past and to assume a self-critical stance vis-à-vis their parents and their grandparents. Because of the closer generational proximity in Japanese society, there is a stronger tendency for the Japanese to avoid the emotion of anger toward those with whom they are closely related. This, in turn, makes it more difficult for one to take a self-critical position vis-à-vis the national past.[35] Other scholars have previously noted the lack of intergenerational conflict in Japan, compared to West Germany, but without tracing it back to relationships within families.[36]

Although there have been many significant changes in Japanese society over the course of the twentieth century, the principles of loyalty and filial piety remain quite important to many Japanese.[37] When small shoots of individualism and the questioning of the givenness of Japanese society did begin to break out as part of the popular rights movement in the first couple decades of the Meiji regime, very few in the movement were willing to question these core values of loyalty and filial piety.[38] The same remains largely true today as well; Bellah notes of the postwar period with its improvements in civil liberties through the 1946 constitution, "but the givenness of Japanese society has not been broken through. Postwar democracy was not the popular enactment of the democratic visions of the Japanese intellectuals. . . . Though enjoying an unprecedented degree of freedom the Japanese intellectuals have most of the same problems they have always had. They have yet to find the organizational forms through which they can have a decisive impact on their own society."[39]

Richie's careful observations regarding Japanese cinema offer us yet another important insight into how the Japanese relate to family relations compared to Westerners. Richie writes, "The concern for the concepts of inside and outside is also a very Japanese one. *Uchi* (inside) and *soto* (outside) are considered much more defining, and limiting, than they are in the West. There is also a Japanese assumption that the former is safe and the latter is not. The assumption therefore fittingly delineates a story where the outside is a repressive governmental area distinguished by its lack of ninjo, the quality of human feeling so touchingly depicted inside the tenement, the closed quarter."[40] Thus, the Japanese have even that much more of a desire to protect the family against an outside world that is viewed as far more hostile than is the case in the Western world. To abandon the family for a political cause is often, literally, beyond reasonable thought. For example, during the militarist period, most Japanese communists abandoned their cause once their captors reminded them of the shame that their family would face through their imprisonment. As we will see elsewhere in this chapter, scholars of Japanese politics and culture have often noted that the Japanese are more apolitical and disengaged from politics than is the case in Western democracies. The Japanese may certainly express frustration with their political leadership, but they are often at a loss as to how they should respond or bring about effective change.[41] Richie has brought our attention to a fundamental predisposition that helps us to understand why political engagement, which has to take place "outside" (*soto*), is something that one might quite logically wish to avoid. The *ideal* of civic engagement as a political orientation is not one that is highly valued in Japanese life. As I will discuss below regarding the postwar youth revolts and postwar social movements, these have not been driven by the ideal of a broader civic engagement, but rather because the outside world (*soto*) has forced itself into the inside of life (*uchi*) in an unwelcomed manner and needs to be beat back. When the private realm is once again secured, the citizens tend to withdraw from civic engagement, leaving the existing political arrangements largely as they were before.

## Chronological Development

The immediate postwar years in Japan under the US occupation were very dynamic in terms of the willingness of many Japanese to demand that the wartime leadership be held accountable for the disaster that had befallen the country. The true extent of the disaster and Japan's wartime crimes were not immediately known due to the effectiveness of wartime censorship and propaganda. Japanese educators immediately demanded that Supreme Commander of Allied Powers (SCAP) begin purging those who had supported the militarist policies in the schools.[42] In October 1945, members of the opposition to the militarist leadership were released from prison, and the Japan Communist Party was reconstructed. The prewar teachers' unionists, the Communist Party members, and left-wing intellectuals all came together as a loose coalition demanding change for their society.

In an important move, the emperor renounced his divinity on January 1, 1946, thus opening up some further possibility for critical voices to be raised against him and the institution he represented. And in May 1946, the International Military Tribunal for the Far East (IMTFE) began its prosecution of top-level militarists. The IMTFE remained active until November 1948. In the end, the tribunal was far less successful than the Nuremberg trials, which were taking place at the same time in Germany.[43]

The first postwar years were marked by a significant amount of activism on the part of Japan's civil society, especially between 1946 and 1950.[44] One of the most important civil society groups to form in these early years was the Japanese Teachers' Union (JTU), which defined itself as supporting democratic values, serving the people and not the state, and fighting against the remilitarization of Japan. At the same time, the JTU came to focus much more on the domestic victims of Japan's disastrous war rather than those living in other countries.[45] Many teachers felt motivated to struggle against remilitarization and the Japanese state because of their failure to do so during the war. They focused on the theme of never having their students sent to war again. While the JTU became an important voice for democratization, it was not a force in Japanese society that was pushing for an understanding of wartime responsibility that included the broader population.[46] With the growing anti-communist and anti-leftist policies of the American occupation, the JTU found its ability to shape postwar debates quickly curtailed when they lost the right to strike in 1948, thus severely weakening their ability to wield political power. But the position of the JTU is very important to note, especially in contrast with the position of teachers in the other cases. For example, teachers and educational institutions in Turkey view themselves as an extension of state power, not something that should question or check state power. In Spain, it has taken many years for educators to extract themselves from the influence of the Catholic Church, which was closely allied to Franco's regime.

Another civil society organization that came to play an important role in shaping the more liberal and progressive side of the discussion was the Wadatsumikai, or the Japan Memorial Society for the Students Killed in the War.[47] This organization had a very small membership when compared with that of the JTU, but they were very active in publishing books, producing films and plays, and setting up other artistic exhibits. They fully utilized the free and open space provided by Japan's civil society to offer a critique of the war and the loss of Japan's students. While the first postwar years were marked by a great deal of dynamism on the part of civil society and a willingness to engage critically with the war years, these critiques were somewhat limited in that there were very few attempts to identify with the victims of Japan's war of aggression who were not themselves Japanese.

The most notable and partial exception to this was the formation of the Japan-China Friendship Association in October 1950. This organization explicitly sought to draw attention to Japanese war crimes against the Chinese, but almost exclusively crimes against Chinese forced laborers in Japan and not elsewhere outside of Japan.[48] Thus, while there were pro-peace and anti-militarist groups, they were almost wholly silent on Japanese war crimes outside of Japan. These groups hardly set the national tone going forward into the 1950s, which took a decidedly conservative turn, not unlike what was seen in West Germany during the same decade. During this decade, there was a turn against the "detestable and distasteful" discussions of the war.[49]

As with each period in Japan, there are dominant trends and counterexamples. The publication of *Sanko* in 1955 by Japanese POWs, who had returned from camps in China, talked explicitly and in graphic detail about Japanese war crimes in China. It was also during this decade that Junpei Gomikawa published a six-volume novel called *Ningen no joken* (*The Human Condition*) between 1956 and 1958. The novel was immensely popular, especially with university students.[50] Masaki Kobayashi turned the novel into a lengthy film version comprised of three separate films between 1959 and 1961. Kobayashi's film gives one of the clearest portrayals of the Japanese as perpetrators, with graphic displays of beatings, torture, and horrible work conditions for Chinese slave laborers as well as the sexual exploitation of women. Up to this point in West and East German cinematic history, there was nothing that showed German war crimes in the same light. The film was very successful and paved the way for Kobayashi, always an outsider in the studio system dominated by large film corporations, to produce two more masterpieces in the 1960s, *Hara-Kiri* and *Joiuchi* (*Samurai Rebellion*), both of which fit into the antifeudalist samurai genre.[51] Kobayashi was working against the broader mainstream, although not without success. Richie wrote of Kobayashi's earlier film *Kabe atsuki heya* (*The Thick-Walled Room*) (1956) that it was "one of the very few Japanese films to raise the question of responsibility for the war."[52] As a result, Kobayashi's film company, Shochiku, withheld the release of the film for several years, perhaps under pressure from the Japanese government or the US occupation authorities.[53] Kobayashi's studio-based film career ended after *Samurai Rebellion* (1967), even though his films had been commercially successful. His final release was an independent project.

In contrast to Kobayashi's iconoclasm, mainstream cinema was far less confrontational with popular sentiments. In his survey of the 1950s film landscape, Michael Baskett writes that the "postwar antiwar films" became popular mixtures of remorse for the defeat, while also filled with a nostalgia for empire.[54] This is not unlike some of the more right-wing cinema that we can find in West Germany during the same decade. This is not to say that there were not brutal portrayals of war and its costs, as in *Nobi* (*Fires on the Plain*) (1959), which gives a graphic view of how many Japanese soldiers felt abandoned by their leadership at the end of the war, in this case in the Philippines. The film was based on the novel of the same name by Shohei Ooka. But films like *Fires on the Plain* tended to focus on Japanese suffering without investigating how one had arrived at such a state in the first place. The setting of the film at the end of the war leaves open the question of how one came to the point of wandering hopelessly through a barren landscape, a problem that Kobayashi avoids in *The Human Condition*. Kobayashi has his main character making compromises with the regime from the beginning, as he struggled to maintain his humanity while also seeking accommodation with the regime. The narrative of *Fires on the Plain*, which clearly demonstrates the horrors of war and thus can be labeled "anti-war," is very similar to the one that former Japanese soldiers wrote about themselves, which was to portray them as powerless victims.[55] In this manner, *Fires on the Plain* and others match closely a pattern in postwar West German cinema in which soldiers find themselves fighting a hopeless war against a terrible enemy with no clear understanding of how they had arrived at that point. There is also a partial and notable parallel between Japanese war films and West German war films in that the identity of the enemy is often blurred or absent. For example, in many Japanese war films and, for that matter, Japanese war memoirs, the enemy is almost wholly absent from the picture. Van C. Gessel notes that while very few Japanese novels deal with Japanese war atrocities, they also deal little with the enemy in general.[56] The struggle to stay alive is portrayed more as a survival narrative in a natural catastrophe or a lost in the wilderness story.

Perhaps the most popular Japanese film set in the prewar and wartime is *Nijushi no hitomi* (*Twenty-Four Eyes*) (1954), directed by Keisuke Kinoshita and based on the 1952 novel by Sakae Tsuboi. The story is set on the Shodo Island in the Inland Sea of Japan, a rural setting far from the big cities and the industry necessary for making war. The twenty-four eyes in the title refer to the eyes of the twelve students in a young teacher's classroom in her rural school. The children are just beginning school in 1928 when the film opens and the war is still far away. Indeed, the war and the harsh economic conditions imposed by first the economic depression and then the war itself are only seen indirectly in the film through the suffering and tears of those in the village and town. The film foregrounds the life of Mrs. Oishi, with the events of the wider world moving forward quietly in the distance. The outside events are brought to the viewer through on-screen texts that notify us of the Manchurian Incident in 1931 and then the coming of the wider war, but always in the passive voice with the perspective of great events far beyond the village—forces that no one can control.

Mrs. Oishi is not someone who betrays great political awareness, but she pushes back against the school administrator when word spreads that a colleague now finds himself in trouble for having used "red literature" in his class. Mrs. Oishi does not like being told what to do, and she begins to use some of the "red literature" in her class. In a scene in front of her colleagues, she openly confronts the school administrator saying that she sees nothing wrong with the poems. When she is rebuked by the principal, her colleagues remain silent, and she is quickly isolated in her opposition. Eventually, she decides to leave the school, to retreat from the relationship she has no hopes of changing. The film ends with a class reunion after the war. Mrs. Oishi has grown older, lost her husband and son to the war, as well as many of her male students. The female students invite her to tea where they reflect on what has happened, and they are joined by one surviving male student, who is now blind. The film is a beautifully wrought tale of the costs of war and touches on the special bond that exists between teachers and students in Japan, as reflected in the JTU campaigns and the Wadatsumikai organization. This special bond is defined by the Confucian virtue of *zunshi* (in Chinese), which places the student and teacher in a relationship similar to that of a child and a parent. The teacher is responsible for the overall well-being of her students.[57] But it is also a film that feeds the tendency toward victim consciousness present in much of the Japanese postwar culture. Tadao Sato, one of Japan's best-known film critics, while recognizing the clear merits of the film, also comments that it "has probably wrung more tears out of Japanese audiences than any other postwar film."[58]

Kon Ichikawa directed two of the other best-known anti-war films of the 1950s, *Biruma no tategoto* (*Harp of Burma*) (1956) and *Nobi* (*Fires on the Plain*) (1959). The *Harp of Burma* is based on the 1946 novel of the same name by Michio Takeyama.

In the film, Mizushima, the hero of the story, is a member of a military company in Burma when they learn that the war is over. Everyone in Mizushima's company is relieved that the fighting is over, but there is another Japanese military company up in a cave that refuses to accept the end of the war. They are prepared to continue the fight in order to honor their fallen comrades. Mizushima is given the task of climbing up to the mountain cave where the holdouts are in order to convince them to surrender. If he fails, the British will begin to fire artillery on the position of the holdouts in the cave. Despite Mizushima's entreaties for them to surrender, the fanatics prefer death and honor over the promise of a new beginning after the war, and the shelling begins. Mizushima barely escapes with his life, but his comrades assume that he has been killed. Through the telling of the story, Mizushima first accidently adopts the outward appearance of a Buddhist monk but then decides to take this on as his new identity, with the mission of burying the war dead in Burma, while his comrades return to Japan to begin the rebuilding of the country. By the end of the film, Mizushima's survival is revealed to his comrades when the captain reads Mizushima's letter to them in which he asks, "Why does tragedy exist on this earth and why do we have to suffer it?"

The film has several significant features. First, it reminds us of the importance of taking each of these cases and respecting their cultural differences, which as we will see, exist among the Western Christian countries as well. To put it bluntly but to make the point, the Japanese are not going to primarily use the lens of Christianity to understand their experiences and the end of the war; this is not primarily part of their cultural tradition, although there are Japanese who have converted to Christianity. This is not without significant consequences because Christian converts have gained an outsider perspective, an Axial Age perspective, which has helped them to be some of the leading critics of Japanese society, as we have seen above with the refusal of the Christian University to reinforce the emperor cult. Of course, for the vast majority of Japanese, they will work on understanding the end of the war through the lens of Buddhism. As we can see in the case of Germany, Christianity did not necessarily encourage postwar Germans to confront the wartime atrocities that they had committed, instead intoning the importance of Christian forgiveness in the Dachau concentration camp, for example. And, sometimes, this so-called Christian propensity for forgiveness was contrasted unfavorably with the "avenging Jew," who was demanding justice for the crimes committed in the past. But embedded in both the Christian and the Jewish traditions, the demands for justice *and* the responsibility for seeking to transform the world from what it is into something better is an important contrast with the general Buddhist orientation.

The Buddhist tradition encourages more of an acceptance of the way things are, rather than an emotional energy to transform the world. At the core of the Buddhist tradition is the enlightenment that comes from recognizing that suffering is what defines the human condition, as expressed in Mizushima's letter to his comrades. The film sets up the contrast between the company of fanatics that prefer death and honor, on the one hand, and Mizushima's company that accepts the end of the war as an inevitable outcome. Here, we can see an example of the hindsight bias discussed in the section on psychology. In her essay on the film, Keiko McDonald observes the following:

> These soldiers surrender to the British because they accept defeat as an inevitable consequence of the human condition. They accept the progression of time, seeing in its insistent turning toward the future a confirmation of the value of the individual life. When they are relocated in the POW camp later, these soldiers sing a song about the wheel of a mill. Significantly, the song's recurring image of the turning wheel expresses a natural and spontaneous feeling about the passing of time and human destiny.[59]

This future-oriented fatalism is very much reflected in the "fortunate fall" myth discussed by Hashimoto and is one that is popular across ideological divisions in Japan. These things have come to pass; we must accept them because this is how history has unfolded. But it is a perspective that is very much at odds with the Western view of needing to assign responsibility and blame to those who have caused harm in the past. And here we come to the paradoxes of the two approaches, which I have labeled broadly as the Eastern and Western cultural traditions. The Eastern tradition has the potential to escape the endless pull back into the past and past wrongs but orienting oneself and one's society toward the future, but at the cost of perhaps failing to bring about the transformation of one's society to try and prevent these same wrongs from happening again. The Buddhist tradition is very much in harmony with one of the lessons of *Antigone*: that all of the dead deserve their proper burial. The dead need to be buried, and we need to turn toward the future.

There is significant evidence that the Buddhist tradition has had a deep impact on how the Vietnamese and Cambodians have dealt with their respective recent histories of war and genocide. Like the character of Mizushima, they appear to show a great deal of willingness to treat all deaths in the war and from genocide as the same—that they all require equal respect and concern. As is expressed in *Harp of Burma*, there is a profound concern in the Buddhist tradition for making sure that the spirit of the dead is at peace, which means a proper burial at home. A "good death" is one that occurs "at home," while a "bad death" is one that occurs "in the street" or away from the home of the ancestors. What is important is to return to the harmonious wholeness of the family and the ancestors so that they continue to reside together and rest peacefully after their death.[60] If Mizushima is not able to provide a burial at home, he is at least able to offer a burial for the war dead where they fell. Still today, the Japanese government will make sure to repatriate the corpse of any Japanese soldier found in one of the former battlefields of the empire.

Even with this brief discussion of Japanese films, we can see a clear emphasis on discussion of the Japanese as victims of war as a natural catastrophe rather than something that one might be responsible for in some manner. Hijiya-Kirschnereit finds a pattern in the Japanese transformation of "history into nature" through literature, noting, "The attitude of regarding war as a category of nature is also characteristic of many descriptions of war. . . . A resigned aestheticism has marked the Japanese attitude toward natural catastrophes."[61] Here, we can see the role of *social contagion*, *reinforcement*, and also SS-RIF as images and narratives of Japanese victims tend to dominate the discussion to the almost total exclusion of the Japanese as perpetrators, with Kobayashi's *The Human Condition* being the most notable exception. *Harp of Burma* takes us to the very end of the war without any inquiry into how the main characters have arrived at this point. *Fires on the Plain* echoes the story of Stalingrad in Germany, where soldiers are stuck in a hell-on-earth struggle for survival, with no investigation into how this hell was created. Although very subtle, *Twenty-Four Eyes* does raise the question of resistance against militarism through the character of Mrs. Oishi, but we are kept at a very safe distance from the battlefield. There are many Japanese victims in *Twenty-Four Eyes*, but we are left wondering what the young men might have done in the war. Some things are revealed; others remain hidden and obscured.

It was within this context that in August 1953 the annual pensions were restored to the war-bereaved families, and in 1955 the law was revised so that war criminals also became eligible as well as the survivors of those who had already been executed, as "deaths incurred in the line of duty."[62] We can see a similar trend in West Germany in the 1950s, when former Gestapo officials had their pensions restored along with performance bonuses for deporting Jews to the death camps. The shift in the general cultural matrix toward a decriminalization of the wartime past created the political setting in which such policy decisions could be moved through democratic legislatures. It was also during this decade, as conservatives began to return to power in government, that any discussion of Japanese perpetrators in the school textbooks was significantly toned down.[63]

The year 1954 also marked another important turn toward a further strengthening of the victim consciousness with the so-called *Lucky Dragon* incident. The *Lucky Dragon 5* was a Japanese fishing vessel that was well outside the recommended zone of exclusion around the American testing of the hydrogen bomb at the Bikini Atoll on March 1. Nevertheless, the radioactive fallout from the explosion fell on the ship, eventually giving the crew radiation sickness and contaminating their catch of tuna. When the radio operator on the ship died in September 1954 from radiation sickness, the agitation in the society at large exploded into an outpouring of antibomb fervor. Antibomb petitions began to collect millions of signatures, ten million by October 1954, and eventually thirty million by August 1955, the tenth anniversary of the atomic bombings of Hiroshima and Nagasaki. It was at this point that the *hibakusha*, the scarred survivors of Hiroshima and Nagasaki, gained national prominence. The impact of the American postwar censorship on the bombings began to dissipate.

Although there would continue to be bits and pieces of stories related to Japanese perpetrators, these were clearly overwhelmed by narratives of Japanese victims that dominated the national discussions of the 1950s and 1960s. The turning point would come in the early 1970s and build dramatically through the 1980s to the present, but first the focus was on Japanese victimhood. The point is not to criticize an individual or a population for mourning their own suffering; indeed, I have argued that the ethnocentrism of death is an inevitable and necessary outcome of mass violence. In the case of the Japanese and the memorialization of the atomic bombings, there has been a strong tendency from the beginning to view the atomic bombings as something akin to a natural disaster, which was beyond human agency. This goes so far in some Japanese narratives as to even remove the United States as a source of the bombing. The intense focus on the victims of the bombings did not lead to a discussion of how it came to be that the bombs were dropped in the first place. It is simply enough that it happened. Keiji Nakazawa's graphic novel *Barefoot Gen* (*Hadashi no Gen*) (1973–1987) has achieved an iconic status in Japan, equal to that of Anne Frank's story in the West. The narrative is semiautobiographical. Through the novel, Nakazawa tells the story of his family and his own personal survival after the atomic bombing of Hiroshima. The graphic details of the bombing and its effects on human beings are some of the first images that grade school children have of the events, and they stay with them many years later. While *Barefoot Gen* is very clear about the evils of war, it remains, like many other Japanese narratives, disconnected from the events that led to the bombing in the first place.[64] We can again see the influence of a Buddhist orientation toward a catastrophe in which the search for causes is left to the side and a focus on human suffering is moved to the fore.

There is a whole series of films that have dealt with the bombings and the long suffering of the survivors. The JTU actually sponsored two of these films as part of their attempt to fight against militarism and the state. Kaneto Shindo made *Gembaku no ko* (*Children of Hiroshima*) in 1952, based on a best-selling book of children's testimonies compiled by Arata Osada. Richie writes that the film failed to achieve the political goals of the JTU, which was to create a stick "with which to beat Uncle Sam."[65] Therefore, the JTU sponsored another film, Hideo Sekikawa's *Hiroshima* (1953), with which the JTU was far more pleased. The fact that both of these films were made immediately after the end of the US occupation demonstrate that the atomic bombings were already part of the discussion before the *Lucky Dragon* incident, reminding us that this event occurred within a cultural context already primed to explode. Akira Kurosawa responded immediately to the shift in the national mood with his film *Ikimono no kiroku* (*The Record of a Living Being*) (1955) in which an aging family patriarch is eventually driven insane by his fears of a nuclear war. In 1989, Shohei Imamura filmed *Kuroi ame* (*Black Rain*) based on the prize-winning novel of the same name by Masuji Ibuse from 1966. The opening scenes of horror remain indelible images throughout the film as the focus shifts to the inability of a family to find a marriage partner for their daughter, who is a *hibakusha* and dying of radiation sickness. Some of Japan's most famous and skilled film directors eventually turned their talents in this direction with startling effect, especially Imamura.

Whatever critical perspective had been gained on the war through the 1950s began to be lost in the war films of the 1960s and 1970s, when the war simply became a setting for adventure, rather than stage for critical moral reflection.[66] At the outset of the 1960s, one might reasonably have expected a different outcome based on the events around what became known as the Anpo crisis. In May and June 1960, there were mass protests against Prime Minister Kishi, a former top-level government official during the war, and his plans to sign a revised US-Japan Security Treaty. For the progressive forces in Japanese society, this marked, yet again, as with the rearming of the country in response to the war in Korea, a potential return to militarism. Kishi eventually signed the treaty, and the crowds dispersed without any lasting effect.

This was another example of the expressive protests that J. Victor Koschmann has written about in which there is a near hysterical and passionate emotional commitment to a cause, but rather than this leading to a well-structured, institutionalized social movement designed to bring about meaningful change, one simply moves on.[67] Whereas in the Western context one would expect a further rational instrumentalization of these social energies into a transformative project, in Japan one has already achieved all that one can hope to achieve simply by expressing one's opposition. For example, the youth revolts of 1960, the Anpo crisis, and the 1968 student protests were brief, had a low level of participation (perhaps about 5 percent of the youth cohort), and none of those who participated later found themselves involved in politics.[68] Hashimoto finds the Japanese population particularly disengaged from politics and the idea of social change, and she traces this back to the endless theme of "powerlessness" that pervades Japanese narratives about the war. Shunsuke Tsurumi echoes these observations and suggests that the roots of such behavior exist in the premodern history of Japan.[69] The Japanese, Tsurumi observes, can be roused to political action, but only if there is some specific issue that impinges directly on their own life. Such mobilization does not result in a broader, general political awareness and engagement.[70]

This is in stark contrast to the pattern in West Germany where the youth revolts of the 1960s, defined by intergenerational turmoil and attacks on the "capitalist-fascist state," led to future political careers and a deep commitment to political change. In Japan, the pattern has been the rise of expressive protest movements that yield little change in Japanese society or long-lasting civil society organizations. For Bellah, this is yet another sign of Japan's nonaxial nature.[71] Returning to the 1960s Anpo crisis, Seraphim writes, "The peace and student movements shifted their activism in ways that paid lip service to the memory of the war but focused exclusively on the failures of postwar democracy."[72] Therefore, while there may appear to be strong similarities between the youth revolts in Germany and Japan, they have different roots and very different outcomes. For Wadatsumikai, this meant a continued confrontation with the emperor system as a serious flaw of the postwar democracy. The broader point to appreciate is that we need to take cultural differences into consideration when studying social protest movements in non-Western countries. The social movement literature was developed in Western countries and contains within it certain biases.[73]

As we can see in the German case, the Nuremberg trials and the later domestic trials had a very mixed reception in West Germany,[74] something far less positive than is often assumed in the Western academic literature. But the trials did take place, and there were Germans who used the legacy of the Nuremberg trials to justify a further confrontation with Germany's difficult past. This has not been the case in Japan. While many Japanese were pleased to see their own leadership put on trial at the Tokyo trials, this was because they were relieved to watch those who had led a catastrophic war punished based on their own sense of suffering and victimhood, not because of what their leadership or they themselves had done in the war.[75]

Over time, many Japanese came to see the Tokyo trials as a crude victor's justice, and the dissenting voice of Justice Pal became more popular. Pal had argued in his dissent that the Western imperial powers were hardly likely to give up their colonial ambitions in the region and that they could hardly sit in judgment of those who fought against them. The potential liberalizing influence of the trials was further undermined by the US war in Vietnam, which was widely viewed in Japan and elsewhere in the world as a massive criminal and imperial adventure by the United States. Who was now going to sit in judgment of the United States? This question entered the popular culture through a play by Junji Kinoshita called *Kami to hito to no aida* (*Between God and Man*) (1970). The Vietnam War, in this manner, became another source of exculpation for the Japanese.[76]

But beyond the failure of the Tokyo trials to educate the local population about the ways of justice was the fact that the Japanese never engaged in a series of domestic war crime trials; they never undertook a legal judgment of their own war criminals. One very likely reason for this was the strong continuity that existed in state institutions in terms of personnel and leadership. This was also a problem and explanation for the lack of trials and their mixed results in West Germany. We should also remember that the Japanese have a very different sense of what they want their courts and the law to achieve, which is a return to communal harmony rather than the Western preference for establishing enduring, universal principles to guide future decision making. The Japanese court does not establish and does not seek to establish new principles that can be applied to future cases but rather to restore the harmonious relationships of the society, which may require very different answers to rather similar cases. Japanese court cases focus much more on context and situational ethics. Whereas the Western preference would be to establish principles that could be applied to other future similar cases, the Japanese preference is only the immediate repair in social relations. Westerners tend to view and celebrate their courts as institutions of transformation; the Japanese tend to avoid the use of courts, but when they are used, the goal is to restore social harmony, not to transform society.

There is a near consensus among scholars on Japan that the economic growth of the 1960s acted to suppress discussions of the wartime past. The rapid economic expansion and increasing affluence of the population led to the escapist consumerism, which also came to play an important role in West Germany around the same time. Kato Shuichi sees in the expansion of the consumer society "an illusion of individual freedom," where one can exercise choice as a consumer but not as a citizen.[77] The 1964 Tokyo Olympics also helped the Japanese feel that they had fulfilled their postwar promise of peace and prosperity for themselves and the broader global community.[78]

The next sparks that would reignite a fuller confrontation with Japan's wartime history came from outside the country, the expanding US war in Vietnam. Seraphim writes that the Vietnam War "resulted in a more critical consideration of war victimization, including questions of the Japanese people's complicity in and perpetration of war crimes," and the period from 1968 to 1972 saw "intensified public uses of war memory."[79] Saburo Ienaga had begun his textbook trials against the Ministry of Education in 1965; Makoto Oda founded the citizen's movement Citizens' Federation for Peace in Vietnam, also known as Beheiren, although this remained an organization defined by decentralization and volunteerism; and the first accounts of the so-called comfort women's experiences during the war began to appear.[80] While the issue of the comfort women would reach international prominence in the 1990s, it is important to recognize that there was some movement in Japanese civil society prior to this but always from those in the civil society, not the state. Again, these themes began to find their expression in Japanese popular culture as well. Kei Kumai directed *Sandakan hachiban shokan: Bokyo* (*Sandakan 8*) in 1974, in which an elderly woman tells a journalist about her experiences during the war as a "comfort woman." The previous year, Shohei Imamura made a documentary on the same material, *Karayuki-san: The Making of a Prostitute* (*Karayuki-san*) (1973). Kei Kumai would later make *Umi to dokuyaku* (*The Sea and Poison*) (1986) in which he shows the wartime medical experiments that the Japanese Imperial Army conducted on American POWs.[81] These were explosive narratives that returned to Kobayashi's attempts to examine the Japanese as perpetrators against not only their own people, as in the state against society, but also against the people of other countries.

As with the showing of *Holocaust*, the American television miniseries, on West German public television in winter 1979, the reason that Katsuichi Honda's articles in *Asahi Shimbun* in 1971 had the effect that they did needs to be seen in context. In both cases, it was not simply the narrative of *Holocaust* or Honda's reporting that forced new issues onto the social agenda. Rather, it is the quality of their narratives coupled with a social context that was ready to hear what these works had to say. Honda's reporting on massive Japanese war crimes in China during the war was not the first time that the Japanese had had a chance to respond to such claims. When one thousand war criminals returned from China in 1956, they published an account of their war crimes in the *Three Alls* in March 1957.[82] At the time, the response was very hostile.

With the improving relations between Japan and China and the official normalization of relations in 1972, Honda was able to travel to China and to interview Chinese witnesses and victims of Japanese wartime atrocities, including the Nanking massacre. Here, we can see how changes in the realm of international relations played an important role in shifting the debate within Japan. Up to this point, the Japanese had largely been cut off from any interaction, direct or vicarious, with the Chinese, who had experienced the Japanese invasion and occupation of their country. Honda interviewed Chinese survivors and thus challenged the mainstream consensus that had formed around the victim consciousness in Japan. Part of what motivated Honda to do this reporting was his experience in reporting on the US war in Vietnam, which challenged the myth that the United States only fought just wars for democracy and justice. The articles received a very warm welcome from the more liberal readers of *Asahi Shimbun*,[83] and Honda's follow-up book, *Chugoku no tabi* (*Journey to China*) (1972) was also a best seller. But both also attracted harsh criticism from conservatives, who seized on some of the more sensationalistic aspects of Honda's reporting, which turned out not to have any basis in fact, such as the killing competitions among soldiers during the Nanking massacre. Nonetheless, the way was clearly open for further investigations in the narratives of Japanese war crimes, which had been closed off during the previous two decades. His reporting clearly put the Nanking massacre on the agenda for historians.

The 1970s were clearly marked by an increasing divide between a conservative Japanese state, on the one hand, and a civil society that was becoming far more open to critical narratives about Japanese behavior during the war, on the other hand. While the Japanese prime minister Tanaka gave a strongly worded acknowledgment of Japanese responsibility for the war in 1972, as part of the normalization of relations with China, other Japanese prime ministers would begin to court criticism for their visits to the Yasukuni Shrine on the anniversaries of the defeat, August 15. The Yasukuni Shrine along with a whole system of nation protecting shrines throughout the country were established by the state after Japan's victory over Russia in the Russo-Japanese War of 1904–1905. The shrines were to house the spirits of the war dead and became part of the cult of the war dead. The natural desire on the part of the population at large and the state to recognize the sacrifice of the war dead in specific memorials became more complicated when the cause for which those war dead gave their lives was questioned in later years. The situation at the Yasukuni Shrine became more controversial after October 1978, when there was a secret enshrinement of fourteen class A war criminals. This only became public in 1979.

For those who had suffered at the hands of Japanese imperialism during the war, the enshrinement of war criminals in the national memorial for the war dead could easily and understandably be interpreted as nationalistic posturing by the Japanese. But there are also other interpretations that one cannot simply dismiss, even if those who carried out the secret enshrinement had clear nationalistic motives. As I mentioned above, the Buddhist tradition of focusing on compassion and the equal treatment of all the war dead is something that resonates very clearly with many Japanese. As in *Harp of Burma*, where Mizushima tries to correct the "bad deaths"—deaths away from the ancestral home and the family—by burying all of the war dead where he finds them, the inclusion of all the war dead in the Yasukuni Shrine and other shrines can be, for many Buddhists, an attempt to bring a correct order to the world. American servicemen have often been surprised and deeply touched by the willingness of the Vietnamese people to meet and talk with them when they visit Vietnam. The Vietnamese understand the desire on the part of the Americans to correct the "bad deaths" of their comrades in the war with proper burials at home with the ancestors. The Vietnamese people, in contrast to the state, often demonstrate a great willingness to aid the search for the American war dead. The Westerner can, perhaps, hear in this Buddhist dedication to trying to correct "bad deaths," a bit of Antigone's voice, where she calls for the honorable burial of all the war dead as a means to overcome the desire for revenge and the threat of the Furies. I am not proposing a solution to the Yasukuni Shrine controversy but rather simply offering a different cultural interpretation.

There is a consensus in the literature that the 1980s became a very different decade from everything that had preceded it in terms of how Japanese society dealt with its difficult history during World War II.[84] First, this was aided by a change in the realm of international relations, as Japan continued to develop closer relations with a still-Communist-but-far-more-open China and a democratizing South Korea. As both of these countries opened up, their citizenry began to engage their own difficult histories and sense of victimization at the hands of the Japanese during the war. The weakening of the cold war divisions helped this process.

It was also a decade during which Japanese victimization of others became far more openly discussed within Japan. Historical debates about the Nanking massacre exploded,[85] discussion about the forced prostitution of "comfort women" continued, and more information continued to come to light about Unit 731 and its gruesome biological experiments on POWs. In summer 1982, Ienaga's two-decade judicial challenge against the Ministry of Education became a source of debate not only in Japan but also an international diplomatic event.[86]

Discussions of Japanese war crimes also continued to find expression in the popular culture. In the early 1980s, Seiichi Morimura began research for a short story by looking for the surviving members of Unit 731, which was almost wholly unknown in Japanese society at the time. It had not been mentioned, for example, in Japanese textbooks. He later met the well-known composer Shin'ichiro Ikebe, who wrote the music for the choral work and together they produced *Akuma no hoshoku* (*The Devil's Gluttony*) in 1983. The work grew in popularity over the following decade as the general attitude in the society moved toward recognizing the criminal aspects of Japan's wartime policies, although neither Morimura nor Ikebe had set off with the intention of wanting to engage in the debates about war responsibility.[87] This new concern with Japanese perpetrators was also echoed on Japanese public television, with documentaries about Unit 731 as well as the "comfort women."[88]

As with nearly all aspects of Japan's engagement with its difficult history, for each example one can find of dealing with an unpleasant part of that past, one can find a more nationalistic response, or one that again focuses on Japanese suffering. The key distinction is almost always the division between the more challenging initiatives that come from the side of the civil society and the more neutral and victim-centered narratives supported by the state. Take for example the proliferation of small, private museums all over Japan, or those supported by municipal governments during the 1980s and 1990s.[89] Japanese schoolteachers are very fond of taking their students to museums, so the role of museums in Japanese society is probably more significant than is the case in other societies. Indeed, in his research into how the Japanese have dealt with their past, Seaton notes that in a survey of more than our hundred Japanese university students, they ranked their visits to museums as equal to documentaries and films in terms of the impression they left on them.[90] Many of these private and municipal museums show a great deal more willingness to discuss difficult aspects of Japan's wartime history without a sole focus on the suffering of the Japanese.[91] In contrast, the new state-supported Showa-kan museum, which opened in spring 1999, avoids anything provocative and focuses on the everyday life of the Japanese from 1935 to 1955.[92]

The most recent decades have seen an increasing willingness on the part of Japanese society to go still further in the discussion of what the Japanese did to others during the war. For example, the NHK, Japan's public broadcaster, produced a documentary about the extraordinary case of a former soldier who felt the need to be clear about the horrible things he had done and witnessed during the war. He died in the mid-1980s and left his family a written testimony of what he had done and witnessed, which was extremely upsetting for his family. Broadcast in December 2000, *Hitoheishi no jugun nikki: sofu no senso wo shiru* (*A Soldier's Diary: Learning about Grandfather's War*) tells the story of Takeshi Yamamoto's eight hundred–page diary, which he left for his family after he died in 1986.[93] In 2001, Minoru Matsui released his documentary film, *Riben guizi* (*Japanese Devils*) in which he compiled interviews from fourteen former soldiers about their experiences of fighting in China.[94] In a book, *My Father's Dying Wish: Legacies of War Guilt in a Japanese Family*, from 2002, Ayako Kurahashi investigated the difficulties her family had in dealing with the knowledge that her father had committed and witnessed horrible war crimes while fighting in China.[95] Although other men have admitted to similar war crimes, they have only done so in an anonymous fashion, not because they feared prosecution, but because they were deeply ashamed of what they had done and did not want this to affect their families. Concern for the honor of the family has placed a powerful cultural break on discussions of these difficult aspects of Japan's past.[96]

These narratives by perpetrators tend to be very rare compared to the far more voluminous writings by women about their wartime experiences. Roughly 85 percent of the population experienced the war on the home front, and this is primarily where the women were. Seaton reports that most of the Japanese testimony about the war has been written by civilians and from the perspective of victimhood.[97] Hashimoto and Chino Kaori have also found a preponderance of female narratives about the war, which Kaori has characterized as the feminization of war memories.[98] This same domestic perspective dominates the Showa-kan museum exhibits. This again illustrates the important contrast between the German and Japanese cases and those of Spain, Yugoslavia, and Turkey, which experienced civil wars. With Germany and Japan, there was a more clearly defined home front and battlefront until the very end of the war, which helped to intensify a sense of pure victimhood in wartime.

The discussion of perpetrator memories has become more common in the past two decades and has been met by a nationalist backlash, which has been stronger than what we can see in Germany.[99] Nonetheless, the victim consciousness that has tended to dominate and define the Japanese orientation toward its wartime history has weakened. The problem, which remains, is for the Japanese to develop the skills for critical thinking about violence and when resistance to state authority might be possible and legitimate. We can see this in the way that the wartime resistance has been wholly neglected for the entire postwar history. If the Japanese were to engage in a discussion about the legitimacy of wartime resistance against the state, it could force a broader discussion about the nature of resistance and when it is justified.

## Conclusion

The Japanese case helps to highlight the manner in which the different components of our model have played a role in shaping how the Japanese have approached their difficult legacy of war and mass atrocities. The domestic political situation has fostered a democratic pluralism, which has permitted the generation of countermemory narratives, perhaps best represented by the films of Kobayashi, but also the publications of the Japan-China Friendship Association or the activities of the JTU. For those individuals and groups that have been able to mobilize the necessary resources, they have been able to bring their memory narratives into the marketplace for general consumption. As suggested by the memory-market dictum, the primary censoring effect will not come from the state but rather from the perception of mass attitudes and the ability to sell one's memory product.

The primary restraint on Japanese discussions about the difficult legacy of the war has come from the cultural realm, where there is a strong emphasis placed on the maintenance of personal relationships and the restoration of harmony after conflict. Hashimoto's work helps to explain why there was so little intergenerational conflict in Japan compared to Germany. Because the generational proximity between the living generations and between the living and the dead is much closer in Japan, it becomes far more difficult for children to question or criticize their parents.

While Western observers might quickly dismiss the myth of the "fortunate fall" as self-serving, this ignores the cultural context within which most Japanese operate, which is fundamentally different from Western expectations. Just as Westerners suffer more from the fundamental attribution error, where an individual's character and principles should override all contextual constraints, the Japanese are more inclined to exhibit a hindsight bias, which inhibits counterfactual reasoning. There is a tendency in Japan not to engage in "what if" types of argumentation about how the past may have unfolded differently than it has. For many, Japanese soldiers and the Japanese at large cannot be criticized for their past actions not only because of the closer generational proximity, but because this is a senseless exercise.

The Buddhist orientation, as represented in the film *Harp of Burma*, works to orient the survivors of catastrophe toward the future and away from deep reflection on the past. As things are the way they are and have unfolded only as they could, there is little value in spending a great deal of time working back over what has already happened. What matters most is that harmonious relationships are restored as quickly as possible and that all the dead are given their proper burial.

At the same time that these cultural orientations push the discussion in a particular direction, they are not determinative. We need to recognize the role that cultural differences play in how difficult legacies of war and genocide are processed by a society, while not turning the culture into an essential, unchanging force. Indeed, this chapter has pointed out numerous counterexamples of when Japanese took positions somewhat at odds with the dominant culture and its expectations.

We have seen how the ethnocentrism of death has played a key role in how the Japanese have dealt with their violent history, which is a pattern we can see in all of the cases in this comparative research. There is an intense focus on one's own suffering, which tends to block out a recognition of what one has done to others. The externalization of blame is also present through the Japanese tendency to naturalize disastrous events. For the Japanese, the externalization of blame fits into a more fateful reading of how history unfolds, which is in line with the "fortunate fall" myth.

But even given these tendencies, we have also seen how the social-psychological processes of social contagion and reinforcement have had a significant effect in Japan in the past several decades. As popular and public knowledge of Japanese atrocities became more widely known over time, this has opened up new lines of understanding in Japan about the role that the Japanese have played as perpetrators. Because of the cultural constraints in Japan, this probably will not lead to a vigorous investigation of what went wrong in the past and the search for the guilty parties, but it can continue to serve as the basis for deepening Japan's commitment to a more peaceful future. Whether or not this is enough of a basis on which to build better relations with its regional neighbors remains a far more open question.

# 3 Spain

*what I decree: let no one honor him*
*with burial or mourning; rather leave*
*his corpse exposed and watch as hungry dogs*
*and vultures rip his flesh disgracefully.*

—Creon in *Antigone*[1]

*My nature calls for sharing love, not hate.*

—Antigone to Creon in *Antigone*[2]

## Introduction

The Nationalist, pro-Francoist forces launched their military coup on July 18, 1936, beginning what they called the "Glorious Uprising," but what is more commonly known as the Spanish Civil War. The military launched the coup against the legitimately elected Republican government with the support of different rightist forces in Spanish society, each concerned with preventing Republican reforms that threatened their positions of authority and power. The wealthy elites sought to maintain their privileges through their extensive landholdings or control of industry and the banks. The Republican support for land reform and trade unions threatened the wealthy elite in both the rural countryside and the cities. The military was particularly concerned with maintaining a centralized state, against the Republican move for some level of regional autonomy and recognition of Spain's linguistic and ethnic diversity. The unity of the Spanish state had long been challenged by subnational groups in the Basque Country, Catalonia, and Galicia, resulting in a couple of centuries of significant political upheaval, which weakened the future prospects for democratization.[3] And the Catholic Church feared the wide-ranging liberalizing tendencies within the Republican movement, which supported the right of women to vote, along with a broader modernizing and liberalizing program including education.[4]

The war involved fighters from outside Spain who supported both the Republican and Nationalist sides in the war. The Republicans gained the support of various anti-fascist forces from other Western countries, including the United Kingdom, the United States, and France, as well as the Soviet Union. The Nationalists pulled in support from fascist Germany and Italy. In the end, the Republican forces suffered a total defeat, and the war ended on April 1, 1939, although armed guerilla groups, known as the *maquis*, continued to fight Franco's regime throughout the 1940s, especially up until 1945, while there was still hope that the Allied forces in World War II would intervene in Spain. The last of the *maquis* were killed in 1951. We will want to return to the *maquis* later in the chapter, as they represent a form of resistance to Francoist Spain for more than a decade after the end of the war.

The Spanish case offers interesting comparative insights for all of our cases, but it is in the first instance most clearly comparable to what happened in Yugoslavia in the context of World War II. Both cases are examples of civil wars, with competition among national groups and the involvement of outside intervention. The nationalist competition in Spain did less to define the civil war than was the case in Yugoslavia, and the outside interventions were on a far smaller scale than what Yugoslavia experienced, where the state was destroyed and the country was occupied by fascist Germany and Italy. Nonetheless, the outside intervention in Spain played an important role in terms of how the war was discussed in the immediate postwar years, *not* as a civil war, but as a war against outside invaders. As we have seen in each of these cases, there is a clear attempt to externalize blame for the sources of evil and violence that threatened to destroy the national community. The *externalization of blame* in the case of civil wars plays an important role in masking the internal divisions that remain after the fighting has stopped. Indeed, the externalization of blame for the war is an attempt not to recognize the fighting as a civil war at all.

While any civil war is a horrific event and a difficult one to overcome, the Spanish case involves levels of violence and humiliation that go well beyond the normal violence of war. This is another important similarity with the civil war in Yugoslavia during World War II, where the Serbian population suffered the genocidal campaign managed by the Croatian Ustasha, which became a key stumbling block for the development of Yugoslavia after the war. This was on top of the widespread, intimate violence that had existed in many parts of the country, where violence was carried out against neighbors on a very local level, rather than by anonymous military forces. Much of the same is true in Spain as well. In addition to the normal deaths on the battlefield, both Republican and Nationalist forces carried out extensive rearguard massacres of civilians, although the scale of killing was weighted heavily toward the Nationalists. The level of the Nationalist violence has only become far clearer since Franco's death in 1975. One of the primary sources of this information has been local historians operating outside the official academy of the universities, who began to publish their work in the 1990s. As a result of this local historical research, it became increasingly difficult to maintain the narrative of everyone having behaved in an equally bad manner during a period of collective insanity.

During the civil war, the Republican rear guard killed about 55,000, while the Nationalist rear guard killed approximately 150,000.[5] The bodies were frequently dumped in mass graves, often on the outskirts of the village or town, which came to serve as a painful reminder for the families of how their loved ones had been "buried like dogs." The treatment of the war dead in Spain followed very much the vengeful spirit represented by Creon in *Antigone*. As we will see later, giving these murdered Republicans a proper burial today is an important part of the exhumation drive that has taken off since 2000. *Antigone*'s warning about leaving the enemy dead without dignified burial was ignored in Spain for decades, leaving deep and lasting wounds. The massacres were then sometimes followed by "liberation celebrations" in which the wives of murdered men were forced to serve meals to the killers, exposed to sexual violence, and had their heads shaved to further the public humiliation.

Moreover, the Nationalists continued to execute and massacre Republicans after the war was over. Between 1939 and 1944, another twenty thousand men and women were executed by the victorious Nationalists. Only more recently have we learned the scale at which babies and children were taken away by force from Republican mothers while they were imprisoned. Approximately thirty thousand children were taken by force from their families between 1944 and 1955.[6] The Francoist state sought to force Republican families further and further into poverty so that they would have to beg for assistance from their persecutors, or the women would be forced into prostitution to support their families. The Catholic Church played a central role in both of these campaigns of taking the children from Republican families and placing them in non-Republican households as well as serving as a vehicle for delivering "charity" to Republican families after they had been pushed into extreme poverty. The country was also filled with slave labor camps for Republicans. When Franco conceived of a national "reconciliation" memorial to be built close to Madrid, twelve thousand Republican prisoners were brought in to work on its construction, with not an insignificant number of them dying in the process. The Valley of the Fallen memorial was opened on April 1, 1959, to mark the twentieth anniversary of the Nationalist's victory. But the memorial had little to do with reconciliation. Instead, it came to represent the continued humiliation of the losers in the war and their forced penitence by the victorious.[7]

This leads to an interesting paradox when we compare the Catholic Spanish case with the officially atheist Yugoslav case. In Yugoslavia, the official narrative of the state was an open one in which all the peoples of Yugoslavia were encouraged to identify with the partisan victory and the liberation of the country. The partisans certainly extracted revenge against the members of the Croatian Ustasha, and there were certainly low-level revenge killings that took place after the war, but in general, things calmed down fairly quickly. The next round of repression was unleashed after Tito's break with Stalin in 1948, which resulted in the Goli Otok prison camp; but again, this level of state violence does not compare with what happened in Spain after the war. In relative terms, Tito's Yugoslavia sought to integrate the entire population, as far as possible, into the brotherhood and unity promised by the new socialist state. In contrast to Tito's Yugoslavia, Franco's Spain continued to wage a fierce campaign against Republicans and their families. The killing, imprisonment, slave labor, and forced removal of children from families continued for decades after the war.

How are we to explain this stark contrast? The answer again lies within the realm of cultural analysis and the importance of understanding Spain as a deeply Christian and, even more importantly, Catholic country. Suffering and martyrdom have extremely deep roots in Christianity and have to do with the founding of the Jesus movement in the ancient world and the persecution of the early Christians within the Roman Empire. The Catholic Church places an even greater emphasis on the suffering of Christ on the cross as the means through which all of humanity is redeemed for its sins. Suffering can be redemptive and meaningful for Christians,[8] but this is even more central for traditional Catholics than Protestants and Orthodox Christians. Moreover, according to the traditional teachings of the Catholic Church, this redemptive salvation through the suffering of Christ can only come through the institutions of the Catholic Church and its control of the sacraments.

If we look at the actions of the Francoist state after the war through the lens of Spanish Catholicism, we can see that suffering and the infliction of suffering was a purifying mission for the state. This is clearly how Franco viewed the situation, commenting, "the suffering of a nation at a particular point of its history is no caprice: it is a spiritual punishment, the punishment which God imposes upon a distorted life, upon an unclean history."[9] As the scholar Michael Richards put it, "Redemption and regeneration, in individual and national terms, were seen as only achievable through suffering and sacrifice."[10] Franco, as God's representative and agent on earth and savior of Spain, was responsible for inflicting meaningful, redemptive suffering on the degenerate Republican body. The Spanish Catholic Church clearly believed in this mission, and the church served the Franco state well, although younger priests in the postwar period would begin to question the church's support of the regime in the 1960s.

Given the complete collapse of the Republican side by the end of the war, with its supporters either in exile, imprisoned, or living under extreme duress in Spain, the master narrative of the conflict came to be wholly dominated by the Francoist state. The state used its control over all media outlets to propagate its version of the war. The print media, film, and television in the 1960s carried only the regime's version of events. The state and Catholic Church also had absolute control over the production of school textbooks. Both institutions used extreme measures of repression to silence and atomize Republican supporters.[11] Recent work by Layla Renshaw suggests that, at least in rural areas, Republican families silenced discussion of the war even within the family, where dead or disappeared fathers were not frequently talked about. Renshaw writes, "My hypothesis contends that the sustained repression experienced by Republican families engendered a condition of atomisation, dismantling memory communities and creating a hostile memory environment. This presents challenges for a Republican memory campaign. Collective and political representations of the dead were not permitted in this environment."[12] In this manner, the level of repression generated by the Francoist regime approached that of the worst years of Stalinist repression in Russia, where the intergenerational discussion about disappeared or murdered family members was also largely silenced.

## Psychological and Social-Psychological Processes

As we see in each of the cases discussed in this research, the externalization of blame plays a role in Spain as well. As much as the Francoist state turned its violence against its own citizens, the official narrative focused far more on the invasion of the country by communists and other atheist nonbelievers, who were supported by a few internal collaborators. This is very similar to the strategy pursued by the Yugoslav state after World War II in which a great deal of the blame for the horrific violence of the war was placed on the external invading forces and their internal collaborators, who were kept to a minimum and treated as ideological rather than national enemies of the people. Paloma Aguilar writes:

> An attempt was made to convey the image that the battle was not fought against an internal enemy, against a Spanish opponent, but that the "Nationalists" were forced to confront foreign invading forces (thus the expression "War of Liberation" and the parallels that were very often drawn with the War of Independence against the French). At best, the enemy was anti-Spanish, a traitor to the Patria who had conspired with the greatest communist power, the USSR, to set up a proletarian dictatorship in Spain. It was a matter of good against evil, of Spanishness against anti-Spanishness, of believers against atheists (thus the expression "the crusade," which was coined by the Spanish Church), of law-abiding people against anarchists, of reason against barbarism.[13]

Whereas salvation came in the form of commitment to the new socialist Yugoslavia, which permitted sincere converts to join their ranks, in Spain, Republicans could be saved by rededicating themselves to the Catholic faith, after the appropriate amount of suffering had been imposed. Indeed, Franco eventually permitted the burial of Republicans, who could prove their Catholic faith, in the Valley of the Fallen memorial. As with the other cases, the externalization of blame helps to restore a community of the good after the period of mass violence has passed.

The *ethnocentrism of death* also plays a critical and reoccurring role in the Spanish case. Each of the groups tends to engage in a process of competitive victimhood in order to establish their own innocence and to shift the blame onto others. The atrocities committed by others against oneself or the members of one's group once again serve as a way of blocking out recognition of what harm "we" may have caused others. The Catholic Church plays a central role here as the core "victim," which again fits within the Christian framework of suffering like Christ and for Christ. The Nationalists justified the uprising as a defense of the church and the clergy against massacres and anticlerical actions being taken by the Republicans, which did happen. But the Catholic Church has used this suffering as a way to block out discussion about its support for the Nationalists, their massacres, and postwar repression, which the church actually facilitated through the delivery of "Christian charity" to impoverished Republican families and the mass, forced removal of children from Republican families. While critical voices began to be raised by younger priests in the 1960s, demanding a national strategy of reconciliation, even today the church continues to play up its martyrdom during the civil war. For example, during a papal visit to Spain in 2011, the handouts produced for young people again framed the suffering and martyrdom of the church in the context of the civil war.[14]

We will return to the changing arc of the postwar narrative later in this chapter, but we only need to note here that as part of the national reconciliation campaign that began in the 1960s, the Nationalists started to relent a bit in their triumphalism, and the Franco regime began to promote the narrative of the war as a collective insanity in which everyone had behaved in a horrible fashion. This collective insanity and equal responsibility narrative has begun to collapse since the 1990s. As local historians uncovered more information about the scale of the Nationalist repression, both during and after the war, it became harder to sustain the claims of "collective insanity" and "equal responsibility." The fact that the Nationalists carried out far more massacres during the war and continued the massacres, executions, enslavement, and humiliation long after the war has forced Franco's supporters onto the defensive in the past two decades. In order to try and balance off these claims, present-day defenders of the Nationalists try to shift the blame back onto the Republicans by focusing on the Paracuellos de Jarama massacres that the Republicans carried out against Nationalists in Madrid, as the Nationalist forces prepared to besiege and enter the city. The Republicans massacred thousands of conservatives in the city. In this way, we can see an attempt to balance one atrocity against another.

There is also ample evidence of the role that *social contagion, reinforcement*, and *socially shared retrieval-induced forgetting* (SS-RIF) have played in the postwar discussions of the civil war in Spain. Over the course of this chapter, we will have multiple chances to bring these concepts into our analysis, so I will take just a couple of examples here to illustrate their roles. Social contagion is the best way of understanding what has happened in the mainstream society, especially since 2000. We will return to this in greater detail in the chronological section of this chapter, but it is worth noting here that in 1991 Román Gubern, a well-known Spanish professor of cinema, wrote an article in which he concluded, "In 1976 that episode [the Civil War] seemed very recent and demanded to be re-examined in depth from a new perspective, but by 1987 the majority of the public and most critics already considered it outdated and exhausted. It seemed as if ten years had been sufficient to dilute an obsession and to retire an historic ghost. It could be said that the ghosts of the past had been exorcised. Or at least some of them."[15] Gubern was not alone in reaching such a conclusion. Victor Pérez-Díaz made a similar set of observations around the same time noting that there was little contestation in Spanish society over the civil war or its symbolism and monuments.[16] Their observations help us to understand how unexpected the explosion of interest in the civil war and especially the crimes of the Nationalists were after 2000, when the exhumation of mass graves began to gain much more widespread interest. What is important to note here is that the social contagion effect as well as reinforcement began to gather momentum in the 1990s and were in full force after 2000.

But prior to this phase of intense and widespread engagement with the civil war and the new, popular knowledge about the crimes of the Nationalists, there was a much broader period of time marked by silence, forgetting, and marginalization of the civil war, and again the social-psychological phenomenon of SS-RIF played a key role. Not only did Spaniards avoid discussion of the war in public life but also private family life, at least within Republican families. We will give a great deal of attention to this silence within families and communities later in this chapter. The exhumation of mass graves in a much more public manner since 2000 has shattered this pattern of silencing the past violence, as by now five thousand corpses have been exhumed, identified, and buried. The fact that tens of thousands more remain is now general knowledge for the first time since the end of the war.

## Politics

We will first look at the development of state-society relations from the founding of the Francoist system in 1939 through to Franco's death in 1975 and the beginning of the transitional period through to institutionalized democracy. Whereas Yugoslavia failed to find a peaceful transition from authoritarianism and Turkey may be slipping back into a new period of increased authoritarianism, Spain today is a well-established democracy and a member of the European Union. Spain offers a hopeful example of how it is possible to transition from authoritarian rule to democratic rule. The moderation of different political forces in Spanish civil society and the rediscovery of civil society over the course of Francoist rule were key components of this transition. Spain was also helped in the transition process by having West European democracies as a model to which to aspire. The opening of Spain's borders to the people and ideas of the rest of Europe helped Spain in its process of Westernization. The same open borders had helped democratic civil society forces in Yugoslavia, although that country took a tragic turn over the course of the 1980s. Both Spain and Yugoslavia have and have had difficult histories with which to deal. Perhaps fortunately, in the case of Spain, the increasing knowledge about the extent of the Nationalist violence has emerged only after the transition to democracy had been achieved and the institutions strengthened. For Yugoslavia, open discussions about the horrific violence that had occurred during World War II burst into the open in the 1980s, when the economic conditions were deteriorating rapidly and the transition to greater democracy was coupled with rising nationalist resentment.

### *State-Society Relations*

The Nationalist forces set about establishing an authoritarian state centered on a National-Catholicism ideal, which was to emphasize the unitary nature of the state and the nation. We can see the institutional legacy of this in Spain today, as the church and the state continue to be closely connected, with the church competing with the state to deliver social, educational, and cultural services.[17] The Franco regime created an authoritarian system that was composed of different components or "families," whose interests did not necessarily always coincide or remain stable over time. The growing impoverishment and international isolation of the country during the first two decades of the dictatorship led to a shift in policy in 1959, when the International Monetary Fund (IMF) extended a much-needed loan to the regime that became part of a "Stabilization Plan," which ushered in an end to economic autarky. The severe repression of the society by the state and the church during the first twenty years of the regime began to give way.

The 1960s saw the reemergence of a more open civil society, in large part encouraged by the growth of the tourism industry, which brought much-needed foreign capital into the country. As Spaniards began to have contact again with Europeans coming from the more successful capitalist and democratic West European countries, they began to question increasingly the conditions in their own country. The opening of the country improved the prospects for economic growth, which led to more Spaniards working abroad as well, thus again encouraging interaction with other Europeans in far more open and democratic countries. As with the Yugoslavs who went to work elsewhere in Europe, they began to appreciate what was lacking and or seen as backward back home. The late Francoist period from 1965 until Franco's death in 1975 was marked by the further weakening of the authoritarian coalition and a growing level of criticism of the regime within the Catholic Church.[18] The weakening of official censorship in the 1960s also led to increasing cultural creativity and a willingness and ability of artists, authors, and filmmakers to help the society process the difficult legacy of the civil war. Whereas Yugoslavia would also experience a period of greater openness in the 1960s, this was brought to a sharp end by the regime at the very end of the 1960s and into the 1970s, as the regime felt its legitimacy was being challenged too directly, especially over the issue of Goli Otok.

In contrast to Yugoslavia, Spain continued on a path toward some form of greater openness as pro-regime elements and dissident groups engaged in extended negotiations about what was to follow Franco's death, with the eventual agreement on a transition toward democracy and national unity along with an amnesty for everything that had happened during the Franco years. After Franco's death on November 20, 1975, the process of institutional democratization moved forward with the legalization of the Spanish Communist Party in 1977, while in the same year the Amnesty Law was passed by Parliament blocking any prosecution of crimes committed during the war or during the postwar years. A new constitution was agreed to in 1978, followed by an attempted military coup on February 23, 1981, which quickly collapsed when the Spanish king went on television and firmly stated his support for the 1978 constitution. Then, in October 1982, the opposition Socialist Party of Spain (PSOE) won the first completely open and free national election. Previously held local elections had already started a shift in power and the acceptance of political pluralism. These earlier local elections were important because as soon as opposition candidates won in some parts of the country, a process of removing the symbols of Francoism began almost immediately, including the first exhumations of mass graves in localities where family members felt free to do so for the first time since 1939.

### *Schools and Education*

As with the other cases, the schoolroom has been a site of important contestation over the meaning and portrayal of the civil war. And it is in this location that the mixed authority of the Catholic Church and the Francoist state becomes very clear. Furthermore, the system of education in Spain has, until more recent times, been far more centralized and unified than was the case in Yugoslavia, and has tended more in the direction of extreme centralization we can see in Turkey, the difference being that the Turkish system remains highly centralized, whereas local initiatives of engaging the civil war in Spain have begun to be an accepted part of the school curriculum. For example, a group based in Barcelona has organized more than four hundred school visits by living witnesses of the war, thus reaching more than twenty-five thousand students.[19] But in trying to understand the Spanish case, one needs to appreciate that the vast majority of Spaniards were heavily influenced by the narrative of the war that they received at school because of the lack of competing narratives in the society at large *and* at home. From 1939 to 1969, for an entire generation, the regime exercised almost total control over the narrative of the war in the public sphere. And because of the atomization of former Republican families and the resultant silence, there was not much of a counternarrative even within families.

Spain entered the twentieth century with a massive deficit in terms of investment in education. The political instability and relative poverty of the country left Spain far behind other Western countries at the beginning of the century, with total educational spending at only 20 percent of that in the United Kingdom and 10 percent of that in the United States.[20] As late as 1932, only about half of school-age children were in school,[21] and illiteracy remained a problem holding back economic development even in the 1960s.

With the victory of the Nationalists in the civil war, the Catholic Church was again given firm control over educational institutions. Although a state sector of education had been expanded over the course of the first three decades of the twentieth century, especially during the Republic, the private, church-controlled sector continued to dominate. In fact, the church was able to recapture the position it had

had before the establishment of the Republic, which meant that the church exercised control over the public schools as well. Catholic dogma remained the general ideological guiding principle in both the public and private schools. This also included the continued segregation of education for men and women, with women given special instruction in the maintenance of the home and the moral life of the family. In terms of postsecondary education, the stated goal of a university education in the 1940s was to create a "spiritual aristocracy."[22] Education was designed to reproduce existing hierarchies and gender roles, as well as the state and church version of the civil war.

As the first postwar generation moved into the universities in the 1950s, they began to rebel against the extreme control being exercised over their lives and their education, even though most of them came from Falangist families and the winning side of the war. Students began to organize against the Falangist Spanish University Student Union (SEU) with the encouragement of the Communist Party, which was illegal and operated underground. This led to an ongoing crisis at Spanish universities, with the future elite of the society rebelling against the tight strictures of a church-dominated educational system. As the country continued to open up to the outside world and the rest of Europe in the 1960s, the student protests changed along with the curriculum at the universities, with a movement away from creating "a spiritual aristocracy" rooted in the humanities, to one more focused on technology and the sciences. This was seen as necessary to support the growing needs of the economy. There was also a dramatic growth in the social sciences.

Spanish university students captured part of the international wave of growing leftist radicalism in other countries through their opposition to the US war in Vietnam and the rise of guerrilla movements throughout Latin America that challenged US imperialism.[23] But not unlike the student movements in Germany, the Spanish radicalism on university campuses was not so much focused on reworking the Spanish past as engaging in radical political action in the present. The reevaluation of the Spanish past was going to require far more freedom in the civil society and several more decades of time. One reason for this was that the professoriate in Spain did not support a reevaluation of the Spanish past. They were, by and large, far more conservative and very much in line with the regime in terms of politics. Second, even if some professors had wished to conduct research and publish on the more recent past, they would have found the archives closed to them. Furthermore, any critical work regarding the war or the regime had almost no hope of being published in Spain.

At the primary and secondary level, the Francoist state established and maintained a firm control over the narrative of the most recent Spanish past. The disorder, chaos, and illegitimacy of the Republican government was emphasized, with reminders of how Spain's greatness had been destroyed by nearly two centuries of political turmoil. The growing disorder of the Republic justified the military coup, known as the "Glorious Uprising," which the military began to fight against the "Red

Terror." A great deal of emphasis was placed on the role that external forces played in stirring up trouble within Spain. The textbooks made sure to highlight the Republican atrocities against Catholics and the church clergy, and then celebrated the reestablishment of order through the Caudillo, Francisco Franco, who exhibited the virtues of bravery, heroism, and self-denial.[24] Of particular importance was the emphasis placed on the fact that the "enemy" in the war was always identified primarily with outside forces.[25] The image that the regime tried to create was one of outside invaders, who were supported by some, but not many, misguided internal collaborators. This helps to explain why the regime studiously avoided the term *civil war* in describing the conflict. It was known as "the crusade," the "Glorious Uprising," and "the war of Spain."

The fact that the content in the classroom gave frequent and specific attention to the crimes against Catholics and the church is hardly surprising when one considers that educational institutions were put into the hands of the church by the state, thus giving another example of how state and religious authority were combined in Spain.[26] This relationship gave a strong Nationalist bias to education in Spain, with long-term consequences. For example, it was still common to find Francoist language in school textbooks in the late 1980s, such as describing the war as a "national uprising" or calling it an "anti-communist crusade." The turning point appears to have been around 1990, when the antidemocratic nature of the Francoist regime began to receive more emphasis.[27] While the textbooks made sure to focus on the Red Terror and the violence against Catholics and the church during the war, very few secondary students actually study the Franco dictatorship that followed the war.[28] All of the new history about the nature of the dictatorship and the continued violence and repression after the war has had to be learned through the popular culture or the new histories that began to appear in larger numbers in the bookstores during the 1990s. By the end of the 1990s, the Franco-Nationalist repression had been extensively documented in about 60 percent of Spain's provinces.[29] But it would take more time for this information to be integrated into the general educational program. Nonetheless, there are still examples of textbooks today that continue to obscure the nature of what happened during the war, with the causes of death and the reasons for forced exile left unmentioned, although these are now met with protest.[30] But these protests are also met by well-organized conservative forces in Spanish society, which have slowed the pace of change.[31]

These new histories about the Franco dictatorship were largely being written by historians outside the official academy, which has remained far more conservative and reluctant to engage these aspects of recent Spanish history. The change, as is so often the case, has come from the margins and the periphery. Nonacademic historians in local areas have played a primary role in uncovering many aspects of the Franco dictatorship, and some of this material has begun to filter into local schools, where the local politics supports a more critical view of the Franco regime and the civil war. For example, in the Rioja region, La Barranca, the Association for the Preservation of Historical Memory in La Rioja (APHM), which is the current legal association that grew out of a committee originally formed in 1977, almost immediately after Franco's death, produced a booklet and DVD in 2010 that they shared with secondary school students.[32] It includes detailed information about Republican victims of the Nationalist violence and a tour of local sites related to the war, including a prison. This local initiative and others like it have been criticized by the Royal Academy of History for teaching a biased view of history.[33] Clearly, the schoolroom and the field of history remain areas of intense contestation in Spain today.

### *International Relations*

Pressure for and against change in Spain has come from several different directions. First, there were the diplomatic relations between the Franco regime and the Western powers after the end of World War II. Then there was also the role of the Spanish Republican emigrant community that lived in exile but continued to work to foster change within the country. And finally, the growing strength of the global human rights movement, which was still weak in the 1970s, helped to encourage local Spanish organizers and nongovernmental organizations (NGOs) in the 1980s and 1990s. This globalization of a human rights discourse has had an impact on each of the countries that we have discussed, although their success has depended on the openness of the civil society in each case.

At first, the Franco regime received very little cooperation and recognition from France and the United Kingdom, and in the context of World War II, the *maquis* were able to continue their struggle against the regime. But after the end of World War II, Spain found itself increasingly isolated for having remained neutral during the war and because of the clearly antidemocratic nature of the regime. But by 1949, the United States had shifted its position toward the regime to one that was more positive in light of the anti-communist credentials of Franco. This change in the US position helped to set up the IMF loans and Stabilization Plan in 1959.

This recognition also came with demands that Spain open up its internal, autarkic markets to outside competition and investment, which helped to usher in the greater opening of the civil society in the 1960s. This was an important step toward laying the groundwork for the transition from the dictatorship after 1975. There were similar consequences for Turkey after the opening up of the economy after the 1980 military coup. In both cases, it took a full decade or more for the greater openness in the civil society to help foster more open discussions about the country's difficult past; but in both cases, the results were positive in terms of allowing a more open and free-flowing discussion.

Whereas the potential memory community of Republicans living in Spain was atomized, those living in exile in democratic countries worked to keep the Republican memory alive and to push for change in the country. Republicans living in exile in Paris established the Éditions Ruedo ibérico in 1961 and began to smuggle Spanish publications and translations into the country, in a manner similar to what happened in Yugoslavia with the publication of Milovan Djilas's works alongside other regime dissidents. There was even a meeting between regime sympathizers and members of the exile community over three days from June 5 to 8, 1962, in Munich, Germany, to discuss accommodation and ways to further open up the country for change. There were clearly those within the Francoist regime who recognized that Spain needed to rejoin the postwar West European path of democratization and economic growth. The regime found out about the Munich meeting and those who returned to Spain found themselves in trouble, but what this demonstrates is that there were attempts more than a decade before Franco's death to try and pull the country back together. This is in stark contrast to what happened in Yugoslavia, in which those living in exile continued to plan for the destruction of the regime, and the Yugoslav state returned in kind by killing members of the exile community.

## Culture

As with the other case studies in this research, a strong, national father figure has played a role in suppressing discussion about Spain's difficult past. Spanish culture, buttressed by Catholic patriarchal authority, has long been supportive of existing hierarchies. Spanish scholars talk of a "sociological Francoism" to highlight the overlap between political and cultural authority in Spain. These patterns of authority are again replicated within families, so we will give attention to the family as a special location for discussing the national history, although surviving Republican families probably left much of this difficult past buried until very recently. Finally, we will take a look at how the civil war has been handled in Spanish popular culture. As in the other cases, discussions about Spain's difficult past in the broader society have helped to spur debates within families.

### *Franco's Cult of Personality*

One striking feature of each of the cases in this research is the central role that a single male, father figure has played in shaping the discussion about each country's difficult history. Although to different degrees, these father figures during their lives and after their deaths restrained the investigation into their society's difficult history. This has been a combination of love, respect, and fear. Of the five cases, Franco's cult appears to have been the weakest, although he certainly gave himself the grandest mausoleum in the Valley of the Fallen, where the body of the great leader was symbolically combined with those of his fallen Nationalist comrades, and in a token of reconciliation, Catholic Republicans.

The physical death of the father figure and national leader in the cases of Japan, Yugoslavia, and Spain appeared to break a sort of spell that had held certain social forces in check. The death of each of these individuals did not immediately transform any of the state structures or their capacity for repression and discipline. But in a spell-breaking fashion, each of their deaths appears to have almost immediately freed up critical discussions about the country's difficult past. Respect for the Japanese emperor appears to have long muted such critical discussions in Japan. In Yugoslavia, it was immediately after Tito's death that stories about Goli Otok began to appear alongside an increasingly bitter ethnonationalist narrative about the violence in World War II.

Franco's death appears to have had a similar effect in Spain. Susan Friend Harding had conducted ethnographic research in rural Spain in the mid-1970s, and she noticed almost immediately a stark change in the nature of her conversations with the villagers. In 1976, there was a willingness on the part of villagers to talk about political matters that they had always avoided before. Harding writes, "Almost overnight, the double thinking disappeared."[34] Meirian Jump notes in the Rioja region that the families of those murdered by Franco's forces had risked placing flowers at the site of their mass grave during the dictatorship but that they established a committee in 1977 to officially mark the site and then had a monument dedicated in 1979.[35] The year 1979 was a key turning point because the first freely contested municipal elections were held, and there were significant victories for anti-Franco candidates. This led not only to the marking of mass graves but also the first exhumations in Rioja, Calahorra, and Nájera.[36] *Interviú* is a Spanish magazine that was founded in 1976 and quickly became the most widely read publication during the years of the transition, in part because of its aggressive and irreverent reporting. *Interviú* covered some of these early exhumations, but this coverage failed to spark the widespread confrontation with the dictatorship, which followed a later round of exhumations beginning in 2000.[37] The broader cultural realm was not yet prepared to support these revelations of mass graves, and the uneasy silence of the transitional years was maintained. Others also date the first round of exhumations as having begun in the late 1970s,[38] although there were some clandestine exhumations even during the dictatorship.[39]

While the fear of Franco has obviously disappeared with the establishment of stable democratic institutions in Spain and especially after the failed military coup of 1981, the love or respect has not completely disappeared. As the antidemocratic and repressive nature of the regime becomes better known to the general public, Franco's stature continues to decline (see Figure 2), but there are two key myths that continue to support Franco's reputation and leave many people feeling ambivalent or even positive about his legacy: (1) he is credited with saving the country economically by ushering in the first period of real economic growth in Spain during the 1960s, and (2) he fought the civil war to prevent a communist takeover of the country.[40] Another piece of Franco's postwar legacy that is widely viewed in a positive light is the peace and prosperity that the country eventually experienced, which helped Spaniards overcome some of the shame and stigma that they felt compared to other Western countries for their supposed propensity for violence, anarchy, and self-destruction.[41] Obviously, another important component of becoming more Western includes developing democratic institutions, so the Spanish have developed a narrative some-

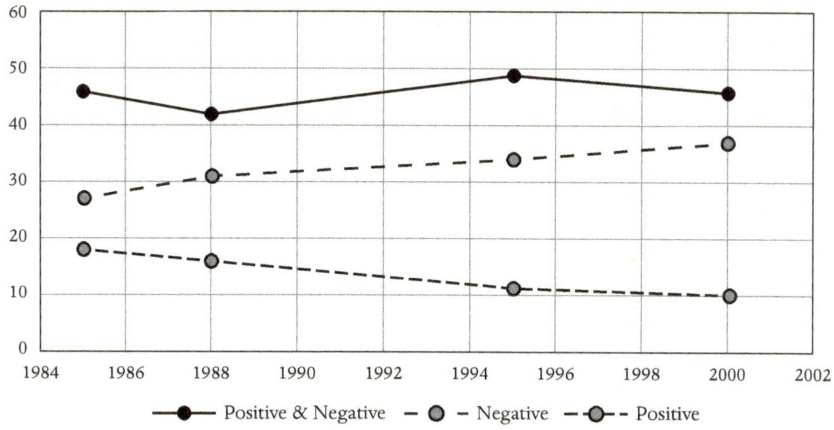


Figure 2 Spanish attitudes toward the Franco regime.
*Source*: Félix Moral, Veinticinco Años Después—La memoria del franquismo y de la transición a la democracia en los españoles del año 2000 [Twenty-five years after—the memory of Francoism and of the transition to democracy in the Spanish people for the year 2000] (Madrid: Centro de Investigaciones Sociológicas, 2001), 12.

what similar to the "fateful fall" myth, as discussed in the chapter on Japan, through which the war and Franco brought about the conditions necessary to bring democracy and prosperity to the country.

While it is hard to detect a broad sense of love and affection for Franco in the present, it is quite striking to see how stable the memory landscape of Spain has been since the transition to democracy. Whereas regime change in Central and Eastern Europe ushered in the wide-scale destruction and removal of communist memorials, and the destruction of memorials to the Yugoslav partisans in Croatia has been particularly thorough,[42] one study finds that 79 percent of provincial capitals still have references to the Franco regime in their street names. Most interestingly, there appears to be no variation between regional governments headed by the socialists or the conservative People's Party. The only places where there has been a systematic removal of Francoist symbols has been in Catalonia and the Basque Country.[43]

### *Cultural Values that Continue to Support Francoism*

General cultural attitudes in Spain continue to support what some scholars have called "sociological Francoism," and obviously also help to support a positive evaluation of Franco's legacy for the country. There is a tendency in Spain to value existing hierarchies, to show respect for authority, and to give due deference.[44] Obviously, these values are also reinforced by Spanish Catholicism, which remained central to the educational curriculum for most of the twentieth century. For example, the textbooks during the dictatorship emphasized the need to purify the country of unwanted cultural pluralism. When looking back at earlier Spanish history, one textbook commented, "Another decision made by the Catholic monarchs, to purify strange elements and to unite the Spanish race spiritually, was to expel the Jews and the Moors."[45] We can see here how the state and religious authority are combined in the Catholic monarchs, just as the Franco regime sought to rule through National-Catholicism, along with a clear antipluralist position. Just as previous Catholic monarchs had fought against cultural and religious pluralism, Franco sought to maintain a unified Spain by suppressing regional identities.

Spanish Catholicism has also encouraged a more fatalistic view of life. Biblical characters are often portrayed as having played out roles that were predetermined by providence, rather than caused by personal will. We can see echoes of this pattern of thinking in ethnographic studies. Renshaw's ethnographic fieldwork offers numerous examples of how rural villagers use religious stories and imagery to understand what happened during the civil war, rather than a political and ideological framework. For example, Renshaw shows how the villagers viewed betrayal through the lens of a fatalistic, material transaction rather than one defined by competition between contrasting political ideologies: "By invoking Judas's betrayal of Jesus, my informants communicate the conviction that their relatives were not simply betrayed but were sold, and that a material transaction of some kind surrounded their deaths. There are also parallels between the two tropes in the invocation of fatalism or inevitability, of people simply 'playing their part.'"[46] We can also see this fatalism in how the civil war was discussed in its entirety, with it increasingly becoming naturalized as something similar to a natural disaster, and thus certainly something beyond human control.[47] Here, we can see strong parallels with a Japanese tendency toward fatalism and hindsight bias, which has come to view the Asia-Pacific war as unavoidable, or the atomic bombings as something akin to a natural disaster, without human agency. There are also examples of this in Turkey as well, with the idea that one's future is written on one's forehead. Fatalistic narratives and the naturalization of war are other examples of how the externalization of blame helps to exculpate human agency and responsibility. The fatalism that can be embedded in certain cultural and religious orientations contrasts sharply with Enlightenment modernism and specifically the communist movement in Yugoslavia, which placed human agency and political ideology at the center of explaining the events during World War II.

### *Silence within Families*

The dynamics within the family play an important role in how the difficult Spanish past has been discussed or silenced. A survey of the literature provides evidence that SS-RIF played a significant role within Republican families. Numerous authors point toward a long-lasting silence within Republican families that continues to stretch into the present, although that has begun to change with the exhumations since 2000. But even here, Renshaw notes that many of those who have become involved with the Association for the Recovery of Historical Memory (ARMH) have done so as a way to deal with the issue while at the same time avoiding direct discussions within their own families.[48] This is similar to what we can see in the German and Austrian cases where some children opt for political engagement in the broader society while avoiding a direct confrontation with family members, although it is always important to emphasize that while there are patterns of similarity, these exist within a wide diversity of responses within families.[49] A review of the literature on Spain gives strong evidence that there has been a significant break in the intergenerational transmission of family history largely out of fear of state repression or social exclusion. It is very important to emphasize that Republican families, especially those that continued to live in rural areas in close proximity to the perpetrators and their relatives, have lived with a deep fear and shame of what happened in the past. Direct state repression was less of a threat than the far more immediate potential for social sanction from one's neighbors.

It seems reasonable to assume that the silence within Republican families was greatest within small local communities, where the victims and perpetrators continued to live in close proximity to each other. Harding reports from her field research in a rural Spanish community in the 1970s that those who had been most politically active had left for larger urban areas, especially Barcelona, which became a center for anti-Francoist activity, or exile in France.[50] She also reports that the remaining "reds" in Ibieca, the site of her ethnographic field research, could not talk openly about their experiences in the early 1970s, although this changed very quickly after Franco's death in 1975.[51] While Franco's death provided a sense of release for some of those who wanted to talk about the past, it also came, retrospectively, to represent a clear end of one period and the beginning of a new period.[52]

However much this changed with Franco's death in 1975, it is very clear from Renshaw's work that the fear and tension about the past remains very intense, even in the last decade, when she conducted her ethnographic field research around the exhumation of mass graves in rural areas. She reports, "I was unprepared for the reality of the pact of silence in a small rural community, and felt initially overwhelmed by the rawness of the emotions, particularly of fear and anxiety, that talking about the past elicited in my informants."[53] She traces this in part to the deep atomization of the Republican community, which she sees as a potential memory community that had nearly been completely destroyed.[54] Part of this involved how families were cut off from significant public rituals around the burial of the dead and the maintenance of family gravesites. Republican families may very well have known where the mass graves were, but they were in the earliest years of the regime denied any right to mourn publicly for their family members.[55] Just as Antigone was denied the right to bury and mourn the death of her brother, many Republican families had their relationship with their dead ancestors and family members cut off by fear of state reprisal and social isolation. The fact that their loved ones had been denied a proper burial and that the family was unable to visit the grave on All

Saints Day, an important Catholic ritual, reminded them on an annual basis, in a very emotionally poignant manner, that they were not full members of the community. This led to significant feelings of shame toward the neighbors for failing in their public duty and a deep sense of guilt toward the dead.[56]

We do not have a good picture of how information about the civil war has been transmitted in Nationalist families. The existing literature has focused on the silences within Republican families. To the extent that the difficult past is discussed, it seems reasonable to assume that a similar dynamic exists in Spain as with what we can see in Germany in which families steer clear of conversations that could implicate family members in criminal acts. To the extent that violence is discussed, it probably is justified through *tu quoque* (you also) argumentation of Republican violence and the threat of Soviet communism.

Given the lack of clear information about the civil war in the broader society for most of Spain's history in the twentieth century and the silences within the family, the postwar generations began to adopt the Francoist propaganda for interpreting their own history, while also trying to recapture the goodness of the family and the injustices that they had been subjected to. Renshaw reports that children, now adults, would declare that their father had been a good man and *not* a communist or red.[57] Ángela Cenarro also reports evidence showing how Republican victims sought to interpret their own personal narrative within the broader social framework, which clearly recognized that the communist movement had been a threat to the survival of the nation.[58] The end result is that the children develop depoliticized narratives about why their parents were killed by their neighbors, which instead focus far more on personal narratives of sexual jealousy, material resentments or other personal grievances.[59] The political nature of the massacres is largely lost because of the atomization that Renshaw claims has so seriously fractured the potential Republican community, at least in some rural communities. The process of the exhumations, the public meetings that follow, and the ritual of a proper reburial is helping to breakdown this atomization and for former Republican families to recognize their common fate.[60] But it is a process that is still fairly recent.

### *Memory Traces in the Popular Culture*

The state's control over the public narrative of the civil war was extensive and has had long-lasting consequences for Spain. All public media were brought under state control through a 1941 censorship law, which formalized the power that the regime already exercised over all public discussions of the civil war. All material related to "the crusade" first had to gain the approval of civilian and military leaders. This censorship only began to be relaxed between 1964 and 1966, as a partial response to the near continuous protests that existed on university campuses, where Spain's elite youth and future leaders expressed their dissatisfaction with this constant control over what could be said, discussed, and read. In this manner, the totalitarian drive to control all aspects of Spanish society lasted even longer than was the case in Yugoslavia, where the communist leadership surrendered attempts to strictly control the cultural sphere by the early 1950s, although discussion of nationalism remained tightly monitored. From the cases in this study, only Turkey has exercised a more repressive framework for a longer time. Scholars of Spain agree that this period of state control over the cultural sphere has left a long legacy of repressed memories, fears, and resentments, which exploded with the exhumation campaign that began in 2000. Núria Triana-Toribio writes, "The regime's censorship placed obstacles in the way of national and foreign films that questioned, even slightly, the benefits of this concept of the nation [one, great, free, and Roman Catholic]."[61] Paul Preston comments, "To this day, its [Francoist propaganda and censorship] powerful residual effects hamper the ability of mainstream contemporary society to look upon its recent violent past in an open and honest way that could facilitate the necessary social and political closure."[62]

There is no question that the civil war continues to haunt Spanish popular culture today. Sometimes this involves a dramatic narrative being located just before, during, or after the war, but there is no shortage of material that suggests the ghosts of this past are still very present in Spain today, if not more often in the background of the story. Novelist Javier Marías draws on the consequences of Francoist repression for his father, who was imprisoned and then blacklisted by the regime in his trilogy *Tu rostro mañana* (*Your Face Tomorrow*) (2002, 2004, 2007). Two other recent novels that deal with the civil war have been made into successful films as well: Manuel Rivas's *El lápiz del carpintero* (*The Carpenter's Pencil*) (2000), which was filmed by Antón Reixa in 2001, and Javier Cercas, *Soldados de Salamina* (*Soldiers of Salamis*) (2001), which was filmed by David Trueba in 2003. In her research into Spanish literature, Ofelia Ferrán notes that there is a recurring image of improper burials.[63] In a manner not all that unlike the "bad deaths" that occur in public and away from home in Buddhist cultures, there is a deep sense that the dead are not resting peacefully in Spain, that there is work that remains to be done.

When one surveys the Spanish cultural landscape, we can see a further confirmation of the *memory-market dictum*, which suggests that the more capital intensive a given medium is, the more it will tend to soften the edges of its engagement with the difficult past so as to appeal to as broad an audience as possible. During the years of heavy censorship, it was first in the form of the novel, and not cinema or television, that one saw challenges to the regime's preferred narrative. For example, Ramón J. Sender was able to publish his novel in 1953 in which he pointed to the role that the Catholic Church played in carrying out the regime's repression in the countryside. However, what the regime permitted in the form of a novel did not find its film adaptation until 1985 with *Réquiem por un campesino español* (*Requiem for a Spanish Peasant*).[64] This is not unlike what we see in Yugoslavia with Dragoslav

Mihailović's novel *Kad su cvetale tikve* (*When Pumpkins Blossomed*), which was published, but then the theater production was blocked.

Another more recent example of the memory-market dictum has been the TVE public television series *Cuéntame cómo pasó* (*Tell Me, How It Was*), which began in 2001 and continues to run after fifteen years with 271 episodes. The soap opera follows the three-generation Alcántara family during the late Franco years, beginning in 1968, through the transition years, and now into the 1980s. While the show does portray the limitations on freedom, the family is largely apolitical and the show focuses on their struggle for self-actualization within the limits defined by the regime. The triumph of the democratic transition is clearly celebrated in the show, and the civil war is touched on in the third season, although the roots of the dictatorship are never explored. In one third season episode, the Alcántara family travels back to the village from which Antonio, the father, comes. Antonio's mother is ill. During the visit, he is summoned to the bedside of a terminally ill Don Mauro, the local political boss, who is known to have sided with the fascists during the war. Antonio is shocked to learn the real reason for his father's death from Don Mauro, which his mother had always hidden from him. Don Mauro had ordered the soldiers to shoot Antonio's father because he was in love with Antonio's mother. The murder is driven by passionate jealousy, not politics or ideology. This echoes the pattern Renshaw discovered in her ethnographic work; the potentially political nature of the violence is removed or minimized and turned into personal jealousy. The family tragedy remains a private affair, as fear about the consequences of this knowledge in the late Franco years is too great for Antonio. We learn other details about the violence in Spain's past through other characters in the series, through the grandmother's anxiety or the experiences of other relatives, one of whom was a union leader killed at the beginning of the war.[65] While there is some engagement with Spain's violent past, some scholars argue the television series has traded more in the nostalgia of the time by commercializing products related to the show, such as CDs featuring music from the 1960s and 1970s.[66]

In this manner, the television series fits a broader pattern in which television programs tend to be the least confrontational in terms of challenging mainstream attitudes, because of their even higher level of commercialization and need to pull in large audiences. An example from Brazil helps to underscore this fact. The first television serial drama dealing with the military dictatorship addresses the torture used by the regime, but none of the perpetrators in the show are members of the military.[67] The counterexample of West German public television and its more open confrontation with the past reminds us that it is not necessarily the medium of television that tends to soften the edges but rather the funding model for television that is at issue. As public television stations face more commercial pressures and the withdrawal of public funding, it is less likely that they will play the role that they once did in West Germany.

The development of a narrative arc in Spanish cinema regarding the civil war was heavily influenced by the role that the censors played in postwar Francoist Spain. Unlike in Yugoslavia, where the standard was postproduction censorship, in Spain the screenplay had to pass through the hands of the censors before the filming could even begin. The government and the censors were especially keen to maintain control over the narrative about the war. The most important early "crusade" film was *Raza* (*Race a.k.a. Pure Blood*) (1941), which was actually written by Franco under a pseudonym. The film's narrative follows the story of the bourgeois Churruca family, which has made sacrifices for the nation from Trafalgar (1805) to Cuba (1898) and finally the civil war. The initial triumphalist phase, in which the Republican view was rejected by the censors, eventually gave way by the end of the 1950s to more of a tragic tone. Pedro Lazaga's film *La fiel infantería* (*The Proud Infantry*) (1959) was dedicated to "all Spaniards who fought in this war, wherever they are dead or alive." Bernard Bentley writes of the film, "This film takes the reasons for the conflict for granted without presenting any anti-communist agenda. It occasionally shows Republicans in uniforms that are far too clean and only as depersonalised enemy fire, but never demonises them as in previous films. It prefers to focus on personal relationships and with its concluding sequence of slaughter and death together with the final intertitle manages to acknowledge regrets for all those who had died."[68] The film was a rare and expensive color production to celebrate the twentieth anniversary of the war's end and Franco's victory, but it also marked the direction of the next decade, which would see the emergence of a reconciliation-oriented cinema.

Bentley writes of the films produced between 1961 and 1969: "These are films that mention the importance of reconciliation but on Nationalist terms within the dominant ideology."[69] An important film from this period was *España otra vez* (*Spain Again*) (1968) by Jaime Camino. The film gave the first positive portrayal of a Republican soldier in the figure of an American doctor who had served in the Lincoln Brigade. Not only was there a positive portrayal of a Republican, but he was a foreigner, although as a doctor, not strictly a combatant. The film was also significant for its inclusion of dialogue in Catalan, as the story takes place in Barcelona, to which the American doctor returns. It was one of the first films to allow for the use of a language other than Castilian. The censors demanded massive cuts to the script and gave the following warning: "In making the film, care must be taken to avoid anything that could implicitly or explicitly, be taken as a mention or interpretation of our war that is not clearly in a reconciliatory spirit, as well as any depiction of negative aspects of Spanish life that, in the film's context, could take on an inappropriate meaning."[70] For the censors, "reconciliation" meant reconciliation on the terms set by the victors, which meant the continued recognition and justification for "the crusade," although the tone had begun to shift in the direction of a tragedy that had befallen the country.

At the very end of the dictatorship in the early 1970s, one could begin to see further cracks in the Francoist control over the narrative of the war and some of the directions this would take in the coming decades. Carlos Saura's film *La prima Angélica* (*Cousin Angelica*) (1974) is frequently seen as the first film that openly identified with the Republican side, while also portraying the Nationalists in a ridiculous manner. The negative portrayal of the Nationalists helped to provoke some extreme-right denunciations of the film as well as some riots.[71]

Víctor Erice's enigmatic film *El spíritu de la colena* (*Spirit of the Beehive*) (1973) is set in the immediate postwar years. The film's location and time are established in some opening texts: "Once upon a time" followed by, "Somewhere on the Castilian plain, around 1940." In an interview with Erice, the director said of the censors, "I have to say they didn't cut a single frame. It's all there. Just to set the record straight. However, it seems they considered banning it, but they could find no explicit reasons to cite. They discussed the fugitive's death at length. But what I think carried the day—and they made note of this—is that they felt no one would go see it. That the film was . . . simply unwatchable."[72] The movie opens with the presentation of the film *Frankenstein* in the small village by a traveling cinema company. The film makes a strong impression on two little girls, who are sisters, and results in their exploring the differences between fantasy and reality. One of the little girls imagines that she has brought her "own Frankenstein" into existence, in the form of a fugitive, perhaps a member of the *maquis*, in an abandoned farmhouse. The little girls' mother has a former lover who has fled into exile. At the beginning of the film, she tries to send him a letter, but later in the film, perhaps after having not received any response, she throws the envelope into the fire, with the postage stamp bearing Franco's image clearly going up in flames.

During the years of the transition, films with a pro-Nationalist bend to them completely disappeared, while films taking a clear Republican point of view became more common but not necessarily more common than films that tended to take a more balanced view. With the rise of the exhumation movement in 2000, there has been a renewed energy poured back into discussing the civil war but again from multiple perspectives. José Luis Cuerda's film *La lengua de las mariposas* (*Butterfly*) (1999) gives a view of village life before the war told in a nostalgic framework and from the perspective of a delicate little boy, Moncho, who suffers from asthma. The film was based on a novel of the same title by Rivas. Characters in the film take on their roles of supporting or opposing Republican reform efforts; the village priest and a wealthy businessman are set in opposition to the Republic and the figure of Don Gregorio, who is the village teacher and is rumored to be an atheist and a pacifist. What Don Gregorio is first and foremost is a representative of the hopes put forward by the Enlightenment and the promise that a better educated Spanish population would be more willing to support the Republic and liberal principles in general. Some of the village women speak in favor of their new-won right to vote, although others disagree and raise concerns about Republicans burning churches in Barcelona. The relatively gentle pace of the film and village life is shattered at the end, when the Nationalist uprising begins. Don Gregorio and other village sub-

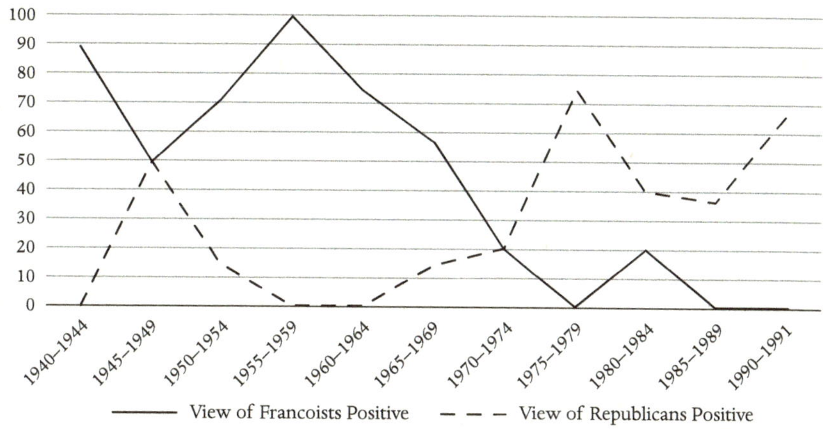


Figure 3 Spanish Civil War films.
*Source*: Juanjo Igartua and Darío Páez, "Art and Remembering Traumatic Collective Events: The Case of the Spanish Civil War," in *Collective Memory of Political Events: Social Psychological Perspectives*, ed. James W. Pennebaker, Darío Páez, and Bernard Rimé (Mahwah, NJ: Lawrence Erlbaum, 1997), 85.

versives are shown bloodied and being loaded onto the back of a truck. Moncho's mother and others have gathered to denounce and shout at the men in the back of the truck, and she encourages her son to do the same, to throw rocks at them with the others. Perhaps she is motivated more by fear than conviction, but it is heartbreaking to see Moncho pick up a stone and throw it at Don Gregorio, who had treated him with such tenderness and encouraged his love of learning.

Other novels and films have addressed the violence during the war and immediately after the war as the new fascist regime continued the fight against the *maquis*. Rivas's novel *The Carpenter's Pencil* (2001) and Cercas's novel *Soldiers of Salamis* (2003) were both successful novels that were turned into films with the same titles. In *The Carpenter's Pencil*, Rivas sets some of the same forces in opposition to each other as he did in *Butterfly*. The Republic is associated with artists, doctors, schoolteachers, reason, and the Enlightenment, and thus the future and love. The Nationalists, in contrast, are associated with the past, the military, the Catholic Church, superstition, and unreason. Rivas's Nationalist character in *The Carpenter's Pencil* is Herbal, who is motivated more by his resentment and jealousy toward Dr. Daniel Da Barca, who has attracted the attention of the woman whom Herbal also desires. Rivas clearly shows that the political and the personal both explain the violence in the war. In the character of Herbal, he reflects a point made by Renshaw, where she talked about how villagers at the sites of the exhumations tended to depoliticize the violence, seeing it not as a struggle between Republicans and Nationalists but rather as violence provoked by personal jealousies and rivalries. Rivas also gives the massacres and killings that occurred behind the official battle lines clear attention in his novel with a character commenting, "The main struggle is waged in the rear guard," with the violence clearly extending beyond military necessity.[73]

Cercas's novel *Soldiers of Salamis*, as well as the film based on the novel, also addresses the question of war crimes, the massacres that both Nationalists and Republicans perpetrated against each other. In the case of Cercas's novel, he deals with one specific massacre carried out by some Republican soldiers at the very end of the war in 1939, when they took a group of high-level Nationalist prisoners out into the woods to kill them. Cercas likes to mix fiction and reality in his novels, and he places himself in this novel as a journalist and somewhat successful novelist. In the novel, Cercas becomes fascinated with a story told by Rafael Sánchez Mazas, who was a real-life member of the early fascist movement in Spain even before the war. Sánchez Mazas was in Madrid at the beginning of the war, when the city was seized by the Republicans. He eventually made his way to Barcelona in an attempt to escape but was captured. Along with other high-level prisoners, he is taken to the woods by the Republicans to be killed, but he escapes in the confusion. His escape is noticed, and he is pursued, but when a Republican soldier sees him, he decides not to shoot and tells his comrades that he sees no one. Cercas places this moment and the look in the eyes of the Republican soldier at the center of the novel, along with the question, "Why does he decide not to shoot Sánchez Mazas?" The novel plays with the difficulty of uncovering the past and raises questions about whether or not Sánchez Mazas is even telling the truth, and who the Republican soldier might be.

Part of the significance of *The Carpenter's Pencil* and *Soldiers of Salamis* is that both the novels and the films shift the attention away from a tragic, but perhaps noble, struggle between two sides in a war in which each thought their ideals worth fighting for. In her study of contemporary Spanish novels, Sarah Leggott finds in both these novels and still others a greater willingness to move beyond simple portrayals of good and evil.[74] In this manner, these writers are striving for the balance suggested by Haemon and Ismene in *Antigone*. The "reconciliation" cinema of the 1960s, which favored reconciliation on Nationalist terms, later gave way to narratives that allowed a positive portrayal of the values supported by the Republicans, which in turn placed the reasons for the Nationalist struggle in doubt. But as attention has shifted from the war and the tragic but perhaps legitimate killing of the battlefield to tens of thousands of murders through rearguard actions, the war has begun to take on a very different tone. As the specter of violence with genocidal overtones begins to appear, the basis for a reconciliation grounded on a "collective madness" becomes more difficult to sustain.

The terrain that remains largely left unexplored at this point in Spanish popular culture is the scale of the violence and repression that continued after the end of the war in 1939. The attention has now shifted from the civil war itself to the repressive aftermath. While the postwar violence has been uncovered by historians and generated some powerful documentaries, these stories have not yet found their expression in dramatic cinematic form.[75] One partial exception to this general pattern is Guillermo del Toro's film *El laberinto del fauno* (*Pan's Labyrinth*) (2006), which is similar to Erice's *Spirit of the Beehive* (1973) in that it combines a little girl's fantasy world with reality but with far more deadly consequences. Whereas *Spirit of the Beehive* could only hint at the continuing resistance of the *maquis* against the fascists, del Toro puts their continued struggle against the fascists at the center of his story, which is set in 1944. The film's narrative leaves no doubt that they are justified in their fight against extremely brutal and ruthless Nationalists.

The question of what came after the end of the war in 1939 remains a period that is largely underexplored in Spain today. In some ways, the difficulty in engaging the continued repression, killing, and torture that followed the end of the war is similar to what we see with the Goli Otok debate in Yugoslavia. Within the context of war, fighting and dying in combat can be more easily accommodated than war crimes, massacres, and genocide. The fact that the violence of Franco's regime extended far beyond the war itself is a more difficult legacy to address.

## Chronological Development

Given the dominance of the state over societal relations, the periodization of Spanish public representations of the civil war are largely driven by changes in state policy until the period of democratization after Franco's death in 1975, the first free democratic elections in 1977, and the writing of a new constitution in 1978. The dominance of the state also limits our ability to gauge what changes were taking place within Spanish families and among Spanish citizens. What we can clearly observe are, however, some definitive trends in terms of how the war was discussed in literature and film. As suggested by the memory-market dictum, the state's control over cinema was much more extensive than compared to novels, where little bits of countermemory narratives could begin to take shape.

The first period stretches from the end of the war in 1939 through 1959 and the first years of the 1960s. The early postwar years, especially until the end of World War II in 1945, was particularly repressive, and scholars have named it the "Time of Silence," although the regime did make sure to put its view of the war on the record and in the cinemas. Although relatively few films were actually made dealing with the war, those that were made came to be known as the "crusade cinema," after the Nationalist's preference for referring to the civil war as something other than a civil war. In his study of Spanish literature, Maryse Bertrand de Muñoz discovered a pattern of novels that supported the regime's view of the war, and the justification of their cause, from 1939 through 1949, and then a period of relative silence, or "amnesia" from 1950 through 1960.[76]

In fact, it was the regime's own censorship policies that helped to encourage this period of amnesia or forgetting with the passing of a strict censorship policy in 1941, which required any material related to "the crusade" to first gain approval of both the civilian and military leaders, a policy that was only relaxed between 1964 and 1966.[77] That did not mean that the regime was shy about promoting its own narrative of the war, and Franco himself wrote the script, under a pseudonym, for one of the most important crusade films of the time, *Raza* (1941). The film follows the story of a family from the loss of Cuba and empire in 1898 through to the conclusion of the civil war, which finally made the country safe, thanks to the Nationalist rebellion. The empire may have been lost due to prior mismanagement, but the promise for the future greatness of Spain is clear.

It was also a period of extreme economic autarky and social isolation for Spanish society. The regime only began to move away from this in 1959, when the government received a stabilization loan from the IMF to help with the increasing domestic economic crisis. During the period of autarky, the ability of external forces to act on Spanish society was minimal. Those living in exile had little ability to communicate with those living inside Spain, and the government was not only determined to use censorship to shape Spanish cinema, but also to severely curtail the importation of any material that could be seen as a threat to the regime.

After the beginning of the 1960s, the regime began to open up Spain to the rest of Europe to deal with the economic crisis brought on by extreme autarky and an increasingly inefficient agricultural sector, which was still based on large landowners and poor peasants. The growing tolerance for anti-communist dictatorships on the part of the United States and its West European allies also aided this process. One primary goal was to attract foreign tourists to Spain to help bring in much-needed foreign currency, and the film industry was used as a vehicle to create a positive image of Spain for external audiences, while continuing to avoid internal social problems.

The increasing openness of the country also helped the significant Republican population living in exile to reconnect with the country or, if direct travel back to Spain was too dangerous, to begin to send their literature and publications into the country. The late Francoist period from 1965 until Franco's death in 1975 was marked by the further weakening of the authoritarian coalition and a growing level of criticism of the regime within the Catholic Church.[78]

The Francoist version of the war remained well anchored in the national narratives, but with the lightening of the censorship laws after March 1966, there was room for greater expression. Aguilar notes that April 1 continued to be referred to as "liberation day" throughout the decade, and the regime sought to legitimize itself by reminding Spaniards that they had now experienced twenty-five years of peaceful development, something unique in Spanish history.[79] But it was also a decade during which the regime's narrative about the war began to face some challenges. Both Aguilar and Bentley note that the theme of reconciliation began to appear after 1966 in films as well as other mass media, suggesting that the losers deserved to be reintegrated into Spanish society, although clearly on the terms established by the regime.[80] A 1969 poll showed very strong support across the population for a general amnesty for all crimes committed prior to 1939, with 71 percent endorsing this proposal as a "very good" idea.[81] Aguilar sees this as a transition from the mode of creating heroic myths to one of creating tragic myths in which the civil war came to be seen as a period of "collective insanity."[82] The war increasingly became seen as a tragic, fratricidal conflict in which it was not necessary to sort out victims and perpetrators. This shift left the identity of the perpetrators masked, and the post-war crimes of the regime were certainly not yet being addressed. Nonetheless, by the end of the decade, Bentley argues we have the first positive portrayal of a Republican in Jaime Camino's 1968 film, *España otra vez,* in which a former member of the Lincoln Brigade returns to Barcelona.[83] It was also one of the first films to include dialogue in Catalan, also challenging the regime's extreme aversion to any reminders or representations of regional differences. Camino would return to the topic of the civil war on several occasions after the end of the dictatorship. Igartua and Páez's data about civil war films support Bentley's observation, as they show that the period between 1965 and 1969 included the first positive portrayal of the Republican side since the early 1950s, alongside some increasingly ambivalent portrayals of the Nationalist side (see Figure 3).[84] The growing ambivalence confirms the impression of others that the war increasingly became one in which neither side was to blame, that the war was somehow akin to a natural disaster. This naturalization of war is something that we can also observe in the cases of Germany and Japan.

Another reason for these changes was that the broad coalition that had initially supported the regime during and immediately after the war began to have some serious divisions. The last decade of the regime's existence was marked by growing dissent within the Catholic Church. While the Catholic Church had initially been one of the regime's strongest supporters during and after the war, the post-war generation of clergy had increasingly come to feel alienated. A 1969 poll of eighteen thousand clergy found that 24.8 percent thought of themselves as socialists and only 2.4 percent as Falangists.[85] At the same time, the Spanish Communist Party, which would remain illegal until after Franco's death, began to recruit youthful rebels, who were prepared to challenge the regime.[86] Student protests at the universities had begun around 1956 and had become endemic by 1962.[87] The regime was clearly losing its struggle to socialize the new governing elite of middle-class university students to their worldview.

These pressures from above and below were preparing the way toward democratization, which became possible after Franco's death on November 20, 1975. The internal weakness of the regime's hold on the narrative of Spain's history would become immediately apparent after Franco's death. In 1974, even a year before his death, the first film that was openly critical of the Nationalist forces was released. Carlos Saura's film *La prima Angélica* was released because of a change in the leadership in the Ministry for Information and Tourism in January 1974. The film took the point of view of the Republicans and portrayed the Nationalists in a ridiculous fashion. The film was so provocative that the extreme-right reacted vehemently against the film, and there were even riots.[88] Pío Cabanillas, the new head at the Ministry for Information and Tourism, only survived in office until October 1975.

But with Franco's death on November 20, 1975, elites began to negotiate earnestly about the transfer of power to new democratic institutions. Far-right gunmen murdered five people, four of them communist labor lawyers, in what became known as the Atocha massacre, after the eponymous district where the shootings took place in Madrid. Alongside the far-right violence, there was the continued terrorist campaign run by Euskadi Ta Askatasuna (ETA), the Basque separatist, nationalist fighting force. There was a clear sense by all those involved that widespread violence could return to the country. Nonetheless, the Spanish Communist Party was legalized in April 1977, in time for the first free elections at the local level that same year, and by 1978 a new constitution had been written. The period that followed came to be governed by the *pacto del olvido* (pact of forgetting) during which elites avoided engaging the legacy of the civil war. After a failed military coup on February 23, 1981, the Spanish Socialist Party won the next election in 1982, and the democratic transition began to look more and more solidified as the Socialists governed from 1982 to 1996. The first non-Francoist government since the end of the civil war in 1939 showed every intention of holding to the pact of forgetting. Although the government sponsored the building of a monument to the civil war dead in the Plaza de la Lealtad in 1985, it was a monument dedicated to all of the civil war dead. There was no attempt to sort out the justice of either cause or to identify perpetrators and victims. Although the crusade master narrative of the Francoist regime had lost its legitimacy, the fratricidal war framework with its undercurrent of naturalism and viewing the war as something like a natural disaster, left the question of victims and perpetrators unanswered.

While the state and political elites largely removed themselves from the history debates, the rest of Spanish society was not respecting this pact of silence to the same degree. The push for memory from below began to expand with many local initiatives even as early as the 1970s,[89] which then laid the groundwork for the widely recognized "memory boom" that became more obvious between 1995 and 2000. What is striking is how quickly the Francoist version of the civil war was removed from some aspects of Spanish society. From 1975 to 1991, there were twenty-seven films that dealt with the civil war, but only one of them gave a positive portrayal of the Nationalist forces. All of the other films were either ambivalent, supporting the tragic or "collective insanity" narrative, or they clearly supported the Republican view of history (see Figure 3).[90] These changes were not always apparent to observe at the time. In 1991, Gubern, a very well-known Spanish professor of cinema, wrote an article in which he concluded, "In 1976 that episode [the Civil War] seemed very recent and demanded to be re-examined in depth from a new perspective, but by 1987 the majority of the public and most critics already considered it outdated and exhausted. It seemed as if ten years had been sufficient to dilute an obsession and to retire an historic ghost. It could be said that the ghosts of the past had been exorcised. Or at least some of them."[91]

The timing of Gubern's article is useful, for it suggests that a very careful observer of the Spanish popular culture and its engagement with the civil war did not foresee what was coming next. Whereas Gubern saw a denouement of the civil war narrative in Spain, other forces in Spanish society were pushing to dig even deeper into the past. Within the civil society, members of Republican families, by this time often the grandchildren, began asking for information about where their family members were buried, or even discovering for the first time that a father or grandfather had been a Republican. As mentioned above, the Francoist regime's earliest years had tried to impose a "time of silence" on the entire society, with family members often never being given any official word of their loved one's death, frequently by execution. And they were humiliated by having no right to reclaim the body of their loved one, which they could bury properly. Beginning in the late 1970s and early 1980s, relatives had already begun the process of trying to find the remains of their family members, who had been killed during the war or after the war in the prisons and labor camps. But these were localized activities that failed to gain the attention of the whole society. The search for the dead ancestors, which had begun much earlier, had by 2000 become a national movement.

Rather than a denouement, the early 1990s was in fact the beginning of a memory boom, which took off between the mid-1990s and 2000.[92] By 1991, family members with connections to the *maquis* had formed La Gavilla Verde (The Green Sheaf), which set about trying to recapture the history of the *maquis* through oral history projects and the building of a monument in memory of the freedom fighters. Relatives of dead Republicans had begun even earlier to gather information about the mass graves, which are scattered around Spain's rural countryside. Although unmarked, local oral history often had maintained stories about massacres, executions, and mass burials.

With the explosion of interest in the civil war in the broader society, those who held this local knowledge became more willing to share this information with others. The macrolevel of the collective memory model began to cause a shift in the interpersonal dialogues that were occurring at the microlevel. The macrolevel and the microlevel began to create a positive feedback loop that encouraged more discussion about the civil war in ways that had long been suppressed. As discussions about the civil war became more common in the broader society (macrolevel), individuals (microlevel) felt freer to discuss it as well. But most importantly, all of this was taking place in the society without the encouragement of the state or political elites. The government was not leading this process. The Spanish People's Party, the right-of-center party, had defeated the Socialists in the 1996 election, and they would remain in power until 2004. The Socialists would then govern again from 2004 to 2011. But it is important to emphasize, again, that while the Socialists had been in power, they also had avoided encouraging any sort of deep investigation into the history and legacy of the civil war.

In the civil society, there was an explosion of activity during 1999 and 2000 in terms of radio and television programs, films, books, and touring exhibitions.[93] The period between 2000 and 2009 saw thirty-two theater productions dealing with the civil war, more than a 50 percent increase compared to any previous decade since the war.[94] Then, in October 2000, thirteen bodies were exhumed from a civil war grave in Priaranza del Bierzo in the province of León. In December of the same year, two grandchildren of men who had disappeared during the civil war, Santiago Macías and Emilio Silva, formed the nonpartisan ARMH. Other more partisan organizations also formed, such as the Forum for Historical Memory, sponsored by the Spanish Communist Party. Since the exhumation at Priaranza in October 2000, 171 graves have been opened and more than 4,000 bodies have been recovered.[95] In 2001, La Gavilla Verde succeeded in having the label "bandit" lifted from the *maquis*, who were finally recognized as legitimate freedom fighters.

The broader changes in the society began to be transmitted to the state and legal institutions. Although the People's Party had refused to back an earlier motion in the parliament condemning the 1936 military coup, on November 20, 2002, marking the twenty-fifth anniversary of Franco's death in 1975, a similar motion passed unanimously. The social pressure to condemn the Francoist regime and war increased rapidly after 2000, and the People's Party needed to clearly establish itself as a democratic party of the right by breaking with the Francoist legacy. But the People's Party also knows that part of their support comes from those who continue to support exactly such a linkage. Thus, when the Spanish Parliament permitted a series of speeches about the anti-Franco fighters in December 2003, members of the People's Party in Parliament stayed away. The People's Party tried to find a middle ground of condemning the military coup in 1936, while avoiding any further investigations into what had happened during and after the war.

In 2004, the Socialist Party, led by José Luis Rodríguez Zapatero, began to engage with this broader change in the society by making the recovery of Spain's historical memory part of their official party platform, in an election that they won. Zapatero is the grandson of Spanish army captain Juan Rodríguez Lozano, who was executed by a Francoist firing squad because of his loyalty to the Republic in August 1936. Soon after the Socialists formed a government, they established a commission that began drafting legislation that would work toward the moral and judicial rehabilitation of the victims, of both Nationalist and Republican violence. In 2007, the government passed the Ley de Memoria Histórica (Law of Historical Memory). In the end, the law did allow for the moral and judicial rehabilitation of victims, whose family members could petition for a "victim certificate," which would be granted by a five-person panel of experts. However, no financial compensation was to be offered, and furthermore, the perpetrators were to be left unnamed and unidentified. The survivors of the victims could be from any side in the conflict, so the law and the government sought to avoid any particular stance vis-à-vis the causes and justifications for the war. Last, those groups engaged in the recovery of historical memory and the exhumation of mass graves were to be helped by local authorities, although the government would not provide financial resources toward this end.

The political battle lines that were drawn around this piece of legislation are instructive, for they demonstrate the continuing divisions in Spanish society regarding the history of the civil war and its commemoration. Amnesty International began to use external pressure on the government, and represented the growing international movement for applying human rights norms to past cases of human rights abuses. Within Spain, the ARMH and other NGOs also supported development of the legislation and drew inspiration from what was happening in Argentina, where local activists were pursuing more information about the military regime that ran the country from 1976 to 1983.[96]

Not everyone was pleased by these developments. In opposition were representatives of rightist forces in Spain that had previously aligned themselves with the Francoist regime. One of those voices came from the *El Mundo* newspaper, which claimed in an editorial that Amnesty International was only interested in the Republican victims and not the Nationalist victims of the war. The editorial read at one point, "During the war all sorts of atrocities were committed by both sides. Since the arrival of the Zapatero government, however, there has been a climate of skewed historical revisionism aimed at remembering the past in an unfair and selective manner."[97] In addition to the editorial, *El Mundo* began publishing in memoriam notices from family members whose relatives had been killed by Republican death squads. Spain's Catholic bishops also began to lobby against the proposed legislation demanding that the 6,500 martyrs of the church be remembered as victims of Republican violence. Although the church had backed the transition to democracy, the institution remained conservative and hostile to many of the Socialist's other political programs over same-sex marriage and easing the divorce laws. The church accused Zapatero's government of drawing the "reconciliation" of the transition period into question, and thus damaging Spanish society. The People's Party, now in opposition, represented these voices in the parliamentary debates.

Since 2007, the overall economic situation in Spain has deteriorated rapidly. The Socialist government long remained in denial, at least in public, about the problems with Spain's banks and financial sector, which had run up massive levels of debt during an extended construction and housing boom. While the current setting is not conducive for the further investigation of the civil war and its legacy, what is of significance is that some Spaniards see the current financial crisis as rooted in the weak level of democratic culture in Spanish society, the roots for which they trace back to the Franco regime. This shows that the shifting framework of understanding the civil war and the following years of dictatorship is playing a role in modern-day Spanish politics. The reasons for the Catalonian government's decision to push forward with an independence referendum on October 1, 2017, against the explicit warnings not to do so by the People's Party government in Madrid and the Spanish courts, are more complex than what can be discussed here. But it is worth noting that whether or not the legacy of the civil war entered directly into these debates, the revival of Catalan identity since 1978 has been part of a process on the part of many Catalans to try and overcome suppression of the region's language and identity during Franco's regime.

## Conclusion

The Spanish case helps us to see more clearly some of the tensions embedded in *Antigone* and the long legacy that a civil war can leave for a society.[98] As with the case of Yugoslavia, the dead who have not been given a proper burial continue to haunt the imaginations of their relatives for many years after the war. A sense of unease and a world not yet properly ordered continues to linger, to haunt the present. The rural landscapes of Spain and Yugoslavia were filled with mass graves from the wars, the location of which could remain firmly anchored in local knowledge and memory, despite the attempts of the state to try and set the issue to rest. In each their own manner, Franco and Tito sought to play the role of Creon in giving very open and proper burials for those who had fought for the city, while denying the same for their enemies. The unburied or disrespected dead continued to haunt both countries for decades.

As in *Antigone*, Spanish families are split over what to do. Some, like Antigone, were not able to rest until they had given their family members a proper burial. Others, like Ismene, feared not only the power of the state, which forbade for many decades the proper burial, but also the broader social implications of literally digging up the past. The perpetrators of the massacres or their decedents were likely to be very fearful of what might follow, thus raising the specter of further violence. The Furies remained loose and barely hidden.

One strategy that the Franco regime attempted to employ was the externalization of blame. By shifting the blame for the war onto outsiders who intervened in Spanish affairs and threatened to impose a Stalinist dictatorship, the regime hoped to limit the discussion about internal victims and perpetrators. But this effort was somewhat undermined by the ethnocentrism of death on the part of the Nationalists and their supporters, as their first impulse was to impose further suffering on the Republican survivors, in a dark inversion of Christ's suffering leading to redemption of all humanity. The regime sought to impose suffering and humiliation on Republicans and their families as a form of redemption for the nation.

This extended period of postwar repression against Republican families effectively atomized this group in Spanish society. Fear and shame led to a widespread silencing of Republican family histories. Moreover, the Francoist propaganda firmly anchored in the popular imagination the links between Republicans and the Soviet Union so that they both became simply the "Reds" and anti-Spanish. As Renshaw's work demonstrates, Republican families, at least in rural areas, are often reluctant to claim a political reason for the killing of their loved ones, preferring instead to find other reasons to explain their murder and to avoid the taint of being labeled a "Red."

Nonetheless, the Spanish understanding of the civil war underwent a significant change approximately twenty years after Franco's death, through the actions of many different individuals and groups in the civil society. Political elites have not led this change. Instead, individuals and families sought to give a proper burial for their loved ones, as Antigone does in the play. With Creon gone and a new political regime in place, Spaniards have sought to bring order again to the world of the dead. Local historians, rather than members of the academy, began to investigate the scale of the violence in their region. Over time, enough information was gathered so that the processes of social contagion and reinforcement began a positive feedback loop between individual, microlevel activities and societal, macrolevel representations of Spain's difficult past. While well-placed commentators thought the issue had been settled at the beginning of the 1990s, new information about the war, the postwar period, and the Franco regime began to pour forth over the following decades. The legacy of the war remains very much with Spanish society still today.

# 4 *Yugoslavia*

*The other states are all convulsed with hate.*
*Their mangled sons receive their final rites*
*from dogs and beasts, or else some wingèd bird*
*defiles the city's hearth with putrid flesh.*
—Tiresias to Creon in *Antigone*[1]

*Step back from anger. Let your feelings change.*
—Haemon to Creon in *Antigone*[2]

## Introduction

Our discussion of the Yugoslav case will focus on the development of communist Yugoslavia after World War II. There will be reasons for us to look back to the Balkan Wars of 1912 and 1913 as well as World War I, but the primary focus will be on the invasion of the country by Germany and Italy in the context of World War II, the destruction of the Yugoslav state, and the civil war that erupted after the Axis invasion. The civil wars in Spain and Turkey, as with the Yugoslav case, all involved outside interventions, although this was far less the case in Spain than in Turkey and Yugoslavia. In the latter two cases, the continued existence of the state was thrown into question by the invading armies and their respective occupations. While the Turkish state would have continued to exist even with the implementation of the Treaty of Sèvres, the Yugoslav state was completely destroyed as a result of the Axis invasion, with serious consequences for the postwar situation. While outside forces also intervened in the case of Spain and became an exaggerated part of the Francoist interpretation of the civil war as "a crusade," the Yugoslav case differs in that the outside invasion and dismemberment of the country was far more traumatic. But what unites these cases is that there is a clear external enemy to the nation or the national community that can be blamed for much of the violence that occurred. The *externalization of blame* plays a key role in each of these cases.

In contrast with the cases of Japan and Germany, the resulting civil wars that erupted after the invasions vastly complicated the position of perpetrators and victims in the postwar setting and left these two groups, never completely distinct, living in close proximity to each other after the mass violence had ended. While Japan and Germany had to deal with the legacy of defeat after wars that largely became seen as unjust in later years, the legacy of a civil war is different. There is still a defeated side, but that defeated side remains a neighbor in the village after the war is over. The relationships between the victorious and defeated sides in each of these civil wars differed significantly in terms of the paths of reconciliation that were sought, if at all, after the killing had stopped. In the case of Turkey, the lines were drawn starkly between those who had "betrayed" the Ottoman Empire and those that had remained "loyal." Moreover, the Turks, the largest ethnonational group, set about establishing their domination of the new Turkish Republic after the successful War of Liberation. They had no need for reconciliation with the Armenians or Greeks, and in the coming decades the minorities that remained in the Turkish Republic were marginalized and expelled. The Spanish case is somewhat more similar to the Yugoslav situation in that both ideological and ethnonational divisions had to be dealt with after the war ended. The Franco regime opted for a path of no reconciliation in the first instance and, in fact, continued a pattern of extreme violence and repression that would last for a couple more decades after the war had ended. The regime reversed Republican decentralization and began to suppress regional identities and languages in Catalonia and the Basque region.

In contrast to these other two cases, the postwar Yugoslav situation was far more complex in terms of its diversity, with different linguistic, religious, and ethnonationalist groups, all of which had fought on multiple sides in the war. While there were severe problems of postwar violence and repressions—points that we will return to throughout this chapter—the victorious forces around Tito's partisans took a very different path from those of the victorious forces in Spain and Turkey. Unlike in Turkey, no ethnonationalist group emerged as the dominant force in postwar Yugoslavia that sought to impose its will on all the other groups. Unlike in Spain, there was a far greater willingness on the part of the Yugoslav partisans to reintegrate as many of the people of the region into the new Yugoslav state as possible. The official position of the state was "brotherhood and unity," which expressed a focus on the multiethnic, victorious, partisan forces, with which everyone was encouraged to identify.

While Tito's partisan forces fought against the occupying armies of Italy and Germany, they also fought against those that collaborated with the occupiers, the Croatian Ustasha and the Serbian-royalist Chetniks. The Croatian Ustasha were given their own so-called Independent State of Croatia, while the Serbian-royalist Chetniks fought against both the occupiers and the partisans. The Chetniks also sought accommodation from both the Ustasha and the partisans in hopes of reestablishing a Serbian monarchy.

Those who had fought and supported the Ustasha and the Chetniks certainly found themselves in a precarious position at the end of the war, and many, who could, fled the country. Once in exile, they reorganized and became a steady external force for anti-Communist agitation from outside Yugoslavia. Within the country, there was no shortage of violent retribution carried out against those who could not flee, especially against the Croatian Ustasha. The most infamous massacre took place at Bleiburg, which included many thousands of victims.

The official partisan position was to encourage as broad a mass identification with the victorious all-Yugoslav forces as possible. Even those who had remained ambivalent or joined the fight at a late date were encouraged to identify with the collective victory over the foreign occupiers and their collaborators. The victorious partisans had a great deal of legitimacy and popularity at the end of the war, and they used this to emphasize the all-Yugoslav nature of the struggle. They also attempted to smooth over the ethnonationalist divides that had opened up during the war. This was very different from the situation in Spain, where Franco, inspired by Catholic and Christian notions of redemption through suffering, continued measures of harsh repression against entire Republican families for decades after the end of Spain's civil war.

## Psychological and Social-Psychological Processes

As we have seen in each of the other cases, the process of externalizing blame for the mass violence became an important tool in trying to reestablish a community of the good after the killing had stopped. As the Kingdom of Yugoslavia was invaded and destroyed by outside forces, this part of the externalization process is rather obvious and straightforward. What became more difficult in the case of Yugoslavia was how to deal conceptually with those who had collaborated with the occupiers, carried out massacres, and in the case of the Independent State of Croatia, had committed genocide. The solution to this problem was to focus on the slogan of "Brotherhood and Unity," encourage identification with Tito and the partisans, and to turn the internal collaborators into ideological others. There was an attempt to remove the ethnic identification of the Ustasha with Croats and the Chetniks with Serbs, and to focus on the "fascist" characteristic of both of the movements, which the communist, anti-fascist, partisan movement had overcome.

The partisan movement was indeed multiethnic in its makeup, so Croats, Serbs, and Slovenians were encouraged to view this as their movement, whatever their level of participation in the actual fighting or their identification with the partisans during the war. This identification with the partisan movement remained somewhat more difficult for the ethnic Albanians, primarily located in Kosovo, and Bosnian Muslims, some of whom had fought on the side of the Ustasha. Yugoslavia's Muslim population remained associated in the minds of many Catholic and Orthodox Christians with the "five hundred years of domination" by the Ottoman Empire. But the postwar communist movement was nonconfessional and antireligious, so Yugoslavs with a Muslim background were also welcomed into the new party organizations.

What is curious about the Yugoslav case and distinguishes it from the Spanish and Turkish cases is that it became much more difficult to establish the problematic *ethnocentrism of death*. The clearest example of this, which we will deal with extensively below, is the difficulty that the Yugoslav state had in coming to terms with the mass extermination camp of Jasenovac, which was established by the Ustasha regime to kill Serbs, Jews, and Roma in a genocidal campaign. Furthermore, any discussion in the general population about massacres that had been perpetrated by one ethnic group against another was strictly forbidden. These massacres of villagers against one another or against neighboring villages along ethnic lines had been quite common, especially as the Ustasha-led genocide began to accelerate against the Serbs. Given that the competing groups were most intensely mingled in Bosnia, and as the fear of massacres by "rival" groups spread, a logic of striking first began to take hold, especially because such mass killings had occurred in the prior conflicts of the Balkan Wars, World War I, and during the rule over the region by the Ottoman Empire. Because the state tried to minimize the ethnic identities of the domestic perpetrators, there was a repression of the ethnocentrism of death in the public sphere. The official position was to encourage an ethnocentrism of death vis-à-vis the outside occupiers represented by the Germans and Italians. This does not mean, however, that these perspectives were absent from the general population, a point that we will return to later. Oral histories of the massacres and mass graves remained alive within families and networks of intraethnic trust, and they exploded into public discussions in the 1980s. Thus, the ethnocentrism of death remained a key feature of the Yugoslav case, but it remained hidden for many of the postwar decades. In the official public discussions, perpetrators were mentioned in ideological terms, not ethnic terms.

Thus, *socially shared retrieval-induced forgetting* (SS-RIF) played an important part in suppressing discussions of interethnic violence during World War II. Prior to the 1980s, this was not something that could be discussed in public, in the media, and through theater, film, or other arts and entertainment media. This is one reason why, for many Yugoslav citizens, the return of discussion about interethnic violence in the 1980s and then actual fighting in the 1990s came as a surprise. This was especially true for the postwar generations, for whom being "Yugoslav" appeared more natural, although this was more so in more urban and cosmopolitan centers than rural areas.[3] Unless one lived in a family or region that had experienced this type of violence in the context of the war, it was absent from one's historical perspective and the collective memory of the broader society. Although we cannot know this for certain, it is probably the case that these submerged tails of mass violence were most prevalent in Bosnia and in the Krajina region of Croatia, where there was a significant Serbian minority population. What is clear is that once these narratives of interethnic violence broke into the open in the 1980s, the *social contagion* and *reinforcement effects* were very powerful.

Yugoslav intellectuals, artists, and thinkers did much to orient the country toward European ideals of the Enlightenment throughout the nineteenth and twentieth century. While intraethnic solidarity remained strong prior to World War II, especially because each ethnic group closely identified with different religious institutions and practices, an increasing number of urbanized and educated Yugoslav citizens began to identify themselves as Yugoslavs and also as "cultured."[4] People in Yugoslavia were very concerned with distinguishing themselves along a continuum of "culturedness," meaning that one had an extended formal education and had separated oneself from the ways of the village and peasant life. And the openness of the country to the West allowed Yugoslavs to travel freely and study at Western universities. Indeed, the flow of people went in both directions, as Yugoslavia became a popular destination for Western scholars, artists, and tourists. Yugoslavia was far more open to Western Europe and for a longer time than was the case with Spain. Communist ideology also did a great deal to emphasize human rationality and mastery over nature, so that the classics of the Western philosophical tradition became a regular part of the educational system. Unlike in Spain, where the Catholic Church along with Franco's regime sought to blunt the forces of modernity, Yugoslav communism was explicitly modern in its outlook. Rational debate was seen as a way of moving human society forward, and Yugoslav artists and intellectuals engaged in vigorous debates about their society and the future direction of socialism. As we will see, the state sought to set some clear boundaries to these discussions, but reason-based debate was seen as a way of arriving at new truths.

## Politics

Communist Yugoslavia clearly remained anti-democratic and authoritarian in nature until the collapse of the Yugoslav state in a series of wars throughout the 1990s. But this is not to say that the level of state repression and control remained the same from the beginning to the end. Just as can be seen with a partial opening of Turkish state-society relations in the context of the 1960s, only for this to be crushed by a series of military coups, the level of Yugoslav authoritarianism changed over time. There were periods during which questions about the Yugoslav past and the war started to come into the open, and public debate about the direction of the society was explored in the arts, if not so directly in politics.

From the end of the war in 1945 to 1948, the partisan movement struggled to gain control over the country and to establish the institutions necessary for governing. The official plan was to integrate the country within what was becoming the Soviet sphere of influence in Eastern Europe. But in 1948, Tito dramatically decided to break with Stalin and to establish Yugoslavia outside the Soviet sphere of influence. The pathway was to remain socialistic in its orientation, but the country would find its own revolutionary path. This led to a period of severe repression for anyone who was denounced as being too close to Stalin or showing allegiance to the Soviet Union. The Yugoslav communists began to establish a system of prisons in which to hold those suspected of Soviet loyalties, and thus potential internal traitors. The best known of these camps was Goli Otok, or the "naked island." This period of repression became something that the Yugoslav communists wished to silence in later years, but the survivors of the camps and their largely arbitrary and torturous violence would continue to come forward and demand accountability.

This period of repression can be roughly dated from 1948 to 1953. It ended in part because of Stalin's death in March 1953 and the retreating fear that the Soviet Union would invade the country. By the end of 1953, Milovan Djilas, one of Tito's closest advisers during the partisan war and the head of the party's propaganda department, took his concerns about the direction that the communist revolution was taking to the public in a dramatic fashion. Through a series of eighteen articles that were published in the Belgrade-based newspaper *Borba*, Djilas began to make an argument for the rule of law and democratic socialism.[5] His agitation for a change in direction began in 1950 with the introduction of the self-management system of economic organization. But his failure to move the party internally led him to launch his challenge through public appeals in late 1953. In January 1954, Djilas was expelled from the party and began a series of four court trials and nine years in prison, which finally ended in 1966. During this period, he became known as Yugoslavia's best-known dissident, although he was far from alone, as we will see in a moment.

The introduction of the self-management system, which was an attempt to move away from the disastrous central planning model, set Yugoslavia on the route toward ever greater decentralization, which meant the devolution of power from the federal center in Belgrade to the republics. This greatly complicates our discussion of state-society relations as the level of freedom in the different republics varied over time. For example, Yugoslavia did not develop a centralized censorship regime along the lines of what was established in Spain or Turkey. With time, and especially by the mid- to late 1960s, novelists, playwrights, and filmmakers became freer to critique Yugoslav society *and* to begin to ask difficult questions about the country's past. As Goran Miloradović put it, "Despite state and party control, a critical spirit managed to survive and develop in the arts, sometimes creating masterpieces. Film was here often in the forefront."[6] It also permitted nationalist sentiments to begin to take shape again, especially in Croatia. In 1966, Aleksandar Ranković, the vice-president and head of the state security forces, was removed from office by Tito. Ranković had been the primary opponent to further decentralization and the opening-up of civil society.

With greater openness came an ever louder expression of dissatisfaction with different parts of the current situation in Yugoslavia, along with grievances about the past. During the 1960s, Serbia and Slovenia became far more lenient in terms of what could be discussed in public, while Croatia and Bosnia, also known as the "dark kingdom," faced more significant repression.[7] This was because the expression of dissatisfaction with Yugoslavia took on more nationalist tones in Croatia, whereas in Bosnia the republic's rulers kept a firm lid on any nationalist expressions. From 1967 to 1971, there was an outburst of Croatian nationalism in which the republic's political leadership became unified with the intellectuals and wider segments of the society in forging a new nationalist project.[8] Whether or not these nationalist aspirations could be satisfied within Yugoslavia, the demands were for greater decentralization and recognition of Croatian as a separate language from Serbo-Croatian, which had been an attempt to create a more unified language between two variations that were very similar.[9]

From the perspective of the federal communist leadership, these openly nationalist expressions in Croatia and the increasingly critical discussions in Serbia, which did not have the same nationalist bend, became seen as too much of a threat, and a new series of repressive measures and reversals against increasing openness in the civil society were put in place by late 1971. After a period of repression, the 1974 constitution gave new powers to the republics and created two new "autonomous regions" in Kosovo and Vojvodina, which both remained nominally part of Serbia but could now vote against the Serbian republic at the federal level, which they did with increasing frequency. The granting of greater autonomy to Kosovo was designed to deal with rising ethnic Albanian nationalism but only served to sharpen the relations between Serbs and Albanians in the region, which would explode again in the 1980s and 1990s.[10]

These changes bought the Yugoslav state and Communist Party another decade before all of these various ethnonationalist dissatisfactions began to find more open expression after Tito's death on May 4, 1980. With the central, unifying figure of Tito gone, the ability of the old supraethnic partisan leadership to hold the country together began to collapse. The ethnonationalist resentments going back to the war years began to explode into the public realm, and the legitimacy of the Yugoslav Communist Party was shaken with the growing public reevaluations about Goli Otok and the mass repression at the founding of the regime. The civil society uprising against the communist leadership certainly had the potential to move in a more liberal, democratic direction, and those voices were not absent from the scene. Yugoslavia's open borders had long allowed Yugoslavs to travel and study abroad, and there was a great appreciation for what had been achieved in Western Europe. But the unresolved nationalist resentments and fears that remained from World War II had the far stronger, emotional pull, as fear became the most powerful political tool available to the political leadership that was able to seize power.

In terms of international relations and attempts to shape internal discussions about the World War II past, the Serbian and Croatian diasporas, both radically anticommunist and anti-Yugoslav in their orientation, carried their bitter resentments with them into exile. Significant Ustasha leadership figures, including Ante Pavelić and Dinko Šakić, the former commander of the Jasenovac extermination camp, continued to live in exile and to plot against communist Yugoslavia while also seeking to keep core partisan war crimes, such as the mass killings at the end of the war, in the public mind. Serbian exiles tended to come from the Chetnik faction and remained loyal to the idea of reestablishing the monarchy but with far less influence than the Croatian diaspora. But in terms of the global consciousness of what had happened in Yugoslavia during the war, these were extremely parochial concerns. Unlike the case with Spain, where members of different Western countries had fought on the side of the Republicans in the civil war and wrote about their experiences, such as George Orwell and Ernest Hemmingway, there was no similar memory group from outside Yugoslavia. And unlike the Armenian diaspora, which began to organize and demand recognition of the genocide in the 1960s, there was no single, crystallizing war atrocity around which to rally, except for the partisan killing of fascist collaborators at Bleiburg at the end of the war. The horrors of the German occupation of Yugoslavia only began to take on a more international dimension with the development of the Wehrmacht exhibit in Germany in the 1990s, after Yugoslavia had ceased to exist. In part, the lack of external knowledge about the depth of the suffering that had occurred in Yugoslavia during World War II led external observers who sought to intervene in the crises of the 1990s to underestimate the deep emotions and fears that moved many of the participants. This frequently led the Western powers to dismiss ethnonationalist fears as mere propaganda efforts, rather than recognizing that there was a logical and rational basis for these fears for many of the local participants.

## Culture

The Yugoslav case falls more within the Western cultural tradition of modernity and open rational debate about the nature of the social and natural world. Yugoslav communism certainly ushered in a modernist mentality toward what the future had to offer and a turning away from tradition. Nonetheless, certain cultural traditions remained very salient for different segments of the Yugoslav population, especially religion. During the period of communist Yugoslavia, adherence to religious practices was forbidden for party members, but the Yugoslav state remained much more accepting of continued religious practices than was the case in most of Soviet-dominated Eastern Europe. For example, each of the different religious faiths was allowed to maintain religious schools, while public schools were strictly secular. Nonetheless, adherence to religious practices remained weaker and declined, especially among the more cosmopolitan, urban population.

Religious differences have played an important part in Yugoslavia's history. Although there is a division in the country between Western Christianity, with Slovenes and Croats being overwhelmingly Catholic, and Eastern Christianity, with Serbs, Montenegrins, and Macedonians being primarily Orthodox Christians, these differences do not matter that much in terms of the issues that we are discussing in this book. What matters most is that the Christianity that dominates in Yugoslavia is not the more individualistic Protestantism, which took root in northern Germany, the Netherlands, and throughout Scandinavia. Both Catholicism and Orthodox Christianity tend to reinforce the acceptance of existing social hierarchies.[11] Beyond Christianity, Yugoslavia also had a significant Muslim population, especially in Bosnia and among the ethnic Albanians in Kosovo. A significant proportion of the Muslim population of Bosnia is composed of Slavs who converted to Islam after the invasion of the region by the Ottoman Empire in the fifteenth and sixteenth century.

One way to contrast the Yugoslav case with that of Turkey and Japan is to think, again, about the role that a dominant father figure played in the society following the period of mass violence. While the emperor in Japan was blamed by some for having led the country into a disastrous war and having waited too long to bring the war to a close, the emperor and the imperial institution have survived into the present, although with a much diminished stature. In contrast, Atatürk was a heroic and national messianic figure, who has obtained the status of an immortal in Turkish life.

In the Yugoslav case, by contrast, there was an attempt to build up a cult of personality around Tito, but he remained much more of a human figure, open to question and occasional critique and ridicule, although this was very muted during his life and something to be avoided in public. During the "black cinema" phase mentioned above, during the late 1960s and early 1970s, numerous critiques of Yugoslav society poured forth, including the first critical reflections on Goli Otok, which exposed Tito and the party to the critique that they, too, were Stalinists in their methods of rule. The weakness of the Tito cult is apparent in terms of how quickly it disappeared after his death in May 1980. Tito, while alive, certainly acted as a dam against a flood of grievances that were building up in the country. Given the outpouring of critical, creative work that appeared immediately after his death, the 1970s had been a time for fertile reflection on the problems of Yugoslav communism.

Djilas opened the decade with his critical biography, *Tito: The Story from Inside*, which was published immediately in 1980 in the West. A Serbo-Croatian version was published in Paris in 1982 and certainly found its way back into the country. There was also an outpouring of literature on the Goli Otok prison and labor camp. Djilas was aware of Antonije Isaković's novel prior to its publication in 1982, as he writes about it in his critical Tito biography, reflecting, "The subject is truly important in every respect. I cannot avoid it here, not only because of Tito's involvement, but also because of my own: Goli Otok has haunted me both intellectually and morally since my own break with the system, and my reevaluation of it."[12] We will return to the issue of Goli Otok and its discussion in Yugoslavia later in this chapter. At this point, it is important to simply note that certain things were expressed after Tito's death that were not discussed openly during his life.

## Chronological Discussion

One fundamental factor to keep in mind while thinking about Yugoslavia and the different national groupings that made up the country is that each of the constituent populations has a psychocultural narrative rooted in the fear that the national group had nearly been destroyed in the past and could face such destruction again in the future. At the core of each national group is a fundamental trauma narrative of outside domination and cultural, if not physical, genocide.

With the rising tide of national consciousness throughout the course of the nineteenth century and into the twentieth century, the constituent national groups began to take shape and with it the fear that complete cultural assimilation into one of the two great empires that occupied the region—the Austro-Hungarian Empire or the Ottoman Empire—might be their fate. Some Slovene and Croatian intellectuals feared the further assimilation into the Germanic culture of Vienna, while Serbs continued to hold on to their cultural traditions in opposition to the domination of the region by the Ottoman Turks. One reason that the Kingdom of Serbs, Croats, and Slovenes was first formed in 1918, with some popular support, was that it provided each of the Slavic peoples a chance to maintain and foster their own national cultures within the new kingdom after the collapse of the two great empires in the West and East. The kingdom changed its name simply to the Kingdom of Yugoslavia in 1929.

Although the kingdom officially carried the name of each of its constituent Christian nationalities at its formation, the kingdom was governed by the Serbian dynasty that had established the Serbian state through the Balkan Wars in 1912 and 1913 against the Ottomans. Debates about the heritage of the South Slavs have raged over the course of the nineteenth century and into the twentieth century. Whether these peoples should or did "naturally" form a nation remained a contested issue throughout the first part of the twentieth century and into the communist Yugoslavia of the post–World War II period. During the interwar period when the threat of external domination receded, debates revolved around to what extent the kingdom should work toward creating a new national culture to foster political unity. While one could find Croats and Slovenes who also supported the idea of some greater South Slav entity, both in terms of culture and politics, most of this discussion for greater unity came from the largest population, the Serbs. For Croatian and Slovene nationalists, the fear of disappearing under Serbian "hegemony" continued to resonate for some, while others embraced the unification of the language into Serbo-Croatian. For the Slovenes, cultural assimilation or unification was less of an issue as their language remained significantly different. No one disputed the religious, cultural, and linguistic differences that existed. The question always remained, what should the nation-building project look like?[13]

These disputes helped to define the battle lines that developed in the region after the invasion and destruction of the Kingdom of Yugoslavia by the German and Italian forces in April 1941. Some Croatian nationalists rushed to the new Ustasha regime, which then engaged in a genocidal campaign against the Serbs, Jews, and Roma within their zone of control. The Serbs split between the Chetniks, those who wanted to fight for the restoration of the monarchy, and what eventually became the partisans under Tito's command, with their commitment to a communist revolution. The mass violence that engulfed the region in the context of World War II left a huge burden for the new Yugoslav state.

The foundational narrative of the new postwar Yugoslavia was the success of the partisans during the War of National Liberation in which the partisans defeated the outside occupiers and the internal traitors. These narratives of a pan-Yugoslav movement were encouraged by the partisan leadership but also found a spontaneous echo in the general population. The stories and poetry about the partisan struggle, some of which were even published during the war, were very popular with the general population, as were the partisan films that immediately followed the war.[14]

Although the plot structures could vary quite a bit, there are some common features to the partisan novels. The focus is frequently on small, isolated bands of partisan fighters, almost always of a single national group, who fought, at great odds, against either the external invaders or the internal traitors. Women are given an equal standing as fighters, and many of the most attractive and positive partisan fighters are killed along the way, emphasizing the sense of loss.[15] While the narratives never fail to identify the national identity of the outside occupiers, there is an attempt to focus on the ideological motivation of the Ustasha and Chetnik fighters. The fact that the Ustasha are Croats and that the Chetniks are Serbs would have been well known to the readers, but there is an attempt to avoid an essentialist argument about the Ustasha *as* Croats or the Chetniks *as* Serbs. There is also an attempt to emphasize that the internal traitors had been equal in their brutality and killing. As we will see in a moment with our discussion of the Ustasha extermination camp at Jasenovac, this distinction became more difficult to maintain over time.

The attempt by the postwar partisan leadership to strike a tone of moderation and inclusion is quite striking, especially when contrasted with postwar Spain. It helped to create a positive foundational myth for rebuilding Yugoslavia after the war. More recent work by Scott Straus on cases of where genocide did and did not occur in Africa, points to the critical role that the leadership plays at the founding of the state in which the foundational narrative can be used to encourage cooperation across ethnic groups or set up the conditions for future violence.[16] Yugoslavia provides a depressing counterexample to Straus's results in that the Yugoslav partisan leadership worked to construct a positive, inclusive foundational narrative to transcend the wartime interethnic violence. Nonetheless, with the passage of time, the foundational narrative of Yugoslavia was rejected by Creon-like nationalist leaders and intellectuals for reasons that we will explore in the rest of this chapter. They set the Furies loose once again.

A deep story narrative for the South Slavs involves their persistent resistance against outside occupiers in both battle and attempts at religious conversion. We can see a great deal of this reflected in one of the most celebrated epic poems of the nineteenth century, Petar Petrović Njegoš's *Gorski vijenac* (*The Mountain Wreath*) (1846). It may be difficult for outsiders to appreciate the importance of this epic poetry for the local population, but folk poetry and its theme of resistance against outside invaders became a powerful motivating narrative in the context of World War II. The partisan leadership used the characters, narratives, and images of the folk poems to help mobilize the peasant population and to bring female fighters into the partisan ranks.[17] The epic poems were not mere instrumental tools for the partisan leadership but also sources of personal motivation; Djilas carried a copy of Njegoš's work with him during the war.[18]

Njegoš dedicated his epic poem to Karađorđe, who had led the Serbs in an uprising against Ottoman rule in 1804, thus striking the first blow toward the creation of an independent Serbian state. Set in eighteenth-century Montenegro, the Orthodox bishop Danilo, the central character in the story, is concerned not only with the threat of defeat in military battle against stronger external enemies but also the loss of his people through conversion to Islam after centuries of occupation. Who are these South Slav converts to Islam? As Andrew Baruch Wachtel observes, "In Danilo's mind, however, the desire to rid his land of converts to Islam is tempered by a recognition that although they may be traitors to the nation, these men and women are blood relations."[19] This narrative theme and tension about national identity as a process of acculturation, as through religious conversion, and blood relations, is one that would return again and again in postwar Yugoslavia as well. It is also central to Vuk Drašković's novel *Nož* (*Knife*) (1982), which we will return to later in this chapter.

If we apply the memory-market dictum to Yugoslavia, the country's cultural production in terms of novels, plays, and films increasingly became driven by market forces. In the first part of the 1950s, film producers were almost wholly dependent on state subsidies, but over time, the film industry became more commercialized, with filmmakers maintaining an eye on attracting large audiences, engaging in coproductions with foreign companies, taking out bank loans, and giving attention to the potential of the export market. After the early years of the regime, there was no fixed model of state subsidies that authors and producers could count on.[20] They needed to make a profit with their work to survive. At the same time, state censorship could and would be applied if the work was seen as a threat to the government. But this censorship was never centralized in the federal government. It was up to the individual republics to monitor their own standards of what would be allowed, and this varied from one republic to the next. Therefore, the cultural production in Yugoslavia does tell us something important about popular tastes and tolerance for different narratives about the past, although with the sharp edges trimmed from time to time by the state. Therefore, an analysis of film production and the popularity of partisan, wartime narratives can tell us something about popular tastes as well as the limits of what the state would tolerate at any given time.

Wachtel's observation that partisan novels were indeed very popular in the immediate postwar years is further supported by the fact that partisan films were also very popular in the early years. Between 1945 and 1989, Yugoslav filmmakers made 863 films, with around 200 of those films dealing with the war and the partisan movement in some way.[21] Between 1947 and 1982, about 180 films qualified as war films, or about 20 percent of the total output for those years.[22] But between 1945 and 1955, the percentage of war films was even higher. During this first decade, when the number of films being produced on an annual basis was lower than would be the case in the 1960s, there were fifty-six films made, of which twenty-one were war films, or 37.5 percent of the total.[23] In these early films, seventeen of the main characters were peasants, while only four were workers, reflecting the reality of a largely rural and peasant country.[24] It also meant that the viewers could see themselves and their experiences reflected in the films.

The lower number of films created during the first decade reflected the early orientation in postwar Yugoslavia toward centralization, strict party control, and bureaucratic oversight. For example, in the first five years after the war, there were only thirteen films made, almost all of which dealt with the war or socialist reconstruction. After Tito's break with Stalin in 1948, the country began to move away from centralization and more toward a federal model, with the party remaining as the central, unifying force but one that was organized on a republican basis. The movement toward self-management in nearly all areas of the economy in 1950 affected the film industry as well, and in 1952 the party made it clear that the cultural sphere should be allowed to develop in a largely independent manner.[25] Another component of this was that film critics in newspapers and other publications were given more freedom to express their evaluation of films in terms of their content and quality.[26] This is far from a trivial development because permitting and accepting criticism becomes an important part of furthering the development of any cultural, social, or political project. Domestic film production climbed to around thirty films per year during the 1960s, but then fell to around eighteen films per year in the 1970s, due to the increasing popularity and availability of television programming.[27]

The process of decentralization in the cultural sphere had its first impact on literature and the fine arts and then later film,[28] again offering a confirmation of the memory-market dictum, that forms of expression that have a lower capital intensity will be the first areas to express more critical voices. We can see this, for example, in Dobrica Ćosić's book, *Daleko je sunce* (*Far Away Is the Sun*) (1950), which marked a clear transition away from the heroic romanticism of the early partisan novels, plays, and films toward a darker, self-critical evaluation of the war years. After first appearing as a novel in 1950, Radoš Novaković made a very successful film adaptation in 1953, but only after the liberalization had proceeded further. Challenges to the mainstream always arrive from the margins, so it is not surprising that a wholly positive view of the partisan struggle was first challenged in the form of a novel, even if it came from an insider. Ćosić's stature among the former partisans gave him the standing to raise some less comfortable truths about the partisan war and current issues in postwar Yugoslavia. For example, Djilas reported on learning more about Goli Otok from Ćosić. "In September 1953, I spent some time at the resort of Niška Banja with the writers Dobrica Ćosić and Oskar Davičo. We talked about the new, liberal trends that resistance to Stalin and the Soviet bloc had unleashed in our Communism. I heard that Ćosić, out of curiosity, had visited Goli Otok. He told me that the security service, the UDBA, had devised and applied corrective methods that were possibly the most diabolical in history."[29]

Before I say more about Ćosić's *Far Away Is the Sun*, it will be useful to situate the book and the film in a broader series of changes that would take place in the war narrative genre. Andrew Horton has suggested the following periodization and categorization of Yugoslav war films, based on a two-volume study of Yugoslav war films by Milutin Čolić, with a clear temporal progression: (1) heroic romanticism, (2) deromanticism, (3) antiheroic negativism, and (4) spectacle, action films. The heroic romanticist phase began with the end of the war and with the early partisan film *Slavica* (1947) by Vjekoslav Afić, which helped to establish the ideal of the female partisan fighter, the *partizanka*.[30] Slavica is the name of the leading *partizanka* in the film, who joins the partisans in Dalmatia and fights against the Italian and German occupying forces, only to be killed toward the end of the war. During this earliest phase, the film industry was trapped in the Yugoslav adaptation of Stalinist centralization and the explicit politicization of culture. *Slavica* was a hugely successful film that attracted nearly two million viewers from all parts of Yugoslavia.[31] Ćosić's work, *Far Away Is the Sun*, marked the transition to the deromanticist phase in which the partisan war was shown as also filled with cruelty and a lack of idealism.[32]

The next phase of antiheroic negativism began to take hold more in the context of the mid-1960s with Aleksandar Petrović's 1965 film *Tri* (*Three*), which was based on the stories of Isaković. Isaković worked with Petrović on creating the screenplay for the film. As we will see later, Isaković also made a significant contribution to the Goli Otok literature, which began to appear after Tito's death in 1980. Isaković's writings also served as a basis for Stole Janković's film, *Partizanske priče* (*Partisan Stories*) (1960), which also was praised for its portrayal of the war as tragedy. Janković was a former Serb partisan fighter who became an important part of the political establishment. As with Aeschylus, Janković was a veteran who knew the nature of war. While he did not glorify the war, he also recognized the necessity of defending his country against a brutal outside invasion and occupation. In *Three*, Petrović and Isaković go further in showing war as filled with tragedy, disillusionment, and cruelty. The film is divided into three segments, showing the invasion of the country by German forces in 1941, followed by the partisan resistance, and then the mass execution of collaborators at the end of the war. With the exploration of the topic of mass summary executions, the film opened up a new self-critical reflection on the costs of the war and leaves open the question as to whether or not such actions were justified. The film gained critical success both inside Yugoslavia and outside the country when it was one of five finalists for an Academy Award in 1967 for the best foreign language film category. As we will see, the regime later turned against the "black wave" in the arts because of its self-critical perspective, and Petrović lost his position at the Belgrade film academy in 1973.[33]

The final category of war as spectacle and action is one that stretches across the entire history of the war film genre in Yugoslavia but is probably best represented by two films from Veljko Bulajić, *Vlak bez voznog reda* (*Train without a Timetable*) (1959) and *Bitka na Neretvi* (*Battle of the River Neretva*) (1969). These films became more common in later years. While there is not a strict linear decline in the partisan mythology, the general trend is away from heroic romanticism, to deromanticism, toward antiheroic negativism. Jelena Batinić has found a similar pattern in terms of how the *partizanka* were portrayed in the postwar years, with a movement from a heroic revolutionary icon between 1945 and 1962, toward more of a romantic and sexual object, and finally simply obscurity after 1987.[34] With the passage of time, the foundational mythology of the all-Yugoslav partisan movement fragmented into nationalistic-specific narratives of victimization at the hands of the partisans, the communists, or the other ethnic and religious groups, especially in the context of the 1980s.

Ćosić's *Far Away Is the Sun* tells the story of conflict among the partisan fighters about the goals of the war and the means to achieve them. The conflict is thus as much internal to the movement as it is against the German occupiers and their Chetnik collaborators. Comrade Paul represents the interests of the all-Yugoslav partisan movement with his universalistic outlook. He is set in contrast to the very brave peasant partisan Gvozden, who is more particularistic and local in his perspective. The question becomes whether or not this group of partisans should stay where they are and defend their own homes and families, the position supported by Gvozden's character, or whether they should seek to link up with the other all-partisan Yugoslav forces. The conflict between Paul and Gvozden is resolved when Gvozden is put on trial for treason and is executed.[35]

Vojislav Nanović was another former partisan who made his way into the filmmaking industry in the postwar years. He had considerable success with his autobiographical film *Besmrtna mladost* (*Immortal Youth*) in 1948, which attracted close to three-quarter of a million viewers in just six months.[36] In his 1955 film *Šolaja*, he focused on a local partisan hero from western Bosnia who rose up with other peasants against the Ustasha genocide and the Italian occupiers.[37] Not only did the film deal with the Ustasha genocide against the Serbs, Jews, and Roma but also the Serbian civil war between the partisans and the Chetniks.

What is striking about the development of the Yugoslav partisan war films is that they became a cultural model within which to explore important questions about the postwar society and the building of socialism in the country. Although the genre could generate pure entertainment, spectacle, and escapism, it also set different forces and themes in opposition to each other that the audience was left to wrestle with, not unlike the samurai films in Japan or the western in the United States. Whereas the partisan genre within the Soviet Union and other East European countries became stultified, the Yugoslav partisan film genre showed quite a wide variation in terms of the themes covered and the self-critical stance that was developed, especially in the antiheroic negativist phase. Unlike in the defeated countries of Germany and Japan in which it became extremely problematic, although not impossible, especially in the case of Japan, to create heroic war narratives, it is quite striking to find Yugoslav novelists and filmmakers raising questions about the costs of the war. While the justification of fighting the War of National Liberation is never questioned, the characters that survive are deeply marked by their experiences.

What does become questioned, eventually, is whether or not the outcome of the war has led to a just society. Have the promises of the revolution been upheld by the communist leadership? Or was there a betrayal of the cause? If one found a betrayal of the revolution, with its universalistic commitments, this then could lead to the search for new universalistic principles and rights that could be upheld, either within the revolution, through reform, or by recognizing the inherent authoritarianism in the communist movement, which was Djilas's argument. But there was also another possible answer to the question of betrayal, and that could take on more nationalistic and particularistic tone. This is where Ćosić and other intellectuals moved over the course of Yugoslavia's postwar development. Once they felt that the all-Yugoslav partisan struggle had been betrayed by growing nationalism, they too defected and took an increasingly nationalistic posture.

The partisan foundational narrative and the slogan of "Brotherhood and Unity" faced a number of challenges in the postwar years. First, there were the deep divisions that had existed in the different national communities during the war, which had led to a civil war alongside a war against the outside occupiers. This meant that many former collaborators remained in the country, living alongside those they had fought against.

Second, there was the attempt through the partisan mythology to assign equal blame to both Ustasha Croat and Chetnik Serb collaborators for atrocities committed during the war. If this had been accepted by everyone, it may have led to some form of reconciliation along the lines of everyone having behaved badly in equal measure. The main challenge to this narrative was the Ustasha genocide against Serbs, Jews, and Roma, as symbolized by the extermination camp of Jasenovac. Talking about the Ustasha genocide risked upsetting this balance and generating antagonism between Serbs and Croats; not talking about the Ustasha genocide risked leaving victims and survivors suffering in silence.

The third challenge was the treatment of those deemed to be supporters of Stalin after the Tito-Stalin split of 1948 at the prison camp of Goli Otok. Some would later try to justify Goli Otok as a tragic historical necessity by arguing that without the vigorous suppression of Stalin's supporters in Yugoslavia, the country would have fallen to Stalinists and a new round of Stalinist terror. Djilas took this position in 1980, writing, "In retrospect, and with all the self-criticism of which I am able, I must admit that we could not have avoided a concentration camp for the Cominformists. . . . The ascent to power of those forces [the Cominformists]—and there could have been no doubt in anyone's mind about that—would have meant not only the removal of our present leadership and bloody purges within the Party, but also the subjugation of Yugoslavia to the Soviet Union."[38] For others like Isaković, who would publish his novel about Goli Otok in 1982, too many innocent or marginal people were swept up, as witch-hunts led to the settling of other scores between competing factions within the party. As Isaković said in 1982, "We were fighting Stalinism with Stalinist methods when the real weapons against Stalinism are greater freedom and greater democracy."[39]

One of the benefits of a democratic society, as we have seen with the cases of Germany and Japan, is that forces in the civil society are able to organize and generate narratives about their grievances vis-à-vis the past. There are ways for their voices to be heard in the broader public, through the writing of novels, the production of theater plays, the screening of films in cinemas, and the opening of museum exhibits. They can also lobby the government for recognition of these past crimes. This does not mean that these challenges will be accepted by the broader society or the state, or that future violence can be avoided, but a democratic society and state provide more channels for the expression and the negotiation of these disagreements. Turkey's troubled path to democratization clearly demonstrates the costs of not addressing these past grievances and their continued suppression in the present. Spain offers a more hopeful example of how a democratic transition can eventually lead to a fuller discussion of the past along with the deepening of democracy.

Yugoslavia, in contrast, offers a warning that a failure to address such grievances can lead to a deepening sense of victimization, which can in turn lead to ever more particularistic and nationalistic narratives. As with Antigone's speculation about her own "madness" given her grief for her unburied brother, a sense that the issues of past violence remain unresolved can threaten to reemerge in the future. What makes the Yugoslav story particularly tragic is that the opening of the country in the 1960s began to allow forces in the civil society to articulate their grievances about the past as well as their dissatisfaction with the development of socialism in the country. If the regime had risked allowing these developments to continue, there was a chance that the society could have renewed itself and found solutions to its problems by allowing for contentious politics and an opening toward democratization.[40] However, the regime closed this pathway.

The greater openness of the 1960s led to a number of critical reevaluations of the past as well as the present. Two difficult topics for discussion related to the past were the Ustasha genocide against the Serbs and the Yugoslav Communist Party's repression of Cominform members at the Goli Otok prison camp. As we have seen above, the Ustasha genocide against Serbs and Jews was being directly addressed in films as a justification for the partisan movement, but in some ways these films, although stark in their portrayal of the violence, tended to avoid the scale of the killing and especially the extermination camp of Jasenovac. In this manner, the Yugoslav films that touched on the Ustasha-led genocide tended to deal with the material in a manner similar to the early West German films that did address the persecution of the Jews but failed to express the scale of the killing that occurred. As long as the Ustasha violence was limited to "normal" repression, combat, and collaboration with the Germans, they could be placed on par with the actions of the Chetniks. But there was no moral counterweight to Jasenovac or the nature of the Ustasha violence, which went beyond "rational" wartime killing to wholesale massacres of Serbian civilians. The Ustasha embraced the racial ideology of the German fascist movement, sometimes with such enthusiasm and brutality that it even gave the German commanders in Yugoslavia pause. The communist partisan leadership realized that it was going to be difficult to deal with this genocidal program and its core symbol of Jasenovac, and they tried to avoid the subject.

The same was true for Goli Otok, which became something that the communist leadership preferred to suppress when it began to appear in public discussions in the late 1960s. The difference between Jasenovac, as a condensation symbol for the Ustasha genocide, and Goli Otok, for illegitimate Yugoslav communist repression, is that the Croatian republic would eventually build a memorial at Jasenovac in response to public pressure from camp survivors and their families. In contrast, Goli Otok remained a taboo subject until after Tito's death in 1980, when discussion of the prison camp and what it meant for the legitimacy of the Yugoslav state exploded onto the scene. The 1980s also witnessed an eruption of long-suppressed discussions about the Ustasha genocide and the interethnic massacres that had marked fighting in the country during World War II. The "brotherhood and unity" mythology had always tried to mask the interethnic killing as driven by ideology, but this was not primarily how many of those who experienced the violence remembered it. Both topics began to be raised in the context of the greater openness experienced in the 1960s.

This leads to some interesting what-if questions about how Yugoslavia might have developed.[41] Counterfactual argumentation and reasoning is not merely a fanciful academic exercise but rather a useful way of thinking through what factors may have led to a different outcome. When decisions of individuals play a critical and pivotal role in the unfolding of history, it is certainly reasonable to think about how things may have unfolded if they were no longer living or in a position of power. The life course and survival of any given individual is a rather haphazard affair. If, on the other hand, there are larger systemic forces at work, which are far beyond the control of a single individual or group, then it becomes more difficult to imagine a different course of events.

Djilas, someone who was very much aware of both the systemic nature of communist power as well as the personalities within those systems, engaged in exactly this type of counterfactual thinking in his book on Tito. As a result of the weakening of the revolutionary policy system after 1966, "Democratic trends soon began to make themselves felt within the Party—nationalistic in Croatia, liberal in Serbia, technocratic in Slovenia. . . . This most liberal period of Tito's rule was marked by diminished personal and doctrinal aggression."[42] Djilas continues, "In the late sixties, Yugoslavia had another chance, the most promising if also uncertain, at democratization with the rise of national Communism in Croatia . . . and the democratic movement in the Party's leadership in Serbia."[43] He also saw what he called "Democratic nationalistic" trends in Slovenia and Macedonia.[44] There were movements both within a nascent Yugoslav civil society, which was beginning to look at its past and present in a more critical light, and there was movement within the different national, communist, republican parties, toward critical discussions, contentious politics, and the possibility of democratization. Yugoslav intellectuals, writers, filmmakers, theater producers, and journalists all demonstrated the *potential* for real creative energies and critical discussions, which are essential to democratic transformations. The systemic features were showing promising developments, but Djilas is clear in assigning the blame for shutting down this opening to Tito: "he was a major and irreparable failure within the broader scope of what is democratic and what is humane."[45] Tito used his direct authority over the army and the soon-reconstituted secret police to purge party members who showed any initiative in self-critical reflection.

Does Djilas exaggerate the role of Tito here over the systemic factors? I would suggest he does not, given what happened after Tito's death in 1980. Immediately after his death, critical intellectual and artistic works that were blocked from production at the end of the 1960s began to appear after a lost decade, as we will see in our discussion of Goli Otok and Jasenovac in both the 1960s and the 1980s in the next two sections. But by the 1980s, the broader economic conditions had grown far worse, and the situation was ripe for a new round of nationalistic recriminations by opportunistic leaders. This is not to argue that events would have unfolded in an unproblematic manner in the 1960s, but it was, as Djilas argues, a second chance for moving in a more democratic direction—one that was not taken.

### *Jasenovac and Goli Otok in the 1960s*

Heike Karge has provided us some rich insights into the nature of the memorial culture in Yugoslavia at the end of the 1950s and the beginning of the 1960s through her research into the veterans' organizations. The veterans of the People's Liberation War were concerned that the positive legacy of the war was being lost in the postwar years, and they set out to investigate how the war was being remembered around the country. While they hoped to find echoes of the "brotherhood and unity" theme and the universalist aspects of the struggle as a Yugoslav struggle that transcended national differences, they actually found very little of this. For example, most of the memorial objects in Croatia and Serbia focused on local fighters or the victims of the fascist terror.[46] Religious and local traditions dominated the memorials,[47] although this was not the case in Slovenia, where the process of building memorials had been centralized by the republic beginning in

1950.[48] The contrast of Slovenia with the rest of the country is instructive, because it shows that absent the hand of a centralized state, the people naturally gravitated toward a local understanding of the war and its consequences.

Another very important contrast between the republics was that the memorials in Serbia tended to combine remembrance of the Balkan Wars of 1912 and 1913, along with World War I and World War II.[49] In contrast, there were almost no memorials to World War I in either Slovenia or Croatia.[50] The combining of these multiple wars in the Serbian culture of remembrance is critical because it shows that all of these events are clearly linked in the Serbian appreciation of the past and that Serbs, from their perspective, had constantly been at war to initially create the first independent South Slav state in Serbia, and to also fight for the liberation of the other South Slavs from Ottoman and Austro-Hungarian domination. The Serbian sense of a massive national sacrifice that was not appreciated by the other South Slav nationalities would explode in the context of the crisis over Kosovo in the 1980s.

There was little that connected these memorials to the idea of brotherhood or a broader Yugoslav unified partisan struggle. In further studies of the mass media, memorial buildings, school books, demonstrations, museums, and films, the veterans' organization found the same deficits.[51] They were specifically concerned that the Croatian school system lacked a book on the People's Liberation War, with the first high school book about World War II only appearing in 1972, after the Croatian nationalist uprising had been crushed in 1971.

Karge's study of the memorial culture of Yugoslavia through the work of the veterans' organizations helps us to appreciate that what was happening at the local level was perhaps something very different from what was happening at the more national or federal level, where the party was clearly in control and fully capable of mobilizing the masses for public demonstrations of brotherhood and unity. But where was the memorial for the Jasenovac extermination camp, which one would have assumed could serve as clear evidence of the importance of brotherhood and unity and justification for the partisan struggle? Karge aptly notes, "Given the fact that thousands of monuments were built in the country elsewhere at this time the official disregard towards commemorating the victims of the former Jasenovac Concentration Camp during the 1950s demands an explanation."[52] It was not that the facts about the camp were so much in dispute, taboo, or hidden. The postwar Croatian State Commission estimated that between 500,000 and 600,000 people were murdered at the Jasenovac camp, or approximately one-third of all the wartime deaths in the country, which was estimated at 1.7 million.[53] And as we have seen with the discussion of the films, the nature of the Ustasha regime was not in dispute or something that was avoided in the popular culture. Yet, there was no memorial at the camp. Karge argues that this was because there was no symbolic counterweight to Jasenovac; there had been no Serbian equivalent of genocide against another ethnic group.[54]

The solution to the interethnic wartime violence had always been to try and keep the nationalities submerged when talking about the war atrocities and to balance the Ustasha with the Chetniks. Once the party did decide to place a memorial at Jasenovac, they tried to obscure the identity of the perpetrators. The solution, as Karge demonstrates through her study of the veterans' organizations, was the following: "In order to reduce Croatian responsibility for the cruelties committed there, the perpetrators were overwhelmingly given the labels of 'aggressor,' 'occupying force' and 'degenerate individuals' or even the completely abstract term, 'enemy.'"[55] The memorial probably would never have come into existence except for the survivor organizations and their families, which began to mobilize for some recognition of their suffering. Survivors and their relatives began to hold commemorative events at the former location of the camp, which lacked any surviving structures, on two separate dates, July 4, which was a national holiday marking the beginning of the partisan uprising, and the end of April, which marked an uprising among the camp inmates in 1945. We do not know when these commemorative activities began, but Karge has found evidence that a group of approximately seven hundred people had gathered at the site in 1956 and that this had grown to about ten thousand people by 1963 for the July 4 ceremony.[56] Karge has also found letters dating back to the beginning of the 1950s that were addressed to the War Veterans Union in which the writer was upset that there was no official recognition of the Jasenovac camp.[57]

Eventually, the political elites relented, although as noted above, the language they chose was extremely circumspect. The first official memorial ceremony took place on July 4, 1965, and the official memorial and museum were opened in 1966. Whereas the entire federation paid for the massive memorial project at the Sutjeska battle site, the Croatian Republic alone paid for the building of the Jasenovac memorial, and Tito never attended any of the memorial ceremonies.[58] In 1966, Bogdan Bogdanović's concrete flower memorial was unveiled. Bogdanović was Yugoslavia's best-known sculptor at the time, and he also designed many of the other partisan monuments. A Yugoslav publication from 1968, in English, titled *Yugoslavia Monuments to the Revolution*, gave the Jasenovac monument a prominent place alongside the Mostar partisan necropolis and the Sutjeska monument. The entry for Jasenovac reads: "Genocyde [*sic*] of monstrous proportions took place in the concentration camp Jasenovac. In the part of occupied Yugoslavia where the Italian and German invaders installed the quisling Ustashi government, headed by Ante Pavelić, and established the puppet Independent State of Croatia, the Jasenovac camp was set up in the summer of 1941, modelled on Nazi concentration camps."[59]

The monument was established, but its carefully crafted narrative could not contain the diversity and emotionally raw experiences that many continued to carry with them. The oral history of the genocide probably did not conform to the official narrative. When individuals tried to express their grief and rage outside the official narrative, they could quickly be repressed. But given that the cultural realm remained relatively more open, especially toward the end of the 1960s, some did make this attempt. For example, Vojislav Lubarda published an excerpt from his then unpublished novel *Gordo posrtanje* (*Proud Stumbling*) in Sarajevo in 1969 in which he graphically described the massacre of Bosnian Serbs at the hands of a Muslim Ustasha group, which included witnessing his own father being led away for execution. Lubarda also described the Serbian partisan reprisal attacks and even went on to name the prominent Muslims who had participated in the initial massacre. The Muslim perpetrators were at the time in public positions in Bosnia.[60] Having angered everyone with his publication, Lubarda faced years of persecution, the loss of his job, the inability to publish anything for ten years, and threats of imprisonment. All of this came to light when he published *Anatema* (*Anathema*) in 1982. We will return later to his story and those of others that were published at the beginning of the 1980s. What is important to realize at this point is that there were others like Lubarda who carried around deep psychological wounds from the war and that he was not able to express these in public—or to challenge the legitimacy of former perpetrators, who now held political positions in Bosnia. One can easily see how the Jasenovac memorial failed to address people like Lubarda. The fact that war criminals were serving in official capacities in Bosnia must have been particularly difficult to bear.

While limited public discussion of Jasenovac and the Ustasha genocide had begun earlier in the mid-1950s and continued into the 1960s, the topic of Goli Otok only appeared in public toward the end of the latter decade. As with the push for the Jasenovac memorial, the drive for more memory in terms of Goli Otok and what it represented, the criminal founding of the Yugoslav communist regime if not its continued criminality, came from the civil society and novelists who were finally able to tell their story—for a limited time. Two novels appeared in 1968 that threatened the Communist Party establishment and began to create a strong backlash against the "black wave" that had swept across the arts scene: (1) Slobodan Selenić's *Memoari Pere Bogalja* (*Memoirs of Pera the Cripple*), and (2) Dragoslav Mihailović's *Kad su cvetale tikve* (*When Pumpkins Blossomed*). The Serbian literary critic Sveta Lukić, writing at the time, identified a definite shift in the willingness of the authorities to intervene in the cultural sphere in a repressive manner beginning in summer 1968, around the time of the student demonstrations at the University of Belgrade.[61] Selenić's novel offered a critique of the nice living that former peasant partisans were enjoying in the old homes of the former Belgrade upper classes. In this manner, he created a dramatic portrayal of the "new class," which Djilas had written about in the late 1950s. Selenić also touched on the twisting of historical truths about the nature of the partisan struggle and the persecution of the Cominformists, beginning in 1948. The book went on to win a literary prize in Belgrade, and Selenić's next novel was going to be an even more direct confrontation with Goli Otok; however, this second novel was removed from publication and destroyed in 1970. Selenić managed to save one copy of the manuscript, and it served as the basis for his novel *Pismo/Glava* (*Heads/Tails*), which was published in 1982.[62] *Pismo/Glava* became part of the Goli Otok literature that burst onto the scene after Tito's death in 1980.

Selenić may have been at first encouraged and then discouraged with what had happened to Mihailović during the same time. The year 1968 appeared to offer new possibilities in terms of how the regime could be confronted and challenged, but by 1970 there was a definitive turn by the regime against the "black wave" negativism. Mihailović's *When Pumpkins Blossomed* also appeared in 1968 and was again an immediate popular and critical success. The book even received a quick English translation and appeared in 1971. His novel drew on his own life experiences as he was imprisoned at Goli Otok for fifteen months when he was in his twenties. After his release from a horrifying period of captivity, he faced years of unemployment and ostracism. The novel tells the story Ljuba Šampion, whose family is destroyed after his brother and father are imprisoned at Goli Otok. His father returns a broken man, and the fate of his brother remains unknown. Ljuba tries to find out more information about his brother from state officials, but he is blocked and warned not to ask any more questions. In addition to dealing with Goli Otok, the book portrays the gang violence of Belgrade's poorer neighborhoods, painting a less-than-ideal picture of present-day socialism. The past and the present are both set in a very negative light. Based on the success of the novel, Boro Drašković, one of the best-known directors at the time, made preparations almost immediately to turn the novel into a play. Just before the play was to open in 1969 at the Yugoslav Drama Theater in Belgrade, the theater withdrew the production, with a couple of sources stating that Tito himself had intervened.[63] If Djilas is correct in assigning direct personal blame to Tito for the construction of Goli Otok, we can see why Tito was as concerned as he was. As a result of the play being banned, Drašković withdrew from involvement with the theater.[64]

The banning of theater productions was not an uncommon practice, and it clearly led to patterns of self-censorship because of political concerns rather than concerns about box office success and marketability. But the bans tended to be regional and haphazard. Aleksandar Popović became one of the most prolific playwrights in Yugoslavia but one who was also burdened with his own experiences of imprisonment in Goli Otok, perhaps between 1950 and 1955, after he published a paper, "Crveno jeste" ("Red Truth").[65] Popović had seven of his forty plays banned and was put under near constant pressure by state authorities through surveillance and questioning by the police. His experiences at Goli Otok and subsequent treatment clearly dimmed his view of the Communist Party in Yugoslavia, although he remained a committed leftist. He was an anti-Titoist.[66] In his 1967 play *Razvojni put Bore Šnajdera* (*The Development of Bora Šnajder*), he created a farce that criticized the economic mismanagement of the country by inexperienced and unqualified managers but also the political forces that allowed these people to take their positions. The play premiered at the Atelje 212 theater in Belgrade and was pulled by the theater after three performances, apparently after some political pressure.[67] The exact reasons for such actions are rarely known, but Alexandra Jovićević suggests that one of the characters wore a hairstyle that was too close to Jovanka's, Tito's wife. But the play had immediately struck a chord with the audience, and it went on to win the best play award at the 12th Yugoslav Theater Festival in Novi Sad in 1968. When Petar Marjanović assembled an anthology of Yugoslav playwrights with English translations of their works in 1984, he chose to include a play by Popović, and this play in particular.[68] Popović's personal connection to Goli Otok and his critical stance toward the regime help to remind us of the resistance and countermemories that existed in the society because of what had happened in the past.

While the Communist Party was willing to tolerate for several years the development of the "black wave" in the arts, it was not willing to accept the growing national awakening that was taking place, primarily in Croatia. Croatian intellectuals and party members started to come together in the late 1960s. While there were Croats who were dedicated to a more unitary vision of the country and sought to bridge the cultural and linguistic divisions between Serbs and Croats, Croatian nationalists had long been suspicious of the "Yugoslav project" as an attempt at Serbian hegemonic governance in both politics and culture. Discussion of "Yugoslav" projects, culture, or identity was viewed by some Slovenes and Croats as a code for Serbian domination. The roots of these tensions go back to the formation of the first Yugoslav kingdom after World War I.

By 1969, the idea that Croatia was "an exploited nation" had gained a strong following among the intellectual class as well as members of the Croatian political class.[69] Concerns were growing that the development of the Serbo-Croatian language was being used as a tool to destroy the ethnic identity of Croats. There was also a backlash against the Jasenovac memorial, which was perceived by some as an attempt to burden the Croatian nation with the legacy of genocide and thus to make them the perpetrators and the Serbs the victims, therefore justifying Serbian domination inside the Yugoslav state. Croatian historians actively began to try and remove the perceived stigma of the genocide from Croatian nationalism in the context of the 1960s.[70]

At some point during 1971, Tito decided that the threat of "Croatian separatism" had gone too far, and in December of that year, there was a large-scale suppression of what some called the Croatian Spring. Intellectuals were put under pressure to calm nationalist language, and Croatian party officials, who had let things not only get out of hand but had encouraged their development, were purged. The repressive actions of the state were not limited to Croatia. There had been nationalistic-themed ethnic Albanian demonstrations in Kosovo going back to 1968. The Communist Party also brought the intellectual challenges to state and party authority that had become more common in Serbia and Belgrade to an end. There was widespread repression throughout Serbia into 1972 against "black wave" intellectuals, the leaders of the student demonstrations from 1968, the Praxist philosophers, and nonconformist writers such as Dobrica Ćosić. Ćosić had become increasingly nationalistic in his outlook over the course of the 1960s in reaction against what he saw as the nationalistic separatism inherent among Slovene and Croatian writers.[71] As Jasna Dragović-Soso makes clear in her wonderful intellectual history of Serbian nationalists, the long-term consequences of this period of repression was that many gave up hope of changing the system from within, and this resulted in a new class of "extra-systemic" dissidents.[72] The nationalists in each of their camps began to react more and more negatively vis-à-vis the others. The new 1974 constitution gave the republics more powers, which many Serbs bitterly saw as rewarding the Croatian nationalists after a period of repression. Furthermore, and of greater concern for a growing group of Serbian nationalists such as Ćosić, Serbia was broken apart, with greater autonomy given to the regions of Vojvodina in the north and Kosovo in the south. Although the national competition between Serbs and ethnic Albanians in Kosovo had been a problem since the formation of the first Yugoslav kingdom, these tensions accelerated in the 1960s. For many Serbs, the 1974 constitution was seen as an abandonment of their copatriots to the ethnic Albanians, who gained more control over the autonomous region. While Yugoslavia had been a solution to Serbian national aspirations, the growing trend toward fragmentation and the fact that 40 percent of the Serbian population now lived outside of the Serbian republic led to a growing sense that the Yugoslav state had betrayed the Serbian sacrifice in the Balkan Wars of 1912 and 1913 as well as World War I and World War II. As we have seen in Karge's research, Serbs tended to combine these wars into a single narrative in their memorials.

In terms of how Yugoslav society dealt with the legacy of these earlier periods of mass violence, and especially World War II, 1974 to 1980 was not a time without artistic interventions into this debate, but it was nothing in comparison to what was to explode after Tito's death in May 1980. For example, Mihailović had *Petrijin venac* (*Petrija's Wreath*) published in 1975, which served as the basis for a film of the same name directed by Srđan Karanović in 1980. But it was clear that the film industry was suffering as a result of the new repression of the cultural sphere, with a dramatic drop-off in terms of film productions.[73] This was probably a consequence of several factors: (1) greater political uncertainty about what was acceptable, (2) the market pressures of a growing television entertainment market, and (3) the increased difficulty of maintaining cooperation across the different republics, thus creating problems with coproduction and funding.

But there was no question that the legacy of the past continued to have a strong pull on the country and the film-going audiences. The Croatian film director Lordan Zafranović began a film trilogy in 1978 with *Okupacija u 26 slika* (*Occupation in 26 Pictures*) along with the Serbian writer Mirko Kovač. The other two films were *Pad Italije* (*The Fall of Italy*) (1981) and *Večernja zvona* (*Evening Bells*) (1986). *Occupation in 26 Pictures* was a huge commercial success, attracting more than six million viewers, which was six times the usual box office draw for domestic productions at the time. The film offered a strong warning about the consequences of extreme nationalist passions and the violence that this had previously resulted in. The film gives an extremely graphic portrayal of the Ustasha violence. The domestic perpetrators are shown in a far worse light than the foreign occupiers. The most violent scene in the film, perpetrated by the Ustasha, is directed against a group of people, representing all the different segments of Yugoslav society, including the main Jewish character and his family. They have been loaded into a bus and are being driven out into the countryside when the Ustasha members attack them in the most brutal, primitive, and barbaric manner. The main Jewish character is able to escape out the back of the bus and joins the partisans. The extreme brutality and sadism of the Ustasha violence continues to haunt the region and its popular culture today, as in Miljenko Jergović's novel *The Walnut Mansion*, with a horrific scene of Ustasha violence against a group of Gypsy musicians.[74] Similar war atrocities within the local village and Jasenovac also continue to haunt the main characters in one of Vuk Drašković's new novels set in the early 1990s, *The Memoirs of Jesus*.[75]

Mihailović's novel *Petrijin venac* was turned into a very successful film by Srđan Karanović in 1980. The story focuses on the life of Petrija, an illiterate peasant woman, and her life before, during, and after World War II. In this case, we see the struggle of a single, vulnerable individual against the harsh realities of rural poverty and the war, which in different ways contribute to the death of two of her children. She is turned out of the house by her husband with almost no resources and manages to find work in a local tavern run by an elderly man. He shows her the first human kindness that she has experienced in years. But with the end of the war and the rise of the new communist regime, he is denounced as a capitalist and his tavern is destroyed. In this manner, Mihailović returns to a self-critical view of the founding of the Yugoslav state and the lawlessness that followed the end of the war.

These two works are just a sample to remind us that the investigation of Yugoslav's history by its novelists, playwrights, and filmmakers had not ended with the more repressive period following the end of the Croatian "great awakening" in 1971. What became clear was that there was a pent-up frustration with the repression in itself, as well as a desire to discuss matters related to the country's history that had been marginalized or repressed in the past. After Tito's death in May 1980, the cultural landscape changed significantly, and frustrations with the current economic and political context blended with unresolved anger about the violence that had occurred during World War II as well as the state repression that had followed, most clearly symbolized in the Goli Otok prison camp.

As we have already seen, Goli Otok and the repressive nature of the Yugoslav state had already become a topic as part of the "black wave" in the late 1960s. This discussion about the past repression and how it related to the current society was cut short by state authorities. This demonstrated a clear capacity on the part of Yugoslav society to generate self-critical discussions about the past, but a capacity that was frustrated and blocked by an authoritarian state, which had no interest in encouraging an examination of its own past harsh measures and crimes. While the discussion of Goli Otok was completely blocked by state repression, the discussion around wartime atrocities continued during the course of the 1970s, as demonstrated by Zafranović's film *Occupation in 26 Pictures*. Clearly, this remained a traumatic event, which many in the society felt needed further discussion but the resolution of which was far from clear.

It is important to see these two discussions in relationship to each other. Clearly, there remained in the society a deep need to talk about the horrific violence that individuals had witnessed during the war. But where was this discussion going to lead? Based on what had happened in the past, what was one to do in the present? The fear on the part of the Yugoslav political elite had always been that such discussions, if not bounded by the "all were equally bad" argument, could lead to antagonizing nationalist sentiments in the country. For the political elite, the answer was to try and limit discussions about past crimes and, when necessary, balance the bad actions of the Ustasha with those of the Chetniks. The answer for the future was the unity of all the Yugoslav nations in a new state of peace and prosperity.

### *Jasenovac and Goli Otok in the 1980s*

But by the 1980s, this answer to the past trauma was appealing to fewer and fewer people. The claim to prosperity was clearly false. Significant portions of the population had been forced to leave the country since the 1970s to work in Western Europe as guest workers. Their extra income, which they sent back home and then later brought with them if they repatriated, helped to stabilize the situation for a decade. But the problem of nonexistent economic growth in the country was reaching a crisis point. Domestic consumption was maintained only for a period of time through significant borrowing from international capital markets, which was encouraged by the Western powers as long as nonaligned Yugoslavia was seen as an asset in the cold war context. Heavy debts owed to foreign creditors combined with nonexistent domestic economic growth were a serious problem in the 1980s.

It is important to recognize the economic crisis as part of what led to the disintegration of Yugoslavia in a series of wars in the 1990s. The unresolved issues of what had happened during World War II were not enough on their own to bring about the frustrations and nationalist tensions of the 1980s. But these unresolved issues did create a framework in which a nationalist solution rather than a pan-Yugoslav solution to the crisis appeared to make more sense to many of the local participants. The discussions that developed around Goli Otok and Jasenovac in the 1980s mattered because they raised serious doubts about the possibility and desirability of a pan-Yugoslav solution to the economic and political crisis. As suggested previously, once Tito moved against the civil society opening and the critical and creative discussions that appeared between 1966 and 1971, the chances for a more democratic direction were put off for another decade, during which the economic conditions in the country continued to deteriorate.

Why did Goli Otok still matter to so many people in the 1980s? Certainly, there were more than a few survivors and their families that were left around such as Aleksandar Popović and Dragoslav Mihailović. But this was clearly an issue that mattered to a far broader population than those that had been directly affected. Although compared to the total population of Yugoslavia, the number of survivors and family members of those who were killed was very small, there was something about the Goli Otok story that resonated in a powerful way with the broader public. The popularity of the films and novels that dealt with the theme of Goli Otok requires an explanation. One important part of the Goli Otok narrative is that it is almost always an *innocent* victim that is portrayed. Someone is humiliated, tortured, or punished unjustly. This is something that many people in Yugoslavia could relate to in some manner, the sense that the state had in some way unjustly abused its power over them as well. Not only had horrible crimes been committed against innocent or marginal supporters of the Soviet Union, but no one had ever been held accountable for these crimes. The theme of innocent victims and unaccountable perpetrators had a strong popular appeal with which many people could identify.

It is difficult to know which Goli Otok narrative first hit the shelves or found its way into the hands of Yugoslav readers, but Djilas's *Tito: The Story from Inside* was immediately available in 1980 in English and banned in the country. The book is not specifically about Goli Otok, as it includes a wide-ranging discussion of Tito's merits and faults as a wartime partisan leader and a postwar political figure, but there is no question that Djilas's claim that Tito alone was responsible for setting up the camp was explosive material. Criticism of Tito, while he was alive, was strictly forbidden. Although a Serbo-Croatian version of the book would only appear in Paris in 1982, one can well imagine that English-language copies immediately began to circulate in Yugoslavia in 1980. In these passages, not only does Djilas blame Tito and recognize his own sense of guilt and shame, but he also argues that a Yugoslavia independent of Soviet influence probably would not have existed without these measures.[76]

Within Yugoslavia, works that had previously been banned by government authorities began to appear. In Slovenia, Branko Hofman's novel *Noč do jutra* (*Night till Dawn*) appeared in 1981, after six years of rejections, and then went on to be praised as the best Slovenian novel of the year.[77] Other previously banned works also began to appear, such as the autobiographical work of Vitomil Zupan, who was a camp survivor as well as a Slovenian partisan, imprisoned for a joke he made about Tito in August 1948. His work, previously completed in 1972 but banned, began to appear in 1983.[78] In January 1982, Isaković published *Tren 2* (*Instant 2*), which was based on interviews with camp survivors. It immediately became a best seller. The preparation of the manuscript was done in close supervision with twenty-three official readers, and Isaković himself made sure in his public pronouncements to try to set the context within which the repression took place.[79]

In 1982, Slobodan Selenić published *Pismo/Glava* (*Heads/Tails*), which was based on the sole manuscript he had saved from the suppression of his 1970 novel dealing with Goli Otok. In the novel, Selenić argues that only pluralism and personal freedom can guard against such horrors in the future.[80] Whereas Selenić's first novel of the 1980s could be seen as a call for greater freedom and democracy, he became more fearful and nationalistic over the course of the 1980s. In his next novels, he argued that the Yugoslav state was a failure and that the Serbs had been the greatest losers. His 1985 novel *Očevi i oci* (*Fathers and Forefathers*) offered a severe criticism of the Yugoslav communist movement.[81] And then in 1989, with *Timor mortis*, he focused specifically on the Croatian massacres against Serbs that occurred during World War II, in graphic detail, and framed it within the context of ancient hatreds that were tragic but eternal.[82] These last two novels were written at a time during which the nationalism crisis in Yugoslavia was reaching a new high point over the situation in Kosovo.

Goli Otok also began to appear in theater productions and films, again with protagonists with whom the audience could easily identify. Although hard-core Stalinists, who probably were a serious threat to the regime, did end up in Goli Otok, deservedly or not, the narratives of the 1980s focused on outright innocent characters or simply those that were taken by surprise by the sudden shift from "Stalin Hero!" to "Stalin Pig!" This is the case of the main character in Dušan Jovanović's Slovenian play *The Karamazovs*, which opened in 1980. In the play, Svetozar Milić is imprisoned simply because he hesitates to suddenly denounce Stalin after years of having been told otherwise. The play portrays his psychological and physical destruction before he finally dies in prison.[83] The play, based on Dragoslav Mihailović's 1968 novel *When Pumpkins Blossomed*, which at the time had been set to open in Belgrade and was closed down by state authorities, finally was produced in 1984. And there were also films that dealt with the subject matter. Lordan Zafranović, the director of *Occupation in 26 Pictures*, closed his trilogy about the wartime past with a story about Tomislav K. and his life between 1926 and 1948, when he is wrongly accused of being a Stalinist and dies in prison. The theme of innocent prisoners continued with Emir Kusturica's film *Otac na službenom putu* (*When Father Was Away on Business*) (1985). The main character in Kusturica's film is a loyal Yugoslav communist, but one who is competing for the affection of a woman who is not his wife, with another party member. One day, he makes an offhand comment about a cartoon, and this is used to question his loyalty to the party. The idea that one could be sent to prison for making a joke or offhand comment is one that is repeated in several of these narratives. Stole Popov took the 1985 prize-winning Macedonian play by Gordan Mihić, *Srećna nova, '49* (*Happy New Year 1949*) and turned it into a powerful film of the same name a year later. The story is more complicated than one of simple wrongful imprisonment, as the play and film demonstrate how friendship, family, and intimate love relationships were destroyed in the chaos unleashed by Tito's break with Stalin in 1948. In this sense, the play and the film do not fit into the Goli Otok literature, but it does show the damage the continued political conflict after the war had on personal relationships.[84]

Goli Otok exposed the regime to the charge that it had participated in mass crimes against, at least sometimes, innocent victims for which no one had been held accountable. Moreover, as became increasingly clear in the 1980s, this was coupled with a growing rage against the suppression of such topics by the state. There were clearly positive, more democratic trends that began to emerge as a result. Dragović-Soso summarized the situation as follows: "In contrast to the 1960s, however, liberalisation [in the 1980s] was this time taking place in a very different Yugoslavia—one that was ridden by economic problems, a crisis of legitimacy and worsening centrifugal tendencies. . . . This situation of flux and greater openness created the space for the forging of a wide, though informal, opposition umbrella movement within the intelligentsia, which was initially focused on the defence of civil rights."[85]

The engagement with Goli Otok reflected a concern with civil rights and how they had been seriously violated in the past. The answer to this dilemma was to improve the condition for civil rights in Yugoslavia, which would require some sort of political transformation. The Jasenovac narrative stream and discussion of the Ustasha genocide during World War II was far more complicated. What was the "solution" to dealing with this extremely difficult part of the country's history? There had been some acknowledgment of the crimes on the part of the state and the society since the mid-1960s, but the depth of the anguish that many still felt over their experiences and those of their families remained very raw. The fact that the state appeared to have suppressed "the truth" about Jasenovac and the extent of the Ustasha crimes left many Serbs feeling betrayed. And the emotional tenor of the conflict was again accentuated by an ongoing, multidecade drama in the province of Kosovo, where Serbs again felt themselves to be victimized and unprotected by the state. The present political reality of the crisis in Kosovo and the reemergence of narratives about the Ustasha genocide began to flow into each other in a particularly toxic manner.

I want to give some specific attention to the narratives that developed about the Ustasha genocide in the 1980s, but first, it is important to have some further understanding of the political context in the 1980s and what was happening in Kosovo. Kosovo, for many Serbs, is considered the birthplace of the nation, and there is the famous defeat of a South Slav army at the hands of the Ottomans in 1389 in Kosovo. For many Serbs, this marked the beginning of five hundred years of subjugation to the Ottoman Empire, which is the background for Ivo Andrić's *The Bridge on the Drina*. It also sets the context for his novel *The Days of the Consuls*, which again shows the native population of Bosnia being subjugated to Ottoman rule and the more "enlightened" French occupying forces of Napoleon Bonaparte. Part of the key to understanding the logic and reasoning of all the national groups in the former Yugoslavia is this sense of constantly being subjugated to far more powerful outside forces that threaten the very existence of the nation. When the outside forces appear less threatening, the fear turns more inward into what the other regional groups are doing to gain the upper hand. Although Serbs constituted the largest ethnonational group in Yugoslavia, they also constituted significant minorities in Croatia, Bosnia, and Kosovo. Yugoslavia could be the Serbian answer to their insecurity that was in turn viewed as a potential threat to the other national groups. In a state and a society without clear civil liberties, democratic citizenship, and protection for minorities, a sense of security often came through the maintenance of in-group solidarity.

All of this background can help the outside observer hopefully better understand the dangerous dynamics that developed in Kosovo between Serbs and ethnic Albanians over the course of the post–World War II period. Serbs identify with Kosovo as their homeland, and indeed the landscape is filled with hundreds of Serbian Orthodox monasteries, many of them dating back to the fourteenth century. While Kosovo was still part of the Serb Republic within the Yugoslav federation system in the 1960s, the region itself was about 65 percent Albanian and 25 percent Serb. Aleksandar Ranković, the vice-president of Yugoslavia and the head of the state security forces, had long made sure that Serbs were in charge of running Kosovo. After Ranković's removal in a 1966 purge, there was an eruption in Albanian violence against Serbs in 1967 and 1968, which led the federal government to begin shifting the power balance in the region to the Albanians and the granting of the region the status of an autonomous region, just below that of a republic, in the 1974 constitution. As the ethnic balance of institutional power shifted in favor of Albanians in Kosovo, Serbs began to leave the region in significant numbers from the end of the 1960s forward. The Serbian exodus was driven by a combination of failed economic development and continued interethnic violence. The new Albanian leadership wasted economic development funds on prestige projects while neglecting basic infrastructure. Furthermore, Albanian separatist violence remained unappeased by the 1974 constitution, and attacks against Serbs and Serbian institutions continued. The 1970s and 1980s were marked by Albanian separatist violence followed by state repression and arrests.[86] By 1981, when a new round of Albanian protests turned violent, the Serbian population constituted only 13.2 percent of Kosovo's population.[87] The pressure that the Serb population felt to emigrate from Kosovo only grew in the face of renewed Albanian violence, and Serbs called on the Yugoslav federal government to help them.

This created an ongoing crisis, which in large part led to the collapse of Yugoslavia. Serbs in the rest of Yugoslavia saw their compatriots being persecuted, harassed, and threatened by the Albanian leadership in Kosovo as well as by the general Albanian population. They called on the leadership in the Serbian Republic to act, but the political leadership was at first unwilling to acknowledge a problem. Then, as Slobodan Milošević came into more of a leadership position in the mid-1980s, he was blocked by the other republics from acting within the federation, as all of the other republics plus Vojvodina and Kosovo, regions that had once been part of Serbia, voted against Milošević and the Serb Republic. What further enraged ordinary Serbs and Serbian intellectuals was that Slovenes and Croats took the side of the Kosovar Albanians against the local Serb population. Moreover, and here we come to a key point, the symbolism and narratives that were mobilized against the Serb position on Kosovo all made reference back to World War II. For example, in February 1989, Slovenian intellectuals organized a protest in which they wore the yellow Star of David in solidarity with the Albanians whom they argued were being treated like the Jews in Hitler's Germany. The sense that Serbs were again being betrayed by the other national groups exploded in Belgrade. The Slovenian pro-Albanian, anti-Serb protest was broadcast on television. Dragović-Soso writes, "Within a few hours of the television transmission of the Ljubljana manifestation, Belgrade was in uproar. The seething volcano of pent-up frustration, sense of injustice and bitterness blew its top, unleashing a veritable explosion of insults, denunciations and accusations against the Slovenes. Over the course of twenty-four hours a crowd of a million people gathered in front of the federal parliament chanting 'Slovenia is lying' and 'Slovenia is a traitor' and calling upon the Serbian leadership to stand firm against the Albanians and their 'sponsors.'"[88] Dragović-Soso continues, "It was particularly the Jewish comparison that offended Serbian intellectuals, especially because they had claimed that parallel for their own nation—as victims of Ustasha mass extermination, as well as of present-day 'terror' in Kosovo."[89]

What is essential for the present argument is to appreciate the extent to which each of the ethnonational groups in Yugoslavia began ever more intensely to view their present-day political problems through the lens of what had happened in World War II. What that history had meant had shifted significantly over time. Again, if we return to the beginning of this chapter, we will be reminded of the general sense of relief and solidarity that existed among the survivors of the war and the popularity of those first partisan films, which portrayed an all-Yugoslav partisan force fighting against the outside occupiers and their brutal local collaborators. The sense of victory and national liberation was a deeply held sentiment. The threat of a Soviet invasion after 1948 again helped to pull constituent ethnonational populations together, even as their own state grew more repressive in order to face the challenge of Soviet sympathizers. And in these early years, the party was heavily staffed with veterans of the partisan struggle, who did share a unified Yugoslav vision for the country. During the first phase of Yugoslavia's development, the legacy of World War II was something that unified the country. The solution to the past trauma of the war was "brotherhood and unity."

By the time we reach the 1980s, the legacy of World War II is far different. The ethnonational groups began to engage in a narrative competition of victimization, of what had "really" happened in World War II, but the state did not want you to know about. Furthermore, the present Yugoslav state had continued the victimization and exploitation of the ethnonational community. Slovenes and Croats turned against what they saw as rising Serbian nationalism in the 1980s over the crisis in Kosovo. Serbian nationalism was provoked by a sense of betrayal and having, yet again, sacrificed the most for Yugoslavia but having gained the least.

Given this historical context, we can now better appreciate the impact that a series of novels, plays, and films about the history of World War II helped to feed into these growing tensions. Given what we have seen above, there was clearly an ability for Yugoslav writers, playwrights, and filmmakers to address the extreme violence of World War II. And they were even able to deal quite explicitly with the interethnic violence perpetrated by the Ustasha and the Chetniks, although the Chetnik violence was more of a Serbian civil war rather than an example of interethnic violence. But the Ustasha violence as *genocidal violence* tended to be muted or "balanced" in the earlier decades. The narratives remained similar to the German films of the 1950s and 1960s, which might hint at the persecution of the Jews, but the stories involved the persecution of an individual, not a genocidal campaign to exterminate millions. The genocidal nature of the Ustasha violence had remained somewhat hidden and less clearly articulated. This is what changed radically in the 1980s. The violence became less individualized or contextualized within the setting of combat, as with the partisans fighting against the Ustasha, and shifted to the outright slaughter of masses of innocent people. The genocidal nature of the violence began to come more into focus than had previously been the case, not unlike what happened in West Germany with the showing of the television series *Holocaust* in 1979.

For example, Slobodan Šnajder's play *Hrvatski Faust* (*A Croatian Faust*) was produced in 1982 and used the staging of Goethe's *Faust* in 1942 occupied Zagreb as a way to address the Ustasha genocide. For example, the Walpurgis Night scene from *Faust* is set in the Jasenovac concentration camp, moving directly to the site of mass murder. The genocide is far from the only topic of the play, which has a great deal to say about the relationship between art and politics, and the too frequent subservience of art to politics and ideology in Yugoslavia. Croatian nationalists detested the play, and Šnajder was banned from postindependence Croatia until the end of the Franjo Tuđman regime in 1999.[90]

As with all artistic work except the most didactic, the meaning is left open for the audience or reader to debate and ponder. Was the more frequent discussion of the Ustasha genocide an attempt to stigmatize Croatian nationalists? Was it a blow for political and artistic freedom because such narratives had been banned in the past? Was it an attempt to stir Serbian nationalism? Was it an attempt to offer a warning against extreme nationalist passions? Was it the attempt of an individual artist to exercise some deep sense of personal pain and frustration? As I have suggested in the model outlined in the introduction to this book, the meaning is never *in the object* but rather in the debates that it sparks in the broader society. What is clear is that discussion of the Ustasha genocide became a *meaningful topic* for Yugoslav society, resisted by some and embraced by others for many different reasons.

Jovan Radulović's play *Golubnjača* (*Pigeon Cave*), which opened in fall 1982 in Novi Sad, embraced all of these different possibilities and elicited all of these different reactions. Government officials feared that it was stirring dangerous nationalist passions, and after ten performances in Novi Sad, Vojvodina, the play was closed. Intellectuals rose in defense of the work and saw it as another blow against state censorship and a triumph for artistic freedom. The play then moved to the Student Cultural Center in Belgrade, the site of numerous anti-regime initiatives and confrontations with the past, and faced new political pressure to close. In the end, the play was again hugely successful, playing in theaters all around the country, even playing to sold-out audiences in Slovenia.[91]

The story of the play dealt explicitly with the terrible interethnic violence that had been unleashed in a small village in the Krajina region of Croatia in which Croats from a neighboring village, who had joined the local Ustasha forces, massacred the Serbian population and threw the bodies into a cave near the village. The postwar setting is the 1960s, and the play shows the failure of the Yugoslav state to deal successfully with the legacy of the mass violence during the war. In the present, the survivors and other Serbs live in the village with their unburied relatives still in the cave. Rather than brotherhood and unity, the Serbs and Croats in the play trade insults, and their behavior is mirrored in that of the schoolchildren. The situation was not unlike that in Spain in the 1960s, where the survivors of Francoist-Nationalist massacres in small villages all over Spain continued to live beside the perpetrators and with full knowledge of where the mass graves were but unable to mourn or give a proper burial to their family members. In Titoist Yugoslavia, the survivors of the Ustasha genocide were discouraged from opening up the mass graves and giving their relatives a proper Orthodox burial.[92] The play gave a very frank portrayal of a country that had not dealt successfully with the long legacy of war and genocide.

The improper burial of loved ones is a burden for any society but more so for some than others. In writing about the oral history traditions in Yugoslavia, Krinka Vidaković-Petrov made the following observation:

> The ritual songs performed at funerals and on certain subsequent occasions are especially interesting from the point of view of memory. What is specific to them is the fact that memory is expanded in order to include both the living and the dead. Why? The cult of the dead implies the coexistence of two worlds: the world of the living and that of the dead. . . . The ancestors are, therefore, integrated into the present life of the community. Whenever the individual or the community is threatened, the living can evoke their dead ancestors and secure their protection.[93]

As in *Antigone*, the improper burial of thousands of Yugoslavs after the end of World War II left many local communities with a sense that the coexisting world of the living and the dead had suffered a serious rupture, not yet repaired.

Vuk Drašković's novel *Nož* (*Knife*) also appeared in 1982 and was based on a true account of the massacre of a Serbian family by the neighboring Muslim population on the Orthodox Christmas Eve in 1942 in Bosnia. It was a story that Drašković had heard many times within the confines of the family home while growing up,[94] giving us a clear sense of the role that oral history within families played in keeping memories of the past atrocities alive. Drašković's novel is a literary work of great merit worthy of much more discussion as it deals with not only the legacy of the wartime violence but also the saving of a Serbian baby by the Muslim killers, who is then raised as one of their own. Alija, the Muslim name given to the Serbian baby, grows up hating Serbs for what they did against "his people" in the war but discovers his other identity by the end of the book. Drašković is drawing on many important themes found in other great works of Yugoslav writers. Wachtel observes, "Draskovic appears thus to be deepening and echoing Andric's observations about the paradoxical similarity and difference between the separate Bosnian groups, saying that their very kinship, seen metaphorically as the proximity of the two sides of a knife blade, is what makes possible great connection and empathy *and* the most horrifying and violent enmity."[95]

The existing literature does not give us a clear sense of how widespread such stories were within families or whether they began to circulate only more recently, although Radulović's play and the suppression of Lubarda's work in the 1960s suggest that such conversations, at least within families or among members of one's ethnic group were not uncommon. This is another contrast with Spain where the postwar Francoist repression silenced intergenerational dialogues within families. One reason for this may be that societal discussion of Francoist violence and massacres was blocked from all public discussion for decades, whereas discussion of wartime atrocities in Yugoslavia were permitted in public, if given the proper context. The public discussion of wartime atrocities in Yugoslavia could always serve the function of reinforcement and help to stimulate discussions within families. We have already discussed Vojislav Lubarda's autobiographical *Anatema* (*Anathema*), which also appeared in 1982. In that work, he wrote about how his earlier attempt to write about interethnic wartime violence had been suppressed in Bosnia, in part or especially because he had identified prominent Muslims who had perpetrated war crimes and now had positions of political power in Bosnia.

Ćosić had written a four-volume work in the 1970s called *Vreme Smrti* (*A Time of Death*) in which his characters debate, against the background of World War I, about what should happen among the various South Slav peoples. Some argue for greater unity, while others view this as impossible. By the 1970s, Ćosić was clearly in the camp that viewed Yugoslavia as a failure, and the Serbs were the biggest losers. His views were largely shaped by his relationship with the writers in the other republics, which were not good, and the political crisis in Kosovo after 1966, when more control was turned over to ethnic Albanians and the outward emigration of Serbs increased. Because of his outspoken criticism over the federation's policy in Kosovo, which he viewed as anti-Serb, he was thrown out of the Communist Party in 1968.[96] After an extended time as a regime outsider, Ćosić now found himself on the inside, first in the intellectual opposition and then in the Serbian nationalist government of Slobodan Milošević, in large part because of the crisis in Kosovo in the 1980s. In January 1984, the second volume of *A Time of Death* was given a theatrical treatment. The story focuses on the heroic victory of the vastly outnumbered Serbian forces against the Austro-Hungarian army in December 1914. Dragović-Soso writes, "The play provoked impressive reactions from the audience. Not only was it the main event on the Belgrade cultural scene in this period, attracting the whole spectrum of intelligentsia, but it was completely booked for months on end and every performance was greeted by frenetic applause, exclamations and even tears by an ecstatic audience."[97] Here was the celebration of a Serbian victory against huge odds, not a pan-Yugoslav partisan victory in World War II. The nationalistic particularism that Ćosić had criticized and warned against in *Far Away Is the Sun* had become the only solution he and other Serbs saw in the context of the 1980s.

## Conclusion

It will be worthwhile to reflect, just briefly, on where the successor states of the former Yugoslavia are today. Each of them has developed into a formal democracy driven in part by either realized or hoped-for membership in the European Union (EU). Slovenia joined the EU first and then Croatia. All of the other former republics of Yugoslavia are now in the process of negotiating membership in the EU. Kosovo's disputed sovereignty creates some problems for this region's negotiations with the EU.

All of these newly independent countries find themselves marked by the wars that were fought over the course of the 1990s, some far more than others. The war in Croatia ended after Operation Storm in August 1995, when the separatist Serb leadership in the Krajina region was defeated and the entire Serbian population of more than five hundred thousand was forced out by the Croatian forces. Fighting in Croatia had lasted from 1991 to 1995. The most extensive fighting took place in Bosnia and Herzegovina between 1992 and 1995, as the various ethnic militias battled each other for control of territory and cities, while the Bosnian Croats and Bosnian Serbs both received support from their respective outside patrons. The war in Bosnia ended with the signing of the Dayton Peace Accords in late 1995, which saw the internal division of the country into a Muslim-Bosnian and Croatian section and a Serbian section. Bosnia remains internally divided today.

The end of warfare in Croatia and Bosnia did not resolve any of the problems that continued to fester in Kosovo, which had helped to foster the spiral of nationalist mobilization in the 1980s, but the roots of that conflict go back to the 1960s, if not earlier. Slobodan Milošević sought to reverse the ethnic power balance in Kosovo back to the pre-1968 Serb domination. He reestablished Serb control in Kosovo through military force. Ethnic Albanians were divided among themselves about how to address the situation, with some opting for political engagement and negotiation and others opting for a military solution.[98] By sometime in 1997 or 1998, the Kosovo Liberation Army was carrying out regular attacks against Serbian military and civilian targets, with the fighting accelerating in fall 1998. NATO began a bombing campaign of Kosovo and Serbia in March 1999, which lasted three months and resulted in Milošević agreeing to remove all Serbian forces from Kosovo in June 1999.[99] He was later overthrown through popular demonstrations in October 2000.

The competition between ethnic Albanians and Serbs in Kosovo threatened to destabilize Macedonia as well, which has a significant Albanian minority concentrated along its border with Kosovo. While there was some violence, Macedonia was able to avoid being pulled into a civil war. Last, Montenegro was able to avoid any direct involvement in direct warfare, although it had remained attached to Serbia until 2006, when the region narrowly voted to separate from Serbia.

With the definitive collapse of any Yugoslav narrative or view of the past, each of the national groups has begun the process of writing new national histories and dealing with the most recent wars as well. Unfortunately but not surprisingly, many of the general trends that this research has helped to elucidate further are present in each of these countries today. The externalization of blame is widespread, either blaming the other nations or the machinations of the great outside powers, which fits into the historical framework going back to the beginning of the twentieth century. The ethnocentrism of death blocks identification with members of the other national groups. The building of in-group solidarity is very important for each of the national communities in the current context, which works against those who are trying to develop discussions of a more universal human rights perspective. The International Criminal Tribunal for the former Yugoslavia (ICTY), just like the Nuremburg trials in postwar Germany, has garnered almost universal hatred throughout the region. The ICTY has generally helped to reinforce nationalist narratives of victimhood and exploitation by others. Each nationality feels singled out for prosecution and tends to defend "their people" at the court.[100] While the Nuremberg trials suffered from the charge of "victor's justice" in Germany, this has not primarily been the problem with the ICTY, as the victor is less clear, although for many Serbs there is a strong sense that ICTY represents "Western" interests, which has helped Russia foster a closer relationship with Serbia.

This is not to say that the entire picture is bleak and without hope but rather that it is actually at quite a normal state given the recentness of the mass violence, which has resulted in hundreds of thousands of refugees and tens of thousands dead. For example, some of the more extreme nationalist rhetoric in Croatia during the Tuđman years from 1990 to 1999 has begun to shift toward one more open to engagement with Serbia and away from a purely nationalistic view of history. It is not clear what Tuđman understood about the nature of General Francisco Franco's monument to the Nationalist movement in Spain, which is discussed in the chapter on Spain. The monument, which Franco called one of national reconciliation, was clearly designed to humiliate the Republican side in the civil war, as former Republicans built the monument with their slave labor, with some dying in the process. In any case, Tuđman thought that it would be good to turn the Jasenovac memorial into one of national reconciliation, which meant removing it from a narrative about the Ustasha genocide to a "national memorial" by burying the remains of some Ustasha soldiers from Bleiburg. Bleiburg is located in Slovenia and became a memorial site even during Yugoslav times for the partisan massacre of Ustasha soldiers and sympathizers at the end of the war. The Croats at Bleiburg had tried to surrender to the British in Slovenia but were turned back. The partisans then killed some immediately and then marched others off to labor camps or other fates. For Croatian nationalists, Bleiburg came to represent partisan atrocities and a way to balance the legacy of Jasenovac. Tuđman sought to combine the two narratives in Jasenovac as a site of national reconciliation but eventually had to drop the plan due to international pressure, not least because Jasenovac had also become bound up with the narrative of the Holocaust in the postwar years, as Jews had also been killed at the camp along with Serbs. But that did not prevent the writers of Croatian textbooks in the 1990s from giving graphic details about the crimes of the partisans at Bleiburg and the Chetniks, while ignoring Jasenovac. There was also a huge effort in Croatia to remove all traces of the wartime partisans, with almost three thousand memorial markers removed between 1991 and 1998.[101] A central square in Zagreb lost its name of Square to the Victims of Fascism.

But with Tuđman's death in 1999, things appear to have moved in a far more balanced direction. The Square to the Victims of Fascism had its name restored in December 2000. And the Croatian president at the time, Stipe Mesić, began to make very clear that Bleiburg and Jasenovac were two separate narratives that Croats needed to accept. Mesić made a comment in 2005 that showed a clear understanding that it was not easy to separate victims and perpetrators: "We are not comparing Bleiburg and Jasenovac. None of the victims from Jasenovac were responsible for the people killed in the trenches and in Bleiburg, but a lot of people in Bleiburg were responsible for mass murder. They are victims, but we cannot say they are innocent. They should not have been killed and tormented, but they should have been put on trial."[102]

Even in stable, prosperous democracies, it can take several decades for a society and state to move in a direction that allows for a discussion of past violence and some measures to address the crimes of the past. Yugoslavia did not have the benefit of these conditions in the 1980s and the movement toward greater democracy collapsed into competition among nationalist leaders. The situation in the region has improved somewhat since the end of the 1990s with the death of Tuđman, the removal of Milošević from power, and the slow entrenchment of basic democratic institutions. Spain, in contrast, had a far more stable economic grounding and a couple of decades of democratic entrenchment before an intensive investigation of the nation's violent history began on a large scale, and this was also more than sixty years after the end of the civil war in 1936. The successor states of the former Yugoslavia are still very close to the mass violence of the 1990s as well as the even worse violence of World War II. The cases in this research suggest that this will be a process lasting decades. In many ways, we are at the end of *Antigone*, with the wasteland of war still around the main characters and Tiresias is issuing his warning against vengeance. Those who remain are slowly crafting a view of what the future might become.

# 5 Turkey

*You act outrageously,*
*and therefore Hades' executioners,*
*the gods' destructive Furies, lie in wait*
*to tangle you in evils you create.*
—Tiresias to Creon in *Antigone*[1]

*That's true. I hurt myself when mocking you.*
—Antigone to Ismene in *Antigone*[2]

## Introduction

The Ottoman Empire collapsed as a result of its defeat in World War I, but the end of the war and the occupation of the country by Western allied armies led to an uprising led by Mustafa Kemal in 1919, which turned into a three-year War of Independence (1919–1922). It was in the context of World War I that the Ottoman Turks committed the first genocide of the twentieth century against the Christian Armenians, mostly located in the eastern part of Anatolia. In terms of the present study, it will be useful to think about the Turkish experience in World War I as a civil war, making this case more similar to Spain and Yugoslavia than Germany and Japan. The civil war in the case of the Ottoman Empire and the Turkish Republic was primarily fought against non-Muslim, non-Turkish ethnic minorities, the Jews, Greeks, and Armenians, who were largely removed from the country, followed by a War of Independence against foreign occupying armies.

The few remaining non-Muslim minorities in Turkey have had to remain almost wholly silent about their past suffering until the past decade or so. The destruction and removal of the non-Muslim minorities from what became the Turkish Republic was dramatic. In 1900, 56 percent of Istanbul's population was non-Muslim; today, it is less than 1 percent.[3] In the part of Anatolia that would become the Turkish Republic in 1923, in 1906, about 20 percent of the population was non-Muslim and in 1924 only 2.6 percent.[4] This is a stark difference to the cases of Spain and Yugoslavia where the victims and perpetrators of earlier violence in civil wars continued to live in close proximity to each other after the end of the war. This has meant that the internal pressure for confronting Turkey's difficult history and periods of mass violence has come primarily from outside the country, although an increasing number of Turks are now asking these questions themselves. As we have seen throughout this study, external pressures tend to be the weakest unless they can find internal allies and proponents.

Another aspect that makes the Turkish case similar to that of Yugoslavia and different from Germany, Japan, and Spain is the relationship between the period of mass violence and the founding of a new state. Fatma Müge Göçek and Fatma Ulgen have suggested that because the Turkish period of mass violence took place during the state's founding, this has led to an even deeper silencing or sense that this violence is a taboo subject.[5] It is not merely that there is a difficult history that needs to be addressed, but there is a strong fear in so doing that the very foundation of the state and its legitimacy may be drawn into question. We can see a similar pattern in the Yugoslav case, where the communist regime was particularly sensitive to discussions about Goli Otok as a mass crime that took place at the founding of the Yugoslav state. Moreover, Tito, the founding father in the case of Yugoslavia, was directly responsible for Goli Otok, a foundational crime. In the case of Turkey, while Atatürk was not involved in the Armenian genocide, he did directly participate in its marginalization in official Turkish history. Given that Atatürk has obtained an immortal status in the Turkish Republic, a point that I will expand on in a moment, any risk that his status could become tainted by past crimes is extremely sensitive.

## Psychological and Social-Psychological Processes

As we can see in the other cases, a strong sense of having suffered oneself tends to block identification with others whom one's group may well have harmed. The *ethnocentrism of death* plays a role in all of the cases under consideration in this study, and as we can see, it is a sentiment that can persist over many decades and can be transmitted between generations. Even those who did not directly suffer the mass death that occurred in World War II in Germany and Japan can still have a raw sense of the suffering that their grandparents or parents suffered at the time.

The ethnocentrism of death remains far more acute in Turkey than is the situation in any of the other cases. The reasons for this are complex and will be addressed throughout this chapter, but it will be absolutely essential to recognize a growing divide between how this is expressed by the Turkish state compared to some segments of the civil society. Whereas the Turkish state remains fixated on an aggressive and assertive policy of denying the Armenian genocide along with other anti-minority policies and actions that the state has taken against non-Muslim minorities in Turkey, there is a growing willingness of some within Turkish civil society to discuss these past policies as part of what they see as an essential component of deepening their democracy. At the same time, the vast majority of the civil society remain locked in a deep sense of Turkish victimization and are closed to any discussion of Turks as perpetrators. Whereas the discussion of Japanese and German perpetrators has largely become normalized, if not uncontroversial, this is very much not the case in Turkey today. As we will see later, these sentiments continue to be reinforced through the educational system, which remains very much under the control of the Turkish state. The failure of the Turkish education system to democratize is a serious impediment to broader change in the society.

To the extent that there is any recognition of actions having been taken against non-Muslim minorities in Turkey, there is a very strong tendency to engage in the *externalization of blame* for these actions. Even for those that wish to discuss the Armenian genocide in Turkey, they need to avoid the use of the word *genocide*. Otherwise, they face state sanctions or verbal and physical attacks from extreme nationalists. When the Armenian "massacres" are discussed, the reasons for the actions are usually couched in the language of a military necessity in the context of World War I, with the suggestion that the Armenians were siding with the invading Russian forces. Furthermore, Turkish narratives not only question the level of violence committed by Turks against Armenians but also place the blame on the Armenians who betrayed the Turks and did far more to victimize the Turkish population at the time.[6] The other anti-minority and non-Muslim actions, such as the 1942 wealth tax and the September 6–7, 1955, riots, which were orchestrated by the government, are generally not discussed or given any explanation. While some of these anti-minority measures are discussed by minority authors in Turkey, the general theme in Turkish literature written by ethnic Turks when looking back into the past is to emphasize peaceful coexistence and to leave the question of why this period came to an end not only unanswered but unasked.[7]

Another component of externalizing blame, which is by no means unique to Turkey but may be more heavily accented than the other cases, is the strong belief in destiny, which colors local discussions about why things happen and plays a repeated role in Turkish films.[8] The well-known Turkish author Ece Temelkuran reflects on this, writing, "In Turkish 'destiny' or 'fate' is referred to as *alin yazisi*: 'the writing on one's forehead,' the inscription present at birth. Perhaps societies, too, have an *alin yazisi* from which we're exempt until we've grown up enough to leave our childhood behind. Perhaps one of the rites of passage is to be branded with this sense of historical identity and societal destiny. But, unlike *alin yazisi*, can a society's destiny be changed?"[9]

As we will see in the chronological discussion of the Turkish case, while there has been some discussion of anti-minority actions against the non-Muslim population as well as Kurds, who are Muslim, in more recent years, these have remained extremely sporadic and muted. Thus, the *social contagion* and the *reinforcement effect* have been extremely limited, although since the 1990s there has been an increasing willingness on the part of some in the civil society to engage in self-critical reflection on the treatment of non-Turkish minorities in Turkish history. The more common pattern for most of the history of the republic has been to encourage *socially shared retrieval-induced forgetting* (SS-RIF), the selective remembering that occurs in day-to-day conversations. For example, one will find a fair amount of discussion about Armenians in Turkish history but only as the perpetrators of violence against Turks. The process of SS-RIF has blended the violence committed by Turks against the Armenians in the context of World War I out of the picture. There is sometimes not a silence about Armenians but rather a silence about one part of Turkish-Armenian relations. In other cases, the presence of Armenians in real life or in fiction is simply avoided so as not to begin a conversation that could lead in an uncomfortable direction. During her multiyear attempt to learn about Turkey while living in the country, Meline Toumani, an American Armenian, noted that a typical exchange with a Turk would involve an inquiry into her ethnic identity, followed by her saying that she is Armenian. The Turk would then switch the conversation to the weather.[10] In the world of fiction, Karin Schweißgut notes that the appearance of an Armenian character in a piece of literature published in 1990 was ignored by the reviewers, the interviewers, and the author herself in her memoir. As Schweißgut notes, "In my opinion, the discussions on 'Can Kusu' seem to be—like the Armenian past in the story—part of the self unconscious or unconscious self of Turkish society."[11]

In terms of the dynamics that we can see regarding societies that are more collectivist or individualist in their orientation, Turkey tends more toward the collectivist side of the spectrum and thus is more similar to Japan than the cases of Germany, Spain, and Yugoslavia. Scholars of Turkey continually point to the greater emphasis on collectivism in Turkish society.[12] I already discussed the research of the social psychologists Bertjan Doosje and Nyla R. Branscombe in the introduction, where they point out that more collectivist societies demonstrate a stronger tendency to externalize blame and show a stronger in-group bias. This also means that members of the in-group that break ranks with the broader society are more likely to suffer severe social sanctions for their actions. By striking a self-critical stance vis-à-vis Turkey's history, one puts oneself at risk of verbal abuse, state-sanctioned prosecution, and extreme nationalist violence. It is very important to realize that state sanctions are only part of this assault on those who raise difficult questions; social sanctions are also very widespread and normalized. In the preface to one of her most recent publications on the manner in which the Armenian genocide has been handled in Turkey, Göçek, a Turkish scholar raised in Turkey but now a longtime student and professor in the United States, talks about how her scholarship is seen as a "betrayal" of her people by many of those who had close personal relationships with her in Turkey. Some can only explain her "betrayal" in racialized terms by assuming that she must have Armenian blood in her.[13] In another instance, a Turkish extreme nationalist assassinated the Turkish Armenian journalist Hrant Dink in 2007. Dink's murder was preceded by his continual denouncement in the nationalist media and an official state prosecution for having insulted Turkishness. Orhan Pamuk, the Nobel Prize–winning author, has spoken out about the Armenian genocide on occasion and, after having done so with a Swiss journalist in 2005, found himself being prosecuted by the state and deciding to live outside the country for a time because of threats that were made against him. He now has to have armed protection with him while going for his much-beloved walks in Istanbul. State sanctions combined with social pressure make discussions of Turkey's difficult history a more treacherous terrain than in any of our other cases. Both political and cultural power are exercised to maintain a relative silence.

## Politics

In terms of the balance between democracy and authoritarianism, Turkey is most similar to the case of Yugoslavia in that the authoritarian state has dominated state-society relations for many decades. It also shares some characteristics with Spain in that there has been a noticeable opening up of Turkish civil society since the 1980 military coup, especially in the 1990s and 2000s, but this transition remains far less complete than what Spain has achieved since the death of Franco in 1975. In response to a failed coup attempt in July 2016, the current Recep Tayyip Erdoğan government has swung wildly toward increased authoritarianism and repression, throwing many of the positive developments of the past decade into doubt. While the authoritarian state had previously begun to withdraw somewhat, authoritarianism continues to mark the political landscape in Turkey, even though there are regular elections. The acceptance of political pluralism remains weak in Turkey and compromise is seen as a sign of weakness.[14] The Kemalist secularists and the Islamists have sought to capture state power and then to use that power to marginalize the other side. As Ervin Staub has noted in his work on genocide and violent conflict, a culture and society that is openly hostile toward pluralism is going to be far more prone to mass violence.[15]

### *State-Society Relations*

There are two sites within the emerging civil society in Turkey that deserve special attention: the classroom and the realm of cultural production, which has long labored under highly restrictive state censorship. While the state has recently begun to withdraw somewhat from direct control over the secondary and university classroom, these reforms remain incomplete and appear to be failing. The more promising realm is that of general cultural production, where there is an increasing plurality of voices that are engaging different parts of Turkey's difficult history.

### *The Classroom*

Whereas the classroom eventually became a site of countermemory and resistance against minimizing war crimes in Japan and Germany after World War II, the teaching profession and educational institutions in Turkey have remained very conservative and closely tied to state authority. Education in Turkey is not about the fostering of a sovereign individual capable of independent reasoning and debate but rather creating a subject of the state who must obey. There is a strong authoritarianism rooted in both the family and the classroom.[16] In his study of Turkish textbooks as well as ethnographic fieldwork, Sam Kaplan concludes, "Thus, both the military and state officials considered their task to consist of turning children into law-abiding citizens. To this end, parents, teachers, and officials were mobilized to manage, supervise, and control children. Thus, the family unit, the school, and the state were all depicted in the curriculum as responsible for fostering the same rules, regulations, order, and above all, obedience."[17] In trying to understand the confused response of university students to the film *Bulutari Beklerken* (*Waiting for the Clouds*) (2004), which we will discuss below, Asuman Suner comments, "Formal education in Turkey entails a bombardment of official ideology and the public discussion of the subjects like the history of non-Muslim minorities is still taboo."[18]

These patterns of power are so firmly entrenched that the most recent attempts to introduce more Western forms of education, which focus on the needs of the child and critical thinking, have made very little progress in Turkey. The push for change came from both outside and inside the country. Beginning in 2004, the European Union (EU) began to encourage Turkey to try and foster a more liberal and student-centered education, and this included a pilot program begun in 2008.[19] There was also a realization from within Turkey that changes needed to be made as the country had performed very poorly against other Organisation for Economic Co-operation and Development (OECD) countries on the Programme for International Student Assessment (PISA) examinations. But the reform attempts have been undermined on all levels, by the state, the teachers, and the parents.

Hisham Sharabi notes that one of the characteristics of neopatriarchy is the turning of modernization into a fetish and a model that can be copied but that such efforts at reform will fail because they remain imitations and are based on the passivity of all those involved.[20] For example, the top-down state reformers in Turkey claim that they want to institute more teacher autonomy because this is part of the "Western model," part of the reason why Western countries are having more success than Turkey on the PISA examinations. But there is nothing autonomous about any part of this process, and the state immediately begins to undermine its own efforts and stated mandate. Everyone involved in the process recognizes that one important part of teacher autonomy would involve allowing the teachers to have more control over the curriculum, and theoretically teachers can exercise this choice, except that there is no real choice. Because of the severe underfunding of schools, teachers can only choose the state-provided textbook for history because it is offered free of charge.[21] Teachers and parents are filled with uncertainty as to what this phase of "modernization" should accomplish, especially because it appears to be challenging well-entrenched patterns of patriarchal authority, both inside and outside the classroom.[22]

The dominance of rote learning in Arab and Middle Eastern cultures was identified as a problem in the late 1970s and remains very much the dominant pattern today.[23] Sharabi noted at the time, "Rote-learning and punishment have this in common: Both exclude understanding and emphasize authority; they both cultivate passivity and inhibit change."[24] The Socratic method of open inquiry and questioning is shut down at an early age in patriarchal societies. The quest for understanding, the search for meaning, the openness to questioning, which are taken for granted as part of Western education today, are largely absent.[25] The result is what Sharabi calls monological discourse, which means that the father, teacher, religious leader, or political leader holds forth in a one-sided manner.[26]

Temelkuran finds exactly this same type of father figure in Turkey: "For Turkey, however, it ['father'] has more of a corporeal presence. The speaker at the lectern ought not to talk about economic figures, to display any kind of consistency regarding the past, or to present a rational argument. Let him be as Middle Eastern a father figure as possible and the votes are his."[27] Moreover, Temelkuran argues, politicians are not only fathers, but the voters are overwhelmingly addressed and treated as orphans, desperately in need of a father to love them and to punish them. Candidates literally campaign on "the rights of orphans." Voters are not citizens; they are addressed and treated like orphans.[28]

This does not mean that there is no resistance to this imposition of patriarchal authority, but the resistance, as in Japan, remains largely passive. In Japan, resistance takes primarily the form of ritualism and outward conformity, or withdrawal from the relationship, if possible. Sharabi notes a similar pattern in Middle Eastern societies, where resistance takes primarily the form of gossip, backbiting, storytelling, or silence. The Turkish classroom tends to reproduce the forms of authority that continue to undermine not only the autonomy of the teachers but also the encouragement of autonomous critical thinking on the part of the students.

One characteristic of the Turkish education system that clearly sets it apart from many other countries is the stability of the perspectives expressed in the official textbooks, of which there have been only three editions—1929, 1950, 1986—as of 1997.[29] Indeed, the Turkish education system remains, even today, the most centralized in all of the OECD countries.[30] The perspective established in the 1930s has, by and large, been maintained into the present,[31] although Avonna Deanne Swartz's detailed content analysis suggests some subtle shifts over time.

Unfortunately, one of the characteristics that has remained predominant since the first 1929 edition is Atatürk's mythology about the "murderous Armenians" and the "oppressed Turks." Rather than a silence about Armenians, there is an active state attempt to portray them as murderous traitors of the Turkish nation. It is also essential to recognize that this narrative was established by Atatürk. As seen above, the extreme reverence for Atatürk and all that he said will make changing this narrative very difficult. It will require a rethinking of core Turkish symbols rather than simply marshaling more historical facts. Although Atatürk acknowledged certain "shameful acts" that had occurred during the war, the emphasis has always been to externalize the blame onto the Armenians and the Western powers that sought to destroy the Turkish people. Between 1944 and 1980, the Ottoman deportations and mass killing of Armenians disappeared from Turkish textbooks, while the "murderous Armenians" remained.[32] As recently as 2003, the Ministry of Education held an essay competition on "why the Armenians were traitors, why genocide claims were baseless, and why Turkey needed to secure itself against minority claims to preserve its unity as a nation."[33]

The military has played a central role in shaping Turkish textbooks, and it has used the paternalism learned in the family to support the youth's view of the Turkish state. As Kaplan notes in his study of both the texts and from his ethnographic fieldwork in a Turkish village, "The generals, I suggest here, tapped into the concept of *father-state* (*devlet baba*). . . . That is to say, they drew on a paternalist understanding of power holders as custodians of the people's welfare to legitimate their intervention. . . . This concept of father-state remains a central feature in the official politics of national culture and finds expression in the curriculum."[34] In this way, we can see that the lessons about power and authority in the home find a strong echo elsewhere in Turkish society. All of this is then bound up with the Atatürk cult so that children from the youngest age are encouraged to think of themselves as Atatürk's children. "Understood is that the educational system will beget a future nation of Atatürks for the childless statesman. In first grade, children read out loud that 'we will work hard and show that we are Atatürk children.' Underlying the familial metaphor is that schoolchildren should behave as if they were living extensions of the dead statesman."[35] Students are given constant reinforcement of militaristic notions; they must be willing to sacrifice their lives for the state and Atatürk. Of the ten most frequently used words in one content analysis of Turkish textbooks, three of them are "death," "war," and "hero."[36] Citizenship is equated with martyrdom.[37] Kaplan notes, "Current textbooks graphically and textually immerse this ideal of the Muslim warrior into the moral universe of the modern Turkish child. . . . In this endeavor, textbook writers have reasserted the tradition of the *gazi* and *sehit*, respectively, the warrior fighting and the martyr dying, both on behalf of Islam."[38]

But against whom must the Turkish child-student be constantly vigilant? One of the most damaging parts of the Turkish educational system is the constant reinforcement of the theme of how Turkey faces both internal and external enemies, dark forces that are constantly plotting the destruction of the nation. The internal enemies are Turkey's minority populations, the Greeks, Jews, Kurds, and Armenians.[39] The Armenians, in fact, are singled out for particularly harsh treatment in Turkish textbooks as having been ungrateful for their special position in the Ottoman Empire and for their deceitful betrayal of the Turks.[40] "In these narratives, the Turkish people are portrayed as unsuspecting, innocent victims; the Armenians as brutal, cowardly, and dishonest terrorists"; a third-grade life science textbook reads, "the Armenians who for years had lived with Turks began to oppress and torture the Turks."[41] A 2004 study by Turkish scholars of Turkish textbooks expressed their dismay at the level of what they called racism in Turkish texts: "The scale and depth of the basic attitudes in contravention of human rights, most importantly the right to receive adequate education (also in the field of human rights), the discriminatory rhetoric, and callousness, that we encountered in the textbooks went beyond our expectations that had shaped the project and the first few months of research."[42]

This educational background leaves clear traces on those who pass through it, even those who go to the most liberal institutions or come from intellectual families. Temelkuran, a well-known Turkish writer and journalist from a leftish family observed that she had never drawn a link between the Young Turk movement and the 1915 genocide. Her discovery of this part of her own history came through her friendship with Hrant Dink and his insistence that she travel to Armenia and visit with Armenians in the diaspora. Temelkuran wrote about these experiences in her fascinating book *Deep Mountain*. Regarding her prior inability to draw any connection between the Young Turk movement and the 1915 genocide, Temelkuran notes, "My lack of interest is certainly strange. It's as though I've been programmed not to feel any curiosity. I know terrible things happened but a part of me doesn't want to learn any more. . . . I put down my lack of interest to the awareness that blood has been shed in the lands of Anatolia throughout history, thus further legitimizing my indifference. Are we obligated to know all the details?"[43] Temelkuran continues, "I wondered to myself why, during my hundreds of visits to provinces in the east, I'd never thought, even once, of asking anyone about any of this—even though I knew full well who built those stone buildings, and also knew, in general terms, that there had been great cruelty. So what was the reason for my apathetic silence?"[44]

In her most recent book, Temelkuran continues exactly this thought, pursuing it further. "This lack of curiosity, this ready listlessness and indifference is learned. Just like forgetting was learned in 1915, so too is the reluctance for recollection and the dismissal of curiosity."[45] She continues,

> It had never occurred to me to wonder about this enormous blank space in the middle of the city of Izmir where the Izmir International Fair was situated. This was despite the fact that I had already written the book *Deep Mountain: Across the Turkish-Armenian Divide* and that I was aware that this state of indifference in Turkey was conditioned or learned behaviour. And yet each "Turkish" child is unknowingly instructed in not asking or not thinking to ask why the owners of those beautiful old apartments left and when, or how it was that the congregations of the magnificent churches in Anatolia suddenly vanished, or why those who were once here no longer are. . . . I never wondered how there

> could be such an empty stretch right in the middle of the city. It never even occurred to me to take this as a sign that there was something there to wonder about. . . . So, finding out that the enormous expanse in the middle of Izmir had once been the Armenian and Rum district, that it had been burned to the ground . . . eradicating one's learned blindness could be a greater challenge than one could ever bargain for.[46]

Toumani writes about her friend Fatma Müge Göçek that Göçek did not learn the truth about Armenian life in Turkey even while attending the elite, private Robert College in high school and then later the Bosporus University.[47] While the Turkish state appears to be effectively undermining its latest attempts at modernization and introducing more autonomy into the classroom, there are some signs of hopeful change. The 1990s saw the founding of two independent, private universities in Istanbul: Sabancı University in 1994 and Bilgi University in 1996. It was at Bilgi University that the first academic conference on the Armenian genocide was held in Turkey in 2005. While there has been some change, very recently, we can see in Temelkuran's reflections the passivity that predominates in a society filled with the monological discourse described by Sharabi.

### *Civil Society—Public Space*

The development of a civil society in Turkey has been much delayed over the course of the republic's history in large part because of the authoritarian nature of the state, which took modernization as a project to be imposed on the population. Furthermore, this modernization process included the marginalization or removal of non-Turkish and non-Muslim minorities. Ethnic and religious pluralism was no more tolerated than political pluralism for significant periods. This is not to say that the level of state control over the society has not varied over time, but the control has been sustained over all of the twentieth century.

As our main concern here is with societal confrontations with a difficult history, control over the media landscape and educational institutions are our primary subjects. Here, state control has been persistent and repressive, even outside the immediate periods of the military coups. The control over the primary and secondary education has been highlighted in the previous section and continues into the present, despite announced attempts at reform and the claimed intention of permitting more autonomy for teachers. University instruction has also been shaped by a strong statist and nationalist perspective. This has only recently begun to change with the opening of two new private universities and the Bosporus University, which adhere more to Western notions of academic freedom. The media landscape and artists in the television and film industry have long labored under very restrictive censorship laws, with significant changes only coming in the mid-1980s. Popular, nationalist, and patriarchal attitudes remain widespread in the society, thus maintaining clear limits on what filmmakers and other artists can expect to achieve in terms of producing challenging material and generating the necessary financial resources to continue their work.

When thinking about how different narratives about the past enter the public space, I have emphasized in each of the cases in this book that it is useful to think about the implications of the memory-market dictum: "As memory makers need access to 'capital' to reach the market, the more market dependent and capital intensive a given mode of representation is, the more likely one is to find it in tune with the times, either with mass attitudes (democratic regimes) or state ideology (authoritarian regimes). The 'capital' will take primarily a financial form in a democratic-capitalist system, and primarily a political one in an authoritarian-command economy system."[48] For example, we will expect to find that cinema is far more conservative or less controversial than, say, the realm of memoir writing because of the different level of capital investment needed to make a film compared to publishing a book. If we can find controversial themes being expressed in Turkish cinema, then we should expect to find even more such material in other less capital-intensive forms of talking about the past.

Compared to the other countries in this case study, filmmakers in Turkey have labored under a stricter censorship regime for a longer time, even more so than in communist Yugoslavia. As suggested by the memory-market dictum, the pressure on Turkish filmmakers to avoid difficult historical discussions has come in two forms, official state censorship as well as market pressure and popular expectations. The official state censorship took shape in the early years of the Turkish Republic with a 1932 "Directive Concerning the Control of Cinema Films." In 1939, the state created a censorship board with the power to stop production of domestic films at the script stage and the ability to censor foreign films.[49] There were changes to the censorship policy in 1977, 1979, and 1983, but the strong state control basically remained in place until 1986, when the responsibility for censorship shifted from the Ministry of the Interior to the Ministry of Culture. This was also a period during which the Turkish state began to allow market forces to shape production throughout the economy. While official state censorship continues to play a role in limiting discussions about Turkey's difficult history, the primary force now blocking such discussions remain market-driven forces and the conservative and nationalistic nature of Turkish society. At the same time, some courageous filmmakers are now finally able to work on the periphery of Turkish public life and to challenge their viewers with parts of the country's past, which have been largely absent from Turkish films since the founding of the republic in 1923. Nonetheless, mainstream cinema remains dominated by a nostalgic view of the past, emphasizing the theme of peaceful coexistence between Turks and minorities, while art house cinema takes greater risks by providing the minority's perspective.[50]

From the beginning, censorship was directed against the following topics and themes: anti-militarism, communism, and anti-Turkish sentiment. The result is that even today, Turkish civil society has an impoverished understanding of its own history, as reflected above in Temelkuran's comments. The ban on anti-militarism has been accompanied by an imperative to praise the military, as we have seen above in the school curriculum. Criticism of the military, the use of torture and unlawful detention, the executions without trial carried out by the Liberation Courts in the first years of the republic, and the multiple military coups in Turkish history remain problematic until the present, although since the lightening of state censorship in 1986, there are notable and important exceptions, especially from the mid-1990s and 2000s. There has also been a strong anti-leftist bias in Turkish cinema throughout its history, although this was briefly challenged between 1960 and 1965 with the development of social realist cinema.[51] Last, censorship against anti-Turkish commentary remains part of the country's legal framework and has been interpreted in an extremely broad manner by the courts. Indeed, the EU has requested that the Turkish government reform its legal code, which prohibits insulting Turkishness. This can include any form of self-critical discussion about Turkish history and has severely restricted the ability of all Turkish citizens to enter into discussions about Turkey's difficult history, especially regarding the treatment of different religious and ethnic minority groups, including Muslims, such as the Kurds and Alevis.[52]

For example, it became possible to represent Kurds as Kurds only in the 1990s.[53] Prior to this time, Kurds were portrayed as mountain-dwelling Turks who spoke Turkish poorly and dressed differently, but otherwise their identity remained Turkish. The 1982 film *Yol* (*The Way*), which won the Palme d'Or at the 1982 Cannes Film Festival, touched very briefly on the Kurdish issue and was banned in Turkey until 1999. While discussion of the Kurdish issue has just begun in Turkish cinema, other topics are almost nonexistent. There has been absolutely no discussion of the 1915 Armenian genocide in Turkish cinema, except to portray the official Turkish position in the War of Independence films, which shows the Armenians as murderous betrayers of the Turkish people. Even other less dramatic forms of pressure and violence against non-Turkish groups have also been almost completely absent from Turkish films, although this has again changed in the 1990s and 2000s. We will return to a discussion of some of these films in the chronological section for this chapter.

### *International Relations*

As with each of the other cases in the broader comparative study, the presence or absence of pressure for confronting difficult histories from outside the country has also played an important role in how Turkey has confronted its difficult past. While Armenian communities in France and the United States have long put pressure on Turkey and their own governments to recognize the 1915 Armenian genocide, the government of the United States and Great Britain have long sought to suppress or minimize this pressure for geopolitical reasons, especially during the Cold War, when the Turkish military was seen as an important ally in containing the Soviet Union.[54] This geopolitical importance has returned in the present series of crises in the region unleashed by the 2003 American invasion of Iraq.

Ayşe Zarakol argues that a great deal of the official denial of the Armenian genocide coming from the Turkish state is based on two long-standing worldviews in Turkey, which are still firmly in place. First, there is what many scholars have referred to as the Sèvres Syndrome, which is a reference to the 1920 Treaty of Sèvres signed by the pro-Western Istanbul government during the Turkish War of Independence (1919–1922). The treaty was rejected by the government in Ankara and the military leadership around Atatürk.[55] Jenny White writes of this syndrome in Turkey, "The mutilation of Ottoman territory before and after World War I by European powers has been neither forgotten nor forgiven."[56] This deep sense of Turkish victimization is something that most Western observers fail to appreciate when trying to understand Turkish behavior. The ethnocentrism of death and suffering is a deeply felt sentiment in Turkey. This also creates a strong tendency toward conspiracy theories and paranoid nationalism in the broader Turkish public as well as among the elites, who are convinced that the Western powers are still using the issue of human and minority rights to undermine the Turkish state. Whereas Western powers view themselves as the proponents of universal values that will promote peace and stability, many Turks view the same efforts as part of a long historical project by Western powers to destroy the Turkish nation. We can see this endless focus on "dark forces" and "internal and external" enemies is reinforced not only in the mainstream culture but also in the school curriculum. As a result, any rational and justice-based attempt to recognize past and present crimes and oppression of non-Turkish minorities is frequently dismissed as yet another attempt to undermine the Turkish state.

Second, Zarakol writes about Turkey's obsession with being seen as part of the West and thus civilized. Turks from the common man to state elites desire to be seen as modern, Western, and thus civilized. To have this status confirmed, they seek approval from other Western countries. But this leads to a dilemma. "Turks resent this intrusive gaze, but crave its approval, and suspect the approval when it is dispensed, yet sense discrimination when it is not."[57] Due to this ontological insecurity, the Turkish state and the broader Turkish society lack the self-confidence to engage in self-critical dialogues about the past. As we will see in the section on culture below, the dominance of patriarchal institutions and norms also frustrate self-critical reflection.

In addition to appealing directly to foreign governments to block legislative attempts to recognize the 1915 Armenian genocide, successive Turkish governments, including both Republican Kemalists and the new Islamist governments of the Justice and Development Party (AKP), have sought to shape the development of popular culture in Western countries as well as the intellectual and scholarly debate about the Ottoman Empire, the treatment of minorities, and the genocide itself. The most clearly documented case of the Turkish government trying to prevent the production of a film in the United States was the case of the *Musa Dagh* film project, which was based on the very popular novel by Franz Werfel, first published in German but then translated as *The Forty Days of Musa Dagh*, which became a best seller in the United States in 1934–1935.[58] Based on the popularity of the novel, the Hollywood film company MGM purchased the film rights and planned to move forward with production until they received warnings from the US Department of State and Turkish officials. MGM was warned that moving forward with the project could damage relations between the two countries and that MGM films could face distribution problems in Turkey.[59]

The next clear response to come from the Turkish government came about as a result of the Armenian terrorists who began to assassinate Turkish diplomatic officials overseas, which also resulted in significant loss of other lives as well. In the United States, the Turkish government established the Institute for Turkish Studies in 1982 at Georgetown University and placed Heath Lowry as the director. Lowry's scholarship on the Ottoman Empire is frequently cited by those wishing to question the genocide or the extent of the Armenian deaths. Over the years, the Institute for Turkish Studies has supported a wide range of scholars, including White, who tends to be more critical of current political trends in Turkey. There have been past attempts by Turkish government officials to shape the direction of the institute through the removal of directors who strayed too far in the direction of supporting free academic inquiry, and in November 2015, the Turkish government removed all funding for the institute. The Turkish government also established the Atatürk Chair in Turkish Studies at Princeton University with Heath Lowry as its first holder. The United States is hardly the only target of such pressure. In 1982, the Turkish government asked the Israeli government to cancel a conference on the Holocaust and Genocide Studies that was to take place at Yad Vashem. The conference was to include a discussion of the Armenian genocide. Yad Vashem eventually withdrew its support, and the conference was moved to Tel Aviv University. Furthermore, the Israeli government continues to deny what happened to the Armenians was a genocide.[60]

This leaves the situation largely stuck as it has been for the past one hundred years. As the Western world has moved, over the past several decades, more decisively in the direction of recognizing past crimes in their own societies, this has put added pressure on Turkey to conform to these new developing Western international norms, to the extent that the country wants to continue to pursue Western development and Western modernity. Although there are numerous reasons why the Turkish application for EU membership is moving forward slowly or has perhaps even completely stalled at the moment, the continued failure of the Turkish state to give a definitive recognition of the Armenian genocide *and* to take concrete steps internally to deal with the consequences of this recognition also remain a problem.

## Culture

As we have seen in each of these cases, the structure of authority within and beyond the family has played an important role in shaping how each society has dealt with its difficult history. Questions of what has happened in the past involve potential criticism of the behavior of the ancestors, both living and dead. The bonds that exist between the generations are stronger in some of our cases than others. The Japanese case has helped us to understand why there was effectively no intergenerational conflict in the postwar period, especially when compared with West Germany. Turkey is more similar to Japan than Germany in terms of its collectivism and the closer bonds that exist between the generations in Turkish families.[61] Hashimoto's concept of generational proximity helps us to appreciate some of the additional complications that exist in Turkey when it comes to confronting the country's difficult history. Indeed, because the family bonds and obligations are much higher in Japan and Turkey than in Western societies, psychologists recognize the need to take a different approach in helping their patients deal with psychological distress.[62]

In this section, we will look first at the role that the figure of Atatürk plays in shutting down discussions about the past, similar to the role that the Japanese emperor played in that country. The key difference is that Atatürk has obtained an immortality denied even a Japanese emperor. Then we will look at what scholars of the Turkish family have to say about the dynamics there. This will help us to understand some of the similarities that exist between Japan and Turkey in how cultural norms tend to shut down discussions about the difficult past, even more so than in the three cases that are more Western in their orientation and structure. Hashimoto's concept of generational proximity, which she developed for her discussion of the Japanese case, offers some insights into the Turkish case as well.

### *The Turkish Father Figure: Atatürk*

Turkey is far from the only country that has a central founding father figure who is credited with the creation of the modern state. The difference in Turkey is that empirical and rational discussions about Atatürk's role in founding the Turkish Republic and who he was as a mortal being are nearly impossible to move forward in Turkey. There is still, today, no reasonably authoritative biography about the man, nor an authentic documentary about his life.[63] He remains an unapproachable father figure in a society that remains very patriarchal. That Atatürk also played a key role in establishing a state tradition of denying the Armenian genocide makes it even more challenging to have an open discussion about Turkey's difficult history. In Turkey, one *cannot* engage the topic of the Armenian genocide without touching the most sacred symbol of the country. This is not because Atatürk is implicated directly in the Armenian genocide, as indeed he was at the other end of the country at that time in the war and had had a falling-out with the Young Turk leadership. But Atatürk did establish the historical narrative of the "murderous Armenians," who had betrayed the country, in his *Nutuk* speech before Parliament in 1927. The *Nutuk* speech has inhibited open historiographical research in Turkey, as it created the acceptable boundaries of historical discussion in Turkey. The result has been that the development of history as an evidence-based empirical process in Turkey has been significantly retarded.

Vamik D. Volkan and Norman Itzkowitz write that Atatürk has become immortal in Turkish society. "Atatürk has continued to live as a symbol and a concept. His picture continues to be reverenced alongside the national flag and is displayed beside it on days of national celebration or remembrance. He is omnipresent. He is on postage stamps and money, both bills and coins. . . . Mental and physical representations of Atatürk have fused with and are symbolic of the Turkish spirit, and thus he has indeed become immortal."[64] For those looking to draw parallels between Atatürk and other "founding fathers" in other countries, this misses the point. While the founding fathers, monarchs, or emperors in other countries can play an important role in blocking discussions about the past, none of them has attained the standing that Atatürk has in Turkey. The one exception might be Mao in China, although the Chinese leadership has tried to make a distinction between the early Mao as founding father and his later "errors," which led to the deaths of millions.[65]

Many Americans continue to have problems dealing with the legacy of slavery in the United States because the founding fathers were so intimately bound up with this institution, but that does not prevent Americans and their official state institutions and memorials from recognizing this link today, as we can see with the Independence Mall in Philadelphia, which links George Washington's household with the use of enslaved people,[66] or the incorporation of slave history into the Thomas Jefferson national monument at his home, Monticello. In Japan, the death of the wartime Shoa emperor in 1989 freed up discussions about the wartime past and the role that the Japanese had played as perpetrators in that conflict. As long as the emperor was alive, many Japanese clearly felt uncomfortable engaging in critical reflections about the war, which would necessarily then lead to questions about the legitimacy of the emperor. The point is to recognize that even in democratic societies, the reverence for the founding fathers, emperors, or other male authorities can play a role in blocking discussions about difficult pasts but that these figures have not become immortal and unquestionable in the way that Atatürk has in Turkey. Volkan and Itzkowitz continue, "More than forty years after his death his image is still used to foster a sense of national unity in Turkey. In this sense Atatürk is like a prophet whose mystical image exists as a powerful unifier forever and ever. No other modern leader has achieved the degree of immortality Atatürk enjoys among the Turks."[67]

In her study of the Atatürk personality cult in Turkey, Nazlı Ökten notes the importance of the ancestor cult in Turkish culture and that Atatürk is more than a "founding father"; he is, instead, the ancestor of the Turks. Anıtkabir, his mausoleum in Ankara, has become a site of pilgrimage for those who have complaints and unfulfilled wishes.[68] Ökten observes, "Both Islamists and secularists utilize

November 10 memorials as an opportunity to express their contemporary political agenda."[69] Indeed, anyone can try to win a political debate by arguing that this is what Atatürk would want done. When Ökten tried to encourage her interviewees to talk about possible human faults that Atatürk may have possessed, they generally avoided the question; when an interviewee did mention third-party discussion of his alcoholism or criticism of religion, "They repeated the accusations with the fear of being misunderstood."[70] Temelkuran also offers some personal insights into the consequences of the Atatürk cult, noting that she cannot say whether or not she finds him attractive as a man; "No matter how hard I try, I cannot see Atatürk as a person, as a man. There's an enormous obstacle in the way of my perception. When you see pictures of a figure that often, from morning till night, starting in primary school and going right up until the end of university, it becomes almost completely impossible to think of him as a man, as a person."[71]

Ulgen also links the Atatürk cult to the continuation of genocide denial in Turkey today. In one sense, the discussion of the Armenian genocide and Atatürk should not be so difficult as Atatürk did not play a direct role in the military operations in the east. Although he was a member of the Committee for Union and Progress, he had a falling-out with Enver Pasha in February 1913 and found himself marginalized.[72] The problem emerges in that while seeking to establish the republic and giving the Turks a new history and a new understanding of themselves in world history, Atatürk helped to establish the myth of the "murderous Armenians" and the innocence of the wrongfully betrayed Turks. Ulgen is critical of Taner Akçam, who is often seen as a critical Turkish scholar, because he tries to lean on Atatürk's supposed statement of a "shameful act." Akçam thus remains, for Ulgen, trapped in the Atatürk cult while trying to move Turkish society toward recognition of the genocide, the argument being that because Atatürk recognized the genocide as a "shameful act," Turks today can also talk about this. Ulgen writes, "A more serious ramification of all the works that instrumentalize Kemal in the politics of 'genocide recognition' is that they reproduce his cult status and infantilize the Turks in an ideologically masculine way: the honour of the Father needs to be salvaged first to enable his children to come to terms with their past."[73] As with Volkan and Ökten, Ulgen wants to emphasize that this cult of Atatürk is something more exceptional than what we see in other societies; she calls it "ideological totalitarianism."[74] In a society where discussion of a mortal and fallible Mustafa Kemal is nearly impossible, the mythology established by Atatürk is largely beyond reproach and forms the core of the educational curriculum in Turkey today.

### *The Family: The Consequences of Patriarchy*

For a Western audience, the consequences of extreme patriarchy are now something well beyond the lived experience of the younger generations and somewhat difficult to imagine. Many Westerns have grown so accustomed to the norms surrounding the principles of autonomy, mutual respect, and freedom that it is nearly impossible to imagine what a more extreme patriarchy looks or feels like. Patriarchy, however, is very much on the minds of Turkish intellectuals, writers, thinkers, and social critics—and not just women. For example, Pamuk puts the difficult relationship between fathers and sons, masters and disciples, and political leaders and citizens in Turkey at the center of his new novel, *The Red-Haired Woman*.[75] Turkish discussions of patriarchy make it very clear that men suffer just as much as women under this system of social control focused on obedience, subordination, and dependency. When so much aggression must be repressed, the potential for violence is very real.

To help the reader appreciate the consequences of patriarchy, let me briefly describe some scenes from a film by the Turkish director Reha Erdem. In his film *Beş Vakit* (*Times and Winds*) (2006), Erdem offers not only a critique of patriarchy for his Turkish audience but also a window onto this cultural landscape for the Western viewer. Patriarchy's victims are many, but first and foremost, they are the children. Although set in a rural village, Erdem may want the viewer to think of all of Turkey as "a village" enclosed in on itself. The director clearly does not want simply to critique village ways and life but rather patriarchy itself. Other Turkish directors have raised similar concerns about patriarchy in rural middle-class settings, such as Deniz Gamze Ergüven in her film *Mustang* (2015), or urban middle-class settings as in Seren Yüce's film *Çoğunluk* (*Majority*) (2010). While such critical films resonate with some Turks, the backlash can be fierce. Although Ergüven's film received numerous international nominations and awards, including a nomination for an Academy Award, she and her film received such harsh criticism in Turkey that she has decided not to work in Turkey in the immediate future. *Mustang* portrays the story of five sisters, who are held captive in the family home and married off through arranged marriages at very young ages, as soon as possible, to protect their honor and that of the family.

For Erdem's film, the setting is the present in a small Turkish village, set between the sea and the mountains. But it is only over the course of the film that we come to understand that the film is set in the present and not earlier in the twentieth century, thus potentially shocking the audience with the realization that "this is not once how things were" but rather that "this is how they still are." After watching a film where all of the cues point to the early twentieth century or then maybe the 1950s, the viewer is surprised toward the end to see someone pull out a cell phone. Technological progress is present, but the cultural norms remain deeply embedded.

Early in the film, we are brought into a classroom where young children are reading aloud, when the young, female teacher notices that a little girl has a black eye. When she asks what happened, the other children laugh and cry out that her mother hit her. And then they point at another boy whose arm is heavily bandaged and the children cry out, "And his father beat him!" Casual violence against children by their parents is openly accepted at school and elsewhere.

The children are reading from their textbook about the rotation of the earth, the cycles of night and day, and the heating and cooling of the planet, which causes the winds to blow and brings physical changes to the landscape, even causing rocks to crumble. The entire film is structured around this theme of the cycle of the day, the cycle of the prayers from the minarets, the cycle of birth and death for humans and animals. If the world of nature changes slowly through the heating and cooling of rocks, might not the society of man also change? While the director holds out the possibility of a yes, his transition from the crumbling of the rocks in the school lesson to a conversation between a young mother and an old woman is designed to suggest that the world of men may move even slower, that men may be harder than rocks. The conversation between the young mother and the old woman dwells on the unchanging nature of the men, how the son, even when grown, must submit unquestioningly to endless humiliation from his father, that he will beat his son, and that his son will grow up to be like his father. The women laugh at their observation, but this is exactly the back biting and jokes that remain hidden, which change nothing. What is particularly striking is that throughout the whole film, the subordinate in a relationship *never* questions or challenges the superior directly. The subordinate will cry in silence, plot the death of the superior in secret, curse his name and complain to others, engage in self-mortification, but there is never an open confrontation between the two, which might transform the relationship into one of greater equality, mutual respect, and love. The pent-up aggression is displaced onto the children. There is a clear sense that the days and nights will follow each other, the earth will heat and cool, the rocks will crumble, but the men and their rule will never change.

Erdem does not spare the Turkish state from direct criticism, suggesting that the patriarchal relationships in the families of the village extend to the broader society and the state's relationship with its citizens. The men of the village have gathered in the local café to question one of their own, who has been seen to beat severely a young teenage boy, an orphan, who has been placed in his care. The deep bruises across his back are shown to the village men, and one of them questions the amount of force applied. The caretaker shows indifference and simply leaves. We then hear children's voices in a call-and-response over the scene, "I am Turkish; I am right." The camera then cuts to the schoolyard where the children are gathered in front of the Atatürk bust and reciting the national pledge. The children continue, "I am hardworking. My motto is to protect the younger, to respect the elder, to love my land and my nation more than my own self." In order to underline the incongruous line of "to protect the younger," and what we have just witnessed at the village council, the director cuts to an image of the beaten orphan shepherd with his goats on the mountainside. He begins to move the goats up the hill. But then he stands alone on the steep slope. "My ideal is to rise and make progress. O great Atatürk! I swear that I will follow your path and walk persistently toward the aim you pointed out!

My life is a present offered to the Turkish nation! Happy is he who proclaims himself a Turk!" The ironic tension makes the critique quite clear, if subtle. There may also be further symbolism embodied in the status of the young boy as an orphan, if we remember Temelkuran's earlier observation that political candidates often campaign on the "rights of orphans," as if Turkey's citizens are orphans of Atatürk, in need of a father, in need of discipline by the state.

The film is not without hope for change. If it comes, it will arrive in the form of a little girl who decides to change the direction of her life. Her father shows her greater affection and love than is usual, and the young female teacher loans her a book, *Çalıkuşu* (*The Autobiography of a Turkish Girl*), which was written by Reşat Nuri Güntekin in 1922 and has been filmed and made into a television series twice. The story is of an orphaned young woman who shows greater independence than was usually tolerated at the time. She becomes a teacher and tries to exercise more autonomy over her life. In his critique of neopatriarchy, Sharabi writes the following in his final chapter "What Is to Be Done?": "Of all these groups, potentially the most revolutionary is the women's movement. If this phase of struggle were to open up to radical democratic change, women's liberation would necessarily be its spearhead. Even in the short term, the women's movement is the detonator which will explode patriarchal society from within."[76] Erdem recognizes this as well. If freedom, autonomy, and mutual respect begin to govern the relationship between men and women, then the rocks of patriarchy will begin to crack and society will be transformed; and the relationship between the citizen and the state will also face pressure for change to one based on law and human rights, rather than a subject dedicated to self-sacrifice.

This extreme patriarchy has serious consequences for families and the broader society. If we again remind ourselves that digging around in the national past and addressing it in a self-critical manner is a rebellious act, one that will put one in conflict with existing patterns of authority, we can see how patriarchal authority is more likely to shut down such discussions rather than open them up for investigation.

In their discussion of psychiatry in Turkey, Ibrahim Hakki Öztürk and Vamik Volkan note that Turkish child-rearing practices discourage the development of an "autonomous will and autonomous activity."[77] They are careful to note that the patterns observed should not be classified as psychopathologies but that the development of children tends in the direction of creating a "constricted self" that includes a "lack of curiosity, initiative, and empathy" and fosters a "passive-dependent expectation." "This attribute of passivity and dependence can be seen in attitudes toward the father figure, the elders, the teachers, the state, and God, and in beliefs pertaining to natural phenomena like birth, death, illness, and the catastrophes of life. This passive-dependent expectation and the characteristic of the 'constricted self' seem to suggest a relative lack of basic trust, autonomy, and initiative."[78]

These findings are echoed in Güler Okman Fişek's study of Turkish families where she summarizes, "Regarding the implication for personality development of the above, most authors agree that the traditional Turkish family dynamics would foster the development of a passive, dependent, constricted and somewhat frustrated person without a sense of autonomy and with a reliance on external sources of control and reinforcement."[79] While these patterns are more intense in rural and lower class families, Fişek also notes that,

> while middle class urban parents are more attentive to the development of conceptual skills in their children, they still tend to reinforce reliance on parental authority rather than on the child's own resources, which results in a field of dependent cognitive style among the children. In fact, in this last study it was found that increased democratization in discipline among middle class parents was not accompanied by increased training for autonomy, in contrast to Western studies in which the two child-rearing attitudes have been generally found to co-vary.[80]

Sharabi cites the Lebanese social psychologist Ali Zay'our in looking at the consequences of patriarchy in Arab societies. He quotes Zay'our: "The family is relentless in its repression. [The child] is brought up to become an obedient youth, subservient to those above him—his father, older brother, clan chief, president."[81] Sharabi continues, "Zay'our links repression in the family to the prevalence of 'irrational and superstitious' attitudes in the mass of the population, which facilitates control by the status quo and makes people blindly opposed to social change."[82] While writing specifically about Morocco, Abdellah Hammoudi argued that the relationship of complete subservience between the master and the disciple has deep roots in the Maghreb and Middle Eastern Islam, and is one that is replicated in father-son relationships as well as between the ruler and the ruled in terms of state power.[83] As Elisabeth Özdalga demonstrates in her comparative work, all of these characteristics are far more common in Turkey as well, when compared to Western countries.[84]

As we have seen in the chapter on Japan, the more intense the *generational proximity* is, the less likely one is to find open, intergenerational conflict. This is one reason why Japanese discussions about their wartime past have been more muted, especially regarding the extreme resistance on the part of Japanese children to viewing their parents as anything other than powerless victims of the war and rarely as potential perpetrators. A similar generational proximity exists in Middle Eastern Muslim families as well. Sharabi writes of Arab families and patriarchy, "The cohesion of the family is mainly achieved through the socialization of the child into dependency upon the family—upon the father, the mother, the brothers—and through assuring it his loyalty and support. One important consequence of this dependency is that the child grows up feeling his primary responsibility toward the family and not toward society."[85] Here, we can see a clear reason why Kohlberg was unable to find young Turks who displayed any forms of postconventional reasoning, as we already discussed in the introduction.

And if we transpose the nature of these relationships onto those that should govern the relationship between the citizen and the state, we can see the same dependence and diminution of autonomy in the national pledge that the Turkish schoolchildren recite. Göçek echoes these sentiments as well while giving them an even stronger political tone by noting that the Turkish republican state simply continued to operate like the Ottoman Empire, with the sultan/father at the center of the political power structure.[86] And we have already seen how the state is often thought of as the father-state, the *devlet baba*, in the school textbooks. As with the conversation between the young mother with the old woman in Erdem's film, when questioned by the old woman as to why her husband does not resist his father, the young mother replies, "How can he? It's his father." The old woman does not contradict her, having already known the answer.

Turkish society shares a couple of other characteristics with Japan that help us to understand the difficulties both societies have had in dealing with their violent histories, in that Turkey, like Japan, has a culture and social order founded more on shame than guilt and that honor plays a significant role in one's sense of well-being. Sharabi notes that guilt, an inward sense of self-punishment, is not the dominate sense one experiences for a wrong act in Middle Eastern patriarchal societies. As he writes, "an Arab Hamlet is inconceivable."[87] Rather, one is governed by a sense of shame for a wrong act that has been exposed to others, which then damages one's standing and also the standing of the family in the society. This makes the desire to hide the shameful act all the more necessary and aggressive. Unlike in a guilt-based culture that predominates in the Western world, where an honest apology can set the basis for a renewed relationship, the shame-based culture requires that one resubmit oneself to the superior authority but without a sense of responsibility. Sharabi continues, "Indeed, how can the feeling of responsibility develop if one constantly feels himself powerless? As the individual (unconsciously) repudiates the power that crushes him, he absolves himself of responsibility. And self-absolution automatically shuts off self-criticism, and with it the will to act."[88] What happens if the shamed child or young adult turns against his father and refuses to resubmit? Sharabi writes, "An extreme case, which will illuminate this social syndrome, is the penalty which usually redounds upon the son for violating the father's will in the traditional household: he is reduced to impotence, he has no rights, owns nothing, and is totally at his father's mercy . . . thus as legal opposition is not possible, conspiracy and rebellion become the only possible avenues of action. Similarly, when open discussion is disallowed the remaining form of persuasion is conspiracy and violence."[89] We can see exactly these dynamics in Erdem's film in the Turkish village, as he has the older son of the village imam plotting his father's death by trying to intensify his cold so that he might die, in response to the endless humiliation he faces at the hands of his father, especially as the father favors the younger brother. He feels himself powerless to change the relationship with his father in any other manner, as open dialogue and opposition are disallowed.

The importance of honor, of maintaining face and proper standing before others in the community, and how this is linked to reverence for the father, makes the stakes of confrontations with authority in the household much higher than is the case in the more individualistic Western societies. Moreover, as we have seen above, as the honor of the father has to be sustained under all circumstances, it removes the possibility of a critique or investigation into the wrong behavior of the father. As Ulgen has noted above, this is why attempts to maintain the honor of Atatürk while also investigating the crimes against the Armenians and other minorities in Turkish history becomes an even more difficult task. The two obligations block each other and little meaningful action is taken.

## Chronological Discussion

To understand the Turkish case and the dynamics that have developed between the Turkish state, Turks, and non-Turkish minorities in the Ottoman Empire and the Turkish Republic, one needs to appreciate the extent to which the Turkish population has come to see itself as the principle victim of the collapsing empire, lost wars, and mass expulsions. The ethnocentrism of death and suffering tends to close off any identification with members of other groups, especially if they are seen to be part of the reason for one's own suffering. As we can observe in the German case, the deep sense of German victimhood at the end of the war worked to block an identification with the Jewish victims of German fascism. It was only with a great deal of time and the efforts of those sympathetic to the Jewish position, along with Jews themselves, that the Holocaust moved to the center of the discussions about the legacy of the war; before German society could deal with the Holocaust, Germans had first to process their own suffering and losses. The same is true in the case of Japan, where the Japanese came to view themselves as the primary victim of their own extreme nationalism and imperial project. In both of these cases, the Allies and the United States held an ambiguous position as both punisher and liberator-savior. With the democratization of West Germany and the democratic institutions of the postwar Japanese constitution, both countries came to embrace their democratic future and, with time, to recognize the extreme harm their population and state had caused others.

The case in Turkey is more complicated and helps to explain why this country has made the least progress among our five cases in terms of dealing with its difficult history and especially the harm that Turkey has caused others. In addition to the normal problem of the ethnocentrism of death and suffering, Turks have viewed the Western powers and non-Turkish minorities in hostile terms—as the destroyers and betrayers of the empire and Turks. To appreciate this perspective, one needs to shift the standard framing of history that dominates in the Western world. Just as framing the violence unleashed by imperial Japan does not fit neatly into the Western understanding and time frame of World War II, the Turkish experience of repeated defeats and humiliations at the hands of Western and Christian powers stretches back further than the beginning of World War I and further forward than the end of World War I. At a minimum, the Turkish framing of this history would stretch back to 1912, with the first Balkan War and forward to 1922 with the end of the War of Independence (1919–1922) and the establishment of the Turkish Republic in 1923. It was in 1920 that the successor government of the Ottomans agreed to the terms of the Treaty of Sèvres, which was rejected by Atatürk, who had already launched the War of Independence to drive the Western forces from what remained of the former empire. If one goes back further to the period between 1878 and 1918, Turks will point out that they lost 90 percent of their empire. The Turkish 1915 genocide against the Ottoman Armenians is set within this context and also one that involved Armenian massacres against Turks from 1917 forward. Armenians and Turks were both victims and perpetrators. One way for the Western reader to begin to conceptualize the consequences of this decade of war is to contemplate the deep and traumatic wounds that the far shorter World War I left on the countries of Western Europe. For the Turkish and Muslim populations of the Ottoman Empire, this decade was one of disastrous defeats, mass displacements, and the collapse of the known political order.

With the declaration of the republic on October 29, 1923, Atatürk and the new republic encouraged Turks to dissociate themselves from the entire Ottoman period. Atatürk set the country on the course for Western modernization so that Turks could avoid being dominated by the Western powers in the future. As with Japan in the early twentieth century, Atatürk's Turkey sought to gain recognition and standing in the international community and to reestablish the self-esteem of the Turkish nation that had been so severely threatened over the preceding decades.[90] But in terms of democratic development, the new republic started where the empire had left off. With the destruction of the non-Muslim bourgeoisie of Greeks, Armenians, and Jews through the wars and other anti-minority measures, a new Turkish bourgeoisie was created from the mass theft of this property. This also resulted in the destruction of many of the trade ties that the non-Muslim population had developed with Western countries during the Ottoman Empire. With the only countervailing force in the society to state power deeply indebted to the state for its newfound wealth, there was little in terms of a civil society that could stand in the way of the modernizing power of the new republican state.[91] The primary obstacle remained the vast rural population of Anatolia, which was illiterate and disconnected from the life of the urban centers. They remained deeply religious and traditional in their outlook on the world and resisted the modernization efforts not through coherent action but through passive intransigence. Although thwarted by repeated military coups over the history of the republic, this rural force in Turkish society now finds itself in power since 2002 through the AKP Islamist party.

Atatürk ruled over the new republic for a relatively short time, from 1923 to 1938, although, as we have seen above, he remains an immortal and unifying figure for the country. He also helped to play a direct role in establishing the history for the new republic through a remarkable thirty-six-hour speech and history lesson that he delivered to the parliament on October 15–20, 1927, known as the *Nutuk* speech, which became a sacred text for the new republic.[92] It was in this speech that Atatürk laid the groundwork for the narrative about the murderous and traitorous Armenians, who had fought with the enemy despite having been well treated within the Ottoman Empire. In November 1934, the Grand National Assembly bestowed the title of Atatürk, the father or ancestor of all Turks, on Mustafa Kemal. And on November 10, 1938, the mortal Atatürk died, although his vision for the country remained the legitimizing force for decades to come.

From 1938 to 1950, authoritarian development dominated state policy and the Republican People's Party, which won the first multiparty election in 1946. It was during this period that the authoritarian state gained dominance over the mass media and the cinema industry as well as public education. The censorship law was passed in 1939, and the state remains the only effective source of history textbooks in the country even today. The radical secularism of the party was highly alienating to the vast majority of the republic's citizens, who were overwhelmingly rural and very religious in their outlook. They began to back the Democratic Party. With the full mobilization of the rural population in the next national elections in 1950, the Democratic Party won a significant majority, which they maintained in 1957 as well. As the Democratic Party began to allow religion to play a greater role in public life, the military, which has seen itself as the defender of the secular state established by Atatürk, launched its first coup in 1960 and then continued to involve itself repeatedly in Turkish politics, with military coups in 1971, 1980, and 1997.

The primary tension in Turkish politics has remained between a small, secular, urban elite, largely established and created alongside the republic through the theft of non-Muslim property, thus closely binding this group to the fate of the republic, and the far more religious rural population, which began to migrate in large numbers to the cities in the 1950s and 1960s. Their arrival in Turkey's urban centers did not see a decline in their religiosity. The third component that was added to the mix in the 1980s was the rise of Kurdish separatist nationalism, which remains a problem today. Further complicating the picture is the fact that none of these political forces in Turkey recognize the legitimacy of the other to govern. The idea of a loyal opposition, which is essential to Western parliamentary democracies, is not one shared by any of these factions in Turkish political life. During the 1960s and 1970s, leftist and Marxist ideological parties also played a role in political life, but they were destroyed in the 1980 military coup, which crushed the leftist political forces.

These political and social developments were never conducive to the development of difficult and self-critical reflections on the history of the republic and what had happened to the non-Turkish minorities earlier in the twentieth century.

Indeed, the authoritarian state continued to move forward with other anti-minority measures. There was the 1942–1943 Wealth Tax, which was targeted specifically at Christians and Jews to further impoverish these populations and to add to the wealth of the Turkish bourgeoisie. And then there were the anti-minority, anti-Greek riots of September 6–7, 1955, which were orchestrated by the state. The riots led to the destruction of minority businesses, churches, and cemeteries. The state media spread false stories that there had been a bomb attack on Atatürk's house in Salonica. One hardly needed to name the identity of the supposed perpetrators.[93]

To the extent that Turkish society did look back on its history during these years, it was limited to celebratory films about the War of Independence. Gönül Dönmez-Colin identifies war films and historical action films as a popular genre within the history of Turkish cinema, not unlike the case in other countries. Muhsin Ertuğrul made *Bir Millet Uyaniyor (A Nation Awakening)* (1932), which served as a model for other similar films that followed. One important contrast with the development of the war film genre in Turkey compared to other countries in the West is that they remained largely heroic and positive in their message. The value of the sacrifice for the nation is never questioned, while in Western countries there has been a growing skepticism about the costs of war coming out of World War I.[94] When this skepticism, however minor, did enter Turkish television and cinema, as with Halit Refiğ's filming of Kemal Tahir's novel *Yorgun Savaşçı (Tired Warrior)* (1979) for television, it was burned by the military regime after the 1980 coup for "defaming Atatürk and the War of Independence."[95] This sort of questioning of one's willingness to sacrifice one's life in war has only appeared very recently in Turkish cinema, as with the film *Yazı Tura (Toss-Up)* (2004) from Uğur Yücel, which clearly demonstrates the devastating toll that war takes on veterans.[96] While some war films were given specific settings and historical contexts, others were simply placed in an unspecific heroic past. Dönmez-Colin notes, "Tarkan (created in 1967 and not placed in a particular period) and Karaoglan were played by Kartal Tibet. These heroes fought unknown enemies with fascistic chauvinism; violence was justified by the initial aggression of the enemy—massacre, torture, rape or insult to honour. The three ideologies, nationalism, conservatism and Islamism have been at the core of these films."[97] The popular television series and films called *Kurtlar Vadisi (Valley of the Wolves)* (2006) is a continuation of this tradition, which celebrates violence and revenge.[98]

Although there were carriers of other memories in Turkish society, among those Armenians, Greeks, and Jews who remained, these were populations that existed with very little, if any, voice in the public arena. The censorship laws, if not the threat of nationalist violence, has kept these populations silent until very recently. Within the Turkish Armenian population, the fear of the broader Turkish society has been so great that grandparents refused to share their memories with the younger generation. The intergenerational sharing of family histories became broken and fractured, as the older generation sought to protect the younger generation from knowledge that could only put them in danger in the broader society.[99] This is similar to what we see happening in the case among Republican families in Spain, where Republican parents withheld aspects of the family history from their children to try and protect them in Francoist Spain. The contrast with the Jewish population in postwar occupied Germany and then West Germany is quite clear, as Jews immediately took advantage of their capacity to tell their story to the broader German public. It was the persistence of the Jewish community in West Germany, and in particular Berlin, that eventually began to reach a broader German public in the 1970s and then the 1980s. In contrast, state and societal pressures in Turkey have remained so oppressive that the Armenian and other minority communities could rarely articulate their sentiments and feelings about what had happened in the past.

Therefore, the development of an Armenian narrative about the 1915 genocide had to occur outside of Turkey, thus bringing the international and global role to the forefront. Internal discussion was completely closed off. While there was some discussion of the Armenian experience in the interwar years, as demonstrated by the popularity of Werfel's book *Die Vierzig Tage des Musa Dagh* (1933) and the resulting interest of MGM in the movie rights, the Armenian diaspora community focused primarily on its reconstitution in exile and keeping cultural traditions alive. The Armenian diaspora community in the Western countries, primarily France and the United States, had the freedom to organize and discuss the past. The *Armenian Review* began publication in 1948 but was primarily focused on culture and history, without any specific attention on the genocide until the 1960s. Armenian populations also remained scattered around the Middle East, some of them not even having been touched directly by the genocide, although the Armenian population in the Armenian Republic, which was incorporated into the Soviet Union, was directly affected. Development of the genocide narrative in Soviet Armenia was stifled by the concerns of the socialist state, although eventually this would become the subject of films there as well.

The key turning point for the Armenian diaspora came with the fiftieth anniversary of the 1915 genocide in 1965, which was in itself a significant event. But by 1965, there was also growing global awareness of the Jewish Holocaust in the broader Western consciousness about the legacy of World War II, which added to concerns within the Armenian diaspora community to remember their own traumatic history.[100] Within the Western context, J. Michael Hagopian's short twenty-eight-minute documentary, *Where Are My People?* (1965), may be the first cinematic treatment of the genocide since *Ravished Armenia* was released in 1919, which was based on the memoir of Aurora (Arshaluys) Mardiganian. From this point forward, the diaspora in the West began to recall the genocide in a far more public manner. For example, the French Armenian singer and actor Charles Aznavour recorded "Ils sont tombés" ("They Fell") in 1975. By 1982, the Armenian diaspora in the United States had established the Zoryan Institute in Cambridge, Massachusetts, and began to hold scholarly conferences to expand knowledge about the Armenian experience in the

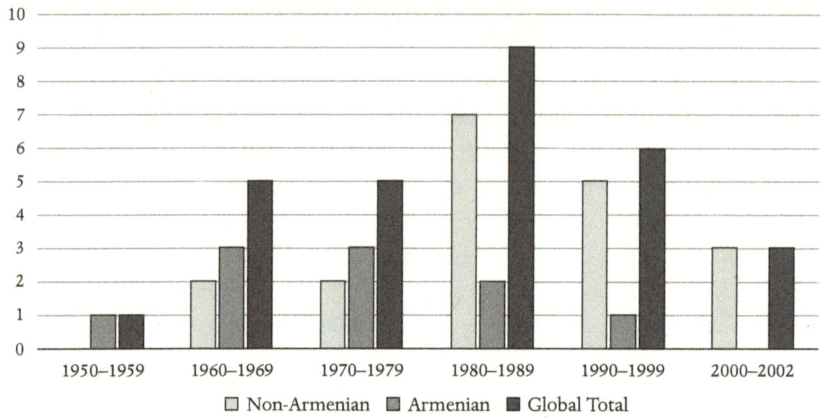


Figure 4 Armenian genocide films.
*Sources*: There is no central source listing all such films. The author collected information from the following: Zaven Boyajyan, *Armenian Cinema Catalogue, 1924–2008: Feature, Documentary, Animation*, 2nd ed. (Yerevan: Armenian Association of Film Critics and Cinema Journalists, 2009); Hovhanness I. Pilikian, *Armenian Cinema: A Source Book* (London: Counter-Point Productions, 1981); *Armenian Cinema*, http://www.arm-cinema.am/en/home/ (accessed November 7, 2017). The following source is part of a Turkish effort to deny the Armenian genocide by labeling the works "propaganda" but nonetheless provides a useful list of films dealing with the genocide: Sedat Laçiner and Şenol Kantarcı, *Art and Armenian Propaganda: Ararat as a Case Study* (Ankara: ASAM Institute for Armenian Research, 2002). Films about the Armenian genocide continue to be produced, but it was too difficult to find consistent sources after 2002.

Ottoman Empire as well as the genocide itself. The *Journal of Armenian Studies* and the *Journal of the Society for Armenian Studies* were established around this time as well. From the 1980s onward, there was a steady stream of documentaries and some feature films that addressed the genocide and Armenian life including *An Armenian Journey*, which was broadcast on the American PBS network in 1987. In this documentary, Theodore Bogosian visits the places where the massacres took place with a survivor of the genocide.

The fiftieth anniversary marked a turning point in Soviet Armenia as well.[101] With some relaxation in the Cold War tensions, members of the diaspora began to reconnect with Armenia and family members in the region, although not in Turkey. The earliest record we have of a film dealing with the Armenian genocide in Soviet Armenia comes from 1950 in an unfinished film project titled, *Yerkrord Karavane* (*The Second Caravan*), directed by Hamo Beknazaryan, who had directed the first Armenian sound film in 1925. The film was to deal with the migration of Armenians from Turkey as a result of the 1915 genocide and their decision to move to Soviet Armenia after World War II. In 1960, Laert Vagharshyan made *Kochvats en aprelu* (*They Are to Live*), which tells the story of two brothers separated during the genocide who never meet again. One of the two brothers dies in World War II, and the other survives to return to Armenia and looks for his brother's children. Other Soviet Armenian films use the events of the genocide as a background for their characters, such as Nerses Hovhannisyan's *A Meeting at an Exhibition* (*Handipum Tsutsahandesum*) (1968) or Henrik Malyan's *Nahapet* (*Life Triumphs*) (1977). Zhirayr Avetisyan's *Dzori Miron/Dzori Miro* (1981) situates the character in the conflict itself as the main character fights against the Turkish militiamen and then decides to begin a new life as a refugee in Soviet Armenia. The clearest foregrounding of the genocide comes in Vigen Chaldranyan's 1985 film *April*, which is set in a small Armenian village on April 24, the day that Armenians use to mark the beginning of the genocide. The film tells the story of the massacres and the desire of the survivors to share their stories with their descendants.

While these activities within the diaspora began to shift the location of the genocide toward the center of Armenian self-understanding, they were having absolutely no impact on the discussion within Turkey. This changed with the eruption of violence by the Armenian Secret Army for the Liberation of Armenia (ASLAN), which began a decade-long campaign of violence against Turkish diplomatic targets outside of Turkey from 1973 to 1985. ASLAN murdered about fifty Turkish diplomats along with others caught in the crossfire. The ASLAN violence led to renewed efforts on the part of the Turkish government to remove references to the Armenian genocide at the United Nations in 1973 and to continue placing pressure on foreign governments not to recognize officially the genocide. For ordinary Turks, the ASLAN violence reactivated a sense of unjustified Turkish victimization at the hands of the traitorous Armenians, which had long been part of the school curriculum and part of the popular culture. The violence worked to further suppress Armenian voices inside Turkey. It was in this context that the state began to combat external demands for the recognition of the genocide more forcefully and also sought other ways to shift the debate by opening and funding the Institute for Turkish Studies at Georgetown University in 1982, with Heath Lowry as its first director. The Turkish government withdrew funding from the institute in November 2015, probably because they felt it had become too independent in terms of the scholarship that it supported under later directors, who allowed for more critical scholarship on Turkey, not only related to the Armenian issue.

While Turkey fought the growing pressure for recognition of the genocide outside the country, the internal restrictions that had been in place since the founding of the republic continued to suppress any potential for critical internal voices from scholars, artists, or social activists. Laws banning the insulting of "Turkishness" or the military continued to be used to intimidate and prosecute those who began to ask questions about Turkish history, even when Turks had been the primary victims, such as the use of the Liberation Courts at the founding of the republic, which the state used to execute anyone who stood in the way of the modernization drive.

The key turning point was the military coup in 1980, which put an end to the running street battles between Marxist leftists and different nationalist and Islamist gangs. While the brutality of the new military regime would later be regretted by many, the steps taken to restore order were quite popular at the time. The military regime implemented measures that would have far-reaching consequences for Turkish society and also bring in a new era in which the difficult past as well as its present could be more widely discussed. These were unintended consequences of the liberalization of the economy.

The balance of power was shifting in Turkey, from the secular state, the military, and the postwar bourgeoisie on the one hand toward the Islamists, with their roots in rural Anatolia. The rural population had been moving to the cities since the 1960s, and some of them were beginning to become successful at business on their own. Whereas the postwar bourgeoisie had depended primarily on the theft of property from non-Muslim minorities, the new business class had begun to develop in the mid-1970s while maintaining their connections to Islam. The old bourgeois class had continued to profit because of Turkey's closure to world markets and their ability to continue profiting from a limited but protected internal market. The 1980 military coup ushered in dramatic changes to the orientation of the Turkish economy away from domestic markets to greater openness to global markets. With the loss of their old protected markets, the secular republican business class was largely replaced by the new business class rooted in the rural Anatolia along with their deeper religious roots.

The liberalization drive also led to significant changes in the media and communication markets and the weakening of state censorship after 1986. Although the state maintained its right to censor media outlets, television, and film production, in reality it largely withdrew from this type of interference. From the 1990s onward, there was a dramatic shift in the openness of discussions about Turkey's history in the twentieth century, although discussion of the Armenian genocide still remains a highly repressed topic. But this is a period during which there is a general freeing-up of discussions on many levels in Turkey. Turkish scholars began to challenge the Turkish Historical Thesis in the 1980s.[102] Ethnic minorities started to be shown as themselves in Turkish films in the 1990s—for example, in having Kurds speak their own language and to be identified as Kurds, something that had previously been censored.[103] There was also an increase in the translation of Armenian authors into Turkish, thus providing some voice for Armenians within Turkey, although the domestic population continued to remain largely silent.[104] In 1994, the Code of Private Radio and Television Broadcasting was passed, ending the state monopoly on broadcasts. And in 1996, the Bolsahay, Armenians living in Turkey, began publication of *Agos* to talk about the difficult position of their community in Turkey. Hrant Dink became the editor of *Agos* and the leading voice for the Bolsahay until his assassination in 2007.

Backed by the new Islamist business class, different iterations of an Islamist party competed successfully for seats in the parliament. The parties would be banned and then reform as a new organization to contest the next election. This resulted in one final military coup on February 28, 1997, but this option for defending the secular state had exhausted itself. In 2001, the AKP was founded, and they have won every election since 2002. In December 2004, the AKP began accession talks with the EU, which again led to an uptick in discussion about the Armenian genocide.[105]

The current and much improved position in Turkey today has little to do with the direct intentions of the secularists or the Islamists in Turkish politics. Both are equally hostile to political and cultural pluralism in Turkey. The Turkish state and whichever party is in control at the time has been of little consequence. The improved conditions have much more to do with the unintended consequences of the economic liberalization program that began in the 1980s, which started to allow for some increasing pluralism in Turkish politics and society and the freeing-up of forces within the civil society to challenge the position of the Turkish state. As with the other cases that we have examined in this book, the change has usually come primarily from the side of the civil society and then, sometimes, been reinforced by state action, as in Germany and Spain.

To get a sense of how things have changed and remained the same in Turkey, let's take a quick look at how the issue of Armenians in Turkey has played out in a couple of public debates in the past decade. At the beginning of the new millennium, the Turkish Ministry of Education felt it was still appropriate in 2003 to hold an essay competition on "why the Armenians were traitors," thus clearly marking the role that the Turkish state has played since the founding of the republic in frustrating discussions about Turkey's difficult history. In April 2004, Hrant Dink and the Turkish Armenian newspaper *Agos* found themselves embroiled in a serious confrontation with the state and extreme nationalists when Dink wrote a story, based on reasonable historical fact, that Sabiha Gökçen, one of Atatürk's adopted children, had Armenian roots. He was charged under Article 301 for having publicly insulted and degraded Turkishness. Gökçen is one of the symbols of the republic, a modern women and fighter pilot, who was frequently photographed at Atatürk's side.[106] The fact that a Muslim Turkish family may have adopted an Armenian orphan was not something that was surprising, as such adoptions are widely known to have taken place at the time of the genocide and the deportations. What made this particular statement by Dink so explosive was that it brought the issue of Armenian history and the genocide into very close and intimate proximity of Atatürk himself.[107] The core symbol of the republic was in danger of becoming polluted. We have seen similar reactions in the United States around the issue of slavery and the founding fathers of the American republic, especially with regard to George Washington and Thomas Jefferson. The reactions in the United States have been similar in that the pollution of slavery has been kept at bay until very recently for both Washington and Jefferson.[108] While the reactions are similar, the intensity of the reaction in Turkey far outpaces the reaction that has taken place in the United States. In July 2006, Dink called the violence against the Armenians in the context of World War I a genocide, and in January 2007, he was assassinated by a young Turkish nationalist with support from others. The initial response to Dink's assassination was hopeful in that over one hundred thousand supporters demonstrated a week later while chanting, "I am Armenian," in solidarity. At first, the situation looked like a breakthrough moment for discussion of the Armenian issue in Turkey, but things quickly turned against the demonstrators and Dink supporters. Prime Minister Erdoğan came out publicly against the "I am Armenian" chant, calling it distasteful, and the nationalist press quickly began to denounce such identification with Armenians as un-Turkish. One recent analysis of the post-assassination debate in Turkey concludes that the anti-acknowledgment group won the public debate.[109]

Nonetheless, the balance of power in Turkish civil society is clearly shifting. Bilgi University, one of the new private universities established in the 1990s, held the first ever conference on the Armenian genocide in Turkey in September 2005. Earlier the same year, Pamuk made reference to the Armenian genocide during an interview with *Das Magazin* in Switzerland. Although the conference at Bilgi was able to go ahead despite threats of violence from extreme nationalists, Pamuk was charged under Article 301 for insulting Turkishness. As a result, he decided to spend additional time outside of the country because of concern for his personal safety. He still has body guards with him today. The charges against him were dropped in January 2006, but the social sanctions and concerns for his personal safety remain with him. As a result of these different debates, in December 2008, about thirty thousand people were willing to put their names on an online petition calling for a public apology to the Armenians and acknowledging the genocide.

While the Turkish state may be bending toward some acknowledgment of the genocide as part of a response to international pressure and the accession negotiations with the EU, internally it continues to act in a repressive and highly nationalistic manner. At the same time, there are clear trends within the civil society that are demanding a fuller accounting and engagement with Turkey's difficult history, not just vis-à-vis the Armenians but also with other non-Muslim minorities, such as Greeks and Jews, as well as Turkey's Kurdish population. The further democratization of the Turkish state and society will necessarily carry with it a further investigation into this difficult past. The success of this movement is not guaranteed in the near or far term, as the Turkish political landscape is dominated by parties that have a long history of denying a role for political or cultural pluralism in the country. The deeply rooted historical narrative in Turkey makes it difficult to view cultural pluralism in a positive light and instead views it as a weakness that outside powers manipulate to weaken the nation.[110]

## Turkish Cinema

One way to gauge the changes that have taken place in Turkey since the mid-1980s has been the dramatic shift in film production and the topics that filmmakers are able to tackle with their work. With the weakening of the official state censorship since 1986 and the expanding of a critical space within civil society, there is an openness in Turkey to dealing with its difficult history that has been absent since the founding of the republic. If we keep the memory-market dictum in mind, we can see how the opening of the civil society has provided some material support for critical filmmakers so that they can continue their work, even if their films are not particularly popular or are barred from state television, which would provide them a far larger audience. The fact that public television has shunned all of the works with a critical engagement with Turkey's history that I will discuss here should remind us of the central role that public television stations played in confronting Germany's difficult history by bringing some films that failed to find distributors or giving other films a broader audience than they otherwise would have had. In Turkey, the state institutions remain very much opposed to the broadening of the public discussion of Turkey's difficult past, thus narrowing the scope and impact that these films have had. While we have seen a rapid proliferation of such self-critical narratives, it is very important to remember that almost all of these films exist well outside the mainstream of Turkish popular culture today. They may very well represent the leading edge of a change yet to come, similar to the film and television programs in West Germany in the 1960s and 1970s that started to address the Holocaust, but they certainly are not part of the mainstream. Indeed, as with the New German Cinema, many of these film directors have had far more success outside the country than within it.

Nonetheless, the changes are dramatic. While the topics of Armenians, Armenian life, and most certainly the genocide remain taboo subjects, filmmakers have begun to address the position of non-Turkish minorities in Turkey, especially the Kurds but also, to a far more limited extent, non-Muslim minorities. Another important part of this also involves Turks having a chance to look at their own victimization at the hands of the Turkish state. Before Turkish society can broaden its circle of empathy to include the victimized minorities, it will probably require more time to process its own sense of victimization at the hands of an authoritarian, militaristic state. These discussions may aid the process of democratization and a growing tolerance for political and cultural pluralism.

### *Turks as Victims*

As with the German encounter with World War II and the Holocaust, and the Japanese struggle with the legacy of Japanese imperialism, it is essential that we recognize the role that the ethnocentrism of death and the externalization of blame play in shaping discussions about difficult national histories. The fact that people will first focus almost solely on their own suffering is probably a universal human trait and perhaps one of necessity, as we need to grieve the deaths of those close to us as well as have our own suffering recognized. Even from an ethical perspective, I would argue that we cannot deny any individual or group the necessary space within which to reflect on their own suffering. Indeed, this is part of Sophocles's warning in *Antigone*. By denying Antigone the right to mourn and honor her dead brother, Creon sets the tragedy of the play in motion.

At the same time, this necessary turning inward can lead to a self-obsessed sense of victimization that blocks identification with others whom one's group may also have inflicted immense harm upon. Although set in motion by Creon, Antigone pushes the tragedy of the play forward when she becomes blind to the interests and needs of those around her as she pursues her confrontation with Creon. As I suggested in the introduction to this book, the promise of the Axial Age is that such identification with others was given a greater potential than had previously been the case in human history. The ancient Greek example of *Persians* or the argument made by Antigone that both brothers be given a proper burial are examples of this capacity. At the same time, as the evidence in this book has shown, this is an incredibly difficult task, one that we are not predisposed to undertake.

If we are to understand Turkish resistance to discussion of their difficult history, we need to recognize this as having two primary sources: the Turkish state and more universal human capacities and limitations. The Turkish state has played a highly damaging role in this process, not only through its undemocratic nature but also through its repressive and aggressive policies. As a result of decades of censorship and a highly nationalistic school curriculum, there has been little development of critical perspectives over the years. Nonetheless, these critical perspectives have become increasingly common over the past two decades. A recognition of the damaging role of the Turkish state in this process will be an important part of turning toward other issues in Turkey's history in the twentieth century. While a focus on Turkish suffering and victimhood helps to feed tendencies that block identification with others, it is also a necessary process that can become the basis for that identification at a later date. If Turks come to recognize that they have suffered just like others because of the lack of democratic institutions in their society, then a basis for future reconciliation can be found. But there is a paradoxical tension in that by turning inward, this can deepen the alienation that is felt by the others who have also been harmed. But to deny any group the right to mourn their own suffering will only breed deep resentment, block accommodation, and set the stage for future violence. This is what we can see particularly clearly from the Yugoslav and Spanish cases, thus echoing the warnings embedded in *Antigone*. All peoples must be allowed to bury their dead with dignity.

Within the Turkish narratives of victimization, there are several important strands to recognize. First is the one that has developed around the Sèvres Syndrome, which I have already discussed earlier in this chapter. The Sèvres Syndrome has been reinforced for many decades through state-sponsored historical narratives in the textbooks as well as in the popular war film genre, which continues into the present with the *Valley of the Wolves* series. These narratives focus on Turks as victims of forces from outside the country. This is the deeply embedded historical fear of domination by outsiders.

More recently, there have also been narratives that focus on the internal harm that the Turkish state has caused, through its founding as a republic and the repeated military coups. At this level, there exists a split between Islamist and non-Islamist narratives of victimization at the hands of the Turkish state. As part of their challenge to Atatürk's secular republican state, Islamists have drawn attention to their persecution at the hands of this state going back to its founding. Then there are also other Turkish narratives of how the republican state has victimized Turks through its repressive measures, with the September 12, 1980, coup and the resulting state violence drawing the most attention.

One way to see this is the way that discussion of the Liberation Courts has been dealt with by both Islamist and secular filmmakers. The Liberation Courts were used to sanction extrajudicial executions, despite being called courts, of those who stood in the way of the secularization and modernization of the country. The subject of the courts has long been a taboo subject in Turkey and involves another example of how extreme violence at the founding of the republic remains a difficult subject but also one that can be used effectively to challenge the legitimacy of Atatürk's secular republic. The Islamist filmmaker Mesut Uçakan uses the subject of the Liberation Courts in his 1993 film *Kelebekler Sonsuza Uçar* (*Butterflies Fly to Eternity*) by talking about the fate of Atif Hodja, who was sentenced to death for his opposition to the Hat Reform.[111] From the secular perspective, Erden Kıral has also approached the subject of the Liberation Courts through his film *Mavi Sürgün* (*The Blue Exile*), also produced in 1993. Kıral is one of Turkey's best-known filmmakers, who decided to live in exile in Germany for a number of years because of the repression after the 1980 coup and the banning of some of his films.[112] In *The Blue Exile*, Kıral tells the story of the Turkish intellectual Cevat Şakir (1890–1973) who was sent into exile for three years because he dared to publish a story about the Liberation Courts, although Kıral's film deals more with the exile than the reasons for the exile.[113]

### *Turks and Kurds: Victims and Perpetrators*

Indigenous non-Turkish voices in Turkey have largely been eliminated or so severely marginalized that they are almost nonexistent in Turkish popular culture, especially in the cinema. This has had serious consequences for the development of a critical discussion about Turkey's past because it means that these non-Turkish filmmakers can only first find their voice outside the country. Then, when they return, they face the charge of being one of the enemies of the state that are trying to undermine the country from the outside. There is even a Turkish publication, available in English, that draws attention to this external "Armenian propaganda."[114]

The Kurds are one exception to this. They constitute about 20 percent of the population and are concentrated in the southeast. Kurds have been able to establish their own political party and to generate their own group of filmmakers. Turks and Kurds are both making films that address the position of Kurds in Turkish society and the consequences of the war that has been waged since the 1980s between Kurdish separatists and the Turkish state. These stories provide a chance for both groups to view themselves as the victims and perpetrators of violence.

In this section, I want to focus on the most recent changes in Turkish society, but it is important to note that one of the giants of Turkish cinema prior to the most recent changes was Yilmaz Güney Putun, who was born to Kurdish parents in 1937. Güney, as he is best known, was raised in a completely Turkish assimilated family. He did not even know his family was Kurdish until he traveled back to his father's village when he was sixteen years old. Within the strict censorship codes that prevented any portrayal of Kurds as Kurds in film, as the Kurdish language was not permitted, Güney nonetheless brought the first portrayals of Kurds into Turkish cinema, although always in subversive ways that may well not have been understood by many of his viewers, through dress and music. His greatest international success came with *Yol*, which won the top award at the Cannes film festival in 1982, although the film had to be directed by Şerif Gören, as Güney was in a Turkish prison at the time of the filming. Gören shot the film, which Güney had written, according to Güney's directions. Through the film, Güney tried to critique the military regime that had seized power in the 1980 coup. He died in exile, in France, in 1984. *Yol* was only shown to domestic Turkish audiences in 1999. There is now a new generation of Kurdish filmmakers that are helping to increase the acceptance of political and cultural pluralism in Turkey: Miraz Bezar, Huseyin Karabey, Orhan Eskikoy, Zeynel Dogan, and Kazim Öz, who has worked with Yeşim Ustaoğlu.

Yeşim Ustaoğlu is Turkey's best-known female director. Her international success has led to charges from some in Turkey that she focuses on only negative stories about Turkey so that she can gain funds from Euroimage, a Council of Europe Fund designed to promote the development of a European cinema.[115] Her film *Güneşe Yolculuk (Journey to the Sun)* (1999) provides a harsh look at the life of Kurds, who try to move to Istanbul to escape the poverty and war in the southeastern part of the country. The story is told through the friendship between a Turk and a Kurd. When his Kurdish friend is killed by the police at a political demonstration, the Turkish friend resolves to return his friend's body to his home village. As the movie shifts from the story in the city to a road movie, he sees parts of his country he knows next to nothing about. The devastation of the war surprises him, and eventually he discovers that his friend's village no longer exists. It existed only in his friend's memory. His village had been "crossed out," meaning that the Turkish government had destroyed it because the villagers refused to join the war against the Kurdish rebels. Due to a hostile political environment in Turkey, the distribution of the film was first delayed and then only eight copies of the film were released to small art house cinemas.[116]

In the same year that Ustaoğlu was able to release *Journey to the Sun*, Nadire Mater, another Turkish woman and an independent journalist, managed to have her book *Voices from the Front: Turkish Soldiers on the War with the Kurdish Guerrillas* (*Mehmedin Kitabı: Güneydoğu'da Savaşmış Askerler Anlatıyor*) published, only to have the book banned and to find herself on trial under Article 159 for belittling the military. She was finally acquitted after a two-year trial, but Mater's case shows the challenges that authors and filmmakers still face when pushing Turkish society toward self-critical reflections. The book was based on her interviews with forty-two former Turkish soldiers who had fought in the southeast between 1984 and 1998.[117] The book went on to become quite successful and helped to open the way for more films about the Kurdish conflict, such as *Yazı Tura* (*Toss-Up*) by Uğur Yücel.

Uğur Yücel is one of Turkey's most popular actors, who has had a long career. His directorial debut was *Yazı Tura*, which dealt directly with the consequences of the war with the Kurds. It was not a popular film, but the film's very existence shows how the boundaries of what is permitted in Turkey continue to expand and open further. It is one of the first Turkish films to question the sacrifice of Turkish lives in the military, something that has been a strict taboo, protected by official censorship, for almost the entire history of the republic. In the film, Yücel shows the costs of the war on young Turkish men, as they return from the conflict damaged and broken. As with other recent films, Yücel also tackles the problems of a repressive, patriarchal society that has no place for wounded veterans. The film won numerous awards but was seen by only about 260,000 people in Turkey.

### *Non-Muslim Victims*

With *Waiting for the Clouds*, Yeşim Ustaoğlu moved away from the present-day conflicts between Turks and Kurds and went back to the end of World War I and the founding of the republic. In this way, the film does even more to challenge the general reluctance or avoidance of the broader Turkish population to recognize the victimization of non-Turkish minorities during that time. The main character was born into a Pontus Greek family around the turn of the century. Later, her family was forcefully deported from Turkish territory along with thousands of other Pontus Greeks. Her parents die as part of the deportation, and she is separated from her brother, whom she also fears died during the deportations, although she does not know his fate. She is taken into a Muslim Turkish family and raised as a Muslim Turk, but she never forgets her own family and brother. The film touches on widely held knowledge in Turkey that many non-Muslim children were taken into Muslim Turkish families as a result of the deportations, massacres, and the Armenian genocide. Many of these child survivors, now very elderly or already dead, never revealed this history to their own children, but some have. In this way, *Waiting for the Clouds* touched on an extremely sensitive topic in contemporary Turkish society, as it links the past violence around the founding of the republic to the present and has the potential of reminding Turks that while they certainly suffered during those years, others also suffered at their hands as well.

The film scholar Suner conducted a brief survey of Turkish university students who had seen *Waiting for the Clouds* and found that they conveyed a great deal of confusion, vagueness, and uncertainty. The fact that the events had occurred during the collapse of the Ottoman Empire rather than in the republic appeared to create a sense of dissociation. And the Greek identity of the main character passed almost without comment. Suner estimates that the film reached only about four thousand viewers in Turkey. She also relates a telling anecdote from the afternoon that she watched the film in a small art house cinema in Ankara. After the completion of the film, a middle-aged woman stood up and said to the audience, "You know, this is all true, what the film shows us is really the case. The Black Sea region, particularly its high plateaus, are as beautiful as they are described in the film."[118]

Tomris Giritlioğlu is another female Turkish director who has given considerable attention to the plight of non-Muslim minorities in Turkish history and not only in the present. She worked for years in the Turkish public television service but has recently used the greater openness to begin her own investigation into Turkey's difficult past. Along with other films, she has made a trilogy that addresses past state actions against non-Muslim minorities, including the population exchanges between Greece and Turkey in her 1991 film *Suyun Öte Yanı* (*The Other Side of the Water*), which also included a discussion of the 1980 military coup. In 1999, she made *Salkım Hanımın Taneleri* (*Mrs. Salkım's Diamonds*), which deals with the 1942–1943 Wealth Tax designed to bankrupt non-Muslim families. This film actually did quite well at the box office with about nine hundred thousand viewers.[119] And then in 2008, she made *Güz Sancısı* (*Autumn Pain*), which examines the September 6–7, 1955, riots that were directed against the remaining non-Muslim population, primarily the Greeks living in the Beyoğlu neighborhood of Istanbul.

Although Ustaoğlu and Giritlioğlu have both made films about the persecution of non-Muslims in the Turkish Republic, neither of them, nor any other Turkish director, has been able to address the Armenian issue in Turkey. As the discussion above about Hrant Dink's assassination and the travails of Pamuk make clear, this discussion is still far too explosive for filmmakers to address. Nonetheless, the increasing prevalence of films addressing non-Muslim and Kurdish victims of Turkish state violence is beginning to create enough material in this subject area that the social contagion and reinforcement mechanisms may begin to make this more common knowledge in Turkey. But this effect will remain far more muted than was the case in Germany in the 1980s because the number of the films and their distribution remain suppressed. They are not being recycled on television, and their distribution within Turkey has remained limited. Furthermore, the narrative that they are trying to advance has to overcome the hostility toward non-Turkish minorities that remains part of the public education curriculum. These films demonstrate the changes that have taken place in the civil society, but they have not yet reached a critical mass that will further this change in a dramatic way.

### *Armenian Voices*

Unlike the case of West Germany, where foreign film productions played a role in how the country came to think about the legacy of the war and the Holocaust, Turkey has remained far more closed to outside productions that go against mainstream culture. As we have seen with the example of Yilmaz Güney and his film *Yol*, even Turkish productions that offended state or mainstream sensibilities have been held at bay until very recently. Thus, the Armenian narrative is almost wholly lost to the Turkish population. Diaspora Armenians and Armenians living in Armenia have been making films related to their experiences since 1965, but I have found no evidence that any of these feature films and documentaries have had any mass audience within Turkey.

The most ambitious and best-known feature film about the Armenian genocide and its legacy for the survivors and later generations is Atom Egoyan's film *Ararat* (2002). Although filmmakers in the Republic of Armenia have made several films that touch on the topic, as has been mentioned above, these films are wholly unknown in the West and probably have never been shown to a wide audience inside Turkey. In the case of *Ararat*, the Turkish government and Turkish nationalists began a campaign against the film even before Egoyan was finished with the postproduction. One Turkish film distributor decided, after seeing the film at the Berlin Film Festival in 2003, to distribute the film in Turkey. First, he had to struggle against official state censors, which blocked distribution. After agreeing to censor a scene of an Ottoman Turkish soldier raping an Armenian woman, the film was cleared by the state censors, but then a campaign by nationalist extremists, with threats of violence, led the distributor to cancel the distribution of the film.[120]

If we look inside Turkey, we have just within the past couple years two films from Özcan Alper, who speaks Hemshin, the language of Armenians who converted to Islam in the seventeenth century. Given the turmoil surrounding Pamuk, the assassination of Hrant Dink, and the threats against Egoyan's film, the production of a couple of films from a director who can trace his family roots back to Christian Armenians living in Turkey is a major achievement and a hopeful sign for the future. As with the Kurdish director Kazim Öz, Alper has worked as an assistant director with Yeşim Ustaoğlu, in his case on *Waiting for the Clouds*. Alper's first film was *Momi* (*Grandmother*) (2000), a short film in which the characters speak Hemshin. Like others, Alper found himself charged by the Court for State Security for "producing material intended to destroy the unity of the state."[121] The charges were dropped when the EU requested that Turkey remove such laws as part of the accession process. In 2007, he made *Sonbahar* (*Autumn*) in which he uses the Hemshin language extensively. The main character in *Autumn* is a man who participated in the student movements of the 1990s and was jailed for ten years before his release on health grounds. Given the nature of the subject matter, the fact that 150,000 saw the film is significant.[122] In 2011, Alper made *Gelecek Uzun Sürer* (*The Future Lasts Forever*), which is even more daring with its direct reference to the Armenian genocide, although most of the focus is on the present and the consequences of the civil war in the southeast. But in the film, the main character, Sumru, meets an old Armenian who is taking care of a collapsing Armenian church. He addresses her in Armenian, and she explains that she is Hamshentsi. On Sumru's third visit to the church, the old Armenian tells her that his mother was a victim of the 1915 *chart*. Given that Armenian characters are almost completely absent from Turkish films, this shows that the boundary of the cultural matrix has been pushed just that much further toward opening up a discussion about Turkey's disappeared non-Muslim populations of Armenians, Greeks, and Jews.

## Conclusion

The Turkish case demonstrates how political and cultural forces have combined to severely limit self-critical discussions of Turkey's difficult history until the very present. The political regime has been authoritarian and repressive for many decades, longer than in any of the other cases. Unlike in the case of Japan, the classroom has not even managed to become a site of resistance against the state's master narrative. Self-critical reflections in mass popular culture have only begun to appear on a regular basis more recently, although their distribution and audiences have been quite limited. As the current conditions in Turkey continue to turn in a more authoritarian direction since the failed 2016 coup attempt, the future of this engagement with Turkey's difficult history is in great doubt. Despite some moves toward the EU and Western norms, Turkey remains far more closed to outside influence than Germany, Japan, or Spain. Indeed, as we have seen, attempts to democratize Turkey's education system and to address the problematic content of Turkey's history textbooks have had minimal results and are being reversed.

On the cultural side, the ethnocentrism of death and the externalization of blame have played a significant role in suppressing self-critical discussions about the past. Moreover, these general human tendencies have been further strengthened in a more collectivist culture in which perceived attacks on the integrity of the nation and its honor are treated in an even more defensive manner. The Turkish case confirms the expectations from Doosje and Branscombe's research, which predicts this sort of reaction in more collectivist societies.[123] As Sharabi, Lawrence Rosen, and others have noted, one is supposed to remain loyal to the family or the nation, not to abstract principles. There is little engagement with Kohlberg's postconventional moral reasoning.

We can also see certain similarities regarding the dynamics within Japanese and Turkish families in that there is a great deal of emphasis placed on honoring and respecting one's parents and ancestors. Although a common trait probably of all human societies, the emphasis on obedience and honor is more intense and less likely to offer opportunities to raise difficult questions about the family's history and its relationship with Turkey's difficult history. As in Japan, the generational proximity in Turkey is closer than in more individualistic Western societies.

All of these political and cultural factors have worked to suppress rather than open up discussions about the past. Nonetheless, in the past two decades, there have been dramatic changes that have allowed for the creation of films that examine the difficult circumstances faced by Turkey's non-Muslim minority populations, both in the present and the past. Books about the war with the Kurds in the southeast have finally begun to appear. The Turkish Armenian population was able to establish *Agos* in 1996. While there is some possibility for the social contagion and reinforcement effects to begin creating a critical mass of information about Turkey's difficult history, the distribution and circulation of this material is still hindered by the state. Public radio and television broadcasters have not taken up this material as an educational mission, as has been the case in Germany, Japan, and Spain. And broad social attitudes continue to be nationalistic and defensive, thus limiting the willingness and ability of those operating in the private market to produce and distribute this material. Creon's dictate to honor those who fought for the city and to dishonor those who fought against it remains much more in force today in Turkey than in the other cases.

# *Conclusion*

*Wisdom's the ultimate source*
*of our happiness,*
*and never committing irreverent acts*
*in matters involving the gods.*
*Bold words of the boastful are punished*
*with blows that are equally bold.*
*They've taught us to cultivate wisdom.*
*It comes with growing old.*

—Chorus in *Antigone*[1]

*I grieve to hear the Persians' many woes,*
*those happening now, and those that are still*
*coming.*

—Chorus in *Persians*[2]

By looking at each of these five cases, we can begin to appreciate just how long the legacy of mass violence can remain for a society. This should serve as a sober reminder for policymakers and activists who seek to deal with postconflict societies. The appropriate time frame for using words such as *reconciliation* is probably measured in decades rather than years, if ever. The primary goal of this research project has been to begin the process of conducting a larger scale comparative study to help identify similarities and differences in terms of how societies deal with their difficult histories over long periods. In this concluding chapter, I want to focus on these contrasts, while also providing some suggestions of what the implications of this research are for those who seek to develop policy responses for societies emerging from periods of mass violence.

The many ghosts of *Antigone* continue to haunt these societies for years after the violence has ended. The human rage against the death of loved ones, the political struggle over who deserves a just burial and who does not, the desire for revenge, often cloaked in the language of "the law and justice," as Creon does in the play, all result in a further unfolding of the tragedy. Creon's mortal law trumps the law of the Gods, and Antigone is buried alive. Despair and suicide rather than reconciliation grip the characters. Creon is left with his "justice" but little else. The future is buried in the cave. What is the way out of this tragic cycle?

The simple answer is the further expansion of empathy and compassion, the core lessons of the Axial Age, of which Sophocles's play is a key part. These are easy words but ones extremely difficult to put into practice. Yet, as we have seen throughout this study, in each case, artists, novelists, playwrights, filmmakers, television producers, and others have all played their part in how each society has encountered and dealt with its difficult history. Not all of this creative energy has been exerted in the direction expanding empathy and compassion, as war films more often than not continue the process of dehumanizing the enemy. Not infrequently, societal narratives about the past continue to focus on the *externalization of blame* and the *ethnocentrism of death*. But among much of the material that tends to feed these problematic reactions, there are also works that seek to expand empathetic identification with others. These are the works, attitudes, and emotions that we need to learn to foster.[3]

There are two powerful social-psychological forces that tend to blunt self-critical and empathy expanding investigations into periods of mass violence, war, and genocide. First, in an attempt to reestablish one's community as one made up of the good, there is a strong tendency to externalize blame for the violence onto other groups or to blame fate or naturalize the conflict as an unavoidable tragedy driven by superhuman or natural forces. While this is a universal human reaction, it differs in its intensity depending on how individualistic or collectivist the society's worldview is.[4] The more collectivist a society's given worldview, the stronger the externalization of blame effect will be. Second, the ethnocentrism of death also works to blunt self-critical evaluations of how one's own group may have contributed to the conflict and the suffering of others.

Both of these social-psychological processes are, in part, driven by different patterns in moral reasoning, with Western and individualistic societies drawn toward Lawrence Kohlberg's postconventional moral reasoning, and Avner Greif and Guido Tabellini's general morality. In contrast, non-Western and collectivist societies rely more on Kohlberg's conventional moral reasoning, and practice more of Greif and Tabellini's limited morality. These points, again, are summarized in Table 2 in the introduction. One consequence of this is that working toward peacebuilding between collectivist societies is going to be even more difficult than will be the case between societies that are more individualistic in their orientation.

One of the most important conclusions that this research has helped to highlight is just how exceptional the case of West Germany is. Unified Germany is often taken as the paradigmatic case of what one might hope to achieve in terms of dealing with a period of mass violence, and the long legacy of war and genocide. But even in the German case, we find that much of what is celebrated as recognition and atonement for the past remains located at the macrolevel and the realm of formal politics. Just as the realization of what the war and Holocaust became more broadly understood in the society as a whole, the knowledge of how one's family history relates to those events remains obscure. Even in the broader society, one can see clear evidence of how Germans steer conversations around the topic of National Socialism and the Holocaust, so as to avoid a difficult topic that may harm social harmony. Getting along with others and reinforcing social solidarity is a necessary part of the human condition, and it is not well suited to difficult conversations, which of necessity include an element of rebellion. The social-psychological process of *socially shared retrieval-induced forgetting* is a very powerful process that works to shut down discussions about difficult pasts at the microlevel of day-to-day conversations. At the same time, people can become very engaged in these issues in the broader society. It is only as this information begins to impinge on the personal sphere of the family and other intimate relationships that a silence again begins to spread. The "success" of the German case is most clearly seen at a distance, at the macrolevel of the society. The correspondence of this with the far more personal world or microlevel cannot be taken as a given.

The phenomena of externalizing blame and the ethnocentrism of death work in coordination with socially shared retrieval-induced forgetting to try and reestablish one's own community as the community of the good. These processes are probably an unavoidable and necessary part of the human process of mourning and dealing with grief. They help to assign a positive value to one's own sacrifice and losses but also, unfortunately, tend to limit identification with the other side in the conflict. The repair of social relationships across the great divide created by mass violence is extremely difficult. Moreover, even decades of time and generational turnover do not necessarily create enough distance from the events. It is only through empathetic identification and the search for compassion that one can bridge a sense of one's own suffering and recognize it in the other as well. This is what Aeschylus sought to achieve with his play *Persians* in 472 BCE.[5] When Atossa, mother of Xerxes, recounts a dream she had at the beginning of the play, she says, "Two women appeared to me, both finely dressed, one in the robes that Persian women wear, the other in Doric dress. . . . They were sisters, born from the same race; one dwelt in Greece, her home by lot; the other, non-Greek land,"[6] is not the playwright asking us to reflect on the unity of humanity and the accidental nature of what appears to divide us?

This comparative study has also emphasized the importance of looking at both the sphere of politics and culture. While democratic regimes clearly provide a far better context within which to have an open, and perhaps self-critical debate, about a difficult history, there is little evidence that democratic states, on their own, take much initiative in this direction. Instead, it has repeatedly been forces in the civil society that have pushed these discussions forward. As we have seen in the cases of Spain, Yugoslavia, and Turkey, even in societies governed by authoritarian governments, individuals and groups in the civil society can find ways, perhaps for limited times, to begin raising new questions about the national past. But the mere engagement with a difficult history does not promise a positive outcome in terms of further peacebuilding and democratization, as the tragic case of Yugoslavia demonstrates.

The *memory-market dictum* suggests that one way to appreciate the changes that take place in the civil society is to look at the relationship between the production and consumption of narratives about the past, and how political, economic, and social forces will shape these debates. Authoritarian states may decide to try and censor and suppress uncomfortable narratives, while market forces in more democratic societies can have their own censoring effect. The importance of the types of narratives being generated has been seen in each of the cases discussed in this study. Moreover, we can find in some of the cases specific periods in which the *social contagion* and *reinforcement effects* become very powerful, thus launching the entire society on a different trajectory.

The most dramatic example of this was in West Germany in the 1980s, when a massive outpouring of material related to the Holocaust finally smashed most of the positive identification with National Socialism and Hitler, both of which had lingered in West German society since the end of the war. In the case of Spain, scholars have identified the mid-1990s through into the 2000s as a period for a memory boom related to the Spanish Civil War, in which far more critical knowledge about the crimes committed by Franco's forces in the war and after the war reached a broad national audience. Prior to the memory boom, scholars of Spain tended to praise the great moderation of attitudes toward the civil war or to simply note that the issue appeared to be resolved. The 1980s in Yugoslavia were also a transformative period, during which the communist state lost control over the narrative of the country's difficult history. The fact that this occurred during a period of uncertain political transformation, from Titoism to something else, along with a severe economic crisis, helped to feed growing nationalist tensions, which eventually led to a new round of wars. There was, perhaps, a chance for Yugoslavia to escape this fate in the 1960s, when these sorts of discussions began to break out into the open during the so-called "black wave" in the arts, but this opportunity was lost when the regime returned to repression and censorship. In Japan, there was a clear shift in the willingness of many to discuss the war and Japanese crimes after the death of the Shoa emperor in January 1989. As with the other cases, the ground had begun to shift much earlier, in the case of Japan in the early 1970s, but the emperor's death seems to have opened up a new willingness to discuss the past in a more self-critical manner. Turkey remains the case where a self-critical investigation into the past has remained the most constrained, although the opening up of civil society since the mid-1990s has led to exactly the sorts of changes we have seen in the other four cases. The problem remains that the state is very ambivalent about allowing these discussions to take place, and there are nationalistic forces in the broader society that also continue to work toward stifling discussion. Unfortunately, Turkey continues to resemble more the case of Yugoslavia rather than Spain. Increasing economic strains, an uncertain international setting, a separatist war in the southeast with the Kurds, and increasing authoritarianism since the July 2016 failed coup do not make one hopeful.

Among all of this diversity in terms of timing and scale, there is a common metaphor that helps us to appreciate the way in which societies come to engage in a more self-critical investigation into their difficult histories. Each period of rapid change, where the social contagion and reinforcement effect becomes far more apparent, has been preceded by at least several decades of slowly accumulating information about the past, which is set to challenge previously accepted interpretations. As suggested by the memory-market dictum, this accumulation of information occurs at first on the margins and in the periphery, in less capital-intensive narrative endeavors such as novels, plays, new histories, or journalistic reporting, before reaching cinema and television. A number of naturalistic metaphors suggest themselves here, from earthquakes, to avalanches or forest fires, in which built-up tensions, energy, and fuel can suddenly be released in the society. This realization is important because quite often one reason that political and social scientists eschew cultural analysis is that they assume that it is largely stable and something that changes very slowly over time. What this research demonstrates is that there can be decades over which very little appears to happen at the macrolevel or societal level, but that change, when it comes, can be quite rapid, unpredictable, and not always with a positive outcome.

These broader social changes may push discussions forward within families, but people in all societies will seek to maintain and protect intimate relationships from these disruptions. This is another crucial lesson to take away from this comparative study, that the microlevel dynamics within the family can have broad social implications. And here, again, we can see an important difference between societies that are more individualistic or collectivist in their orientation. If one lives in a more collectivist society in which the development of an interdependent sense of the self is fostered, there will be an even greater emphasis on the maintenance of personal relationships over any search for eternal or universal truths. At the same time, these universal truths or human rights are more highly valued in more individualistic societies that seek to foster an independent sense of the self. In the individualistic society, being true to one's self and maintaining adherence to specific values, even when they may lead to the destruction of relationships with others can be seen as a social good. In such a society, a mature individual holds to one's principles. In a collectivist society, the maintenance of relationships with others is far more important than strict adherence to one's own principles and sense of self. Indeed, an individual who places his or her principles above the maintenance of existing relationships is likely to be seen as immature and selfish.

Another way in which collectivist sentiments can be expressed is through a deep reverence for a national leader or symbol of the nation. This is an obvious reality for both more individualist or collectivist societies. In the cases of Spain, Yugoslavia, and Japan, the death of a great national leader and symbol led to a freeing-up of societal discussions about the violent history associated with that particular leader or national symbol. Franco and Tito both established new regimes after having led their countries through a civil war and emerging as the victors. In the case of Japan, the institution of the emperor survived the shattering Japanese defeat in World War II, in significant part because the US occupation forces saw him as a useful unifying figure for the defeated country. When each of these national leaders died, there was a marked shift in the way the past was discussed.

Germany is different in that Hitler's death at the end of the war already created a clear break with the past. Nonetheless, in the case of West Germany, a certain level of reverence and fascination with Hitler continued well into the 1970s, although this was eventually destroyed with the widespread acceptance of the Holocaust in the 1980s. The only national figure to have gained an immortal status has been Atatürk, who remains an important unifying figure in Turkey until the present. The power of his figure did not diminish with his death in 1938. He remains a potent symbol of Turkish nationalism, which cannot be approached in a disinterested and scholarly manner within the country. Atatürk's immortality continues to complicate Turkey's engagement with its difficult history.

It is worth reflecting on some of the possible lessons we can take from these five cases as we think about what we might do in terms of policy prescriptions, given that trying to help societies to deal with their difficult histories has become part of postconflict peacebuilding as well as the regular work of building a solid democracy. Americans continue to struggle with the legacy of slavery in their society.[7] The Canadian and Australian Parliaments have issued official apologies to their aboriginal communities for past harmful state policies. Many European countries today are engaged in self-critical reflections on their colonial history. It has very much become the norm in Western democracies for writers, intellectuals, and other artists to begin widening the empathetic identification with those whom the society has harmed at some point in the past. This does not mean that this has led to unified understandings of these histories or that these issues are not controversial. They remain anything but uncontroversial, as Americans and Japanese continue to have very different interpretations of the atomic bombings of Hiroshima and Nagasaki. While Canadian and Australian Parliaments have issued official apologies, the appropriate level of compensation for survivors remains debated. Americans may have a broader understanding of slavery and racial injustice in the past, but action in the present continues to be confused and partial. Protestants and Catholics in Northern Ireland remain very much divided over the meaning of their history and the future direction of the north, although they are increasingly committed to channeling their disagreements into democratic institutions. What has changed—and this places our current era more in line with the beginning of the Axial Age—is that there is more attention focused on self-critical reflections of the past than was the case just a couple of decades ago.

One of the first important lessons to learn is that the legacy of past mass violence can be very long indeed. Even in a situation of stable democratic development supported by strong economic growth, peace, and prosperity, it has taken many decades since the end of World War II for West German and Japanese societies to begin a more wide-ranging discussion about their role as perpetrators. Although West Germans came to identify with the Jewish victims in the Holocaust in the 1980s, the search for German perpetrators has remained far more muted, as the debates about the *Wehrmacht* exhibit demonstrated in the 1990s. The recognition and identification of the victims was far "easier" than dealing with the perpetrators. As Akiko Hashimoto's work has shown, many Japanese remain far more focused on the promise of pacifism and future peaceful relations than demonstrating a strong desire to investigate the crimes of the previous generation.[8]

During the periods of authoritarian rule in Spain, Yugoslavia, and Turkey, discussions about the difficult national history were always blunted and shaped by the imperatives of the state ideology, although each of these societies has also seen periods of greater openness. Only Spain has thus far managed to negotiate its way to a peaceful democratic transition. While this remains a possibility for Turkey, there has been a decided move back toward greater authoritarianism in the past two years.

In the conclusion to their edited volume on postconflict reconstruction in Yugoslavia and Rwanda, Eric Stover and Harvey Weinstein came up with a list of eight key components for reconstruction after periods of mass violence and even genocide: (1) physical security, (2) freedom of movement, (3) the rule of law, (4) access to accurate and unbiased information, (5) justice, (6) education for democracy, (7) economic development, and (8) cross-ethnic engagement.[9] This is an excellent list, and a very difficult one to implement, as those working in the field so clearly understand.

Something that this comparative study has helped to highlight is the role that not only fact-based historiographical research and good journalism can play in helping to provide "access to accurate and unbiased information," but that the stories told by novelists, playwrights, and others have also been extremely important in terms of creating imaginative narratives in which the readers and viewers have been provided the opportunity to expand their empathetic understanding of those whom their own groups may have harmed during the conflict.[10] It is through these imaginative stories that the self-exculpation encouraged by the externalization of blame and the ethnocentrism of death can be blunted and turned in a more helpful direction. As Aeschylus and Sophocles did for their own society, today's artists, novelists, dance choreographers, musicians, playwrights, filmmakers, and television producers can create works that help us to reflect critically on the problem of violence and its damaging legacy. They are potentially just as much a part of the solution as all the other formal institutions of the international transitional justice regime.

In another chapter in the Stover and Weinstein edited volume, Jodi Halpern and Harvey Weinstein appear to despair a bit when they cannot find any willingness among their interviewees in the former Yugoslavia to identify with the other side. "While people from different ethnic groups are working and living as neighbors again, there appears to be a paucity of empathy. Indeed, our data from ninety key informant interviews and twenty-four focus groups in selected cities contain not a single expression of empathy. Nowhere does someone from a particular ethnic group demonstrate curiosity and emotional openness toward the distinct perspective of someone from another ethnic group. This suggests that there are very large barriers to establishing empathy after mass violence."[11] The barriers they note have been identified here as the externalization of blame and the ethnocentrism of death. Halpern and Weinstein discovered this just a mere six years after the end of the fighting, and as we can see in the present comparative study, such lack of empathy or efforts at the rehumanization of the other side can remain absent for more than six decades and even longer.

While many imaginative narratives by creative artists can just as easily reinforce the externalization of blame and the ethnocentrism of death, some works can also help with exactly the empathetic identification that is so much needed. But as the memory-market dictum suggests, these works are likely to remain in short supply, as stories that reinforce feelings of one's own victimhood and the wrong that others have done are likely to remain far more popular.

For those who wish to aid the development of a better future for postconflict societies, the task appears as immense as it in fact is. But this does not mean that there are no means of taking effective action. Unfortunately, much of what needs to be done will require a multidecade effort, which probably will far exceed the ability of outsiders to sustain meaningful programs. Moreover, in none of the cases discussed here have outside forces been determinative of any particular positive outcome. Instead, when there have been positive steps taken toward engaging a difficult history, it has come primarily from within the society rather than from without.

One step that can be taken, by either insiders or outsiders, is to help shift the often unhelpful balance within the memory-market dictum, which tends toward the creation of a mass culture that avoids difficult discussions. Financial support for those who create imaginative narratives that encourage empathetic identification with others and help generate cross-ethnic engagement can be very helpful. In the case of postwar West Germany, the existence of a robust system of public broadcasters played a critical role in bringing more controversial material before German audiences. In the case of Turkey, Euroimage funding has been essential for the production of Yeşim Ustaoğlu's films dealing with violence against Kurds in Turkey today as well as the historical violence against Turkey's Greek population. Ustaoğlu's films along with many other examples in this book demonstrate that change can come from the periphery. Societies are not monolithic, and there will be sympathetic readers of novels, or those willing to go to the dramatic theater or a photography exhibit. By encouraging the production of empathy-expanding narratives, in many different forums, we can work against the hubris and self-focused, destructive passions on display in *Antigone*. By returning to the rule of the gods and allowing all the dead to be buried with dignity, a truly compassionate gesture, the dead and the living will rest better, and the ghosts of *Antigone* will retire to the underworld. With that, a new future is possible.

# Acknowledgments

Work on this project began in different stages over several years, but many of the ideas began to come together during my first sabbatical from Oklahoma State University (OSU). My first book, *"Getting History Right": East and West German Collective Memories of the Holocaust and War* (Bucknell University Press, 2011), offered a comparison that allowed a narrow focus on how political regimes shape discussions about the past. It was during the sabbatical that I began to explore how differences in cultural traditions also shape how human societies deal with their difficult histories. The sabbatical gave me time to read broadly and to take intellectual risks as a political scientist, as I spent almost the entire year reading in almost every field except my own. The ritual slaughter of cattle in Madagascar and its role in reshaping a rural village's memory of French colonialism usually does not show up on the political science syllabus, but it was critical to this research. Once back at OSU, Victoria Trela was a most valuable research assistant for one semester as we began together to gather material for the chapter on Turkey.

From 2015 to 2017, I took an unpaid leave from OSU to work full-time on the manuscript while also being able to live, again, full-time with my wife in Ottawa, Canada. Not unlike many in our profession, we had spent too many years living apart as we pursued our careers in different cities, indeed, in different countries. During this time, I was a visiting professor at Carleton University, which gave essential research assistance. The university's librarians provided a fantastic level of support for a visiting scholar. Not only did a regular stream of interlibrary loan books flow uninterrupted onto my hold shelf, but they also purchased many of my requests for the library, especially newly published books.

I want to thank all of my friends and colleagues who offered to read all or some of the manuscript. It is only through the eyes and thoughts of others that you come to a fuller appreciation of what you have written and where its shortcomings are. Martin Heisler, Marc Howard Ross, and Ned Lebow have provided much support and encouragement over the years in many different ways, and each of them took time to read through the entire manuscript and to share their thoughts and reflections. Many thanks to each of you. Akiko Hashimoto, Jeff Sahadeo, Cody Brown, and Jason Maloy also read parts of the manuscript, and each made very insightful comments that helped guide me to improving the overall text. Greg Clingham, the director and editor at Bucknell University Press, and an anonymous reviewer also provided very important guidance and feedback, which has made the book far better than it otherwise would have been. I also had the chance to discuss parts of this work during invited lectures at the University of Copenhagen and its Centre for the Resolution of International Conflicts, and the University of Zagreb. A special thanks to Nik Emmanuel, Dejan Jović, and Cody Brown for these invitations to talk about my research. I began teaching part-time at McGill University in fall 2017, and I had a chance to present parts of this research to my students, who again provided thoughtful comments that have helped me to make still other improvements.

As always, my deepest thanks go to Vesna, my wife. It is always those who are closest to us who have to give the most to allow the work to go forward. And in her own quiet way, Maza, the household cat, played her role as well, reminding me that it is good to take a moment to stretch out in the sunshine and take a break. We both miss her.

Figure 1 has previously appeared in print. I thank the journal for allowing me to republish this figure here. "A Model for Comparative Collective Memory Studies: Regime Types, Cultural Traditions, and Difficult Histories," *Politička Misao* [*Croatian Political Science Review*] 51, no. 5 (2014): 13–35.

# Notes

INTRODUCTION

1. Hannah Arendt, *The Human Condition* (Chicago: University of Chicago Press, 1958), 241.

2. Sophocles, *Antigone*, trans. David Mulroy (Madison: University of Wisconsin Press, 2013), lines 925–28.

3. Aeschylus, *Persians*, trans. James Romm, in *The Greek Plays: Sixteen Plays by Aeschylus, Sophocles, and Euripides*, ed. Mary Lefkowitz and James Romm (New York: Modern Library, 2016), lines 185–87.

4. Karen Armstrong, *The Great Transformation: The Beginning of Our Religious Traditions* (New York: Knopf, 2006), 225–28.

5. Karl Jaspers, *The Origin and Goal of History*, trans. Michael Bullock (London: Routledge and Kegan Paul, 1953), 6.

6. Sophocles, *Antigone*, lines 450–55.

7. Ibid., line 718.

8. Ibid., line 1080.

9. Mary Douglas, *Natural Symbols: Explorations in Cosmology* (London: Barrie & Rockliff, 1970; New ed., London: Routledge, 1996), 7.

10. Karen Armstrong, *Twelve Steps to a Compassionate Life* (Toronto: Vintage Canada, 2011), 95.

11. Within the existing literature, the field of cultural sociology has been the most sensitive to the potential impact of cultural differences, although even here, most cases at first were rooted in the Western world. See, for example, Jeffrey C. Alexander, *The Meanings of Social Life: A Cultural Sociology* (Oxford: Oxford University Press, 2003); Jeffrey C. Alexander et al. (ed.), *Cultural Trauma and Collective Identity* (Berkeley: University of California Press, 2004). With two later publications, the contrasts between Western cases and others became clearer, especially with the work of Akiko Hashimoto. See, for example, *Narrating Trauma: On the Impact of Collective Suffering*, ed. Ron Eyerman et al. (Boulder, CO: Paradigm, 2011); Jeffrey C. Alexander, *Trauma: A Social Theory* (Cambridge: Polity Press, 2012), 94–96, 169n2.

12. Jennifer Cole, *Forget Colonialism? Sacrifice and the Art of Memory in Madagascar* (Berkeley: University of California Press, 2001), 269.

13. Bertjan Doosje and Nyla R. Branscombe, "Attributions for the Negative Historical Actions of a Group," *European Journal of Social Psychology* 33, no. 2 (2003): 246.

14. Mark A. Wolfgram, *"Getting History Right": East and West Germany Collective Memories of the Holocaust and War* (Lewisburg, PA: Bucknell University Press, 2011), 211.

15. Thomas J. Anastasio et al., *Individual and Collective Memory Consolidation: Analogous Processes on Different Levels* (Cambridge, MA: MIT Press, 2012), 72.

16. Wolfgram, *"Getting History Right."*

17. William Hirst and Gerald Echterhoff, "Remembering in Conversations: The Social Sharing and Reshaping of Memories," *Annual Review of Psychology* 63 (2012): 55–79; Charles B. Stone et al., "Toward a Science of Silence: The Consequences of Leaving a Memory Unsaid," *Perspectives on Psychological Science* 7, no. 1 (2012): 39–53; Alin Coman and William Hirst, "Social Identity and Socially Shared Retrieval-Induced Forgetting: The Effects of Group Membership," *Journal of Experimental Psychology* 144, no. 4 (2015): 717–22.

18. Hirst and Echterhoff, "Remembering in Conversations," 66.

19. Marc Howard Ross, *Cultural Contestation in Ethnic Conflict* (Cambridge: Cambridge University Press, 2007), 24.

20. Ugur Ümit Üngör, *The Making of Modern Turkey: Nation and State in Eastern Anatolia, 1913–1950* (Oxford: Oxford University Press, 2011).

21. Wolfgram, *"Getting History Right,"* 21.

22. Mark A. Wolfgram, "Didactic War Crimes Trials and External Legal Culture: The Cases of the Nuremberg, Frankfurt Auschwitz, and Majdanek Trials in West Germany," *Global Change, Peace & Security* 26, no. 3 (2014): 281–97.

23. Richard Ned Lebow, *A Cultural Theory of International Relations* (Cambridge: Cambridge University Press, 2008); Ayşe Zarakol, *After Defeat: How the East Learned to Live with the West* (Cambridge: Cambridge University Press, 2011).

24. Barry Schwartz and Mikyoung Kim, "Introduction: Northeast Asia's Memory Problem," in *Northeast Asia's Difficult Past: Essays in Collective Memory*, ed. Mikyoung Kim and Barry Schwartz (New York: Palgrave Macmillan), 1–27.

25. Akiko Hashimoto and John W. Traphagan, "Changing Japanese Families," in *Imagined Families, Lived Families: Culture and Kinship in Contemporary Japan*, ed. Akiko Hashimoto and John W. Traphagan (Albany: State University of New York Press, 2008), 1–12; Hazel Rose Markus and Shinobu Kitayama, "Culture and the Self: Implications for Cognition, Emotion, and Motivation," *Psychological Review* 98, no. 2 (1991): 224–53; Richard E. Nisbett et al., "Culture and Systems of Thought: Holistic versus Analytic Cognition," *Psychological Review* 108, no. 2 (2001): 291–310; Elisabeth Özdalga, "Contrasting Modernities," in *Autonomy and Dependence in the Family: Turkey and Sweden in Critical Perspective*, ed. Rita Liljeström and Elisabeth Özdalga (Istanbul: Swedish Research Institute in Istanbul, 2002), 2–15; Harry C. Triandis, *Individualism and Collectivism* (Boulder, CO: Westview, 1995).

26. Thomas U. Berger, *War, Guilt, and World Politics after World War II* (Cambridge: Cambridge University Press, 2012); Carol Gluck, "The Past in the Present," in *Postwar Japan as History*, ed. Andrew Gordon (Berkeley: University of California Press, 1993),

64–95; Carol Gluck, "Operations of Memory: 'Comfort Women' and the World," in *Ruptured Histories: War, Memory, and the Post-Cold War in Asia*, ed. Sheila Miyoshi Jager and Rana Mitter (Cambridge, MA: Harvard University Press, 2007), 47–77; Jennifer Lind, *Sorry States: Apologies in International Politics* (Ithaca, NY: Cornell University Press, 2008).

27. Lind, *Sorry States*, 16.

28. Elazar Barkan and Alexander Karn, "Group Apology as an Ethical Imperative," in *Taking Wrongs Seriously: Apologies and Reconciliation*, ed. Elazar Barkan and Alexander Karn (Stanford, CA: Stanford University Press, 2006), 14–16.

29. Ed Park, "Sorry Not Sorry: Reading Dalkey Archive Press's Library of Korean Literature," *New Yorker*, October 19, 2015, 87–90.

30. Torkel Brekke, "Editor's Preface," in *The Ethics of War in Asian Civilizations*, ed. Torkel Brekke (New York: Routledge, 2006), x–xi; Akiko Hashimoto, *The Long Defeat: Cultural Trauma, Memory, and Identity in Japan* (Oxford: Oxford University Press, 2015).

31. Masao Maruyama, "Theory and Psychology of Ultra-Nationalism," trans. Ivan Morris, in *Thought and Behaviour in Modern Japanese Politics*, expanded ed., ed. Ivan Morris (London: Oxford University Press, 1969), 1–24.

32. Daniel Levy and Natan Sznaider have proposed that the Holocaust has become part of a globalized, cosmopolitan memory and the basis for many universal human rights claims. See, for example, their *The Holocaust and Memory in the Global Age*, trans. Assenka Oksiloff (Philadelphia: Temple University Press, 2006); and *Human Rights and Memory* (University Park: Pennsylvania State University Press, 2010). Levy and Sznaider see this trend expanding beyond Western Europe. Jeffrey C. Alexander also recognizes this trend, but he is more cautious in noting that the Holocaust appears to have very little resonance beyond the West and that even within the West, there is a great deal of variation. See *Trauma*, 94–96, 169n2. The present research suggests clear reasons why the globalization of the Holocaust narrative has been quite limited outside Western countries.

33. Jin Li, *Cultural Foundations of Learning: East and West* (Cambridge: Cambridge University Press, 2012), 8.

34. Ibid., 123.

35. Ibid., 122, 147.

36. Joel Mokyr, *A Culture of Growth: The Origins of the Modern Economy* (Princeton, NJ: Princeton University Press, 2017), chap. 14.

37. Akiko Hashimoto, "Japanese and German Projects of Moral Recovery: Toward a New Understanding of War Memories in Defeated Nations" (Cambridge, MA: Harvard University Press, Edwin O. Reischauer Institute of Japanese Studies Occasional Papers in Japanese Studies, 1999).

38. Lawrence Kohlberg, *The Philosophy of Moral Development: Moral States and the Idea of Justice, Essays on Moral Development*, vol. 1 (San Francisco: Harper & Row, 1981); Kohl-

berg, *The Psychology of Moral Development, Essays on Moral Development*, vol. 2 (San Francisco: Harper & Row, 1984).

39. Kohlberg, *Philosophy of Moral Development*, vol. 1, 24–25.

40. Kohlberg, *Psychology of Moral Development*, vol. 2, 593.

41. Hisham Sharabi, *Neopatriarchy: A Theory of Distorted Change in Arab Society* (Oxford: Oxford University Press, 1992).

42. Joseph Henrich et al., "The Weirdest People in the World?" *Behavioral and Brain Sciences* 33, nos. 2–3 (2010): 73.

43. Triandis, *Individualism and Collectivism*.

44. Avner Greif and Guido Tabellini, "The Clan and the City: Sustaining Cooperation in China and Europe," unpublished manuscript, 2015; Mokyr, *Culture of Growth*.

45. Timur Kuran, *The Long Divergence: How Islamic Law Held Back the Middle East* (Princeton, NJ: Princeton University Press, 2011); Timur Kuran, "Islam and Underdevelopment: An Old Puzzle Revisited," *Journal of Institutional and Theoretical Economics* 153, no. 1 (1997): 41–71; Avner Greif, *Institutions and the Path to the Modern Economy: Lessons from Medieval Trade* (Cambridge: Cambridge University Press, 2006).

46. Greif and Tabellini, "Clan and the City," 3.

47. Lawrence Rosen, *Varieties of Muslim Experience: Encounters with Arab Political and Cultural Life* (Chicago: University of Chicago Press, 2008), 63.

48. Abdellah Hammoudi, *Master and Disciple: The Cultural Foundations of Moroccan Authoritarianism* (Chicago: University of Chicago Press, 1997). The Turkish author Orhan Pamuk puts the potential for destruction and violence that is embedded in the master-disciple, father-son relationship at the center of his most recent novel, *The Red-Haired Woman*, trans. Ekin Oklap (Toronto: Knopf Canada, 2017).

49. Rosen, *Varieties of Muslim Experience*, 44.

50. Mark A. Wolfgram, "A Model for Comparative Collective Memory Studies: Regime Types, Cultural Traditions, and Difficult Histories," *Croatian Political Science Review* 51, no. 5 (2014): 23–30.

51. Hashimoto, *Long Defeat*, 36–37.

52. Ibid., 47–48.

53. Maruyama, "Theory and Psychology of Ultra-Nationalism," 4.

54. Ibid., 5.

55. Anthony Gottlieb, *The Dream of Enlightenment: The Rise of Modern Philosophy* (New York: Liveright, 2016), 127.

56. Akiko Hashimoto, "Culture, Power, and the Discourse of Filial Piety in Japan: The Disempowerment of Youth and Its Social Consequences," in *Filial Piety: Practice and Discourse in Contemporary East Asia*, ed. Charlotte Ikels (Stanford, CA: Stanford University Press, 2004), 182–97.

57. Ibid., 186.

58. Ibid., 191.

59. Markus and Kitayama, "Culture and the Self."

60. Hashimoto, "Culture, Power, and the Discourse," 192; J. Victor Koschmann, "Introduction: Soft Rule and Expressive Protest," in *Authority and the Individual in Japan: Citizen Protest in Historical Perspective*, ed. J. Victor Koschmann (Tokyo: University of Tokyo Press, 1978), 20–21.

61. Hashimoto, "Culture, Power, and the Discourse," 193.

62. Richard Lloyd Parry, *Ghosts of the Tsunami* (London: Jonathan Cape, 2017), 92–107; Blaine P. Connor and John W. Traphagan, "Negotiating the Afterlife: Emplacement as Ongoing Concern in Contemporary Japan," *Asian Anthropology* 13, no. 1 (2014): 3–19; Robert J. Smith, *Ancestor Worship in Contemporary Japan* (Stanford, CA: Stanford University Press, 1974).

63. Hashimoto, "Culture, Power, and the Discourse," 188–89.

64. Sharabi, *Neopatriarchy*.

65. Ibid., 151.

66. Kuran, "Islam and Underdevelopment," 66–67.

67. Sharabi, *Neopatriarchy*, 154.

68. Güler Okman Fişek, "Psychopathology and the Turkish Family: A Family Systems Theory Analysis," in *Sex Roles, Family, and Community in Turkey*, ed. Çiğdem Kağıtçıbaşı (Bloomington: Indiana University Press, 1982), 296.

69. Ibid., 302.

70. Orhan M. Öztürk and Vamik Volkan, "The Theory and Practice of Psychiatry in Turkey," in *Psychological Dimensions of Near Eastern Studies*, ed. L. Carl Brown and Norman Itzkowitz (Princeton, NJ: Darwin Press, 1977), 340.

71. Sam Kaplan, *The Pedagogical State: Education and the Politics of National Culture in Post-1980 Turkey* (Stanford, CA: Stanford University Press, 2006); Jenny White, *Muslim Nationalism and the New Turks* (Princeton, NJ: Princeton University Press, 2013), 75–77.

72. James Georgas, "Differences and Universals in Families across Cultures," in *Fundamental Questions in Cross-Cultural Psychology*, ed. Fons J. R. van de Vijver et al. (Cambridge: Cambridge University Press, 2011), 356.

73. Ibid., 357.

74. Antonio J. Ferreira, "Family Myth and Homeostasis," *Archives of General Psychiatry* 9, no. 5 (1963): 462.

75. Peter Sichrovsky, *Born Guilty: Children of Nazi Families*, trans. Jean Steinberg (New York: Basic Books, 1988); Dan Bar-On, *Legacy of Silence: Encounters with Children of the Third Reich* (Cambridge, MA: Harvard University Press, 1989); Gabriele Rosenthal (ed.), *The Holocaust in Three Generations: Families of Victims and Perpetrators of the Nazi Regime* (London: Cassell, 1998); Harald Welzer et al., *"Opa war kein Nazi": Nationalsozialismus*

*und Holocaust im Familiengedächtnis* ["Grandpa wasn't a Nazi": National Socialism and the Holocaust in family memory] (Frankfurt: Fischer Taschenbuch Verlag, 2002); Margit Reiter, *Die Generation danach: Der Nationalsozialismus im Familiengedächtnis* [The generation after: National Socialism in family memory] (Innsbruck: Studien Verlag, 2006); Harald Welzer, "The Collateral Damage of Enlightenment: How Grandchildren Understand the History of National Socialist Crimes and Their Grandfathers' Past," in *Victims and Perpetrators: 1933–1945: (Re)presenting the Past in Post-Unification Culture*, ed. Laurel Cohen-Pfister and Dagmar Wienroeder-Skinner (Berlin: Walter de Gruyter, 2006), 285–95; Mary Fulbrook, *Dissonant Lives: Generations and Violence through the German Dictatorships* (Oxford: Oxford University Press, 2011).

76. Gabriele Rosenthal, "National Socialism and Antisemitism in Intergenerational Dialogue," in *The Holocaust in Three Generations: Families of Victims and Perpetrators of the Nazi Regime*, ed. Gabriele Rosenthal (London: Cassell, 1998), 241.

77. Reiter, *Generation danach*, 283–87.

78. Sophocles, *Antigone*, lines 21–30.

79. Ibid., lines 450–55.

80. Robert Boyd and Peter J. Richerson, *The Origin and Evolution of Cultures* (Oxford: Oxford University Press, 2005).

81. A. C. Grayling, *The Age of Genius: The Seventeenth Century and the Birth of the Modern Mind* (New York: Bloomsbury, 2016); Gottlieb, *Dream of Enlightenment*.

82. Triandis, *Individualism and Collectivism*, 24.

83. Ibid., 33.

84. Marshall Berman, *All that Is Solid Melts into Air: The Experience of Modernity* (New York: Simon & Schuster, 1982); Russell Shorto, *Amsterdam: A History of the World's Most Liberal City* (New York: Doubleday, 2013).

85. Markus and Kitayama, "Culture and the Self."

86. Sophocles, *Antigone*, line 718.

87. David Desser, *The Samurai Films of Akira Kurosawa* (Ann Arbor, MI: UMI Research Press, 1983), 36–39.

88. Donald Richie, *A Hundred Years of Japanese Film: A Concise History, with a Selective Guide to DVDs and Videos* (New York: Kodansha, 2012), 145.

89. Ian Buruma, *A Japanese Mirror: Heroes and Villains of Japanese Culture* (London: Penguin Books, 1984), 164.

90. Joan Mellen, *Voices from the Japanese Cinema* (New York: Liveright, 1975), 147.

91. Buruma, *Japanese Mirror*, 185.

92. Mellen, *Voices*, 147.

93. Buruma, *Japanese Mirror*, 161.

94. Ivan Morris, *The Nobility of Failure: Tragic Heroes in the History of Japan* (New York: Holt, Rinehart and Winston, 1975).

95. Saburo Ienaga, *The Pacific War, 1931–1945* (New York: Pantheon Books, 1978), 203.

96. Robert N. Bellah, "Intellectual and Society in Japan," *Daedalus* 101, no. 2 (1972): 89–115; Koschmann, "Introduction," 14.

97. Ienaga, *Pacific War*, 123.

98. Yoshiaki Yoshimi, *Grassroots Fascism: The War Experience of the Japanese People*, trans. Ethan Mark (New York: Columbia University Press, 2015).

99. Francis L. K. Hsu, *Americans and Chinese: Passage to Differences*, 3rd ed. (Honolulu: University Press of Hawai'i, 1981), 377–78.

100. Wolfgram, *"Getting History Right,"* chap. 4.

101. Grayling, *Age of Genius*; Gottlieb, *Dream of Enlightenment*.

## CHAPTER I — GERMANY

1. Aeschylus, *Persians*, trans. James Romm, in *The Greek Plays: Sixteen Plays by Aeschylus, Sophocles, and Euripides*, ed. Mary Lefkowitz and James Romm (New York: Modern Library, 2016), lines 272–73.

2. Mark A. Wolfgram, "Didactic War Crimes Trials and External Legal Culture: The Cases of the Nuremberg, Frankfurt Auschwitz, and Majdanek Trials in West Germany," *Global Change, Peace & Security* 26, no. 3 (2014): 281–97.

3. Mark A. Wolfgram, *"Getting History Right": East and West Germany Collective Memories of the Holocaust and War* (Lewisburg, PA: Bucknell University Press, 2011), 105.

4. Ibid., 218–19.

5. Charles S. Maier, *The Unmasterable Past: History, Holocaust, and German National Identity* (Cambridge, MA: Harvard University Press, 1988), 7.

6. Wolfgram, "Didactic War Crimes Trials," 290.

7. Wolfgram, *"Getting History Right,"* 217–32.

8. Mark A. Wolfgram, "The Holocaust through the Prism of East German Television: Collective Memory and Audience Perceptions," *Holocaust and Genocide Studies* 20, no. 1 (2006): 65.

9. Wolfgram, *"Getting History Right,"* 228.

10. Ibid., 35.

11. Ibid., 79.

12. Ibid., 80.

13. Ibid., 80.

14. Ibid., 181.

15. Antonio J. Ferreira, "Family Myth and Homeostasis," *Archives of General Psychiatry* 9, no. 5 (1963): 462.

16. Peter Sichrovsky, *Born Guilty: Children of Nazi Families*, trans. Jean Steinberg (New York: Basic Books, 1988); Dan Bar-On, *Legacy of Silence: Encounters with Children of the Third Reich* (Cambridge, MA: Harvard University Press, 1989); Gabriele Rosenthal (ed.), *The Holocaust in Three Generations: Families of Victims and Perpetrators of the Nazi Regime*, (London: Cassell, 1998); Harald Welzer et al., *"Opa war kein Nazi": Nationalsozialismus und Holocaust im Familiengedächtnis* ["Grandpa wasn't a Nazi": National Socialism and the Holocaust in family memory] (Frankfurt: Fischer Taschenbuch Verlag, 2002); Margit Reiter, *Die Generation danach: Der Nationalsozialismus im Familiengedächtnis* [The generation after: National Socialism in family memory] (Innsbruck: Studien Verlag, 2006); Christiane Wienand, *Returning Memories: Former Prisoners of War in Divided and Reunited Germany* (Rochester, NY: Camden House, 2015).

17. Welzer et al., *"Opa war kein Nazi."*

18. Gabriele Rosenthal, "National Socialism and Antisemitism in Intergenerational Dialogue," in *The Holocaust in Three Generations: Families of Victims and Perpetrators of the Nazi Regime*, ed. Gabriele Rosenthal (London: Cassell, 1998), 241.

19. Mark A. Wolfgram, "Rediscovering Narratives of German Resistance: Opposing the Nazi 'Terror-State,'" *Rethinking History* 10, no. 2 (2006): 201–19.

20. Reiter, *Die Generation danach*, 283–87.

21. Wolfgram, *"Getting History Right,"* 39.

22. Ibid., 52–53.

23. Wienand, *Returning Memories*.

24. Wolfgram, *"Getting History Right,"* 230.

25. Ibid., 116–17.

26. Ibid., 186.

27. Ibid.

28. Wolfgram, "The Holocaust through the Prism."

29. Wolfgram, *"Getting History Right,"* 190.

30. Ibid., 91.

31. Ibid., 80.

32. Ibid., 77–78.

33. Wienand, *Returning Memories*.

34. Wolfgram, *"Getting History Right,"* 119.

35. Wolfgram, "Didactic War Crimes Trials."

36. Wolfgram, *"Getting History Right,"* 121–22.

37. Ibid., 138.

38. Christoph Classen, *Bilder der Vergangenheit: Die Zeit des Nationalsozialismus im Fernsehen der Bundesrepublik Deutschland 1955–1965* [Pictures of the past: The time of National Socialism in the television of the Federal Republic of Germany 1955–1965] (Cologne: Bölau Verlag, 1999), 101.

39. Wolfgram, "*Getting History Right,*" 130.

40. Ibid., 131.

41. Ibid., 199–200.

## CHAPTER 2 — JAPAN

1. Aeschylus, *Persians*, trans. James Romm, in *The Greek Plays: Sixteen Plays by Aeschylus, Sophocles, and Euripides*, ed. Mary Lefkowitz and James Romm (New York: Modern Library, 2016), lines 816–20.

2. Yoshiaki Yoshimi, *Grassroots Fascism: The War Experience of the Japanese People*, trans. Ethan Mark (New York: Columbia University Press, 2015).

3. Saburo Ienaga, *The Pacific War, 1931–1945* (New York: Pantheon, 1978), chap. 10.

4. Yuki Miyamoto, *Beyond the Mushroom Cloud: Commemoration, Religion, and Responsibility after Hiroshima* (New York: Fordham University Press, 2012), 150, 156.

5. Jeffrey C. Alexander, *Trauma: A Social Theory* (Cambridge: Polity Press, 2012), 13–15.

6. Akiko Hashimoto, *The Long Defeat: Cultural Trauma, Memory, and Identity in Japan* (Oxford: Oxford University Press, 2015), 36–37.

7. Akiko Hashimoto, "The Cultural Trauma of a Fallen Nation," in *Narrating Trauma: On the Impact of Collective Suffering*, ed. Ron Eyerman et al. (Boulder, CO: Paradigm, 2011), 31.

8. Richard E. Nisbett et al., "Culture and Systems of Thought: Holistic versus Analytic Cognition," *Psychological Review* 108, no. 2 (2001): 299.

9. Ibid.

10. Hazel Rose Markus and Shinobu Kitayama, "Culture and the Self: Implications for Cognition, Emotion, and Motivation," *Psychological Review* 98, no. 2 (1991): 233–35.

11. Nisbett et al., "Culture and Systems of Thought," 296, 298–99.

12. Donald Richie, *A Hundred Years of Japanese Film: A Concise History, with a Selective Guide to DVDs and Videos* (New York: Kodansha, 2012), 123–24.

13. Philip A. Seaton, *Japan's Contested War Memories: The "Memory Rifts" in Historical Consciousness of World War II* (London: Routledge, 2007), 175.

14. Thomas U. Berger, *War, Guilt, and World Politics after World War II* (Cambridge: Cambridge University Press, 2012); Sebastian Conrad, "Entangled Memories: Versions of the Past in Germany and Japan, 1945–2001," *Journal of Contemporary History* 38, no. 1 (2003): 85–99.

15. Franziska Seraphim, *War Memory and Social Politics in Japan, 1945–2005* (Cambridge, MA: Harvard University Asia Center, 2006), 203, 205.

16. Ibid., 262.

17. Robert N. Bellah, *Imagining Japan: The Japanese Tradition and Its Modern Interpretation* (Berkeley: University of California Press, 2003), 58–60.

18. Ibid., 40.

19. Karen Armstrong, *The Great Transformation: The Beginning of Our Religious Traditions* (New York: Knopf, 2006); Robert N. Bellah, *Religion in Human Evolution: From the Paleolithic to the Axial Age* (Cambridge, MA: Belknap Press of Harvard University Press, 2011).

20. Richie, *Hundred Years*, 114–15.

21. Akiko Hashimoto, "Japanese and German Projects of Moral Recovery: Toward a New Understanding of War Memories in Defeated Nations" (Cambridge, MA: Harvard University Press, Edwin O. Reischauer Institute of Japanese Studies Occasional Papers in Japanese Studies, 1999).

22. Joan Mellen, *The Waves at Genji's Door: Japan through Its Cinema* (New York: Pantheon, 1976), 15.

23. Bellah, *Imagining Japan*, 58.

24. Lisa Wedeen, *Ambiguities of Domination: Politics, Rhetoric, and Symbols in Contemporary Syria* (Chicago: University of Chicago Press, 1999), 6.

25. Seraphim, *War Memory*, 274; Hashimoto, *Long Defeat*, 57.

26. Carol Gluck, "The Past in the Present," in *Postwar Japan as History*, ed. Andrew Gordon (Berkeley: University of California Press, 1993), 89.

27. Takashi Fujitani, *Splendid Monarchy: Power and Pageantry in Modern Japan* (Berkeley: University of California Press, 1996), 244.

28. Hashimoto, *Long Defeat*, 75.

29. Yoshikuni Igarashi, "The Bomb, Hirohito, and History: The Foundational Narrative of United States-Japan Postwar Relations," *positions* 6, no. 2 (1998): 262.

30. Mark A. Wolfgram, *"Getting History Right": East and West Germany Collective Memories of the Holocaust and War* (Lewisburg, PA: Bucknell University Press, 2011), 218.

31. Irmela Hijiya-Kirschnereit, "Post–World War II Literature: The Intellectual Climate in Japan, 1945–1985," in *Legacies and Ambiguities: Postwar Fiction and Culture in West Germany and Japan*, ed. Ernestine Schlant and J. Thomas Rimer (Washington, DC: Woodrow Wilson Center Press, 1991), 110.

32. Richie, *Hundred Years*, 214.

33. Blaine P. Connor and John W. Traphagan, "Negotiating the Afterlife: Emplacement as Ongoing Concern in Contemporary Japan," *Asian Anthropology* 13, no. 1 (2014): 3–19; Robert J. Smith, *Ancestor Worship in Contemporary Japan* (Stanford, CA: Stanford University Press, 1974).

34. Richard Lloyd Parry, *Ghosts of the Tsunami* (London: Jonathan Cape, 2017), 92–107.

35. Markus and Kitayama, "Culture and the Self," 237.

36. Gluck, "Past in the Present," 85.

37. Akiko Hashimoto, "Culture, Power, and the Discourse of Filial Piety in Japan: The Disempowerment of Youth and Its Social Consequences," in *Filial Piety: Practice and Discourse in Contemporary East Asia*, ed. Charlotte Ikels (Stanford, CA: Stanford University Press, 2004), 182–97.

38. Robert N. Bellah, "Intellectual and Society in Japan," *Daedalus* 101, no. 2 (1972): 106.

39. Ibid., 111.

40. Richie, *Hundred Years*, 75–76.

41. Parry, *Ghosts of the Tsunami*, 180–84, 198.

42. Seraphim, *War Memory*, 90.

43. Wolfgram, "Didactic War Crimes Trials."

44. Seraphim, *War Memory*, 5.

45. Ibid., 100.

46. Ibid., 106.

47. Ibid., 136.

48. Ibid., 130.

49. Petra Buchholz, *Schreiben und Erinnern: Über Selbstzeugnisse japanischer Kriegsteilnehmer* [Writing and remembering: Personal testimonials of Japanese combatants] (Munich: Iudicium Verlag, 2003), 263–65; Naoko Shimazu, "Popular Representations of the Past: The Case of Postwar Japan," *Journal of Contemporary History* 38, no. 1 (2003): 105.

50. James J. Orr, *The Victim as Hero: Ideologies of Peace and National Identity in Postwar Japan* (Honolulu: University of Hawai'i Press, 2001), 125.

51. David Desser, *The Samurai Films of Akira Kurosawa* (Ann Arbor, MI: UMI Research Press, 1983), 36–39.

52. Richie, *Hundred Years*, 163.

53. Joan Mellen, *Voices from the Japanese Cinema* (New York: Liveright, 1975), 143.

54. Michael Baskett, *The Attractive Empire: Transnational Film Culture in Imperial Japan* (Honolulu: University of Hawai'i Press, 2008), 132.

55. Hashimoto, *Long Defeat*, chap. 2.

56. Van C. Gessel, "Postoccupation Literary Movements and Developments in Japan," in *Legacies and Ambiguities: Postwar Fiction and Culture in West Germany and Japan*, ed. Ernestine Schlant and J. Thomas Rimer (Washington, DC: Woodrow Wilson Center Press, 1991), 216.

57. Jin Li, *Cultural Foundations of Learning: East and West* (Cambridge: Cambridge University Press, 2012), 51.

58. Tadao Sato, *Currents in Japanese cinema: Essays*, trans. Gregory Barrett (Tokyo: Kodansha International, 1982), 109.

59. Keiko I. McDonald, *Cinema East: A Critical Study of Major Japanese Films* (Rutherford, NJ: Fairleigh Dickinson University Press, 1983), 90.

60. Carol A. Kidron, "Alterity and the Particular Limits of Universalism: Comparing Jewish-Israeli Holocaust and Canadian-Cambodian Genocide Legacies," *Current Anthropology* 53, no. 6 (2012): 723–54; Heonik Kwon, *After the Massacre: Commemoration and Consolation in Ha My and My Lai* (Berkeley: University of California Press, 2006); Heonik Kwon, *Ghosts of War in Vietnam* (Cambridge: Cambridge University Press, 2008), 2–27.

61. Hijiya-Kirschnereit, "Post–World War II Literature," 115.

62. Seraphim, *War Memory*, 79.

63. Takashi Yoshida, *The Making of the "Rape of Nanking": History and Memory in Japan, China, and the United States* (Oxford: Oxford University Press, 2006), 53.

64. Hashimoto, *Long Defeat*, 12.

65. Richie, *Hundred Years*, 150.

66. Shimazu, "Popular Representations," 112.

67. J. Victor Koschmann, "Introduction: Soft Rule and Expressive Protest," in *Authority and the Individual in Japan: Citizen Protest in Historical Perspective*, ed. J. Victor Koschmann (Tokyo: University of Tokyo Press, 1978), 22.

68. Hashimoto, *Long Defeat*, 37.

69. Shunsuke Tsurumi, *A Cultural History of Postwar Japan, 1945–1980* (London: Routledge and Kegan Paul, 1987), 106.

70. Tsurumi, *Cultural History*, 111.

71. Bellah, *Imagining Japan*, 59–60.

72. Seraphim, *War Memory*, 172.

73. Jeffrey Broadbent, *Environmental Politics in Japan: Networks of Power and Protest* (Cambridge: Cambridge University Press, 1998); Jeffrey Broadbent and Vicky Brockman (ed.), *East Asian Social Movements: Power, Protest, and Change in a Dynamic Region* (New York: Springer, 2010).

74. Wolfgram, "Didactic War Crimes Trials."

75. Kato Shuichi, "Mechanisms of Ideas: Society, Intellectuals, and Literature in the Postwar Period in Japan," in *Legacies and Ambiguities: Postwar Fiction and Culture in West Germany and Japan*, ed. Ernestine Schlant and J. Thomas Rimer (Washington, DC: Woodrow Wilson Center Press, 1991), 255.

76. Hijiya-Kirschnereit, "Post–World War II Literature," 105.

77. Shuichi, "Mechanisms of Ideas," 259.

78. Carol Gluck, "The 'Long Postwar': Japan and Germany in Common and in Contrast," in *Legacies and Ambiguities: Postwar Fiction and Culture in West Germany and Japan*, ed. Ernestine Schlant and J. Thomas Rimer (Washington, DC: Woodrow Wilson Center Press, 1991), 74.

79. Seraphim, *War Memory*, 23–24.

80. Ibid., 24; C. Sarah Soh, *The Comfort Women: Sexual Violence and Postcolonial Memory in Korea and Japan* (Chicago: University of Chicago Press, 2008), 145–46.

81. Richie, *Hundred Years*, 151–52.

82. Yoshida, *Making*, 56.

83. Ibid., 82.

84. Seraphim, *War Memory*, 8, 261; Carol Gluck, "Operations of Memory: 'Comfort Women' and the World," in *Ruptured Histories: War, Memory, and the Post–Cold War in Asia*, ed. Sheila Miyoshi Jager and Rana Mitter (Cambridge, MA: Harvard University Press, 2007), 72; Hashimoto, *Long Defeat*; Igarashi, "Bomb," 263; Sheila Miyoshi Jager and Rana Mitter, "Introduction: Re-Envisioning Asia, Past and Present," in *Ruptured Histories: War, Memory, and the Post–Cold War in Asia*, ed. Sheila Miyoshi Jager and Rana Mitter (Cambridge, MA: Harvard University Press, 2007), 3; Sven Saaler, *Politics, Memory and Public Opinion: The History Textbook Controversy and Japanese Society* (Munich: IUDICIUM, 2005), 158.

85. Yoshida, *Making*, 100.

86. Seraphim, *War Memory*, 270; Yoshida, *Making*, 81.

87. Seraphim, *War Memory*, 293.

88. Shimazu, "Popular Representations," 108.

89. Hashimoto, *Long Defeat*, 86.

90. Seaton, *Japan's Contested*, 109.

91. Seaton, *Japan's Contested*, 172–77; Seraphim, *War Memory*, 295.

92. Seraphim, *War Memory*, 301.

93. Seaton, *Japan's Contested*, 193.

94. Richie, *Hundred Years*, 250.

95. Ayako Kurahashi, *My Father's Dying Wish: Legacies of War Guilt in a Japanese Family*, trans. Philip A. Seaton (Sheffield, UK: Paulownia Press, 2009). See also Seaton, *Japan's Contested*, 193–96.

96. Hashimoto, *Long Defeat*, 34.

97. Seaton, *Japan's Contested*, 191.

98. Seaton, *Japan's Contested*, 126–27; Hashimoto, *Long Defeat*, 34–36.

99. Hashimoto, *Long Defeat*, 116.

## CHAPTER 3 — SPAIN

1. Sophocles, *Antigone*, trans. David Mulroy (Madison: University of Wisconsin Press, 2013), lines 203–6.

2. Sophocles, *Antigone*, line 523.

3. Charles Tilly, *Contention and Democracy in Europe, 1650–2000* (Cambridge: Cambridge University Press), 85–86.

4. Paul Preston, *The Triumph of Democracy in Spain* (London: Methuen, 1986), 4.

5. Francisco Ferrándiz, "Exhuming the Defeated: Civil War Mass Graves in 21st-Century Spain," *American Ethnologist* 40, no. 1 (2013): 40; Paul Preston, *The Spanish Holocaust: Inquisition and Extermination in Twentieth-Century Spain* (New York: Norton, 2012), xvi–xviii.

6. Giles Tremlett, *Ghosts of Spain: Travels through Spain and Its Silent Past* (New York: Walker, 2006), 67–68; Helen Graham, *The War and Its Shadow: Spain's Civil War in Europe's Long Twentieth Century* (Brighton, UK: Sussex Academic Press, 2012), 148.

7. Andrea Hepworth, "Site of Memory and Dismemory: The Valley of the Fallen in Spain," *Journal of Genocide Research* 16, no. 4 (2014): 463–85.

8. Elizabeth A. Castelli, *Martyrdom and Memory: Early Christian Culture Making* (New York: Columbia University Press, 2004), 34.

9. Michael Richards, *A Time of Silence: Civil War and the Culture of Repression in Franco's Spain, 1936–1945* (Cambridge: Cambridge University Press, 1998), 50.

10. Ibid., 17.

11. Ibid.

12. Layla Renshaw, *Exhuming Loss: Memory, Materiality and Mass Graves of the Spanish Civil War* (Walnut Creek, CA: Left Coast Press, 2011), 32.

13. Paloma Aguilar, *Memory and Amnesia: The Role of the Spanish Civil War in the Transition to Democracy*, trans. Mark Oakley (New York: Berghahn, 2002), 61.

14. Graham, *War and Its Shadow*, 137.

15. Román Gubern, "The Civil War: Inquest or Exorcism?" *Quarterly Review of Film and Video* 13, no. 4 (1991): 109.

16. Victor M. Pérez-Díaz, *The Return of Civil Society: The Emergence of Democratic Spain* (Cambridge, MA: Harvard University Press, 1993), 21–22.

17. Paloma Aguilar and Carsten Humlebaek, "Collective Memory and National Identity in the Spanish Democracy: The Legacies of Francoism and the Civil War," *History & Memory* 14, nos. 1–2 (2002): 142–43.

18. Mercedes Maroto Camino, *Film, Memory and the Legacy of the Spanish Civil War* (New York: Palgrave Macmillan, 2011), 74; Pérez-Díaz, *Return of Civil Society*, 124.

19. Silke Hünecke, "Überwindung des Schweigens: Verdrängte Geschichte, politische Repression und Kollektives Trauma als Gegenstand der Arbeit der erinnerungspoli-

tischen Bewegung im spanischen Staat" [Overcoming the silence: Repressed history, political repression and collective trauma as the subject of the memory and political movement in Spain], PhD diss., Freien Universität Berlin, 2013, 474.

20. José Alvarez Junco, "Education and the Limits of Liberalism," in *Spanish Cultural Studies: An Introduction, the Struggle for Modernity*, ed. Helen Graham and Jo Labanyi (Oxford: Oxford University Press, 1995), 48.

21. Christopher Cobb, "The Republican State and Mass Education-Cultural Initiatives 1931–1936," in *Spanish Cultural Studies: An Introduction, the Struggle for Modernity*, ed. Helen Graham and Jo Labanyi (Oxford: Oxford University Press, 1995), 135.

22. Alicia Alted, "Education and Political Control," in *Spanish Cultural Studies: An Introduction, the Struggle for Modernity*, ed. Helen Graham and Jo Labanyi (Oxford: Oxford University Press, 1995), 199.

23. Alicia Alted, "Educational Policy in a Changing Society," in *Spanish Cultural Studies: An Introduction, the Struggle for Modernity*, ed. Helen Graham and Jo Labanyi (Oxford: Oxford University Press, 1995), 274.

24. Aguilar, *Memory and Amnesia*, 60.

25. Michael Richards, "Grand Narratives, Collective Memory, and Social History: Public Uses of the Past in Postwar Spain," in *Unearthing Franco's Legacy: Mass Graves and the Recovery of Historical Memory in Spain*, ed. Carlos Jerez-Farrán and Samuel Amago (Notre Dame, IN: University of Notre Dame Press, 2010), 130.

26. Aguilar and Humlebaek, "Collective Memory," 142.

27. Walther L. Bernecker and Sören Brinkmann, *Kampf der Erinnerungen: Der Spanische Bürgerkrieg in Politik und Gesellschaft 1936–1939* [Struggle over the memories: The Spanish Civil War in politics and society 1936–1939] (Nettersheim, Germany: Verlag Graswurzelrevolution, 2006), 305–6.

28. Emilio Silva Barrera, "The Importance of Remembrance in the Transition to Democracy in Spain," in *Diktaturbewältigung und nationale Selbstvergewisserung: Geschichtskulturen in Polen und Spanien im Vergleich* [Overcoming dictatorship and national self-assurance: A comparison of historical cultures in Poland and Spain], ed. Krzysztof Ruchniewicz and Stefan Troebst (Wrocław: Wydawnictwo Uniwersytetu Wrocławskiego, 2004), 73.

29. Meirian Jump, "The Role of Archives in the Movement for the Recovery of Historical Memory in Spain. La Rioja: A Regional Case Study," *Journal of the Society of Archivists* 33, no. 2 (2012): 153.

30. Ruth Sanz Sabido, *Memories of the Spanish Civil War: Conflict and Community in Rural Spain* (London: Rowman & Littlefield, 2016), 160–61.

31. Sarah Leggott, *Memory, War, and Dictatorship in Recent Spanish Fiction by Women* (Lewisburg, PA: Bucknell University Press, 2015), 22.

32. Jump, "Role of Archives," 158–59.

33. Tremlett, *Ghosts of Spain*, 14.

34. Susan Friend Harding, *Remaking Ibieca: Rural Life in Aragon under Franco* (Chapel Hill: University of North Carolina Press, 1984), 181.

35. Jump, "Role of Archives," 153.

36. Barrera, "Importance of Remembrance."

37. Paloma Aguilar and Francisco Ferrándiz, "Memory, Media and Spectacle: *Interviú's* Portrayal of Civil War Exhumations in the Early Years of Spanish Democracy," *Journal of Spanish Cultural Studies* 17, no. 1 (2016): 1–25.

38. Francisco Ferrándiz, "The Intimacy of Defeat: Exhumations in Contemporary Spain," in *Unearthing Franco's Legacy: Mass Graves and the Recovery of Historical Memory in Spain*, ed. Carlos Jerez-Farrán and Samuel Amago (Notre Dame, IN: University of Notre Dame Press, 2010), 308; Jump, "Role of Archives," 157; Sabido, *Memories*, 27n6.

39. Alejandro Baer and Natan Sznaider, "Ghosts of the Holocaust in Franco's Mass Graves: Cosmopolitan Memories and the Politics of 'Never Again,'" *Memory Studies* 8, no. 3 (2015): 340.

40. Preston, *Spanish Holocaust*, xii.

41. Tremlett, *Ghosts of Spain*, 8, 10.

42. Ljiljana Radonić, "Transformation of Memory in Croatia: Removing Yugoslav Anti-Fascism," in *Dynamics of Memory and Identity in Contemporary Europe*, ed. Eric Langenbacher et al. (New York: Berghahn, 2012), 166–79.

43. Bernecker and Brinkmann, *Kampf der Erinnerungen*, 316–17.

44. Graham, *War*, 131.

45. Richards, *Time of Silence*, 51.

46. Renshaw, *Exhuming Loss*, 110.

47. Richards, "Grand Narratives," 134.

48. Renshaw, *Exhuming Loss*, 74.

49. Mark A. Wolfgram, "A Model for Comparative Collective Memory Studies: Regime Types, Cultural Traditions, and Difficult Histories," *Croatian Political Science Review* 51, no. 5 (2014): 25–28.

50. Harding, *Remaking Ibieca*, 178.

51. Ibid., 70, 181.

52. Laura Desfor Edles, *Symbol and Ritual in the New Spain: The Transition to Democracy after Franco* (Cambridge: Cambridge University Press, 1998), 42.

53. Renshaw, *Exhuming Loss*, 50.

54. Ibid., 32.

55. Ángela Cenarro, "Memory beyond the Public Sphere: The Francoist Repression Remembered in Aragon," *History & Memory* 14, nos. 1–2 (2002): 170, 173.

56. Renshaw, *Exhuming Loss*, 67; Tremlett, *Ghosts of Spain*, 6.

57. Renshaw, *Exhuming Loss*, 91.

58. Cenarro, "Memory beyond the Public Sphere," 178.

59. Renshaw, *Exhuming Loss*, 117–18.

60. Ibid., 234–35.

61. Núria Triana-Toribio, *Spanish National Cinema* (London: Routledge, 2003), 95.

62. Preston, *The Spanish Holocaust*, 520.

63. Ofelia Ferrán, *Working Through Memory: Writing and Remembrance in Contemporary Spanish Narrative* (Lewisburg, PA: Bucknell University Press, 2007), 271.

64. Gubern, "Civil War."

65. H. Rosi Song, *Lost in Transition: Constructing Memory in Contemporary Spain* (Liverpool: Liverpool University Press, 2016), 107–9.

66. Bernecker and Brinkmann, *Kampf der Erinnerungen*, 310–11; Ferrán, *Working Through Memory*, 275.

67. Rebecca J. Atencio, "A Prime Time to Remember: Memory Merchandising in Globo's *Anos Rebeldes*," in *Accounting for Violence: Marketing Memory in Latin America*, ed. Ksenija Bilbija and Leigh A. Payne (Durham, NC: Duke University Press, 2011), 41–68.

68. Bernard P. Bentley, *A Companion to Spanish Cinema* (Rochester, NY: Tamesis, 2008), 123–24.

69. Ibid., 170.

70. Román Gubern, "Film Censorship," in *A Companion to Spanish Cinema*, ed. Jo Labanyi and Tatjana Pavlović (Oxford: Wiley-Blackwell, 2013), 399.

71. Bentley, *Companion*, 200.

72. *Huellas de un Espiritu* [Footprints of a spirit]. 1998. CANAL+ Espana. Part of the Criterion Collection for Víctor Erice's film *El spíritu de la colena* [Spirit of the beehive] (1973).

73. Manuel Rivas, *The Carpenter's Pencil*, trans. Jonathan Dunne (New York: Overlook Press, 2001), 46–47.

74. Leggott, *Memory, War, and Dictatorship*, 105, 125.

75. Jo Labanyi et al., "Melodrama and Historical Film," in *A Companion to Spanish Cinema*, ed. Jo Labanyi and Tatjana Pavlović (Oxford: Wiley-Blackwell, 2013), 253.

76. Maryse Bertrand de Muñoz, "Literatura de la guerra civil" [Literature of the civil war], *Anthropos* 148 (1993): 6–24.

77. Aguilar, *Memory and Amnesia*, 129.

78. Camino, *Film, Memory and the Legacy*, 74.

79. Aguilar, *Memory and Amnesia*, 31, 124.

80. Ibid., 134; Bentley, *Companion*, 170.

81. Aguilar, *Memory and Amnesia*, 98–99.

82. Ibid., 137–38.

83. Bentley, *Companion*, 191.

84. Igartua and Páez, "Art and Remembering," 87.

85. Preston, *Triumph of Democracy*, 15.

86. Camino, *Film, Memory and the Legacy*, 74.

87. Preston, *Triumph of Democracy*, 14.

88. Bentley, *Companion*, 200.

89. Hünecke, "Überwindung des Schweigens," 520–21.

90. Igartua and Páez, "Art and Remembering."

91. Gubern, "Civil War," 109.

92. Camino, *Film, Memory and the Legacy*, 1; Georgina Blakeley, "Digging Up Spain's Past: Consequences of Truth and Reconciliation," *Democratization* 12, no. 1 (2005): 44–59.

93. Blakeley, "Digging up Spain's Past."

94. Alison Guzmán, "La memoria de la Guerra Civil en el teatro español: 1939–2009" [The memory of the civil war in the Spanish theater: 1939–2009], PhD diss., Universidad de Salamanca, 2012, 191.

95. Ferrándiz, "Intimacy of Defeat," 308.

96. Baer and Sznaider, "Ghosts of the Holocaust," 330.

97. Tremlett, *Ghosts of Spain*, 332.

98. Alejandro Baer and Natan Sznaider, "Antigone in León: The Drama of Trauma Politics," in *Routledge International Handbook of Memory Studies*, ed. Anna Lisa Tota and Trever Hagen (London: Routledge, 2016), 181–92.

## CHAPTER 4 — YUGOSLAVIA

1. Sophocles, *Antigone*, trans. David Mulroy (Madison: University of Wisconsin Press, 2013), lines 1080–84.

2. Ibid., line 718.

3. Tone Bringa, *Being Muslim the Bosnian Way: Identity and Community in a Central Bosnian Village* (Princeton, NJ: Princeton University Press, 1995), 4.

4. Ibid., 58–65.

5. Milovan Djilas, *Anatomy of a Moral*, ed. Abraham Rothberg (London: Thames & Hudson, 1959).

6. Goran Miloradović, "Stalin's Gifts: Yugoslav Feature Films 1945–1955," in *Osteuropa vom Weltkrieg zur Wende* [Eastern Europe from the world war to the end of the cold war],

ed. Wolfgang Mueller and Michael Portmann (Vienna: Österreichische Akademie der Wissenschaften, 2007), 194.

7. Jasna Dragović-Soso, *"Saviours of the Nation": Serbia's Intellectual Opposition and the Revival of Nationalism* (London: Hurst, 2002), 11–14.

8. Ibid., 47.

9. Ibid., 31.

10. Iain King and Whit Mason, *Peace at Any Price: How the World Failed Kosovo* (London: Hurst, 2006); Mark A. Wolfgram, "When the Men with Guns Rule: Explaining Human Rights Failures in Kosovo since 1999," *Political Science Quarterly* 123, no. 3 (2008): 461–84.

11. James Georgas, "Differences and Universals in Families across Cultures," in *Fundamental Questions in Cross-Cultural Psychology*, ed. Fons J. R. van de Vijver et al. (Cambridge: Cambridge University Press, 2011), 357.

12. Milovan Djilas, *Tito: The Story from Inside*, trans. Vasilije Kojic and Richard Hayes (New York: Harcourt Brace Jovanovich, 1980), 81.

13. Aleksa Djilas, *The Contested Country: Yugoslav Unity and Communist Revolution 1919–1953* (Cambridge, MA: Harvard University Press, 1991).

14. Andrew Baruch Wachtel, *Making a Nation, Breaking a Nation: Literature and Cultural Politics in Yugoslavia* (Stanford, CA: Stanford University Press, 1998), 148.

15. Daniel J. Goulding, *Liberated Cinema: The Yugoslav Experience, 1945–2001*, rev. and expanded ed. (Bloomington: Indiana University Press, 2002), 19–20; Wachtel, *Making a Nation*, 152; Jelena Batinić, *Women and Yugoslav Partisans: A History of World War II Resistance* (Cambridge: Cambridge University Press, 2015).

16. Scott Straus, *Making and Unmaking Nations: War, Leadership, and Genocide in Modern Africa* (Ithaca, NY: Cornell University Press, 2015).

17. Batinić, *Women and Yugoslav Partisans*, chap. 1.

18. Milovan Djilas, *Wartime*, trans. Michael B. Petrovich (New York: Harcourt Brace Jovanovich, 1977), 150, 276.

19. Wachtel, *Making a Nation*, 46.

20. Goulding, *Liberated Cinema*, 36–38.

21. Natalija Bašić, "Der Zweite Weltkrieg im Fernsehen: Filmpartisanen im kroatischen und serbischen Familiengedächtnis" [The Second World War in TV: Film partisans in Croatian and Serbian family memory] *Ethnologia Balkanica* 8 (2004): 57.

22. Andrew Horton, "The Rise and Fall of the Yugoslav Partisan Film: Cinematic Perceptions of a National Identity," *Film Criticism* 12, no. 2 (1987): 21.

23. Miloradović, "Stalin's Gifts," 180.

24. Ibid., 182.

25. Wachtel, *Making a Nation*, 147.

26. Goulding, *Liberated Cinema*, 32.

27. Ibid., 2, 37, 63, 143.

28. Ibid., 38.

29. Djilas, *Tito*, 86.

30. Batinić, *Women and Yugoslav Partisans*, 232–39.

31. Goulding, *Liberated Cinema*, 20.

32. Miloradović, "Stalin's Gifts," 187.

33. Goulding, *Liberated Cinema*, 79.

34. Batinić, *Women and Yugoslav Partisans*, 231–57.

35. Wachtel, *Making a Nation*, 152–54.

36. Goulding, *Liberated Cinema*, 20.

37. Miloradović, "Stalin's Gifts," 188–89.

38. Djilas, *Tito*, 84–85.

39. Goulding, *Liberated Cinema*, 159.

40. Charles Tilly, *Contention and Democracy in Europe, 1650–2000* (Cambridge: Cambridge University Press, 2004).

41. Richard Ned Lebow, *Forbidden Fruit: Counterfactuals and International Relations* (Princeton, NJ: Princeton University Press, 2010).

42. Djilas, *Tito*, 72.

43. Ibid., 177.

44. Ibid., 178.

45. Ibid., 179.

46. Heike Karge, *Steinerne Erinnerung—versteinerte Erinnerung? Kriegsgedenken in Jugoslawien (1947–1970)* [Stony memory—fossilized memory? War commemoration in Yugoslavia (1947–1970)] (Wiesbaden, Germany: Harrassowitz, 2010), 57–58.

47. Ibid., 85.

48. Ibid., 88.

49. Ibid., 90.

50. Ibid., 90, 93.

51. Ibid., 69.

52. Heike Karge, "Mediated Remembrance: Local Practices of Remembering the Second World War in Tito's Yugoslavia," *European Review of History/Revue européenne d'histoire* 16, no. 1 (2009): 54.

53. Ibid., 54.

54. Ibid., 54–55.

55. Ibid., 55.

56. Ibid., 57.

57. Ibid., 57.

58. Heike Karge, "Von Helden und Opfern: Eine Analyse der Erinnerungskultur zwischen Pietät und Ideologie" [From heroes to victims: An analysis of the memory culture between piety and ideology], in *Bogdan Bogdanović: Memoria und Utopie in Tito-Jugoslawien* [Bogdan Bogdanović: Memoria and utopia in Tito-Yugoslavia], ed. Architekturzentrum Wien (Klagenfurt, Austria: Wieser Verlag, 2009), 34–39.

59. *Yugoslavia Monuments to the Revolution*, ed. Miloš Bajič (Belgrade: Subnor Jugoslavije, 1968), xxxii–xxxiii.

60. Dragović-Soso, *"Saviours of the Nation,"* 104–5.

61. Sveta Lukić, *Contemporary Yugoslav Literature: A Sociopolitical Approach*, ed. Gertrude Joch Robinson, trans. Pola Triandis (Urbana: University of Illinois Press, 1972), 182–83.

62. Dragović-Soso, *"Saviours of the Nation,"* 23–24.

63. Ibid., 24; Lukić, *Contemporary Yugoslav Literature*, 183.

64. Naum Panovski, "Prelude to a War," *Performing Arts Journal* 18, no. 2 (1996): 12.

65. E. J. Czerwinski, "Aleksandar Popovic: Belgrade's Poet of the Streets," *Books Abroad* 43, no. 3 (1969): 349; Sterijino pozorje, "56th Sterijino Pozorje 2011," http://www.pozorje.org.rs/2011/predstava8eng.htm (accessed November 7, 2017).

66. Alexandra Jovićević, "Censorship and Ingenious Dramatic Strategies in Yugoslav Theatre (1945–1991)," *Primerjalna književnost (Ljubljana)* 31 (2008): 237–49.

67. Ibid., 243.

68. Petar Marjanović, *An Anthology of Works by Twentieth Century Yugoslav Playwrights* (Novi Sad, Serbia: Sterijino Pozorje, 1984).

69. Dragović-Soso, *"Saviours of the Nation,"* 47, 68.

70. Bette Denich, "Dismembering Yugoslavia: Nationalist Ideologies and the Symbolic Revival of Genocide," *American Ethnologist* 21, no. 2 (1994): 376.

71. Nicholas J. Miller, "The Nonconformists: Dobrica Ćosić and Mića Popović Envision Serbia," *Slavic Review* 58, no. 3 (1999): 515–36.

72. Dragović-Soso, *"Saviours of the Nation,"* 49.

73. Goulding, *Liberated Cinema*, 143.

74. Miljenko Jergović, *The Walnut Mansion*, trans. Stephen M. Dickey and Janja Pavetić-Dickey (New Haven, CT: Yale University Press 2015), 234–39.

75. Vuk Drašković, *The Memoirs of Jesus* [*Isusovi memoari*], trans. Mary Thompson Popović (Belgrade: Laguna, 2015).

76. Djilas, *Tito*, 81–91.

77. Oskar Gruenwald, "Yugoslav Camp Literature: Rediscovering the Ghost of a Nation's Past-Present-Future," *Slavic Review* 46, nos. 3–4 (1987): 519.

78. Ibid., 520.

79. Dragović-Soso, *"Saviours of the Nation,"* 81.

80. Gruenwald, "Yugoslav Camp Literature," 519.

81. Dragović-Soso, *"Saviours of the Nation,"* 96.

82. Wachtel, *Making a Nation*, 221–23.

83. Goulding, *Liberated Cinema*, 159, 239n11.

84. Sterijino pozorje, "30th Sterijino Pozorje Festival 1985—Best Performance," http://www.pozorje.org.rs/arhiva/predstava1985eng.htm (accessed November 7, 2017).

85. Dragović-Soso, *"Saviours of the Nation,"* 53.

86. Jasminka Udovicki and Ivan Torov, "The Interlude: 1980–1990," in *Burn This House: The Making and Unmaking of Yugoslavia*, ed. Jasminka Udovicki and James Ridgeway (Durham, NC: Duke University Press, 1997), 84–87.

87. Dragović-Soso, *"Saviours of the Nation,"* 117–18.

88. Ibid., 224–25.

89. Ibid., 225.

90. Jovićević, "Censorship," 246.

91. Dragović-Soso, *"Saviours of the Nation,"* 105–6.

92. Denich, "Dismembering Yugoslavia," 370.

93. Krinka Vidaković-Petrov, "Memory and the Oral Tradition," in *Memory: History, Culture and the Mind*, ed. Thomas Butler (Oxford: Basil Blackwell, 1989), 87.

94. Dragović-Soso, *"Saviours of the Nation,"* 106.

95. Wachtel, *Making a Nation*, 209.

96. Ibid., 198–203.

97. Dragović-Soso, *"Saviours of the Nation,"* 93.

98. King and Mason, *Peace at Any Price*; Wolfgram, "When the Men with Guns Rule."

99. Mark A. Wolfgram, "Democracy and Propaganda: NATO's War in Kosovo," *European Journal of Communication* 23, no. 2 (2008): 153–71.

100. Wolfgram, "Didactic War Crimes Trials."

101. Radonić, "Transformation of Memory," 170.

102. Ibid., 173.

CHAPTER 5 — TURKEY

1. Sophocles, *Antigone*, trans. David Mulroy (Madison: University of Wisconsin Press, 2013), lines 1073–76.

2. Ibid., line 551.

3. Amy Mills, *Streets of Memory: Landscape, Tolerance, and National Identity in Istanbul* (Athens: University of Georgia Press, 2010), 9–10.

4. Çaglar Keyder, *State and Class in Turkey: A Study in Capitalist Development* (London: Verso, 1987), 79.

5. Fatma Müge Göçek, *Denial of Violence: Ottoman Past, Turkish Present, and Collective Violence against the Armenians, 1789–2009* (Oxford: Oxford University Press, 2014), 18; Fatma Ulgen, "'Sabiha Gökçen's 80-Year-Old Secret': Kemalist Nation Formation and the Ottoman Armenians," PhD diss., University of California San Diego, 2010, 95.

6. Ulgen, "'Sabiha Gökçen's 80-Year-Old Secret,'" 371.

7. Hercules Millas, "Constructing Memories of 'Multiculturalism' and Identities in Turkish Novels," in *Turkish Literature and Cultural Memory: "Multiculturalism" as a Literary Theme after 1980*, ed. Catharina Dufft (Wiesbaden, Germany: Harrassowitz, 2009), 88, 94–95.

8. Gönül Dönmez-Colin, *The Routledge Dictionary of Turkish Cinema* (London: Routledge, 2014), 107, 341, 352.

9. Ece Temelkuran, *Deep Mountain: Across the Turkish-Armenian Divide*, trans. Kenneth Dakan (London: Verso, 2010), 56.

10. Meline Toumani, *There Was and There Was Not: A Journey through Hate and Possibility in Turkey, Armenia, and Beyond* (New York: Metropolitan Books, Henry Holt, 2014), 134.

11. Karin Schweißgut, "Memories of a Lost Armenian Identity: Ayla Kutlu's 'Can Kusu,'" in *Turkish Literature and Cultural Memory: "Multiculturalism" as a Literary Theme after 1980*, ed. Catharina Dufft (Wiesbaden, Germany: Harrassowitz Verlag, 2009), 153.

12. M. Şükrü Hanioğlu, *Atatürk: An Intellectual Biography* (Princeton, NJ: Princeton University Press, 2011), 183–84; Elisabeth Özdalga, "Contrasting Modernities," in *Autonomy and Dependence in the Family: Turkey and Sweden in Critical Perspective*, ed. Rita Liljeström and Elisabeth Özdalga (Istanbul: Swedish Research Institute in Istanbul, 2002), 5; Jenny White, *Muslim Nationalism and the New Turks* (Princeton, NJ: Princeton University Press, 2013), 16–17.

13. Goçek, *Denial of Violence*, x.

14. Ali Çarkoğlu and Ersin Kalaycıoğlu. *The Rising Tide of Conservatism in Turkey* (New York: Palgrave Macmillan, 2009), 27, 48–56; Kaya Genç, *Under the Shadow: Rage and Revolution in Modern Turkey* (London: I. B. Tauris, 2016), 26, 133.

15. Ervin Staub, *Overcoming Evil: Genocide, Violent Conflict, and Terrorism* (Oxford: Oxford University Press, 2011), chap. 8.

16. Özdalga, "Contrasting Modernities," 8; Genç, *Under the Shadow*, 122, 142.

17. Sam Kaplan, *The Pedagogical State: Education and the Politics of National Culture in Post-1980 Turkey* (Stanford, CA: Stanford University Press, 2006), 206.

18. Asuman Suner, "Elusive Fragments of an Uneasy Past: Representations of Non-Muslim Minorities in New Turkish Cinema," in *Turkish Literature and Cultural Memory: "Multiculturalism" as a Literary Theme after 1980*, ed. Catharina Dufft (Wiesbaden, Germany: Harrassowitz, 2009), 143–44.

19. White, *Muslim Nationalism*, 75.

20. Hisham Sharabi, *Neopatriarchy: A Theory of Distorted Change in Arab Society* (Oxford: Oxford University Press, 1992), 24–25.

21. Ibrahim Hakki Öztürk, "Curriculum Reform and Teacher Autonomy in Turkey: The Case of the History Teaching," *International Journal of Instruction* 4, no. 2 (2011): 124.

22. White, *Muslim Nationalism*, 77.

23. Gerald D. Miller, "Classroom 19: A Study of Behavior in a Classroom of a Moroccan Primary School," in *Psychological Dimensions of Near Eastern Studies*, ed. L. Carl Brown and Norman Itzkowitz (Princeton, NJ: Darwin Press, 1977), 142–53; Hisham Sharabi and Mukhtar Ani, "Impact of Class and Culture on Social Behavior: The Feudal-Bourgeois Family in Arab Society," in *Psychological Dimensions of Near Eastern Studies*, ed. L. Carl Brown and Norman Itzkowitz (Princeton, NJ: Darwin Press, 1977), 240–56.

24. Sharabi and Ani, "Impact of Class and Culture," 250.

25. Sharabi, *Neopatriarchy*, 85–87.

26. Ibid., 88.

27. Ece Temelkuran, *Turkey: The Insane and the Melancholy*, trans. Zeynep Beler (London: Zed Books, 2015), 42.

28. Ibid., 41.

29. Avonna Deanne Swartz, "Textbooks and National Ideology: A Content Analysis of the Secondary Turkish History Textbooks Used in the Republic of Turkey since 1929," PhD diss., University of Texas at Austin, 1997.

30. Öztürk, "Curriculum Reform," 117; Meral Ugur Cinar, *Collective Memory and National Membership: Identity and Citizenship Models in Turkey and Austria* (New York: Palgrave Macmillan, 2015), 9–10.

31. Faik Gur, "Sculpting the Nation in Early Republican Turkey," *Historical Research* 86, no. 232 (2013): 353.

32. Ulgen, "'Sabiha Gökçen's 80-Year-Old Secret,'" 402.

33. Toumani, *There Was and There Was Not*, 157.

34. Kaplan, *Pedagogical State*, 176.

35. Ibid., 180.

36. Tanıl Bora, "Nationalism in Textbooks," in *Human Rights Issues in Textbooks: The Turkish Case*, ed. Deniz Ceylan and Gürol Irzık (Nisantasi, Istanbul: History Foundation of Turkey, 2004), 70.

37. Ayşe Gül Altınay, "Human Rights or Militarist Ideals? Teaching National Security in High Schools," in *Human Rights Issues in Textbooks: The Turkish Case*, ed. Deniz Tarba Ceylan and Gürol Irzık (Nisantasi, Istanbul: History Foundation of Turkey, 2004), 78.

38. Kaplan, *Pedagogical State*, 188.

39. Ayşe Gül Altınay, *The Myth of the Military-Nation: Militarism, Gender, and Education in Turkey* (New York: Palgrave Macmillan, 2004), 155.

40. Kaplan, *Pedagogical State*, 198–99.

41. Ibid., 199.

42. Orhan Silier, "Foreword," in *Human Rights Issues in Textbooks: The Turkish Case*, ed. Deniz Tarba and Gürol Irzık Ceylan (Nisantasi, Istanbul: History Foundation of Turkey, 2004), xi.

43. Temelkuran, *Deep Mountain*, 74.

44. Ibid., 88.

45. Temelkuran, *Turkey*, 34.

46. Ibid., 36–37.

47. Toumani, *There Was and There Was Not*, 74.

48. Mark A. Wolfgram, *"Getting History Right": East and West Germany Collective Memories of the Holocaust and War* (Lewisburg, PA: Bucknell University Press, 2011), 21–22.

49. Savaş Arslan, *Cinema in Turkey: A New Critical History* (Oxford: Oxford University Press, 2011), 51–52; Gönül Dönmez-Colin, *Turkish Cinema: Identity, Distance and Belonging* (London: Reaktion Books, 2008), 49.

50. Suner, "Elusive Fragments," 137.

51. Dönmez-Colin, *Routledge Dictionary*, 282–83.

52. Kabir Tambar, *The Reckoning of Pluralism: Political Belonging and the Demands of History in Turkey* (Stanford, CA: Stanford University Press, 2014).

53. Dönmez-Colin, *Turkish Cinema*, 15.

54. Donald Bloxham, *The Great Game of Genocide: Imperialism, Nationalism, and the Destruction of the Ottoman Armenians* (Oxford: Oxford University Press, 2005).

55. Fatma Müge Göçek, *The Transformation of Turkey: Redefining State and Society from the Ottoman Empire to the Modern Era* (London: I. B. Tauris, 2011), 135.

56. White, *Muslim Nationalism*, 12.

57. Ayşe Zarakol, "Ontological (In)security and State Denial of Historical Crimes: Turkey and Japan," *International Relations* 24, no. 1 (2010): 15.

58. Edward Minasian, *Musa Dagh* (Nashville, TN: Cold Tree Press, 2007), 66.

59. Ibid., 127–49.

60. Eldad Ben Aharon, "A Unique Denial: Israel's Foreign Policy and the Armenian Genocide," *British Journal of Middle Eastern Studies* 42, no. 4 (2015): 638–54.

61. Alan Duben, "The Significance of Family and Kinship in Urban Turkey," in *Sex Roles, Family, and Community in Turkey*, ed. Çiğdem Kağıtçıbaşı (Bloomington: Indiana University Press, 1982), 73–99.

62. Orhan M. Öztürk and Vamik Volkan, "The Theory and Practice of Psychiatry in Turkey," in *Psychological Dimensions of Near Eastern Studies*, ed. L. Carl Brown and Norman Itzkowitz (Princeton, NJ: Darwin Press, 1977), 334–35.

63. Dönmez-Colin, *Routledge Dictionary*, 91.

64. Vamik D. Volkan and Norman Itzkowitz, *The Immortal Atatürk: A Psychobiography* (Chicago: University of Chicago Press, 1984), 345–46.

65. Geremie Barmé, "History for the Masses," in *Using the Past to Serve the Present: Historiography and Politics in Contemporary China*, ed. Jonathan Unger (Armonk, NY: M. E. Sharpe, 1993), 262.

66. Marc Howard Ross, *Slavery in the North: Forgetting History and Recovering Memory* (Philadelphia: University of Pennsylvania Press, 2018).

67. Volkan and Itzkowitz, *Immortal Atatürk*, 358.

68. Nazlı Ökten, "An Endless Death and an Eternal Mourning: November 10 in Turkey," in *The Politics of Public Memory in Turkey*, ed. Esra Özyürek (Syracuse, NY: Syracuse University Press, 2007), 102.

69. Ibid., 96.

70. Ibid., 109.

71. Temelkuran, *Turkey*, 67.

72. Hanioğlu, *Atatürk*, 46; Michael Mann, *The Dark Side of Democracy: Explaining Ethnic Cleansing* (Cambridge: Cambridge University Press, 2005); Fatma Ulgen, "Reading Mustafa Kemal Atatürk on the Armenian Genocide of 1915," *Patterns of Prejudice* 44, no. 4 (2010): 373.

73. Ulgen, "Reading Mustafa Kemel Atatürk," 373.

74. Ibid., 375.

75. Orhan Pamuk, *The Red-Haired Woman* [*Kırmızı Saçlı Kadın*], trans. Ekin Oklap (Toronto: Knopf Canada, 2017).

76. Sharabi, *Neopatriarchy*, 154.

77. Öztürk and Volkan, "Theory and Practice," 340.

78. Ibid., 342.

79. Güler Okman Fişek, "Psychopathology and the Turkish Family: A Family Systems Theory Analysis," in *Sex Roles, Family, and Community in Turkey*, ed. Çiğdem Kağıtçıbaşı (Bloomington: Indiana University Press, 1982), 302.

80. Ibid., 302.

81. Sharabi, *Neopatriarchy*, 41.

82. Ibid., 41–42.

83. Abdellah Hammoudi, *Master and Disciple: The Cultural Foundations of Moroccan Authoritarianism* (Chicago: University of Chicago Press, 1997).

84. Özdalga, "Contrasting Modernities," 8.

85. Sharabi and Ani, "Impact of Class and Culture," 244.

86. Göçek, *Transformation of Turkey*, 134.

87. Sharabi and Ani, "Impact of Class and Culture," 248.

88. Ibid., 250.

89. Sharabi, *Neopatriarchy*, 47.

90. Richard Ned Lebow, *A Cultural Theory of International Relations* (Cambridge: Cambridge University Press, 2008).

91. James C. Scott, *Seeing Like a State: How Certain Schemes to Improve the Human Condition Have Failed* (New Haven, CT: Yale University Press, 1998), 4–5.

92. Gur, "Sculpting the Nation"; Ulgen, "Reading Mustafa Kemal Atatürk," 384.

93. Mills, *Streets of Memory*, 119.

94. George L. Mosse, *Fallen Soldiers: Reshaping the Memory of the World Wars* (New York: Oxford University Press, 1990).

95. Dönmez-Colin, *Routledge Dictionary*, 266.

96. Ibid., 349.

97. Ibid., 346.

98. Ibid., 346; Asuman Suner, *New Turkish Cinema: Belonging, Identity and Memory* (London: I. B. Tauris, 2010), 46–48.

99. Göçek, *Transformation of Turkey*, 191; Göçek, *Denial of Violence*, 387.

100. Bloxham, *Great Game*, 215; Richard G. Hovannisian, "Introduction: The Armenian Genocide: Remembrance and Denial," in *Remembrance and Denial: The Case of the Armenian Genocide*, ed. Richard G. Hovannisian (Detroit, MI: Wayne State University Press, 1998), 16.

101. Jack Der-Sarkissian, "Musical Perspectives on the Armenian Genocide: From Aznavour to 'System of a Down,'" in *The Armenian Genocide: Cultural and Ethical Legacies*, ed. Richard G. Hovannisian (New Brunswick, NJ: Transaction, 2007), 215.

102. Ayla Göl, "Imagining the Turkish Nation through 'Othering' Armenians," *Nations and Nationalism* 11, no. 1 (2005): 121–39.

103. Dönmez-Colin, *Turkish Cinema*, 15.

104. Göçek, *Transformation of Turkey*, 185–86.

105. Fatma Müge Göçek "Turkish Historiography and the Unbearable Weight of 1915," in *The Armenian Genocide: Cultural and Ethical Legacies*, ed. Richard Hovannisian (New Brunswick, NJ: Transaction, 2007), 361.

106. Ulgen, "'Sabiha Gökçen's 80-Year-Old Secret,'" 112–13.

107. Ibid., 47.

108. Ross, *Slavery in the North.*

109. Gülay Türkmen-Dervişoğlu, "Coming to Terms with a Difficult Past: The Trauma of the Assassination of Hrant Dink and Its Repercussions on Turkish National Identity," *Nations and Nationalism* 19, no. 4 (2013): 687.

110. Cinar, *Collective Memory and National Membership*, 50.

111. Dönmez-Colin, *Routledge Dictionary*, 317.

112. Ibid., 210.

113. Ibid., 227–28.

114. Sedat Laçiner and Şenol Kantarcı, *Art and Armenian Propaganda: Ararat as a Case Study* (Ankara: ASAM Institute for Armenian Research, 2002).

115. Dönmez-Colin, *Routledge Dictionary*, 126–27.

116. Nicolas Monceau, "Confronting Turkey's Social Realities: An Interview with Yesim Ustaoglu," booklet included with Facets Video DVD, 2004, first published *Cinéaste* 26, no. 3 (2001): 28–30.

117. Suner, *New Turkish Cinema*, 65.

118. Ibid., 143.

119. Dönmez-Colin, *Routledge Dictionary*, 152.

120. Atom Egoyan, "In Other Words: Poetic Licence and the Incarnation of History," *University of Toronto Quarterly* 73, no. 3 (2004): 903–4.

121. Dönmez-Colin, *Routledge Dictionary*, 38.

122. Ibid., 287.

123. Bertjan Doosje and Nyla R. Branscombe, "Attributions for the Negative Historical Actions of a Group," *European Journal of Social Psychology* 33, no. 2 (2003): 235–48.

## CONCLUSION

1. Sophocles, *Antigone*, trans. David Mulroy (Madison: University of Wisconsin Press, 2013), lines 1347–53.

2. Aeschylus, *Persians*, trans. James Romm, in *The Greek Plays: Sixteen Plays by Aeschylus, Sophocles, and Euripides*, ed. Mary Lefkowitz and James Romm (New York: Modern Library, 2016), lines 843–44.

3. Karen Armstrong, *Twelve Steps to a Compassionate Life* (Toronto: Vintage Canada, 2011).

4. Bertjan Doosje and Nyla R. Branscombe, "Attributions for the Negative Historical Actions of a Group," *European Journal of Social Psychology* 33, no. 2 (2003): 235–48.

5. Armstrong, *Twelve Steps*, 188–89.

6. Aeschylus, *Persians*, lines 181–87.

7. Marc Howard Ross, *Cultural Contestation in Ethnic Conflict* (Cambridge: Cambridge University Press, 2007), chap. 10; Marc Howard Ross, *Slavery in the North: Forgetting History and Recovering Memory* (Philadelphia: University of Pennsylvania Press, 2018); David W. Blight, *Race and Reunion: The Civil War in American Memory* (Cambridge, MA: Harvard University Press, 2001).

8. Akiko Hashimoto, *The Long Defeat: Cultural Trauma, Memory, and Identity in Japan* (Oxford: Oxford University Press, 2015).

9. Eric Stover and Harvey M. Weinstein, "Conclusion: A Common Objective, a Universe of Alternatives," in *My Neighbor, My Enemy: Justice and Community in the Aftermath of Mass Atrocity*, ed. Eric Stover and Harvey M. Weinstein (Cambridge: Cambridge University Press, 2004), 332–42.

10. Murray Edelman, *From Art to Politics: How Artistic Creations Shape Political Conceptions* (Chicago: University of Chicago Press, 1995).

11. Jodi Halpern and Harvey M. Weinstein, "Empathy and Rehumanization after Mass Violence," in *My Neighbor, My Enemy: Justice and Community in the Aftermath of Mass Atrocity*, ed. Eric Stover and Harvey M. Weinstein (Cambridge: Cambridge University Press, 2004), 308.

# Bibliography


LITERATURE, MEMOIRS, AND THEATER PLAYS

*Armenian*

Mardiganian, Aurora (Arshaluys). *Ravished Armenia*. New York: International Copyright Bureau, 1919.

*Germany*

Werfel, Franz. *Die vierzig Tage des Musa Dagh* [*The Forty Days of Musa Dagh*]. Berlin: Zsolnay, 1933.

Zuckmayer, Carl. *Des Teufels General: Drama in drei Akten* [*The Devil's General: Drama in Three Acts*]. Frankfurt am Main: Fischer Taschenbuch Verlag, 1996.

*Japan*

Gomikawa, Junpei. *Ningen no joken* [*The Human Condition*]. Bunshun Library. 6 vols. Tokyo: Bungei Shunju, 1979.

Ibuse, Masuji. *Black Rain* [*Kuroi ame*]. Translated by John Bester. Tokyo: Kodansha International, 1979.

Kinoshita, Junji. *Between God and Man: A Judgement on War Crimes* [*Kami to hito to no aida*]. Translated by Eric J. Gangloff. Tokyo: University of Tokyo Press, 1979.

Kurahashi, Ayako. *My Father's Dying Wish: Legacies of War Guilt in a Japanese Family*. Translated by Philip A. Seaton. Sheffield: Paulownia Press, 2009.

Morimura, Seiichi. *Akuma no hoshoku* [*The Devil's Gluttony*]. Tokyo: Kobunsha kappa bukkusu, 1981.

Nakazawa, Keiji. *Barefoot Gen* [*Hadashi no Gen*]. Translated by Project Gen. San Francisco: Last Gasp of San Francisco, 2004–2005.

Osada, Arata. *Children of Hiroshima*. New York: Harper & Row, 1982.

Takeyama, Michio. *Harp of Burma* [*Biruma no tategoto*]. Translated by Howard Hibbett. Rutland: Tuttle, 1992.

Tsuboi, Sakae. *Twenty-Four Eyes* [*Nijushi no hitomi*]. Translated by Akira Miura. Rutland: Tuttle, 1983.

*Spain*

Cercas, Javier. *Soldiers of Salamis* [*Soldados de Salamina*]. Translated by Anne McLean. New York: Bloomsbury, 2004.

Marías, Javier. *Your Face Tomorrow* [*Tu rostro mañana*]. Vol. 1 *Fever and Spear*. Vol. 2 *Dance and Dream*. Vol. 3 *Poison, Shadow, and Farewell*. Translated by Margaret Jull Costa. 3 vols. New York: New Directions, 2005–2007.

Rivas, Manuel. *The Carpenter's Pencil* [*O lapis do carpinteiro / El lápiz del carpintero*]. Translated by Jonathan Dunne. New York: Overlook Press, 2001.

Sender, Ramón José. *Requiem for a Spanish Peasant* [*Réquiem por un campesino español*]. Translated by Graham Whittaker. Oxford: Aris & Phillips, 2007.

*Turkey*

Güntekin, Reşat Nuri. *Autobiography of a Turkish Girl* [*Çalıkuşu*]. Translated by Sir Wyndham Deedes. London: Allen & Unwin, 1949.

Pamuk, Orhan. *The Red-Haired Woman* [*Kırmızı Saçlı Kadın*]. Translated by Ekin Oklap. Toronto: Knopf Canada, 2017.

Tahir, Kemal. *Yorgun Savaşçı* [*Tired Warrior*]. Istanbul: Remzi, 1965.

*Yugoslavia*

Andrić, Ivo. *The Bridge on the Drina* [*Na Drini ćuprija*]. Translated by Lovett F. Edwards. Belgrade: Dereta, 2003.

———. *The Days of the Consuls* [*Travnička hronika*]. Translated by Celia Hawkesworth and Bogdan Rakić. Belgrade: Dereta, 2003.

Ćosić, Dobrica. *Far Away Is the Sun* [*Daleko je sunce*]. Translated by Muriel Heppell and Milica Mihajlović. Belgrade: Jugoslavija, 1963.

———. *Vreme Smrti* [*A Time of Death*]. 4 vols. Belgrade: Prosveta, 1972, 1975, 1979.

Drašković, Vuk. *The Memoirs of Jesus* [*Isusovi memoari*]. Translated by Mary Thompson Popović. Belgrade: Laguna, 2015.

———. *Nož* [*Knife*]. Translated by Milo Yelesiyevich. New York: Serbian Classics Press, 2000.

Hofman, Branko. *Noč do jutra* [*Night Till Dawn*]. Ljubljana: DZS, 2005.

Isaković, Antonije. *Tren 2* [*Instant 2*]. Belgrade: Sabrana dela Antonija Isakovića u 5 knjiga, 1983.

Jergović, Miljenko. *The Walnut Mansion* [*Dvori od oraha*]. Translated by Stephen M. Dickey and Janja Pavetić-Dickey. New Haven, CT: Yale University Press, 2015.

Lubarda, Vojislav. *Anatema* [*Anathema*]. Belgrade: Dečje novine, 1990.

———. *Gordo posrtanje* [*Proud Stumbling*]. Belgrade: Zapis, 1982.

Mihailović, Dragoslav. *Petrijin venac* [*Petria's Wreath*]. Belgrade: Srpska književna zadruga, 1975.

———. *When Pumpkins Blossomed* [*Kad su cvetale tikve*]. Translated by Drenka Willen. New York: Harcourt Brace Jovanovich, 1971.

Njegoš, Petar Petrović. *Gorski vijenac* [*The Mountain Wreath*]. 2nd ed. Translated by Vasa D. Mihailovich. Belgrade: Publishing House Vajat, 1989.

Popović, Aleksandar. *Razvojni put Bore Šnajdera* [*The Development of Bora Šnajder*]. Belgrade: Knjiga Komerc, 1995.

Radulović, Jovan. *Golubnjača* [*Pigeon Cave*]. Belgrade: BIGZ, 1983.

Selenić, Slobodan. *Fathers and Forefathers* [*Očevi i oci*]. Translated by Ellen Elias-Bursać. London: Harvill Press, 2003.

———. *Memoari Pere Bogalja* [*Memoirs of Pera the Cripple*]. Belgrade: Prosveta, 1991.

———. *Pismo/Glava* [*Heads/Tails*]. Belgrade: IP 'Beograd,' 1992.

———. *Timor mortis*. Sarajevo: Svjetlost, 1990.

Šnajder, Slobodan. *Hrvatski Faust* [*A Croatian Faust*]. Zagreb: Centar za Kulturnu Djelatnost, 1982.

NONFICTION

Aeschylus. *Persians*. Translated by James Romm. In *The Greek Plays: Sixteen Plays by Aeschylus, Sophocles, and Euripides*, edited by Mary Lefkowitz and James Romm, 9–43. New York: Modern Library, 2016.

Aguilar, Paloma. *Memory and Amnesia: The Role of the Spanish Civil War in the Transition to Democracy*. Translated by Mark Oakley. New York: Berghahn, 2002.

Aguilar, Paloma, and Francisco Ferrándiz. "Memory, Media and Spectacle: *Interviú*'s Portrayal of Civil War Exhumations in the Early Years of Spanish Democracy." *Journal of Spanish Cultural Studies* 17, no. 1 (2016): 1–25.

Aguilar, Paloma, and Carsten Humlebaek. "Collective Memory and National Identity in the Spanish Democracy: The Legacies of Francoism and the Civil War." *History & Memory* 14, nos. 1–2 (2002): 121–64.

Aharon, Eldad Ben. "A Unique Denial: Israel's Foreign Policy and the Armenian Genocide." *British Journal of Middle Eastern Studies* 42, no. 4 (2015): 638–54.

Alexander, Jeffrey C. *The Meanings of Social Life: A Cultural Sociology*. Oxford: Oxford University Press, 2003.

———. *Trauma: A Social Theory*. Cambridge: Polity Press, 2012.

Alexander, Jeffrey C., Ron Eyerman, Bernard Giesen, Neil J. Smelser, and Piotr Sztompka. *Cultural Trauma and Collective Identity*. Berkeley: University of California Press, 2004.

Alted, Alicia. "Education and Political Control." In *Spanish Cultural Studies: An Introduction, the Struggle for Modernity*, edited by Helen Graham and Jo Labanyi, 196–201. Oxford: Oxford University Press, 2005.

———. "Educational Policy in a Changing Society." In *Spanish Cultural Studies: An Introduction, the Struggle for Modernity* edited by Helen Graham and Jo Labanyi, 271–76. Oxford: Oxford University Press, 1995.

Altınay, Ayşe Gül. "Human Rights or Militarist Ideals? Teaching National Security in High Schools." In *Human Rights Issues in Textbooks: The Turkish Case*, edited by Deniz Tarba Ceylan and Gürol Irzık, 76–90. Nisantasi, Istanbul: History Foundation of Turkey, 2004.

———. *The Myth of the Military-Nation: Militarism, Gender, and Education in Turkey*. New York: Palgrave Macmillan, 2004.

Anastasio, Thomas J., Kristen Ann Ehrenberger, Patrick Watson, and Wenyi Zhang. *Individual and Collective Memory Consolidation: Analogous Processes on Different Levels*. Cambridge, MA: MIT Press, 2012.

Arendt, Hannah. *The Human Condition*. Chicago: University of Chicago Press, 1958.

*Armenian Cinema*. http://www.arm-cinema.am/en/home/ (accessed November 7, 2017).

Armstrong, Karen. *The Great Transformation: The Beginning of Our Religious Traditions*. New York: Knopf, 2006.

———. *Twelve Steps to a Compassionate Life*. Toronto: Vintage Canada, 2011.

Arslan, Savaş. *Cinema in Turkey: A New Critical History*. Oxford: Oxford University Press, 2011.

Atencio, Rebecca J. "A Prime Time to Remember: Memory Merchandising in Globo's *Anos Rebeldes*." In *Accounting for Violence: Marketing Memory in Latin America*, edited by Ksenija Bilbija and Leigh A. Payne, 41–68. Durham, NC: Duke University Press, 2011.

Baer, Alejandro, and Natan Sznaider. "Antigone in León: The Drama of Trauma Politics." In *Routledge International Handbook of Memory Studies*, edited by Anna Lisa Tota and Trever Hagen, 181–92. London: Routledge, 2016.

———. "Ghosts of the Holocaust in Franco's Mass Graves: Cosmopolitan Memories and the Politics of 'Never Again.'" *Memory Studies* 8, no. 3 (2015): 328–44.

Bajič, Miloš, ed. *Yugoslavia: Monuments to the Revolution*. Belgrade: Subnor Jugoslavije, 1968.

Barkan, Elazar, and Alexander Karn. "Group Apology as an Ethical Imperative." In *Taking Wrongs Seriously: Apologies and Reconciliation*, edited by Elazar Barkan and Alexander Karn, 3–30. Stanford, CA: Stanford University Press, 2006.

Barmé, Geremie. "History for the Masses." In *Using the Past to Serve the Present: Historiography and Politics in Contemporary China*, edited by Jonathan Unger, 260–86. Armonk, NY: M. E. Sharpe, 1993.

Bar-On, Dan. *Legacy of Silence: Encounters with Children of the Third Reich*. Cambridge, MA: Harvard University Press, 1989.

Barrera, Emilio Silva. "The Importance of Remembrance in the Transition to Democracy in Spain." In *Diktaturbewältigung und nationale Selbstvergewisserung: Geschichtskulturen in Polen und Spanien im Vergleich*, edited by Krzysztof Ruchniewicz and Stefan Troebst, 69–74. Wrocław, Poland: Wydawnictwo Uniwersytetu Wrocławskiego, 2004.

Bašić, Natalija. "Der Zweite Weltkrieg im Fernsehen: Filmpartisanen im kroatischen und serbischen Familiengedächtnis." *Ethnologia Balkanica* 8 (2004): 57–77.

Baskett, Michael. *The Attractive Empire: Transnational Film Culture in Imperial Japan*. Honolulu: University of Hawai'i Press, 2008.

Batinić, Jelena. *Women and Yugoslav Partisans: A History of World War II Resistance*. Cambridge: Cambridge University Press, 2015.

Bellah, Robert N. *Imagining Japan: The Japanese Tradition and Its Modern Interpretation*. Berkeley: University of California Press, 2003.

———. "Intellectual and Society in Japan." *Daedalus* 101, no. 2 (1972): 89–115.

———. *Religion in Human Evolution: From the Paleolithic to the Axial Age*. Cambridge, MA: Belknap Press of Harvard University Press, 2011.

Bentley, Bernard P. *A Companion to Spanish Cinema*. Rochester, NY: Tamesis, 2008.

Berger, Thomas U. *War, Guilt, and World Politics after World War II*. Cambridge: Cambridge University Press, 2012.

Berman, Marshall. *All That Is Solid Melts into Air: The Experience of Modernity*. New York: Simon & Schuster, 1982.

Bernecker, Walther L., and Sören Brinkmann. *Kampf der Erinnerungen: Der Spanische Bürgerkrieg in Politik und Gesellschaft, 1936–1939*. Nettersheim, Germany: Verlag Graswurzelrevolution, 2006.

Bertrand de Muñoz, Maryse. "Literatura de la guerra civil." *Anthropos* 148 (1993): 6–24.

Blakeley, Georgina. "Digging Up Spain's Past: Consequences of Truth and Reconciliation." *Democratization* 12, no. 1 (2005): 44–59.

Blight, David W. *Race and Reunion: The Civil War in American Memory*. Cambridge, MA: Harvard University Press, 2001.

Bloxham, Donald. *The Great Game of Genocide: Imperialism, Nationalism, and the Destruction of the Ottoman Armenians*. Oxford: Oxford University Press, 2005.

Bora, Tanıl. "Nationalism in Textbooks." In *Human Rights Issues in Textbooks: The Turkish Case*, edited by Deniz Tarba Ceylan and Gürol Irzık, 49–75. Nisantasi, Istanbul: History Foundation of Turkey, 2004.

Boyajyan, Zaven. *Armenian Cinema Catalogue, 1924–2008: Feature, Documentary, Animation*. 2nd ed. Yerevan: Armenian Association of Film Critics and Cinema Journalists, 2009.

Boyd, Robert, and Peter J. Richerson. *The Origin and Evolution of Cultures*. Oxford: Oxford University Press, 2005.

Brekke, Torkel. "Editor's Preface." In *The Ethics of War in Asian Civilizations*, edited by Torkel Brekke, ix–xv. New York: Routledge, 2006.

Bringa, Tone. *Being Muslim the Bosnian Way: Identity and Community in a Central Bosnian Village*. Princeton, NJ: Princeton University Press, 1995.

Broadbent, Jeffrey. *Environmental Politics in Japan: Networks of Power and Protest*. Cambridge: Cambridge University Press, 1998.

Broadbent, Jeffrey, and Vicky Brockman, eds. *East Asian Social Movements: Power, Protest, and Change in a Dynamic Region*. New York: Springer, 2010.

Buchholz, Petra. *Schreiben und Erinnern: Über Selbstzeugnisse japanischer Kriegsteilnehmer*. Munich: Iudicium Verlag, 2003.

Buruma, Ian. *A Japanese Mirror: Heroes and Villains of Japanese Culture*. London: Penguin Books, 1984.

Camino, Mercedes Maroto. *Film, Memory and the Legacy of the Spanish Civil War*. New York: Palgrave Macmillan, 2011.

Çarkoğlu, Ali, and Ersin Kalaycıoğlu. *The Rising Tide of Conservatism in Turkey*. New York: Palgrave Macmillan, 2009.

Castelli, Elizabeth A. *Martyrdom and Memory: Early Christian Culture Making*. New York: Columbia University Press, 2004.

Cenarro, Ángela. "Memory beyond the Public Sphere: The Francoist Repression Remembered in Aragon." *History & Memory* 14, nos. 1–2 (2002): 165–88.

Ceylan, Deniz Tarba, and Gürol Irzık, eds. *Human Rights Issues in Textbooks: The Turkish Case*. Nisantasi, Istanbul: History Foundation of Turkey, 2004.

Cinar, Meral Ugur. *Collective Memory and National Membership: Identity and Citizenship Models in Turkey and Austria*. New York: Palgrave Macmillan, 2015.

Classen, Christoph. *Bilder der Vergangenheit: Die Zeit des Nationalsozialismus im Fernsehen der Bundesrepublik Deutschland 1955–1965*. Cologne: Bölau Verlag, 1999.

Cobb, Christopher. "The Republican State and Mass Education-Cultural Initiatives, 1931–1936." In *Spanish Cultural Studies: An Introduction, the Struggle for Modernity*, edited by Helen Graham and Jo Labanyi, 133–38. Oxford: Oxford University Press, 1995.

Cole, Jennifer. *Forget Colonialism? Sacrifice and the Art of Memory in Madagascar*. Berkeley: University of California Press, 2001.

Coman, Alin, and William Hirst. "Social Identity and Socially Shared Retrieval-Induced Forgetting: The Effects of Group Membership." *Journal of Experimental Psychology* 144, no. 4 (2015): 717–22.

Connor, Blaine P., and John W. Traphagan. "Negotiating the Afterlife: Emplacement as Ongoing Concern in Contemporary Japan." *Asian Anthropology* 13, no. 1 (2014): 3–19.

Conrad, Sebastian. "Entangled Memories: Versions of the Past in Germany and Japan, 1945–2001." *Journal of Contemporary History* 38, no. 1 (2003): 85–99.

Czerwinski, E. J. "Aleksandar Popovic: Belgrade's Poet of the Streets." *Books Abroad* 43, no. 3 (1969): 349–54.

Denich, Bette. "Dismembering Yugoslavia: Nationalist Ideologies and the Symbolic Revival of Genocide." *American Ethnologist* 21, no. 2 (1994): 367–90.

Der-Sarkissian, Jack. "Musical Perspectives on the Armenian Genocide: From Aznavour to 'System of a Down.'" In *The Armenian Genocide: Cultural and Ethical Legacies*, edited by Richard G. Hovannisian, 213–25. New Brunswick, NJ: Transaction, 2007.

Desser, David. *The Samurai Films of Akira Kurosawa*. Ann Arbor, MI: UMI Research Press, 1983.

Djilas, Aleksa. *The Contested Country: Yugoslav Unity and Communist Revolution, 1919–1953*. Cambridge, MA: Harvard University Press, 1991.

Djilas, Milovan. *Anatomy of a Moral*. Edited by Abraham Rothberg. London: Thames & Hudson, 1959.

———. *Tito: The Story from Inside*. Translated by Vasilije Kojić and Richard Hayes. New York: Harcourt Brace Jovanovich, 1980.

———. *Wartime*. Translated by Michael B. Petrovich. New York: Harcourt Brace Jovanovich, 1977.

Dönmez-Colin, Gönül. *The Routledge Dictionary of Turkish Cinema*. London: Routledge, 2014.

———. *Turkish Cinema: Identity, Distance and Belonging*. London: Reaktion Books, 2008.

Doosje, Bertjan, and Nyla R. Branscombe. "Attributions for the Negative Historical Actions of a Group." *European Journal of Social Psychology* 33, no. 2 (2003): 235–48.

Douglas, Mary. *Natural Symbols: Explorations in Cosmology*. New ed. London: Routledge, 1996. First published Barrie & Rockliff, 1970.

Dragović-Soso, Jasna. *"Saviours of the Nation": Serbia's Intellectual Opposition and the Revival of Nationalism*. London: Hurst, 2002.

Duben, Alan. "The Significance of Family and Kinship in Urban Turkey." In *Sex Roles, Family, and Community in Turkey*, edited by Çiğdem Kağıtçıbaşı, 73–99. Bloomington: Indiana University Press, 1982.

Edelman, Murray. *From Art to Politics: How Artistic Creations Shape Political Conceptions*. Chicago: University of Chicago Press, 1995.

Edles, Laura Desfor. *Symbol and Ritual in the New Spain: The Transition to Democracy after Franco*. Cambridge: Cambridge University Press, 1998.

Egoyan, Atom. "In Other Words: Poetic Licence and the Incarnation of History." *University of Toronto Quarterly* 73, no. 3 (2004): 886–905.

Eyerman, Ron, Jeffrey C. Alexander, and Elizabeth Butler Breese, eds. *Narrating Trauma: On the Impact of Collective Suffering*. Boulder, CO: Paradigm, 2011.

Ferrán, Ofelia. *Working Through Memory: Writing and Remembrance in Contemporary Spanish Narrative*. Lewisburg, PA: Bucknell University Press, 2007.

Ferrándiz, Francisco. "Exhuming the Defeated: Civil War Mass Graves in 21st-Century Spain." *American Ethnologist* 40, no. 1 (2013): 38–54.

———. "The Intimacy of Defeat: Exhumations in Contemporary Spain." In *Unearthing Franco's Legacy: Mass Graves and the Recovery of Historical Memory in Spain*, edited by Carlos Jerez-Farrán and Samuel Amago, 304–25. Notre Dame, IN: University of Notre Dame Press, 2010.

Ferreira, Antonio J. "Family Myth and Homeostasis." *Archives of General Psychiatry* 9, no. 5 (1963): 457–63.

Fischhoff, Baruch. "Hindsight Is Not Equal to Foresight: The Effect of Outcome Knowledge on Judgement under Uncertainty." *Journal of Experimental Psychology: Human Perception and Performance* 1, no. 3 (1975): 288–99.

Fişek, Güler Okman. "Psychopathology and the Turkish Family: A Family Systems Theory Analysis." In *Sex Roles, Family, and Community in Turkey*, edited by Çiğdem Kağıtçıbaşı, 295–321. Bloomington: Indiana University Press, 1982.

Fujitani, Takashi. *Splendid Monarchy: Power and Pageantry in Modern Japan*. Berkeley: University of California Press, 1996.

Fulbrook, Mary. *Dissonant Lives: Generations and Violence through the German Dictatorships*. Oxford: Oxford University Press, 2011.

Genç, Kaya. *Under the Shadow: Rage and Revolution in Modern Turkey*. London: Tauris, 2016.

Georgas, James. "Differences and Universals in Families across Cultures." In *Fundamental Questions in Cross-Cultural Psychology*, edited by Fons J. R. van de Vijver, Athanasios Chasiotis, and Seger M. Breugelmans, 341–75. Cambridge: Cambridge University Press, 2011.

Gessel, Van C. "Postoccupation Literary Movements and Developments in Japan." In *Legacies and Ambiguities: Postwar Fiction and Culture in West Germany and Japan*, edited by Ernestine Schlant and J. Thomas Rimer, 207–23. Washington, DC: Woodrow Wilson Center Press, 1991.

Gluck, Carol. "The 'Long Postwar': Japan and Germany in Common and in Contrast." In *Legacies and Ambiguities: Postwar Fiction and Culture in West Germany and Japan*, edited by Ernestine Schlant and J. Thomas Rimer, 63–78. Washington, DC: Woodrow Wilson Center Press, 1991.

———. "Operations of Memory: 'Comfort Women' and the World." In *Ruptured Histories: War, Memory, and the Post-Cold War in Asia*, edited by Sheila Miyoshi Jager and Rana Mitter, 47–77. Cambridge, MA: Harvard University Press, 2007.

———. "The Past in the Present." In *Postwar Japan as History*, edited by Andrew Gordon, 64–95. Berkeley: University of California Press, 1993.

Göçek, Fatma Müge. *Denial of Violence: Ottoman Past, Turkish Present, and Collective Violence against the Armenians, 1789–2009*. Oxford: Oxford University Press, 2014.

———. *The Transformation of Turkey: Redefining State and Society from the Ottoman Empire to the Modern Era*. London: Tauris, 2011.

———. "Turkish Historiography and the Unbearable Weight of 1915." In *The Armenian Genocide: Cultural and Ethical Legacies*, edited by Richard Hovannisian, 337–67. New Brunswick, NJ: Transaction, 2007.

Göl, Ayla. "Imagining the Turkish Nation through 'Othering' Armenians." *Nations and Nationalism* 11, no. 1 (2005): 121–39.

Gottlieb, Anthony. *The Dream of Enlightenment: The Rise of Modern Philosophy*. New York: Liveright, 2016.

Goulding, Daniel J. *Liberated Cinema: The Yugoslav Experience, 1945–2001*. Rev. and expanded ed. Bloomington: Indiana University Press, 2002.

Graham, Helen. *The War and Its Shadow: Spain's Civil War in Europe's Long Twentieth Century*. Brighton, UK: Sussex Academic Press, 2012.

Grayling, A. C. *The Age of Genius: The Seventeenth Century and the Birth of the Modern Mind*. New York: Bloomsbury, 2016.

Greif, Avner. *Institutions and the Path to the Modern Economy: Lessons from Medieval Trade*. Cambridge: Cambridge University Press, 2006.

Greif, Avner, and Guido Tabellini. "The Clan and the City: Sustaining Cooperation in China and Europe." Unpublished manuscript, 2015.

Gruenwald, Oskar. "Yugoslav Camp Literature: Rediscovering the Ghost of a Nation's Past-Present-Future." *Slavic Review* 46, nos. 3–4 (1987): 513–28.

Gubern, Román. "The Civil War: Inquest or Exorcism?" *Quarterly Review of Film and Video* 13, no. 4 (1991): 103–12.

———. "Film Censorship." In *A Companion to Spanish Cinema*, edited by Jo Labanyi and Tatjana Pavlović, 391–401. Oxford: Wiley-Blackwell, 2013.

Gur, Faik. "Sculpting the Nation in Early Republican Turkey." *Historical Research* 86, no. 232 (2013): 342–72.

Guzmán, Alison. "La memoria de la Guerra Civil en el teatro español: 1939–2009." PhD diss., Universidad de Salamanca, 2012.

Halpern, Jodi, and Harvey M. Weinstein. "Empathy and Rehumanization after Mass Violence." In *My Neighbor, My Enemy: Justice and Community in the Aftermath of Mass Atrocity*, edited by Eric Stover and Harvey M. Weinstein, 303–22. Cambridge: Cambridge University Press, 2004.

Hammoudi, Abdellah. *Master and Disciple: The Cultural Foundations of Moroccan Authoritarianism*. Chicago: University of Chicago Press, 1997.

Hanioğlu, M. Şükrü. *Atatürk: An Intellectual Biography*. Princeton, NJ: Princeton University Press, 2011.

Harding, Susan Friend. *Remaking Ibieca: Rural Life in Aragon under Franco*. Chapel Hill: University of North Carolina Press, 1984.

Hashimoto, Akiko. "Culture, Power, and the Discourse of Filial Piety in Japan: The Disempowerment of Youth and Its Social Consequences." In *Filial Piety: Practice and Discourse in Contemporary East Asia*, edited by Charlotte Ikels, 182–97. Stanford, CA: Stanford University Press, 2004.

———. "The Cultural Trauma of a Fallen Nation: Japan, 1945." In *Narrating Trauma: On the Impact of Collective Suffering*, edited by Ron Eyerman, Jeffrey C. Alexander, and Elizabeth Butler Breese, 27–52. Boulder, CO: Paradigm, 2011.

———. "Japanese and German Projects of Moral Recovery: Toward a New Understanding of War Memories in Defeated Nations." Edwin O. Reischauer Institute of Japanese Studies Occasional Papers in Japanese Studies. Cambridge, MA: Harvard University Press, 1999.

———. *The Long Defeat: Cultural Trauma, Memory, and Identity in Japan*. Oxford: Oxford University Press, 2015.

Hashimoto, Akiko, and John W. Traphagan. "Changing Japanese Families." In *Imagined Families, Lived Families: Culture and Kinship in Contemporary Japan*, edited by Akiko Hashimoto and John W. Traphagan, 1–12. Albany: State University of New York Press, 2008.

Henrich, Joseph, Steven J. Heine, and Ara Norenzayan. "The Weirdest People in the World?" *Behavioral and Brain Sciences* 33, nos. 2–3 (2010): 61–83.

Hepworth, Andrea. "Site of Memory and Dismemory: The Valley of the Fallen in Spain." *Journal of Genocide Research* 16, no. 4 (2014): 463–85.

Hijiya-Kirschnereit, Irmela. "Post–World War II Literature: The Intellectual Climate in Japan, 1945–1985." In *Legacies and Ambiguities: Postwar Fiction and Culture in West Germany and Japan*, edited by Ernestine Schlant and J. Thomas Rimer, 99–119. Washington, DC: Woodrow Wilson Center Press, 1991.

Hirst, William, and Gerald Echterhoff. "Remembering in Conversations: The Social Sharing and Reshaping of Memories." *Annual Review of Psychology* 63 (2012): 55–79.

Honda, Katsuichi. *Chugoku no tabi*. Tokyo: Asahi Shinbunsha, 1972.

Horton, Andrew. "The Rise and Fall of the Yugoslav Partisan Film: Cinematic Perceptions of a National Identity." *Film Criticism* 12, no. 2 (1987): 18–27.

Hovannisian, Richard G. "Introduction: The Armenian Genocide: Remembrance and Denial." In *Remembrance and Denial: The Case of the Armenian Genocide*, edited by Richard G. Hovannisian, 13–21. Detroit, MI: Wayne State University Press, 1998.

Hsu, Francis L. K. *Americans and Chinese: Passage to Differences*. 3rd ed. Honolulu: University of Hawai'i Press, 1981.

Hünecke, Silke. "Überwindung des Schweigens: Verdrängte Geschichte, politische Repression und Kollektives Trauma als Gegenstand der Arbeit der erinnerungspolitischen Bewegung im spanischen Staat." PhD diss., Freien Universität Berlin, 2013.

Ienaga, Saburo. *The Pacific War, 1931–1945*. New York: Pantheon, 1978.

Igarashi, Yoshikuni. "The Bomb, Hirohito, and History: The Foundational Narrative of United States–Japan Postwar Relations." *positions* 6, no. 2 (1998): 261–302.

Igartua, Juanjo, and Darío Páez. "Art and Remembering Traumatic Collective Events: The Case of the Spanish Civil War." In *Collective Memory of Political Events: Social Psychological Perspectives*, edited by James W. Pennebaker, Darío Páez, and Bernard Rimé, 79–101. Mahwah, NJ: Lawrence Erlbaum, 1997.

Jager, Sheila Miyoshi, and Rana Mitter. "Introduction: Re-Envisioning Asia, Past and Present." In *Ruptured Histories: War, Memory, and the Post–Cold War in Asia*, edited by Sheila Miyoshi Jager and Rana Mitter, 1–14. Cambridge, MA: Harvard University Press, 2007.

Jaspers, Karl. *The Origin and Goal of History*. Translated by Michael Bullock. London: Routledge and Kegan Paul, 1953.

Jovićević, Alexandra. "Censorship and Ingenious Dramatic Strategies in Yugoslav Theatre (1945–1991)." *Primerjalna književnost (Ljubljana)* 31 (2008): 237–49.

Jump, Meirian. "The Role of Archives in the Movement for the Recovery of Historical Memory in Spain. La Rioja: A Regional Case Study." *Journal of the Society of Archivists* 33, no. 2 (2012): 149–66.

Junco, José Alvarez. "Education and the Limits of Liberalism." In *Spanish Cultural Studies: An Introduction, the Struggle for Modernity*, edited by Helen Graham and Jo Labanyi, 45–52. Oxford: Oxford University Press, 1995.

Kaplan, Sam. *The Pedagogical State: Education and the Politics of National Culture in Post-1980 Turkey*. Stanford, CA: Stanford University Press, 2006.

Karge, Heike. "Mediated Remembrance: Local Practices of Remembering the Second World War in Tito's Yugoslavia." *European Review of History/Revue européenne d'histoire* 16, no. 1 (2009): 49–62.

———. *Steinerne Erinnerung–versteinerte Erinnerung? Kriegsgedenken in Jugoslawien (1947–1970)*. Wiesbaden, Germany: Harrassowitz, 2010.

———. "Von Helden und Opfern: Eine Analyse der Erinnerungskultur zwischen Pietät und Ideologie." In *Bogdan Bogdanović: Memoria und Utopie in Tito-Jugoslawien*, edited by Architekturzentrum Wien, 34–39. Klagenfurt, Austria: Wieser Verlag, 2009.

Keyder, Çaglar. *State and Class in Turkey: A Study in Capitalist Development*. London: Verso, 1987.

Kidron, Carol A. "Alterity and the Particular Limits of Universalism: Comparing Jewish-Israeli Holocaust and Canadian-Cambodian Genocide Legacies." *Current Anthropology* 53, no. 6 (2012): 723–54.

King, Iain, and Whit Mason. *Peace at Any Price: How the World Failed Kosovo*. London: Hurst, 2006.

Kohlberg, Lawrence. *The Philosophy of Moral Development*. Vol. 1. *Moral States and the Idea of Justice*. San Francisco: Harper & Row, 1981.

———. *The Psychology of Moral Development*. Vol. 2. *The Nature and Validity of Moral Stages*. San Francisco: Harper & Row, 1984.

Koschmann, J. Victor. "Introduction: Soft Rule and Expressive Protest." In *Authority and the Individual in Japan: Citizen Protest in Historical Perspective*, edited by J. Victor Koschmann, 1–30. Tokyo: University of Tokyo Press, 1978.

Kuran, Timur. "Islam and Underdevelopment: An Old Puzzle Revisited." *Journal of Institutional and Theoretical Economics* 153, no. 1 (1997): 41–71.

———. *The Long Divergence: How Islamic Law Held Back the Middle East*. Princeton, NJ: Princeton University Press, 2011.

Kwon, Heonik. *After the Massacre: Commemoration and Consolation in Ha My and My Lai*. Berkeley: University of California Press, 2006.

———. *Ghosts of War in Vietnam*. Cambridge: Cambridge University Press, 2008.

Labanyi, Jo, Annabel Martin, and Vicente Rodríguez Ortega. "Melodrama and Historical Film." In *A Companion to Spanish Cinema*, edited by Jo Labanyi and Tatjana Pavlovic, 224–58. Oxford: Wiley-Blackwell, 2013.

Laçiner, Sedat, and Şenol Kantarcı. *Art and Armenian Propaganda: Ararat as a Case Study*. Ankara: ASAM Institute for Armenian Research, 2002.

Lebow, Richard Ned. *A Cultural Theory of International Relations*. Cambridge: Cambridge University Press, 2008.

———. *Forbidden Fruit: Counterfactuals and International Relations*. Princeton, NJ: Princeton University Press, 2010.

Leggott, Sarah. *Memory, War, and Dictatorship in Recent Spanish Fiction by Women*. Lewisburg, PA: Bucknell University Press, 2015.

Levy, Daniel, and Natan Sznaider. *The Holocaust and Memory in the Global Age*. Translated by Assenka Oksiloff. Philadelphia: Temple University Press, 2006.

———. *Human Rights and Memory*. University Park: Pennsylvania State University Press, 2010.

Li, Jin. *Cultural Foundations of Learning: East and West*. Cambridge: Cambridge University Press, 2012.

Lind, Jennifer. *Sorry States: Apologies in International Politics*. Ithaca, NY: Cornell University Press, 2008.

Lukić, Sveta. *Contemporary Yugoslav Literature: A Sociopolitical Approach*. Edited by Gertrude Joch Robinson. Translated by Pola Triandis. Urbana: University of Illinois Press, 1972.

Maier, Charles S. *The Unmasterable Past: History, Holocaust, and German National Identity*. Cambridge, MA: Harvard University Press, 1988.

Mann, Michael. *The Dark Side of Democracy: Explaining Ethnic Cleansing*. Cambridge: Cambridge University Press, 2005.

Marjanović, Petar. *An Anthology of Works by Twentieth Century Yugoslav Playwrights*. Novi Sad, Serbia: Sterijino Pozorje, 1984.

Markus, Hazel Rose, and Shinobu Kitayama. "Culture and the Self: Implications for Cognition, Emotion, and Motivation." *Psychological Review* 98, no. 2 (1991): 224–53.

Maruyama, Masao. "Theory and Psychology of Ultra-Nationalism." Translated by Ivan Morris. In *Thought and Behaviour in Modern Japanese Politics*, edited by Ivan Morris, 1–24. Expanded ed. London: Oxford University Press, 1969.

Mater, Nadire. *Voices from the Front: Turkish Soldiers on the War with the Kurdish Guerrillas* [*Mehmedin Kitabı: Güneydoğu'da Savaşmış Askerler Anlatıyor*]. Translated by Ayşe Gül Altınay. New York: Palgrave Macmillan, 2005.

McDonald, Keiko I. *Cinema East: A Critical Study of Major Japanese Films*. Rutherford, NJ: Fairleigh Dickinson University Press, 1983.

Mellen, Joan. *Voices from the Japanese Cinema*. New York: Liveright, 1975.

———. *The Waves at Genji's Door: Japan through Its Cinema*. New York: Pantheon, 1976.

Millas, Hercules. "Constructing Memories of 'Multiculturalism' and Identities in Turkish Novels." In *Turkish Literature and Cultural Memory: "Multiculturalism" as a Literary Theme after 1980*, edited by Catharina Dufft, 79–104. Wiesbaden, Germany: Harrassowitz, 2009.

Miller, Gerald D. "Classroom 19: A Study of Behavior in a Classroom of a Moroccan Primary School." In *Psychological Dimensions of Near Eastern Studies*, edited by L. Carl Brown and Norman Itzkowitz, 142–53. Princeton, NJ: Darwin, 1977.

Miller, Nicholas J. "The Nonconformists: Dobrica Ćosić and Mića Popović Envision Serbia." *Slavic Review* 58, no. 3 (1999): 515–36.

Mills, Amy. *Streets of Memory: Landscape, Tolerance, and National Identity in Istanbul*. Athens: University of Georgia Press, 2010.

Miloradović, Goran. "Stalin's Gifts: Yugoslav Feature Films 1945–1955." In *Osteuropa vom Weltkrieg zur Wende*, edited by Wolfgang Mueller and Michael Portmann, 173–94. Vienna: Österreichische Akademie der Wissenschaften, 2007.

Minasian, Edward. *Musa Dagh*. Nashville, TN: Cold Tree Press, 2007.

Miyamoto, Yuki. *Beyond the Mushroom Cloud: Commemoration, Religion, and Responsibility after Hiroshima*. New York: Fordham University Press, 2012.

Mokyr, Joel. *A Culture of Growth: The Origins of the Modern Economy*. Princeton, NJ: Princeton University Press, 2017.

Monceau, Nicolas. "Confronting Turkey's Social Realities: An Interview with Yesim Ustaoglu." Booklet included with Facets Video DVD, 2004. First published *Cinéaste* 26, no. 3 (2001): 28–30.

Moral, Félix. *Veinticinco años después: La memoria del franquismo y de la transición a la democracia en los españoles del año 2000*. Madrid: Centro de Investigaciones Sociológicas, 2001.

Morris, Ivan. *The Nobility of Failure: Tragic Heroes in the History of Japan*. New York: Holt, Rinehart and Winston, 1975.

Mosse, George L. *Fallen Soldiers: Reshaping the Memory of the World Wars*. New York: Oxford University Press, 1990.

Nisbett, Richard E., Incheol Choi, Kaiping Peng, and Ara Norenzayan. "Culture and Systems of Thought: Holistic versus Analytic Cognition." *Psychological Review* 108, no. 2 (2001): 291–310.

Ökten, Nazlı. "An Endless Death and an Eternal Mourning: November 10 in Turkey." In *The Politics of Public Memory in Turkey*, edited by Esra Özyürek, 95–113. Syracuse, NY: Syracuse University Press, 2007.

Orr, James J. *The Victim as Hero: Ideologies of Peace and National Identity in Postwar Japan*. Honolulu: University of Hawai'i Press, 2001.

Özdalga, Elisabeth. "Contrasting Modernities." In *Autonomy and Dependence in the Family: Turkey and Sweden in Critical Perspective*, edited by Rita Liljeström and Elisabeth Özdalga, 2–15. Istanbul: Swedish Research Institute in Istanbul, 2002.

Öztürk, Ibrahim Hakki. "Curriculum Reform and Teacher Autonomy in Turkey: The Case of the History Teaching." *International Journal of Instruction* 4, no. 2 (2011): 113–28.

Öztürk, Orhan M., and Vamik Volkan. "The Theory and Practice of Psychiatry in Turkey." In *Psychological Dimensions of Near Eastern Studies*, edited by L. Carl Brown and Norman Itzkowitz, 330–61. Princeton, NJ: Darwin, 1977.

Panovski, Naum. "Prelude to a War." *Performing Arts Journal* 18, no. 2 (1996): 2–12.

Park, Ed. "Sorry Not Sorry: Reading Dalkey Archive Press's Library of Korean Literature." *New Yorker*, October 19, 2015, 87–90.

Parry, Richard Lloyd. *Ghosts of the Tsunami*. London: Jonathan Cape, 2017.

Pérez-Díaz, Victor M. *The Return of Civil Society: The Emergence of Democratic Spain*. Cambridge, MA: Harvard University Press, 1993.

Pilikian, Hovhanness I. *Armenian Cinema: A Source Book*. London: Counter-Point Productions, 1981.

Preston, Paul. *The Spanish Holocaust: Inquisition and Extermination in Twentieth-Century Spain*. New York: Norton, 2012.

———. *The Triumph of Democracy in Spain*. London: Methuen, 1986.

Radonić, Ljiljana. "Transformation of Memory in Croatia: Removing Yugoslav Anti-Fascism." In *Dynamics of Memory and Identity in Contemporary Europe*, edited by Eric Langenbacher, Bill Niven, and Ruth Wittlinger, 166–79. New York: Berghahn, 2012.

Reiter, Margit. *Die Generation danach: Der Nationalsozialismus im Familiengedächtnis*. Innsbruck: Studien Verlag, 2006.

Renshaw, Layla. *Exhuming Loss: Memory, Materiality and Mass Graves of the Spanish Civil War*. Walnut Creek, CA: Left Coast Press, 2011.

Richards, Michael. "Grand Narratives, Collective Memory, and Social History: Public Uses of the Past in Postwar Spain." In *Unearthing Franco's Legacy: Mass Graves and the Recovery of Historical Memory in Spain*, edited by Carlos Jerez-Farrán and Samuel Amago, 121–45. Notre Dame, IN: University of Notre Dame Press, 2010.

———. *A Time of Silence: Civil War and the Culture of Repression in Franco's Spain, 1936–1945*. Cambridge: Cambridge University Press, 1998.

Richie, Donald. *A Hundred Years of Japanese Film: A Concise History, with a Selective Guide to DVDs and Videos*. New York: Kodansha, 2012.

Rosen, Lawrence. *Varieties of Muslim Experience: Encounters with Arab Political and Cultural Life*. Chicago: University of Chicago Press, 2008.

Rosenthal, Gabriele, ed. *The Holocaust in Three Generations: Families of Victims and Perpetrators of the Nazi Regime*. London: Cassell, 1998.

———. "National Socialism and Antisemitism in Intergenerational Dialogue." In *The Holocaust in Three Generations: Families of Victims and Perpetrators of the Nazi Regime*, edited by Gabriele Rosenthal, 240–48. London: Cassell, 1998.

Ross, Marc Howard. *Cultural Contestation in Ethnic Conflict*. Cambridge: Cambridge University Press, 2007.

———. *Slavery in the North: Forgetting History and Recovering Memory*. Philadelphia: University of Pennsylvania Press, 2018.

Saaler, Sven. *Politics, Memory and Public Opinion: The History Textbook Controversy and Japanese Society*. Munich: IUDICIUM, 2005.

Sabido, Ruth Sanz. *Memories of the Spanish Civil War: Conflict and Community in Rural Spain*. London: Rowman & Littlefield, 2016.

Sato, Tadao. *Currents in Japanese Cinema: Essays*. Translated by Gregory Barrett. Tokyo: Kodansha International, 1982.

Schwartz, Barry, and Mikyoung Kim. "Introduction: Northeast Asia's Memory Problem." In *Northeast Asia's Difficult Past: Essays in Collective Memory*, edited by Mikyoung Kim and Barry Schwartz, 1–27. New York: Palgrave Macmillan, 2010.

Schweißgut, Karin. "Memories of a Lost Armenian Identity: Ayla Kutlu's 'Can Kusu.'" In *Turkish Literature and Cultural Memory: "Multiculturalism" as a Literary Theme after 1980*, edited by Catharina Dufft, 147–55. Wiesbaden, Germany: Harrassowitz, 2009.

Scott, James C. *Seeing Like a State: How Certain Schemes to Improve the Human Condition Have Failed*. New Haven, CT: Yale University Press, 1998.

Seaton, Philip A. *Japan's Contested War Memories: The "Memory Rifts" in Historical Consciousness of World War II*. London: Routledge, 2007.

Seraphim, Franziska. *War Memory and Social Politics in Japan, 1945–2005*. Cambridge, MA: Harvard University Asia Center, 2006.

Sharabi, Hisham. *Neopatriarchy: A Theory of Distorted Change in Arab Society*. Oxford: Oxford University Press, 1992.

Sharabi, Hisham, and Mukhtar Ani. "Impact of Class and Culture on Social Behavior: The Feudal-Bourgeois Family in Arab Society." In *Psychological Dimensions of Near Eastern Studies*, edited by L. Carl Brown and Norman Itzkowitz, 240–56. Princeton, NJ: Darwin, 1977.

Shimazu, Naoko. "Popular Representations of the Past: The Case of Postwar Japan." *Journal of Contemporary History* 38, no. 1 (2003): 101–16.

Shorto, Russell. *Amsterdam: A History of the World's Most Liberal City*. New York: Doubleday, 2013.

Shuichi, Kato. "Mechanisms of Ideas: Society, Intellectuals, and Literature in the Postwar Period in Japan." In *Legacies and Ambiguities: Postwar Fiction and Culture in West Germany and Japan*, edited by Ernestine Schlant and J. Thomas Rimer, 249–59. Washington, DC: Woodrow Wilson Center Press, 1991.

Sichrovsky, Peter. *Born Guilty: Children of Nazi Families*. Translated by Jean Steinberg. New York: Basic Books, 1988.

Silier, Orhan. "Foreword." In *Human Rights Issues in Textbooks: The Turkish Case*, edited by Deniz Tarba Ceylan and Gürol Irzık, xi–xiii. Nisantasi, Istanbul: History Foundation of Turkey, 2004.

Smith, Robert J. *Ancestor Worship in Contemporary Japan*. Stanford, CA: Stanford University Press, 1974.

Soh, C. Sarah. *The Comfort Women: Sexual Violence and Postcolonial Memory in Korea and Japan*. Chicago: University of Chicago Press, 2008.

Song, H. Rosi. *Lost in Transition: Constructing Memory in Contemporary Spain*. Liverpool: Liverpool University Press, 2016.

Sophocles. *Antigone*. Translation by David Mulroy. Madison: University of Wisconsin Press, 2013.

Staub, Ervin. *Overcoming Evil: Genocide, Violent Conflict, and Terrorism*. Oxford: Oxford University Press, 2011.

Sterijino pozorje. "30th Sterijino Pozorje Festival 1985—Best Performance." http://www.pozorje.org.rs/arhiva/predstava1985eng.htm (accessed November 7, 2017).

———. "56th Sterijino Pozorje 2011." http://www.pozorje.org.rs/2011/predstava8eng.htm (accessed November 7, 2017).

Stone, Charles B., Alin Coman, Adam D. Brown, Jonathan Koppel, and William Hirst. "Toward a Science of Silence: The Consequences of Leaving a Memory Unsaid." *Perspectives on Psychological Science* 7, no. 1 (2012): 39–53.

Stover, Eric, and Harvey M. Weinstein. "Conclusion: A Common Objective, a Universe of Alternatives." In *My Neighbor, My Enemy: Justice and Community in the Aftermath of Mass Atrocity*, edited by Eric Stover and Harvey M. Weinstein, 332–42. Cambridge: Cambridge University Press, 2004.

Straus, Scott. *Making and Unmaking Nations: War, Leadership, and Genocide in Modern Africa*. Ithaca, NY: Cornell University Press, 2015.

Suner, Asuman. "Elusive Fragments of an Uneasy Past: Representations of Non-Muslim Minorities in New Turkish Cinema." In *Turkish Literature and Cultural Memory: "Multiculturalism" as a Literary Theme after 1980*, edited by Catharina Dufft, 137–45. Wiesbaden, Germany: Harrassowitz, 2009.

———. *New Turkish Cinema: Belonging, Identity and Memory*. London: Tauris, 2010.

Swartz, Avonna Deanne. "Textbooks and National Ideology: A Content Analysis of the Secondary Turkish History Textbooks Used in the Republic of Turkey since 1929." PhD diss., University of Texas at Austin, 1997.

Tambar, Kabir. *The Reckoning of Pluralism: Political Belonging and the Demands of History in Turkey*. Stanford, CA: Stanford University Press, 2014.

Temelkuran, Ece. *Deep Mountain: Across the Turkish-Armenian Divide*. Translated by Kenneth Dakan. London: Verso, 2010.

———. *Turkey: The Insane and the Melancholy*. Translated by Zeynep Beler. London: Zed Books, 2015.

Tilly, Charles. *Contention and Democracy in Europe, 1650–2000*. Cambridge: Cambridge University Press, 2004.

Toumani, Meline. *There Was and There Was Not: A Journey through Hate and Possibility in Turkey, Armenia, and Beyond*. New York: Metropolitan Books, Henry Holt, 2014.

Tremlett, Giles. *Ghosts of Spain: Travels through Spain and Its Silent Past*. New York: Walker, 2006.

Triana-Toribio, Núria. *Spanish National Cinema*. London: Routledge, 2003.

Triandis, Harry C. *Individualism and Collectivism*. Boulder, CO: Westview, 1995.

Tsurumi, Shunsuke. *A Cultural History of Postwar Japan, 1945–1980*. London: Routledge and Kegan Paul, 1987.

Türkmen-Dervişoğlu, Gülay. "Coming to Terms with a Difficult Past: The Trauma of the Assassination of Hrant Dink and Its Repercussions on Turkish National Identity." *Nations and Nationalism* 19, no. 4 (2013): 674–92.

Udovicki, Jasminka, and Ivan Torov. "The Interlude: 1980–1990." In *Burn This House: The Making and Unmaking of Yugoslavia*, edited by Jasminka Udovicki and James Ridgeway, 80–107. Durham, NC: Duke University Press, 1997.

Ulgen, Fatma. "Reading Mustafa Kemal Atatürk on the Armenian Genocide of 1915." *Patterns of Prejudice* 44, no. 4 (2010): 369–91.

———. "'Sabiha Gökçen's 80-Year-Old Secret': Kemalist Nation Formation and the Ottoman Armenians." PhD diss., University of California San Diego, 2010.

Üngör, Ugur Ümit. *The Making of Modern Turkey: Nation and State in Eastern Anatolia, 1913–1950*. Oxford: Oxford University Press, 2011.

Vidaković-Petrov, Krinka. "Memory and the Oral Tradition." In *Memory: History, Culture and the Mind*, edited by Thomas Butler, 77–96. Oxford: Basil Blackwell, 1989.

Volkan, Vamik D., and Norman Itzkowitz. *The Immortal Atatürk: A Psychobiography*. Chicago: University of Chicago Press, 1984.

Wachtel, Andrew Baruch. *Making a Nation, Breaking a Nation: Literature and Cultural Politics in Yugoslavia*. Stanford, CA: Stanford University Press, 1998.

Wedeen, Lisa. *Ambiguities of Domination: Politics, Rhetoric, and Symbols in Contemporary Syria*. Chicago: University of Chicago Press, 1999.

Welzer, Harald. "The Collateral Damage of Enlightenment: How Grandchildren Understand the History of National Socialist Crimes and Their Grandfathers' Past." In *Victims and Perpetrators: 1933–1945: (Re)presenting the Past in Post-Unification Culture*, edited by Laurel Cohen-Pfister and Dagmar Wienroeder-Skinner, 285–95. Berlin: Walter de Gruyter, 2006.

Welzer, Harald, Sabine Moller, and Karoline Tschuggnall. *"Opa war kein Nazi": Nationalsozialismus und Holocaust im Familiengedächtnis*. Frankfurt: Fischer Taschenbuch Verlag, 2002.

White, Jenny. *Muslim Nationalism and the New Turks*. Princeton, NJ: Princeton University Press, 2013.

Wienand, Christiane. *Returning Memories: Former Prisoners of War in Divided and Reunited Germany*. Rochester, NY: Camden House, 2015.

Wolfgram, Mark A. "Democracy and Propaganda: NATO's War in Kosovo." *European Journal of Communication* 23, no. 2 (2008): 153–71.

———. "Didactic War Crimes Trials and External Legal Culture: The Cases of the Nuremberg, Frankfurt Auschwitz, and Majdanek Trials in West Germany." *Global Change, Peace & Security* 26, no. 3 (2014): 281–97.

———. *"Getting History Right": East and West Germany Collective Memories of the Holocaust and War*. Lewisburg, PA: Bucknell University Press, 2011.

———. "The Holocaust through the Prism of East German Television: Collective Memory and Audience Perceptions." *Holocaust and Genocide Studies* 20, no. 1 (2006): 57–79.

———. "A Model for Comparative Collective Memory Studies: Regime Types, Cultural Traditions, and Difficult Histories." *Croatian Political Science Review* 51, no. 5 (2014): 13–35.

———. "Rediscovering Narratives of German Resistance: Opposing the Nazi 'Terror-State.'" *Rethinking History* 10, no. 2 (2006): 201–19.

———. "When the Men with Guns Rule: Explaining Human Rights Failures in Kosovo since 1999." *Political Science Quarterly* 123, no. 3 (2008): 461–84.

Yoshida, Takashi. *The Making of the "Rape of Nanking": History and Memory in Japan, China, and the United States*. Oxford: Oxford University Press, 2006.

Yoshimi, Yoshiaki. *Grassroots Fascism: The War Experience of the Japanese People*. Translated by Ethan Mark. New York: Columbia University Press, 2015.

Zarakol, Ayşe. *After Defeat: How the East Learned to Live with the West*. Cambridge: Cambridge University Press, 2011.

———. "Ontological (In)security and State Denial of Historical Crimes: Turkey and Japan." *International Relations* 24, no. 1 (2010): 3–23.

# Filmography

*Armenia (Soviet Union)*

*April.* Directed by Vigen Chaldranyan. 1985.

*Dzori Miro* [*Dzori Miron*]. Directed by Zhirayr Avetisyan. 1981.

*Handipum Tsutsahandesum* [*A Meeting at an Exhibition*]. Directed by Nerses Hovhannisyan. 1968.

*Kochvats en aprelu* [*They Are to Live*]. Directed by Laert Vagharshyan. 1960.

*Nahapet* [*Life Triumphs*]. Directed by Henrik Malyan. 1977.

*Yerkrord Karavane* [*The Second Caravan*]. Directed by Hamo Beknazaryan. 1950.

*Canada*

*Ararat.* Directed by Atom Egoyan. 2002.

*East Germany*

*Die Affäre Blum* [*The Blum Affair*]. Directed by Erich Engel. DEFA, 1948.

*Ehe im Schatten* [*Marriage in the Shadows*]. Directed by Kurt Maetzig, 1947.

*Ich war neunzehn* [*I Was Nineteen*]. Directed by Konrad Wolf. DEFA, 1968.

*Jakob der Lüger* [*Jacob the Liar*]. Directed by Frank Beyer. DEFA, 1975.

*Die Mörder sind unter uns* [*The Murderers Are among Us*]. Directed by Wolfgang Staudte. DEFA, 1946.

*Nackt unter Wölfen* [*Naked among Wolves*]. Directed by Frank Beyer. DEFA, 1963.

*Professor Mamlock.* Directed by Konrad Wolf. DEFA, 1961.

*Sterne* [*Stars*]. Directed by Konrad Wolf. DEFA, 1959.

*East Germany (TV)*

*Der Staatsanwalt hat das Wort* [*The Prosecuting Attorney Takes the Floor*]. DDR-F.

*Polizeiruf 110* [*Police Call 110*]. DDR-F.

*Wir haben nichts zu bereuen* [*We Have Nothing to Regret*]. Directed by Ulrich Teschner. DDR-F, 1984.

*West Germany and Post-1990*

*Canaris*. Directed by Alfred Weidenmann. Fama, 1954.

*David*. Directed by David Lilienthal. Von Vietinghoff/Pro-ject/ZDF, 1978.

*Des Teufels General* [*The Devil's General*]. Directed by Helmut Käutner. Real-Film, 1954.

*Das Haus in der Karpfengasse* [*The House in the Karpfengasse*]. Directed by Kurt Hoffmann. Independent Film/German TV, 1964.

*Lang ist der Weg* [*Long Is the Way*]. Directed by Herbert B. Fredersdorf and Marek Goldstein. IFO-Film, 1947.

*U 47—Kapitänleutnant Prien* [U47—Lieutenant-Commander Prien]. Directed by Harald Reinl. Arca, 1958.

*Das weiße Band* [*The White Ribbon*]. Directed by Michael Haneke. X-Filme Creative Pool, 2009.

*West Germany (TV)*

*Bernhard Lichtenberg*. By Maria Matray and Answald Krüger. Directed by Peter Beauvais. ZDF, July 20, 1965.

*Bilanz eines Verlustes: Jüdische Mitbürger in Deutschland—gestern und heute* [*Balance of a Loss: Jewish Fellow Citizens in Germany—Yesterday and Today*]. ZDF, November 8, 1963.

*Der Fall Nebe* [*The Nebe Case*]. Part 1 "Glanz und Elend einer großen Karriere" [*Glory and Misery of a Great Career*]; Part 2 "Widerstand, Flucht und Ende" [*Resistance, Flight and End*]. Directed by Georg Tressler. ZDF, November 18–19, 1964.

*Waldhausstr. 20* [*Tree House Street 20*]. Directed by John Olden. NDR, October 23, 1960.

*Japan*

*Biruma no tategoto* [*Harp of Burma*]. Directed by Kon Ichikawa. 1956.

*Gembaku no ko* [*Children of Hiroshima*]. Directed by Kaneto Shindo. 1952.

*Hiroshima*. Directed by Hideo Sekikawa. 1953.

*Hitoheishi no jugun nikki: sofu no senso wo shiru* [*A Soldier's Diary: Learning about Grandfather's War*]. NHK, 2000.

*Ikimono no kiroku* [*The Record of a Living Being*]. Directed by Akira Kurosawa. 1955.

*Joiuchi* [*Samurai Rebellion*]. Directed by Masaki Kobayashi. 1967.

*Kabe atsuki heya* [*The Thick-Walled Room*]. Directed by Masaki Kobayashi. 1956.

*Karayuki-san* [*Karayuki-san: The Making of a Prostitute*]. Directed by Shohei Imamura. 1973.

*Kuroi ame* [*Black Rain*]. Directed by Shohei Imamura. 1989.

*Nihon no higeki* [*A Japanese Tragedy*]. Directed by Fumio Kamei. 1946.

*Nijushi no hitomi* [*Twenty-Four Eyes*]. Directed by Keisuke Kinoshita. 1954.

*Ningen no joken.* [*The Human Condition*]. Directed by Masaki Kobayashi. 1959.

*Nobi* [*Fires on the Plain*]. Directed by Kon Ichikawa. 1959.

*Riben guizi* [*Japanese Devils*]. Directed by Minoru Matsui. 2001.

*Sandakan hachiban shokan: Bokyo* [*Sandakan 8*]. Directed by Kei Kumai. 1974.

*Seppuku* [*Hara-Kiri*]. Directed by Masaki Kobayashi. 1962.

*Umi to dokuyaku* [*The Sea and Poison*]. Directed by Kei Kumai. 1986.

### *Spain*

*El laberinto del fauno* [*Pan's Labyrinth*]. Directed by Guillermo del Toro. 2006.

*El lápiz del carpintero* [*The Carpenter's Pencil*]. Directed by Antón Reixa. 2001.

*El spíritu de la colena* [*Spirit of the Beehive*]. Directed by Víctor Erice. 1973.

*España otra vez* [*Spain Again*]. Directed by Jaime Camino. 1968.

*Huellas de un Espiritu* [*Footprints of a Spirit*]. CANAL+ Espana. Directed by Carlos Rodríguez. 1998. Part of the Criterion Collection for Víctor Erice's film *El spíritu de la colena* [*Spirit of the Beehive*]. 1973.

*La fiel infantería* [*The Proud Infantry*]. Directed by Pedro Lazaga. 1959.

*La lengua de las mariposas* [*Butterfly*]. Directed by José Luis Cuerda. 1999.

*La prima Angélica* [*Cousin Angelica*]. Directed by Carlos Saura. 1974.

*Raza* [*Race* a.k.a. *Pure Blood*]. Directed by José Luis Sáenz de Heredia. 1941.

*Réquiem por un campesino español* [*Requiem for a Spanish Peasant*]. Directed by Francesc Betriu. 1985.

*Soldados de Salamina* [*Soldiers of Salamis*]. Directed by David Trueba. 2003.

### *Spanish (TV)*

*Cuéntame cómo pasó* [*Tell Me, How It Was*]. TVE.

### *Turkey*

*Beş Vakit* [*Times and Winds*]. Directed by Reha Erdem. 2006.

*Bir Millet Uyaniyor* [*A Nation Awakening*]. Directed by Muhsin Ertuğrul. 1932.

*Bulutari Beklerken* [*Waiting for the Clouds*]. Directed by Yeşim Ustaoğlu. 2004.

*Çalıkuşu* [*The Autobiography of a Turkish Girl*]. Directed by Osman F. Seden. 1966.

*Çoğunluk* [*Majority*]. Directed by Seren Yüce. 2010.

*Gelecek Uzun Sürer* [*The Future Lasts Forever*]. Directed by Özcan Alper. 2011.

*Güneşe Yolculuk* [*Journey to the Sun*]. Directed by Yeşim Ustaoğlu. 1999.

*Güz Sancısı* [*Autumn Pain*]. Directed by Tomris Giritlioğlu. 2008.

*Kelebekler Sonsuza Uçar* [*Butterflies Fly to Eternity*]. Directed by Mesut Uçakan. 1993.

*Kurtlar Vadisi Irak* [*Valley of the Wolves, Iraq*]. Directed by Serdar Akar. 2006.

*Mavi Sürgün* [*The Blue Exile*]. Directed by Erden Kıral. 1993.

*Momi* [*Grandmother*]. Directed by Özcan Alper. 2000.

*Mustang*. Directed by Deniz Gamze Ergüven. 2015.

*Salkım Hanımın Taneleri* [*Mrs. Salkım's Diamonds*]. Directed by Tomris Giritlioğlu. 1999.

*Sonbahar* [*Autumn*]. Directed by Özcan Alper. 2007.

*Suyun Öte Yanı* [*The Other Side of the Water*]. Directed by Tomris Giritlioğlu. 1991.

*Yazı Tura* [*Toss-Up*]. Directed by Uğur Yücel. 2004.

*Yol* [*The Way*]. Directed by Şerif Gören. 1982.

*Yorgun Savaşçı* [*Tired Warrior*]. Directed by Halit Refiğ. 1979.

### *Soviet Union*

*Blokada* [*Blockade*]. Directed by Michail Jerschow. 1974.

### *United States*

*An Armenian Journey*. Directed by Theodore Bogosian. 1988.

*Holocaust*. Directed by Marvin J. Chomsky. 1978.

*Jakob the Liar*. Directed by Peter Kassovitz. 1999.

*Ravished Armenia*. Directed by Oscar Apfel. 1919.

*Where Are My People?* Directed by J. Michael Hagopian. 1965.

### *Yugoslavia*

*Besmrtna mladost* [*Immortal Youth*]. Directed by Vojislav Nanović. Avala film, Belgrade, 1948.

*Bitka na Neretvi* [*Battle of the River Neretva*]. Directed by Veljko Bulajić. 1969.

*Daleko je sunce* [*Far Away Is the Sun*]. Directed by Radoš Novaković. Avala film, Belgrade, 1953.

*Okupacija u 26 slika* [*Occupation in 26 Pictures*]. Directed by Lordan Zafranović. Jadran film, Zagreb, 1978.

*Otac na službenom putu* [*When Father Was Away on Business*]. Directed by Emir Kusturica. Forum and OOUR Sarajevo film, Sarajevo, 1985.

*Pad Italije* [*The Fall of Italy*]. Directed by Lordan Zafranović. Jadran film, Zagreb, 1981.

*Partizanske priče* [*Partisan Stories*]. Directed by Stole Janković. Ufus, Belgrade, 1960.

*Petrijin venac* [*Petrija's Wreath*]. Directed by Srdjan Karanović. Centar film, Belgrade, 1980.

*Slavica*. Directed by Vjekoslav Afić. Avala film, Belgrade, 1947.

*Šolaja*. Directed by Vojislav Nanović. 1955.

*Srećna nova, '49* [*Happy New Year 1949*]. Directed by Stole Popov. Vardar film, Makedonija film, Gradska kina, Skopje and Union Film, Belgrade, 1985.

*Tri* [*Three*]. Directed by Aleksandar Petrović. Avala film, Belgrade, 1965.

*Večernja zvona* [*Evening Bells*]. Directed by Lordan Zafranović. Jadran film and Jugoart, Zagreb, 1986.

*Vlak bez voznog reda* [*Train without a Timetable*]. Directed by Veljko Bulajić. Jadran film, Zagreb, 1959.

# Index

# About the Author

Mark A. Wolfgram, PhD, University of Wisconsin-Madison, 2001, has received fellowships from the Charlotte W. Newcombe Foundation, the Joan Shorenstein Center at Harvard University, the German Academic Exchange Service (DAAD), and the Friedrich-Ebert Foundation. His first book, *"Getting History Right": East and West German Collective Memories of the Holocaust and War,* was published by Bucknell University Press in 2011. He is a member of the international Steering Committee for the Historical Dialogues, Justice, and Memory Network, which organizes an annual international conference dedicated to interdisciplinary research on historical dialogues. He currently lives in Ottawa, Canada, with his wife, and teaches part-time at McGill University while working on his next book on the role that creative artists play in the political life of their societies.